# HISTORY

OF THE

# WALDENSES OF ITALY

# AMS PRESS
NEW YORK

# HISTORY

OF THE

# WALDENSES OF ITALY,

## FROM THEIR ORIGIN TO THE REFORMATION.

BY

## EMILIO COMBA, D.D.

*( Waldensian Theological College, Florence, Italy ).*

TRANSLATED FROM THE AUTHOR'S REVISED EDITION
BY

## TEOFILO E. COMBA.

LONDON :

TRUSLOVE & SHIRLEY, 7, ST. PAUL'S CHURCHYARD.

—

1889.

Library of Congress Cataloging in Publication Data

Comba, Emilio, 1839-1904.
    History of the Waldenses of Italy, from their origin
to the Reformation.

    Translation of Histoire des Vaudois.
    Reprint of the 1889 ed. published by Truslove &
Shirley, London.
    1. Waldenses.  I. Title.
BX4881.C713   1978     284′.4     77-84713
ISBN 0-404-16119-7

Reprinted from the edition of 1889, London
First AMS edition published in 1978

Manufactured in the United States of America

AMS PRESS, INC.
NEW YORK, N.Y.

# PREFACE.

"It is a beautiful peculiarity of this little people that it should occupy so prominent a place in the history of Europe." This saying of Michelet expresses so well the opinion commonly held, that a new attempt to write its history may, to some, appear superfluous. It may be urged, that, the history of the Waldenses being well known, there is no need to rewrite it. We reply : The history of the Waldenses is not so well-known as is generally assumed. Their early history has been thoroughly explored and discussed, but has never yet been recounted ; indeed a writer of great authority has said, "The history of the ancient Waldenses certainly remains to be written." This is a grave omission indeed, which may well strike us as singular. Was it worth while, it may be asked, to trace their origin so far back and then leave their history unrecorded ? There has been a desire on the part of some to extend backward their early history ; with this only as a result, that it has been crushed out of all shape. The historian has filled it full of fables and traditions picked up at hap-hazard ; then, as if with trumpet-blast and clarion-ring, its antiquity was blazoned forth. But, although the sound re-echoed far and wide, it could not dispel the thick cloud that overhung that people's origin and early days. Flatterers are more to be feared than assailants. The former would have it credited or imagined that the Waldenses are of a patriarchal age—of great duration ; that they are apostolic in name and in fact, but barren withal ; that they had an existence, but always in the cradle ; that they did not *live* with all the word implies, but *slept* for three, seven, or even ten centuries ! It is quite possible to conceive that such an uneventful existence—if such could be —might well have passed unnoticed ; what we deny is that such an existence was possible. We shall examine facts, and, after all, if we find the antiquity of the Waldenses to be less far reaching than has been supposed, it is none the less grand and venerable.

So much for the early period, but as regards the modern period, its history cannot be said to be unrecorded. It is time, however, that there should now be a complete record, and such is the object of this new essay. The material which new researches accumulate from year to year, has nearly all passed through the crucible of discussion. The work of selection and discrimination is still a difficult one, and much has been discarded, and more will share the same fate, before the task of the critic can be considered complete; the reader is asked to bear this in mind and grant indulgence. We shall be guided by the adage of the poet : " Rien n'est beau que le vrai, le vrai seul est aimable."

We shall here study the early period of Waldensian history. There is an idea with some, that its origin may be traced back to the very time of the first preaching of the Gospel; but it is important that this idea be disentangled from a confused mass of legends. We shall find the first authentic source appearing with Waldo, and the disciples whom tradition has called by his name. From that time onward, we shall follow the sinuous course of their followers' history down to the eve of the Reformation.

Then will come the time for us to examine closely, in order to discriminate between those elements which properly belong to the Waldensian idea, and those which the body has taken to itself, in the fields both of literature and religious observances. Before we have finished we shall be convinced that the Waldensian protest at first aimed only at proclaiming and observing the apostolic ideal—an ideal disowned by the Popes and abandoned by the Church ; but that, meeting with persecutions, it quickly gave way to a movement of dissent, which did not at once culminate in schism but necessarily eventually led to it.

# CONTENTS.

## CHAPTER THE FIRST.
### THE ORIGIN OF THE WALDENSES.

PAGE

The Alps—their legends, like their rivers, have hidden sources—The question of the origin of the Waldenses ; the difficulties which surround it— The report of a monk and the inferences that may be drawn from it— The origin of the Waldenses as recorded in tradition, both as to their decadence and as to subsequent revivals—The echo of this among the primitive Waldenses—How another monk quibbles on this point—The Waldensian tradition properly so called—How it degenerated—The truth which lies beneath it—The source ... ... ... ... ... ... ...     1

## CHAPTER THE SECOND.
### THE POOR OF LYONS.

Lyons before the XII. century—Signs of awakening—Peter Waldo : his origin : his conversion—The song of St. Alexis—The advice of the master of theology—The vow of poverty and what it entailed : the commencement of separation—Waldo's daughters in a convent : his alms—The translation of some books of the Scripture—Reunions— Archbishop Guichard and the Chapter of the Cathedral—The first lawsuit : Waldo, banished from Lyons, appeals to Rome—Alexander III. and the third Lateran Council—Waldo receives the kiss of peace—A scene in the Council—The crisis—Archbishop Jean aux Blanches Mains drives away the Waldenses and retires to a convent—The thunders of the Council of Verona. ... ... ... ... ... ... ... ... ... ... ... ...    14

## CHAPTER THE THIRD.
### THE DISPERSION.

The Exodus—The Waldenses enter into Dauphiny after a protest from Peter of Bruys and Henry of Lausanne—The reactions in Southern France : why the doctrine of the Cathari was propagated there ; its progress and influence—Appearance of the Waldenses : their disputation with the Catholic clergy at Narbonne and what resulted from it—Diego and the new tactics of the missionary Legates—Fresh disputations at Montreal and Pâmiers—Durand of Huesca separates, capitulates to the Pope, and founds the order of the Catholic Poor—Bernard I. follows his example— End of the Catholic Poor ; their principle survives—The Waldenses at Metz—Traces of their mission in Switzerland and the Valley of the Rhine ; The Brethren of the Free Spirit—Milan the centre of dissent— The tendency of Arnaldo and the dissent of the Humiliate—The Poor of Lombardy ; the retrograde party and that of the conservatives and of the progressists—The conference of Bergamo and the circular letter— Mission in the diocese of Passau and in the rest of Germany—The Hussite reaction in Bohemia and its relation to the Waldensian mission : Frederick Reiser—The Unity of Brethren and the Waldenses' participation in it, through their Bishop Stephen of Austria—The clue to the dispersion disappears ... ... ... ... ... ... ... ... ... ... ... ...    39

## CHAPTER THE FOURTH.
### THE ALPINE REFUGE.

Religious ideas, like birds, have a tendency to build nests for themselves— The retreat of the Waldenses into the Valleys of the Alps was occasioned by two facts : their banishment from Lyons and the Crusade against the Albigensis—The Waldenses reach the Italian side and establish themselves there, thanks to the concurrence of diverse circumstances—

PAGE

The configuration of the country—Uncultivated lands—Is there any reason to admit the existence of traces of ancient local dissent in the Italian Valleys?—Discussion upon this point tends to prove the vicinity, if not the presence, of the sect of the Cathari—The Abbey of St. Mary of Pignerol and the Castle of Lucerna—Thomas I., Count of Savoy and the House of Achaia—New Colonies : that of Calabria—First decrees of persecution against the Waldenses of the Valleys : that of Turin, and that of Pignerol—The Inquisition : its " raison d'etre " and its establishment—The strongholds capitulate : Podesta Oldrado in Milan and the repression in the country towns—First assaults of the Monks at Perosa, Angrogna, Pragelas, and in Dauphiny—Two new decrees, one by Louis XI. and the other by the Duchess Iolante—First Crusade against the Waldenses : Innocent VIII. and his Bull : a check in the Valleys of Piedmont and cruelties in Dauphiny—A Waldensian deputation at Pignerol—An inquiry at Freyssinieres and the letter of Louis XII.—Margaret of Foix and the first glorious return—What was going on within—The Barbes, the Mission and the School—Condition of the Waldenses on the eve of the Reformation ... ... ... ... ... ... ... 81

## CHAPTER THE FIFTH.
### LITERATURE.

Preliminary remarks—The Waldensian dialect and a general view of materials—VERSIONS OF THE SCRIPTURES—Early versions which have disappeared—Those of Waldo and the Waldenses of Metz—Ancient versions that have survived, but which are contested—Manuscript versions of Lyons and Paris—More recent but recognised versions—MSS. of Cambridge, Grenoble, Dublin, and Zurich—Comparative specimens—Connection between these versions and what is inferred therefrom with respect to their origin—A version in a foreign tongue—MS. of Tepl.—PROSE WRITINGS—Those which have perished—Gleanings of original writings—Compilations from a Catholic source—The Doctor and the Orchard—Brainless treatise—The commentary on the Lord's Prayer—The Virtues, the Canticles—Compilations from a Hussite source—The epistle to King Ladislas—The treatise upon the cause of breaking with the Romish Church—The collection of the Treasure and the Light of Faith, containing The Ten Commandments, the Seven Sacraments, Purgatory, the Invocation of Saints—The Power granted to the Vicars of Christ, Antichrist, and the Minor Interrogations—POETICAL WRITINGS Contempt for the world—The Bark—The Lord's Prayer or confession of sins—The new comfort—The new sermon—The Parable of the Sower The Father Eternal—Finally, the Noble Lesson, with critical notes—The conclusions from this chapter summarized. ... ... ... ... ... .. ... 160

## CHAPTER THE SIXTH.
### THE RELIGIOUS LIFE.

The materials for this picture refurnished by Waldo—The rule of religious life is Christ's law according to the Scripture—Have the Waldenses adopted the scholastic method of interpretation?—Their articles of faith, mainly derived from Catholic tradition, are reformed as regards two points : eschatology and worship—Their morals, copied from the precepts of the Gospel, give evidence of the influence of Catharism, and are especially marked in the protest against falsehood, oaths, and the death penalty—Divers names : the one that remains—The community and the triple vow of admission--Bishops, Presbyters, and Deacons ; the Bishop and the general administration—The Chapters—Worship ; remarks upon the times, places, and elements—The Benedicite Prayer : the Lord's Prayer only used, the Ave Maria given up—The reading of the Holy Scriptures : reading, learning by rote, preaching—The Sacraments : their number according to Waldensian usage—Variations in the conception and observance of baptism—Ordination by the laying on of hands : rubric—Confession and Penances—The Eucharistic rite and the consecrated bread—Polemics—Ethics : praise and calumny—Diverent usages : costumes, disguises ; the hawker—The epoch of decadence ; religious life in the valleys of the Alps toward the end of the XV. century and at the approach of the Reformation, according to the testimony of Inquisitors, of Bishop Seyssel and of the Barbe Morel—Concluding remarks ... ... ... ... ... ... ... ... ... ... ... .. ... ... ... 240

# THE
# WALDENSES OF ITALY.

## CHAPTER THE FIRST.

### THE ORIGIN OF THE WALDENSES.

*The Alps—their legends, like their rivers, have hidden sources—
The question of the origin of the Waldenses; the difficulties
which surround it—The report of a monk and the inferences
that may be drawn from it—The origin of the Waldenses as
recorded in tradition, both as to their decadence and as to
subsequent revivals—The echo of this among the primitive
Waldenses—How another monk quibbles on this point—The
Waldensian tradition properly so called—How it degenerated
—The truth which lies beneath it—The source.*

THE Alps which mark the boundaries of France, Switzerland,
and Italy, offer one of the most sublime of spectacles to the
eye of man. Nature's temples may be found under all skies, but
there, indeed, stands her cathedral, with its white cupola and high
altar. That altar is common to all Europe. A divine hand has there
gathered together invaluable traditions, truths, liberty and virtue.
If they be lost elsewhere, there at least they may be found; they
may be inhaled with every breath, fresh as the first breeze of
morn. Among those awe-inspiring mountains, nature is so grand,
so towering, that all things save reason and truth seem annihilated
in her presence. All temples made by men are small and puny,
before this magnificent pile, built by the hand of God. Before
this mighty Alpine altar, the Omnipotence of God manifests itself
in all its grandeur, and here, as under the very covert of His
wings, lies the birthplace of the Waldenses. It is owing to its
position that the little Waldensian Church has been compared to
a dove able to find her food even among the rocks.

It is hence that spring the traditions of the House of Savoy,
and those others concerning the Israel of the Alps, that are so
closely united with them in time and place. The course of the
history of the Waldenses may well be typified by that of one of
their own Alpine rivers. Like a river, the history interests us
from the very mystery of its origin. Its source we shall find to
be a distinct one, and the distant rivers unto this day bear that
name which tradition, with ineffaceable seal, has stamped as the
origin of its first waters. From such a place the rivers of
history take their rise, even as at the foot of Monte Rosa—crowned
with her seven-pointed diadem—issue those rivers that bless
Europe, and make it fertile. At distant intervals come the
tributaries which greatly help to swell its volume. Its course is
marked by many, and ofttimes surprising irregularities; but a
vigorous people, like an Alpine river, will make for itself an outlet,
in spite of all obstacles. It is dammed back by every impediment
it meets, and seems to gain in strength thereby. If no struggle
be required of it, it grows feeble and is in danger of being lost.
People who judge only by appearances may be deceived by this;
for, just as in the case of the Rhone, it may happen that defeat is
proclaimed when victory is nearest at hand. Is not the very spot
known as "la perte du Rhône" the scene of its most marvellous
victory? It happens that the naturalist who explains this
phenomenon, is himself induced to make a comparison which has
a material interest for us. He says:—" It might often have
been believed that the extermination of the Waldensians was
complete; but they have always risen again."

We need not multiply the analogies;[2] they are self evident.
Whether we study the course of a history or of a river, we like to
discover the origin, and what wanderings were passed through
before the light of day was reached. We may claim to say in
our turn :—" Such are questions with which an ignorant man
distracts himself, and learned men are far from having solved.
How much study and research are necessary before we can trace,
without fear of being mistaken, the immeasurable circuit followed
by a single drop of water through clouds and rocks."[3] Waldensian
history contains just such obscurities of origin and regions of
cloud. The drop of water represents here the idea, the principle,
which disengages itself, in order eventually to reach the river's
source.

The question of the origin of the Waldenses deserves serious investigation. Natural obscurities render the task a difficult one, and this difficulty is increased by party polemics, the result being confusion worse confounded. Solutions offered are far from agreeing with each other. It has been said :—" There is hardly a sect whose origin has been more disputed over than that of the Waldenses." Disregarding the expression " a sect "—which is here more or less out of place—the above statement is not without foundation. We know that any question of origin contains inherently an element of vagueness, which fascinates the imagination. What religion, city, or family, is not inclined to trace its origin back to mythical sources ? All these had their origin in the womb of time, as the river has its source, and the tree its roots, in the womb of nature. To discover such origin, our investigation must be conducted without prejudice or foregone conclusions. If prejudice be allowed to have a voice in the matter, it will only accumulate legends ; and history can no longer disentangle herself from them. This has too often been the case. Basnage says :—" It is a weakness belonging to all Churches, as well as States, to claim for themselves great antiquity." The reason may be readily divined, for it is nothing new.[4] Let us admit at the outset, that prejudice has taken a very active part in the researches relating to the origin of the Waldenses ; it has exerted its influence, somewhat over everybody, friends as well as foes. But as prejudice has no part in true history, it must be our endeavour to free ourselves of it.

The following words, written more than five centuries ago, are often quoted :—" Among all the sects, there is none more pernicious to the church than that of the Leonists, and for three reasons :—In the first place, because it is one of the most ancient ;[5] for some say that it dates back to the time of Sylvester ; others to the time of the Apostles. In the second place, because it is the mostwidespread. There is hardly a country where it does not exist. In the third place, because, if other sects strike with horror those who listen to them, the Leonists, on the contrary, possess a great outward appearance of piety. As a matter of fact they lead irreproachable lives before men, and as regards their faith and the articles of their creed, they are orthodox. Their one conspicuous fault is, that they blaspheme against the

Church and the clergy, points on which laymen in general are known to be too easily led away."

Here we have an indisputable testimony. It has been erroneously attributed to the Inquisitor Raincrius Saccho, who settled in Milan, and was in contact with the Waldenses of Italy; whereas it was rendered by one of his colleagues in the diocese of Passau in Austria, about the year 1260.[6] We may assent to it, but on one condition, namely, that its meaning be not perverted. The writer in no wise affirms that the Waldenses date back to a period anterior to Waldo; he simply states that some claim that they do.[7] As for himself, he believes in no such thing. His mode alone of expressing himself indicates this, whilst the fact becomes evident as he goes on to give his opinion as to the origin of the Waldenses. He classifies them, without much ceremony, among "modern heretics," and proceeds to state that they are descendants of Waldo. Even in such a shape, this testimony is nevertheless of material value to us; for it offers, as it were, the end of a skein which will have to be disentangled. Unquestionably it was, even at this early time, current among the Waldenses, that they were of ancient origin, truly apostolic. We shall hereafter see how this idea may be entertained, and what may reasonably be inferred from it.

The pretension to apostolic succession in the Church innate, manifests itself in the Catholic party in a way differing from that in the dissenting sections. In the former it takes a more material and gross form of expression than in the case of the latter, in which it has nevertheless a wider basis of truth, notwithstanding the little regard manifested for appearances. According to the popular tradition—which for many years has had an increasing ascendancy over men's minds—the primitive Church, faithful and canonical, goes back to the days of Constantine, under whose reign the great original fall of the Church took place, and the era of apostacy began. At that time the church and the world became reconciled; according to the legend, this was the manner of it:—

Constantine, like his predecessors, had first been an enemy—a persecutor of the church. Being afflicted with leprosy, he imagined that in order to be healed, he must bathe in the purest human blood. The innocents destined to furnish this imperial bath were about to be immolated, when their mothers' cry was heard. The Emperor stopped; he was ashamed. Having been warned in a dream, he applied for healing to Sylvester, Bishop of Rome, and by him was baptized in clear water, which miraculously removed the leprosy. Then Constantine made a public declaration of faith, adding that he recognised the sovereignty of Sylvester, Head of the Church, Lord of Rome, of Italy and of the West.[8] It is even said that taking the golden diadem from his own brow, he crowned Sylvester with it to the glory of Saint Peter. Having done this, he withdrew to the East, in order not to encroach upon the Pontiff's domain. During the ceremony, however, a voice had been heard on high, a cry repeated by the angels in the heavens, saying :—" To-day has poison been poured out in the Church."[9] Sylvester heard it as well as the rest; but notwithstanding the example of his Divine master, of the apostles, and of his own predecessors, he was not ashamed to yield to temptation. This time the devil gained the victory, and Sylvester bowed himself before the Emperor, receiving a crown and earthly possessions. Thus, when Cæsar became a Christian, the Pope became a Pagan. Since that time men began to separate themselves from Sylvester and his successors, because it was through them that decadence and the ruin of faith and morals was brought about.[10]

Such was the original fall of the Church. It opened out a new era of corruption on the one hand, and of reform on the other. The reaction produced by it called generations back to the apostolic faith, and caused it to be mourned as a lost ideal. But, it may be asked, is not the above-mentioned story of the gifts made to the Pope unauthentic ? Undoubtedly; nevertheless, it is the expression of a real truth. At all events, it ministered to the ambition of Popes. It is easily perceived that it was in reliance upon its authenticity and authority that they " originally founded their temporal dominion."[11] Towards the year 1000 its authenticity was already being contested, but still' it was admitted by general opinion. While the disciples of Arnaud rejected it as apocryphal,[12] in the days of Eugene III., St. Bernard in a letter to this pontiff, who had at one time been his pupil, writes :—" Acting as thou doest, thou showest that thou hast not succeeded to Peter but to Constantine."[13] And Dante, a long time after, expresses the legend in those famous lines :—

> " Ah, Constantine ! of how much ill was cause,
>     Not thy conversion, but those rich domains,
>     That the first wealthy pope received of thee."

Tradition, indeed, makes the destinies of the Church depend too much upon the will of two men, who, indeed, deserved "neither such excess of honour, nor such indignity."

Decadence had commenced before their appearance upon the scene of history; they are not the originators of it, but they are its most famous factors. Popular tradition, with its tendency to personify everything, clung to their names, the more naturally, in that they mark a distinct political date; that of the general and definite transition of the free, humble, and poor primitive Church into the enslaved, dominant, and worldly Church. In this change is to be found the prime reason, and the common basis of the reactions, which followed one another through the ages of Roman evolution, from the ancient Cathari to the Middle Ages, from Vigilantius and Claudius of Turin down to Pierre de Bruys, Arnaldo da Brescia, Henry of Lausanne and Waldo, and from Waldo to the Reformation. Those reactions, which ecclesiastic prejudice condemns as novel innovations, are, with a few exceptions, more truly conservative than the dominant church with its constant introduction of innovations; as compared with the latter, they seem even to be retrogressive. We must not be surprised if when the first sects had disappeared, the Waldensian reaction, sprung as it were from the very womb of general Christian tradition, claimed its right to be considered apostolic; and this, not at the moment of its appearance, when it still courted the tutelage of the Pope; but, it must be well observed, only after it had broken off with him in consequence of the sentences pronounced by the Councils and the persecution which followed. Indeed, the first writers who mention the Waldenses—Bernardus Fontis Calidi, Alanus, Peter Vallis Cernaii, Eberhard of Bethune, and others—make no allusion to any pretension on their part to reach back through history to the early days of the Church. And yet that pretension was present in the case of others and was quite noisy and near at hand; it was heard from the mouths of other dissenters, particularly from the Cathari;[14] but at that time, having no use for such pretensions, they had not as yet appropriated them. When they were placed under the ban of Catholic Christendom they changed their attitude and became more resolute. They, too, armed themselves with the tradition then in vogue amongst other bodies; and whilst accusing the dominant Church of apostasy, they claimed for themselves an origin anterior to the period of decadence. From that

moment, that is to say during the thirteenth century, the testimony of history comes to light, as is shown by the words of the
Inquisitor of the diocese of Passau, and as the following citation
will prove:—

"The Church of Christ," says the monk Raincrius Saccho,
" continued in her bishops and other prelates, down to the blessed
Sylvester; but under his reign it declined until the Restoration,
which was their work.[15] They say, however, that at all times there
have been God-fearing people who have been saved."[16] They believe that Pope Sylvester, at the instigation of the devil, became
the founder of the Roman Church.[17] "They say," repeats the
monk Moneta, " that the Church of God had declined in the time
of Sylvester, and that in these days it had been re-established by
their efforts, commencing with Waldo."[18] " They call themselves
successors of the Apostles," adds monk David of Augsburg,
" and say they are in possession of the apostolic authority, and of
the keys to bind and unbind."[19]

It is here evident, at the first glance, to what the Waldenses'
pretension to apostolic antiquity is reduced. It is the religious
idea that is ancient in their estimation, not the fact of their origin
as a people. They plead this antiquity for the sole purpose of
reconnecting the truth of their faith and principles with its true
source; the tradition of which had been interrupted by the Roman
apostasy.[20] So manifest is this fact that in order to refute the
ideal succession claimed by the Waldenses, the Inquisitor Moneta
urges against them the evidence of historical facts. This is what
he says:—

" We shall plainly see, if we inquire into their origin, that
they are not the Church of God. Indeed, their existence dates but
a little way back; because, according to every evidence, their
origin goes back to Waldo, a citizen of Lyons, who opened the
way for them some eighty years ago.[21] Therefore, they are not the
successors of the primitive Church; therefore, they are not the
Church of God. Will they attempt to assert that their mode of
thought is of a date prior to Waldo? If so, let them prove it by
some testimony. But that is impossible. If they be descendants
of Waldo let them tell us whence he himself was descended.
If they say that they are begotten of God, of the Apostles, and of
the Gospel, we answer: God is merciful only through his minister,
according to these words, ' Whosoever sins ye remit, they are

remitted unto them.' Therefore, they can have been remitted to Waldo only through the instrumentality of a minister. Who may that minister be ? Have they the three ecclesiastic orders ? They reply that they have. Then I ask : From whom do they hold them ? Who is their bishop ? If they answer : Such an one, I ask : By whom was he ordained ? If they say : He was ordained by a certain person, I ask again : Who ordained this certain person ? Following them up in this way, they are compelled to go back to Waldo. Then we ask : From whom did he hold orders ? If they say that he took them unto himself, it is clear that they are at variance with the Apostle, who writes :— ' And no man taketh this honour unto himself, but he that was called of God, as was Aaron.' Will they say that Waldo holds orders directly from God ? If they do, they will not be able to prove it by the testimony of the Scriptures. Some have claimed that Waldo was ordained by the community of his brethren, and the first to reason in this way was a certain heresiarch, belonging to the order of the ' Poor of Lombardy '—a pervert doctor called Thomas. They may say, perhaps, that their congregation and that of the Roman Church are one, both Holy and Catholic ; although divided into two sections, one of which, the. Roman Church is that of the wicked ; and the other, the Waldensian community, that of the righteous. But this is contradicted by the fact that the existence of such a community, from the time of Sylvester to that of Waldo, cannot be demonstrated.[22] They say that the Church of God declined in the days of the blessed Sylvester. Let us see : How do they know that to be the case ? It cannot be proved by any testimony, and therefore they are obliged to be silent. A wicked life does not prevent a minister from being efficacious in his office ; and even though Sylvester had been sinful and wicked, are we bound to conclude that in him the Church had fallen ? " [23]

This monk's polemics permit us to form some conception of the opinion held in the thirteenth century concerning the Waldenses' origin.

But, some may say that this is not the common opinion ; and that it is only the notion of fanatic monks and absolutely unworthy of credit.

That is not exactly so ; Moneta relates current opinions. Furthermore, we are dealing here with judges of heresy, who base their testimony upon what they heard a thousand times in the course of their prosecutions ; and this proves that they are not absolutely incompetent. Are they truthful ? Not always ; far from it ; but two things are worthy of notice, namely, that in this case their testimony is unanimous, and that their object is to direct the members of the Inquisition in the examination and refutation of heretics. Indeed, in this case, one can hardly see what they could gain by concealing acknowledged facts. The Waldenses were there to produce such facts, if there be any that indicate an ancient origin, prior to Waldo. They did not do so, and this is an important point. The first forefathers of the Waldensian Church were quite as anxious as anybody to appeal to apostolic tradition, unpractised, but unforgotten. They cherished the thought of reviving it again, this cannot be doubted ; but nowhere do we read that, on either side of the Alps, they claimed upon historical ground, an origin anterior to that of Waldo. Did they but produce their testimony we should stand convinced. Let us first cite a fact.

In the year 1218, the Waldenses held a conference with their brethren of Lombardy ; the name they then bore was that of *Valdesians* or *Associates of Valdes*. Together they composed the *Valdesian Society*.[24] In their debates, not the slightest allusion is found to a time anterior to Waldo. To him, as to the leader and founder of the institution, more than one question was referred. He was the leader then according to the avowal of these early Valdesians.

To this fact we can add a piece of explicit testimony, taken from a Waldensian document, with two readings, one of which bears the date of 1404. It reads as follows :—

" We do not find anywhere in the writings of the Old Testament that the light of truth and of holiness was at any time completely extinguished. There have always been men who walked faithfully in the paths of righteousness. Their number has been at times reduced to a few ; but has never been altogether lost. We believe that the same has been the case from the time of Jesus Christ until now ; and that it will be so unto the end. For if the Church of God was founded, it was in order that she might remain until the end of time. She preserved for a long period the virtue of holy religion, and, according to ancient history, her directors lived in poverty and humility for about three centuries ; that is to say, down to the time of Constantine. Under the reign of this Emperor, who was a leper, there was in the Church a man named Sylvester, a Roman. Constantine went to him, was baptized in the name of Jesus Christ, and cured of his leprosy. The Emperor finding himself healed of a loathsome disease, in the name of Jesus Christ, thought he would honour him who had wrought the cure by bestowing upon him the Crown of the Empire. Sylvester accepted it, but his companion, it is said, refused his consent, separated from him, and continued to follow the path of poverty. Then, Constantine went away to regions beyond the sea, followed by a multitude of Romans, and built up the city, to which he gave his name—Constantinople—so that from that time the Heresiarch rose to honour and dignity, and evil was multiplied upon the earth. We do not believe that the Church of God, absolutely departed from the way of truth ; but one portion yielded, and, as is commonly seen, the majority was led away to evil ; the other portion remaining long faithful to the truth it had received. Thus, little by little, the sanctity of the Church declined. Eight centuries after Constantine,. there arose a man named Peter, a native, they say, of a country called Vaud." [25]

Such is the primitive tradition of the Waldenses with regard to their origin. It springs from general tradition, floating in the minds of men for generations. It took root in Lombardy during the XIV. century, and only later, as we shall see further on, did it make its appearance in the valleys of the Alps.[26] Moreover, it has no reference to the isolated existence of any particular religious sect, and not even to their creeds ; but solely to the vow of poverty, which Waldo certainly did not invent, but merely re-established.[27] The testimony of the primitive Waldenses does not, when it is well authenticated, differ materially from that of their judges.

It may be perceived from the Waldensian document quoted above, that the tradition concerning their origin had already begun to degenerate. The imaginary personage, at one time placed side by side with Sylvester, and at another confronted with him, was at first only used to represent uprightness, as the Roman Bishop represents the fall. There is this difference, however, that whereas Sylvester is a man of flesh and blood, the first of a branch like Cain, his companion, having succumbed, like Abel, leaves but a tradition without genealogy. At first he is anonymous; later he is called Leon, perhaps to explain the name of Leonists, at a time when it had already been forgotten that the disciples of Waldo were so named because they came from Lyons.[28] Perhaps in pursuance of a still more whimsical idea, the time of Waldo's appearance was antedated to the time of Sylvester; then he and this so-called Leon constitute one and the same man. Such an hypothesis could only be tenable upon the assumption that Waldo had grown old *backwards*, and that to about the age of Methuselah.[29] The tradition, started in this manner, was still more perverted by the men of the Reformation. Adopting the Waldenses as their precursors, they endeavoured, by that means, to create for themselves " a secret perpetuity during the middle ages, vying with Catholic perpetuity."[30] This purpose was easily attained, thanks to the confounding of the Waldensian reaction with those that, especially during the stormy days of persecution, preceded it. Legend, like Pharaoh's lean kine, swallowed up history; the date of Waldensian writings were confused, and false quotations did the rest.[31]

The legend is at least useful as showing an abhorrence of the vacuum, the abyss formed by Romish decadence. A bridge thrown over an obstacle, or a subterranean way beneath it, are something more than artifices. There is something real going on there which constitutes the link between the Waldensian reaction and the primitive Church. But what is it? One might think a mystery was being unfolded, and that mystery truth itself— imperishable truth. In the struggle for existence, it is truth that constitutes the future; although forced under by oppression, sooner or later it must come to the surface reverberating from distance to distance, like the echo of the apostolic voice; transmitted from hand to hand by its wonderful messengers, it traverses the night as did the fiery cross of the clans. " Et quasi cursores, vitaï lampada tradunt." The tree of life may fall alas! but it lives again in its offshoots. " Uno avulso, non deficit alter." Having whole centuries in which to work, its action is slow and gradual, but sure, notwithstanding the different reactions which seem to impede its progress. Everything surrounding its varied development is bound together and interwoven like the links of a chain; not that of the Popes, but the golden chain of the free Gospel. This is the real, the living, and legitimate succession. The Waldensian reaction is its middle link, long and precious; still that link does not constitute the chain.

The oracles of Rome have verified these successive reactions, without discovering anything good or logical in them. They acknowledge that there exists between them a certain bond of union; but, if we believe them, this bond is purely negative—mutual hatred or vanity; the heretics being only rebels or conspirators. They are compared, with much monotony of iteration, to the little foxes which are tied together by the tail and devastate the mystic vineyard.[32] The comparison is out of place, notwithstanding its Biblical colouring. It is true that Sampsons have never been wanting to tie the tails together, and Papacy has had her giants, and the giants have had their Delilahs. Equally applicable would be another figure, furnished by a great poet, held in high esteem during the middle ages. It might be said that when the Romish Church of decadence is not as furious as a bull of Bashan, it resembles the quadruped described by Virgil, when he recounts how bees come to life. "Procumbit humi bos." There he lies, his entrails exposed and smoking. Suddenly swarms of winged insects fly thereout with a buzzing sound; these are the bees and drones that form the great army of heretics. If fables must be used, it is well to use such as, like this latter one, have at least a basis of truth. But we have nothing to do with fables when it is a question of emerging from the cloud-land of legend to place our foot on the *terra firma* of reality.

To sum up : we assert, that if the antiquity attributed to the Waldenses, by tracing their genealogy back to the early days of Christianity, be only a fable, the gradual preparation of their protest during the centuries of the middle ages is an historic fact.

So much for the subject of the origin of the Waldensian reaction. In a limited sense their antiquity may be admitted ; but Waldo is the source, properly so-called, and therefore, with him the narrative must commence ; this much may as well be admitted with a good grace. Moreover, let us add with one of its critics :—" The Waldensian Church does not need, in order to render herself glorious, that her historical period should be preceded by a sort of mythical era, dating back from the time of the Apostles. It seems to us sufficiently worthy of respect, even though it be descended from a simple layman of Lyons, whose piety, moderation, and courage may be held up as an example to all. To have brought the Gospel to light again, three centuries before the Reformation, and to have preserved it ever since with heroic faithfulness, in the midst of persecution and torture, seems to us sufficiently lovely to restrain us from embellishing that undeniable fact by associating with it a long period regarding which there is no certainty. Now, we have the positive fact of Waldo; why should not that suffice so long, at least, as it cannot be proved that the Waldenses existed before him ? " [33]

# CHAPTER THE SECOND.

## THE POOR OF LYONS.

*Lyons before the XII. century—Signs of awakening—Peter Waldo : his origin : his conversion—The song of St. Alexis —The advice of the master of theology—The vow of poverty and what it entailed : the commencement of separation— Waldo's daughters in a convent : his alms—The translation of some books of the Scripture—Reunions—Archbishop Guichard and the Chapter of the Cathedral—The first lawsuit : Waldo, banished from Lyons, appeals to Rome— Alexander III., and the third Lateran Council—Waldo receives the kiss of peace—A scene in the Council—The crisis—Archbishop Jean aux Blanches Mains drives away the Waldenses and retires to a convent— The thunders of the Council of Verona.*

THE city of Lyons is one of the most ancient capitals of France. "Uniting together nations as well as rivers," as early as the time of the Romans, it attracted a varied population, eminently industrious and given to commerce.[34] During the Middle Ages it became the retreat of a swarm of fugitives, whose sole fortune was their stout arms and the water-way of the Rhone. Opulence, luxury and pleasure were there, elbowing misery, mendicity and fanaticism. The splendour of the Church was not eclipsed by that of the city.[35] The legend of her apostolic origin, the glorious memory of the martyrs, Sanctus, Attalus and Blandine ; of Potin, her first Bishop, a pastor of heroes ; finally, the venerated name of Iræneus, the conqueror of heresy, had crowned her with a brilliant halo. Afterwards came decadence, with new honours in its train. Her Bishop was promoted to the dignity of Archbishop and Primate, and along with him prospered the venerable and fat Chapter of Canons, which mustered on its rolls the sons of Princes and learned men. The

level of morality was sinking lower and lower, whilst that of
superstition was rising, like the threatening tide which no barrier
can stop.　As early as in the days of Charlemagne, efforts had
been made to turn aside the encroachment of idolatry, either by
the Decrees of Councils, or by the authority of the Bishops.
Claudius of Turin undertook this reform on the Italian side ; his
example was followed by Agobard and his disciple Amolus in
Lyons.　It was all in vain.　Zeal for the worship of images
knew no bounds.　God was made to appear to have abdicated His
throne.　Thanks to the ingenuity of the Canons, it was made to
seem as if that Divine power were passing into the hands of the
child Jesus, under the absolute regency of the Madonna.　Indeed,
to the Chapter of Lyons belongs the questionable honour of
having, about the year 1140, corruption being then at its height,
inaugurated the Feast of the Immaculate Virgin, and this notwithstanding the remonstrances of St. Bernard.　But although
the feast was denounced as an innovation, and that by the
most venerated voice[36] amongst them, the Canons of Lyons won
their case.　Did not St. Bernard go so far as to assert that
feasts should be left to the saints in Paradise, and banished
from this vale of exile and misery ?[37]　The Canons were not
troubled with his gloomy disposition.　They did not consider it so
very wrong to anticipate celestial joys.　In their opinion, it be-
hoved men to make merry, and this opinion was shared by many
people in a city like Lyons, who loved to dream of new pleasures.
This novelty, like many others, was not long in becoming a custom ; and early tradition, driven further and further back, seemed
to be swallowed up by a heap of abuses.　To be new, it only had to
come out, but at its own risk and peril ; for the clerical tribe does
not fancy ghosts of that kind, and would have given it the cold
shoulder.[38]　That had happened before, and will happen again.
　　Yet, though in Lyons people accepted the new order, great
signs of a reaction were appearing on the horizon.　After the time
of Berengarius, the word of truth had burst forth in the protest of
Abelard.　He was compelled to give way it is true, but the blow
of his battering ram had been fatal ; the breach made in the walls
of scholasticism was never again repaired; nay, it became enlarged
on all sides, and assailants of every class were seen to be mount-
ing it.　Discussion of the dogmas and customs of the Church
became general.　In 1140, the bishops of France were writing to

the Pope. "Everywhere in our cities and villages, not only in our schools but at the street corners, learned and ignorant, great and small, are discussing the gravest mysteries."[39] It seemed indeed as if the foundations of the Church were being upheaved ; storms of ideas and lurid lights were arising on all sides. " The re-animated fragments of the past came into collision with the germs of the future, which were striving to spring into life under numerous and strange forms. The science of Greek antiquity, as yet ill-understood, the bold conceptions of Arab genius, the distorted traditions of Persian Magianism and of the old mystic theories which had well-nigh ruined Christianity at its birth, were quickly springing up. These were intermingled with new interpretations of the Gospel which were audaciously progressive, and with opinions, which, on the contrary, sought refuge in primitive Christian tradition against the innovations of Rome."[40] It is worth while to pause a moment to contemplate this novel scene.

The Crusades had opened the way for invasions from the East, of the Saracens, the Jews, the Cathari. The latter brought into the field of discussion the Manichean two-fold principle of good and evil, together with a train of Gnostic legends.[41] From Bosnia they spread over Italy like a swarm of grasshoppers, and without losing any time, passed into Provence and Languedoc, where strangers called them after the name of Albi,[42] one of their centres. On the other hand, behold two heroes coming out of the school of Abelard, in the very heart of France. One of them, the younger, will by-and-by go to Rome, and there at the end of his troubled career proclaim the separation of the Church from the world, and in principle that of the Church from the State.[43] The other as firm as his predecessors in repelling the idolatry which is invading Divine worship, goes so far as to reject even the symbol of the Cross. More resolute than Berengarius, he rejects too the dogma of transubstantiation. With the Albigenses he condemns the above-mentioned superstitions, as also that of the salvation of children by the sprinkling of water; but while he condemns these he is tolerant of Pagan dualism and the mania for celibacy. Peter died in 1126, the victim of a mob, while Arnaldo died in 1155. Yet ere that fire was kindled which was to burn Peter de Bruys at the stake, Henry of Lausanne—also called the Italian—had arisen. At first he was thought merely to have been won over to the general reform, promulgated by

Gregory VII., against the dissolute priesthood; but men soon discovered in him the elder Peter de Bruys' disciple, successor, and heir.[44] He also succumbed, and that as early as 1148. The reaction went on notwithstanding the checks it had received. Driven out of Toulouse, its centre, it sent out swarms on all sides without materially depopulating the parent hive. One colony is found in Cologne. Bees and drones are all mixed up together. The Albigenses are readily recognized by their parti-coloured dualism; others gradually borrow from them more than one element of reform; and ultimately they reject all the sacraments except baptism, which they reserve for believers; they reject the mediation of saints, and the prayers for the dead, as a consequence of their no longer admitting the doctrine of purgatory, at least as defined by the Church. In this way they attacked the priesthood at a time when it set itself up as more than ever indispensable. They ousted the clergy from their office and made laymen of them.[45] Such actions as these, which are common both to the Albigenses and the Henricians, betray certain points of contact in their principles. The most evident is the common profession of poverty, a direct consequence of the light in which the apostasy of the dominant Church was regarded at that time. To lead a life of poverty is the first symptom of a return to the good apostolic tradition; it is by their poverty, even more than by their love of their neighbour, that at that time the disciples of Christ may be recognized. Hence, poverty constituted their prestige. "We are Christ's poor," said they, as they fled before their persecutors; "we lead a wandering life, and why? Because we are not of this world. You, on the contrary, addressing their persecutors, are at peace with it because you are its friends."[46] The Parthian's dart was not sharper. They styled themselves " apostolic," and this name is of itself a formidable protest, taken with the fact that about the same time Arnaldo da Brescia was preaching to the Romans that the Pope had lost the right of bearing it.[47] St. Bernard, whose mission it was to oppose them, describes them in a few words. " Do you ask what their faith is? Nothing can be more Christian. What their conduct is? Nothing can be more irreproachable; and what they preach they practice. They are assiduous in their attendance at the services, respectful towards the clergy, liberal in their offerings, and they attend confession and communion. They set an example to the faithful themselves by their life and habits ; haggard with abstinence, they avoid idleness, and earn their bread with their own hands."[48] Yet people shunned them and denounced them ; very soon they were contemptuously nicknamed Beghards and Beguines,[49] or were occasionally called by the name of St. Alexis, on account of the veneration in which he was held by them.[50] According to St. Bernard, the reason of all this was that their piety was only an artifice of the devil. These are his words ; but does he really believe what he says ? The Abbot was irritated and ill at ease when he spoke thus. The very ideal which he looks morosely upon, and which he curses in others, lies deep down in his own soul. He sees himself reflected in it as in a glass ; he would like to see it resplendent in the Church, and resting like a halo upon the head of his disciple, Pope Eugene III. It is the only crown he desired for him; but in vain. " Oh! that I might, before dying, see the Church of God led back to the ideal of her early days ! Then nets were cast out, not to gather gold, but to save souls."[51] Towards this point converge all the protests, heard both within and without the Church. From this point went forth a general if not uniform spirit that took possession of Europe. " Hoc Europa quidem fuerat jam dogmate plena."[52]

But Lyons seemed as yet untainted. " Open to all the merchants of the globe," [53] it continued to attract the youth of the neighbouring country, and more than one mountaineer eager to better his condition. About 1150, the Archiepiscopal chair was occupied by Humbert II., who was descended on his mother's side from the house of the Count of Savoy and Maurienne. What is known concerning him amounts to very little. Did he long for the reformation of the Church, as Pope Celestine V. did later on, and did it seem an impossibility to him ? We dare not suppose it. He kept himself quiet, ready at any time to *abjure his high estate* in his own small way. The chronicle says that, weary of government, he retired to a convent to end his life in a manner that was in accordance with his tastes ; and that at his death he bequeathed to the Cathedral of St. Stephen, now called St. John, a small house and a few charitable doles to keep his memory green.[54] At that time, or a little after, there lived in Lyons a man who was about to rise and undertake that which, notwithstanding their prestige, neither Popes nor Prelates had yet succeeded in accomplishing. That man was Peter Waldo.

Whence did he come? That is not known, but his name has given rise to more than one conjecture. More than one person before him had borne the name of Waldo.[55] His name is properly Valdez or Valdesius;[56] that is to say, it might easily be a surname added to the true and only one of Peter; indicating if not his place of birth, at least that of his origin.[57] Now where shall we look for that place? Not far from Lyons; doubtless towards the Alps.[58] On this point we find a diversity of opinion. Some think that Waldo originated from Dauphiny.[59] Others are inclined to believe he was born further off, even in Piedmont, where there were plenty of mountains and wooded dales. Finally, we are reminded that the Canton de Vaud in Switzerland was so called before this period,[60] and that the monk, Henry of Lausanne, came into France by the Valley of the Rhone. From this point, to arrive at the conclusion that Waldo may easily have come to Lyons by the same road, is but a step.[61] Nevertheless, the question is not settled.[62] Let us, therefore, leave it open, and return to Lyons where we find Waldo.

We are told that Waldo lived near the Church of St. Nizier, in a street afterward called Val Grant or Vaudrant, and sometimes Rue Maudite.[63] He was a merchant, and so successful, that he was in a fair way of becoming wealthy. He undoubtedly attended the fairs and markets of the neighbourhood, leading an active and laborious life. The chronicler informs us that Waldo accumulated wealth, without being very particular concerning the means employed.[64] Even if it were true, what of that? Guerrazzi wrote, not long ago, " In a merchant's house all are alike." That may be going too far; but it is certain that if Waldo had been merely a usurer, the clergy would never have thought of casting a stone at him. Had he not friends in high places, both in the city and in the Church? He enjoyed their society, it would seem, without denying himself home comforts. He went to mass like everyone else. But, lo! at a time when he was in the most comfortable circumstances, and flattered on all sides, his conscience began to trouble him. Did he, in the days of his youth, hear the voice of Henry of Lausanne or his disciples, cursing the general worldliness and proclaiming woe to those who treasure up wealth iniquitously? He may have done so, but his soul was asleep. An accident suddenly roused him. One

day, while in the company of some of the leading citizens, one of
his friends fell lifeless at his side.[65] Terrified by the event, he said
to himself: If death had stricken me, what would have become of
my soul? This thought caused him great uneasiness and
anxiety. On another occasion—on his way to or 'from mass
perhaps, for it was a Sunday—he saw a ballad singer, surrounded by an eager crowd, holding forth in the public square.
He drew near and listened; the singer was reciting in dolorous
tones the story, then much in vogue, of a saint named Alexis,
born in Rome, the only son of wealthy parents. Alexis
married, but had hardly descended the steps of the hymeneal
altar, when he turned his back upon his bride and left his parents,
in order to take the vow of poverty and make a pilgrimage to the
East. When he returned, being recognized by nobody, he begged
his relatives to grant him a shelter under the stairs, and there he
died. Then he was recognized; but it was too late.[65] The old
song of St. Alexis has been found.

> " Signour et dames, entendés un sermon
> D'un saintisme home qui Allessis ot non,
> Et d'une feme que il prist a oissor,
> Que il guerpi pour Diu son Creatour
> Saulve en est l'ame el ciel nostre Signour,
> Li cors en gist a Rom a grant hounour."

Thus runs the commencement of the strain. The singer weeps
over the good old times, and denounces the corruption of the
Church. Life is short; he continues:—

> " Al tans de Noé et al tans Abraham
> Et a Davi que Dieus par ama tant,
> Fu bons li siécles: jamais n'iert si vaillans.
> S'est empierés, et li biens va morant.
> Li ordené vont le loi mal menant :
> Trespassé ont le Damediu commant,
> Et saintes glises, filles Jherusalem,
> De tout en tout se vont afoibliant.
> La fois del siécle se va toute falant.
> Fraisle est la vie : ne duerra lonc tans."

What is to be done, but to prepare for heaven? This St.
Alexis did. Rid of his wealth and all earthly cares, he thinks
of nothing but heaven.

" En sainte église converse volontiers ;
Chascune feste se fait acomungier ;
Sainte escriture ço ert ses conseiliers.[66]"

More than one feature of this will be found resuscitated in
the protest of Waldo.   On that Sunday, Waldo greatly interested, took the singer to his own home in order that he
might repeat the whole story, for he had only heard the
end.   During the night his soul was troubled.   The next morning he anxiously wished to consult a master of theology, possibly
one of the Canons of the Cathedral, in order to arrive at
some definite conclusion relative to his salvation.   The theologian was very learned ;   he knew as many roads to heaven as
Waldo had travelled in attending the different markets.   He talked
a great deal.   The merchant's ears were full of his words ; but his
mind remained still undecided, like that of a man who is seeking
his way and suddenly comes to a cross-road.   He was perplexed
at the choice set before him, and yet he had no time to lose.   At
last he said, " Of all the roads that lead to heaven, which is the
surest ?   I desire to follow the perfect way."   Ah ! answered the
theologian, that being the case, here is Christ's precept : " If
thou wilt be perfect, go, sell that thou hast and give to the poor,
and thou shalt have treasure in heaven ; and come take up thy
cross and follow me." [68]

Waldo undoubtedly desired to understand these words more
fully than the legend of St. Alexis.   It is probable that he
left the Canon to his theological studies, intending to meditate in
solitude upon the words of the Gospel which had just been
addressed to him.   He returned home filled with the words of
Christ.   Far from distorting their meaning by giving them a
mystic, allegorical, and especially a less inconvenient meaning,
after the manner of men in all ages who have tried to reconcile
the doctrine of our Saviour, with love for this world's goods, he took
the precept literally, immediately set about putting it into practice,
and cast his eyes over his possessions ; this time, not for the
purpose of taking stock of them, but to see how he might get rid
of them.   He spoke to his wife about the matter.   At first she was
disconcerted, but when she fully understood his intention, she became calmer.   He said to her, " I am possessed of personal property
and real estate, take your choice."   The list of real estate was a
long one, houses, meadows, vineyards, woods, bakehouses, and

mills, with rent arising from all.    The wife did not hesitate long ; she chose the real estate, and did not ever give it up.[69]    Both felt they had chosen the "better part," each from his own standpoint.    There remained the ready money and what might be realized from the sale of the stock-in-trade.    What should be done with that ?    First, he would make reparation for any injustice of which he might have been guilty.[70]    Then he would devote a portion of it to providing a dowry for his two daughters, whom he decided to remove from their mother's influence, and to place without her knowledge in the Abbey of Fontevrault.    This had been founded in 1106, in Poitou, by an eccentric monk, whose name was Robert of Arbrissel, in a spirit that seems to have anticipated the ideas of the " Poor of Lyons." We give here a succinct history of this man.

Robert of Arbrissel had been at the abbey of la Roue, which he quitted for ever, to devote himself entirely to preaching ; in this intent receiving the approbation of Pope Urban II.    He had no fixed place of abode, and was followed about by a great multitude of men and women.    The presence of the latter caused him some annoyance, and he thought of providing them with some fixed dwelling place.    He was blamed not only for a certain indiscreet familiarity, which gave occasion for invidious remark, but also for his strange appearance, long beard, bare feet, and mean and ragged clothing.    These singularities seemed less likely to give him authority among the simple and needy, than to create a suspicion concerning his sanity among such wise men as Bishop Marbode of Rheims, his superior.    Furthermore, he was accused of declaiming against the priests and the higher clergy, " thereby causing several curates to be deserted by their flocks."[71]  Criticized thus, he finally looked for a place of refuge in the desert, on the confines of the diocese of Poitiers, two leagues from Cande in Touraine.    " This spot, called Fontevrault, was uncultivated, covered with thorns and briars, and Robert having obtained possession of it from the owners, at once erected huts as a protection from the weather, and built an oratory.    He separated the women from the men, and shut the former up by themselves, intending that they should devote themselves chiefly to prayer, whilst the men should work.    Ecclesiastics and laymen lived together, the former sang psalms and celebrated mass, the latter performed manual labour ;  and all preserved silence at certain times. They lived very frugally and unitedly, and called Robert ' Master,' simply because he would not allow the title of ' Dom ' or ' Abbot ' to be used. He denounced sin and sinners vehemently, and his discourses displayed marvellous energy ; but he was gentle with the penitent ; indulgent to others, he was stern to himself. Hypocrisy he hated. He would not have his disciples bear any other name than that of the ' Poor of Jesus Christ.' Indeed they lived for some time on what was voluntarily supplied by the inhabitants of the surrounding country."[72] Such was the origin of the Abbey founded in honour of the Virgin Mary. Donations soon began to flow in, thanks to the favour of the Bishop of Poitiers, who revered the memory of Robert of Arbrissel as that of an " apostolic man." In Waldo's time the monastery of Fontevrault was fashionable. It received the daughters of the nobility, widows, and even beggars ; and it is believed that, in certain cases, the pupils were permitted to quit the institution after a certain time and yet retain the name of the " Poor of Christ," which they had learned to love.

To this solitary dwelling-place Waldo consigned his two daughters. He had not as yet parted with all his property, the larger portion of the ready money still remained. This was reserved for the poor, and, as we shall see further on, for a work that rendered his name glorious. At that time famine was raging, and the city of Lyons was swarming with beggars. To relieve them, Waldo did not proceed at hap-hazard but according to certain rules. Nothing in his manner recalls that of some well-known monks who, actuated rather by a desire for show, than by love for their neighbour, did not think of the profit which the poor might derive from the wealth which they gave up. He did not proceed, as did, for instance, Francis of Assise, who threw his father's money out of window ; or like Gerard Segarelli who divided his wealth among rogues, who gambled it away. Such proceedings are so contrary to all reason, that a great wit, though a zealous Franciscan, in remarking upon them, added with a touch of irony, that Christ had indeed commanded us to give our goods to the poor, but not to rogues.[73] Waldo, while conforming to the manners of his age, was more sensible. He planned a regular distribution of bread, meat, and other provisions to the poor. Beginning at Pentecost, this distribution was continued three times a week until the feast of the Ascension of the Virgin, which was at that time celebrated in the middle of August. We read that on that day he distributed the rest of his money to the starving poor in the streets, saying to whomsoever chose to hear him : " No man can serve two masters, God and Mammon." When the crowd thronged him on all sides, and people began to laugh, thinking he had gone out of his mind, he took up a position whence he could be heard by all and spoke as follows :—

" Citizens and friends, I am not mad as you suppose. This is what I have done : I have revenged myself on enemies, who had reduced me to such a state of servitude as to make me more heedful of money than of God ; more subject to the creature than to the Creator. I know that not a few will blame me for doing these things publicly ; but I have acted in this manner for my own sake, who now speak to you, and for yours, who hear me ; for myself, that anyone may call me mad who in future shall see me possessed of money ; for you also, in a measure, that you may learn to put your trust in God and no longer run after wealth."[74]

That was the end. The next day as he returned from mass, Waldo asked a friend to give him something to eat. His friend took him to his house, received him like a brother, and said :— " Now ask for anything you require ; as long as I live you shall not want for the necessaries of life." Waldo's wife, however, got wind of this, and was almost distracted. She ran to the Archbishop, and told him with tears of the affront that had been put upon her. On a sign from the Archbishop, the hospitable host was ordered to give up his guest and to bring him before the Prelate. When Waldo's wife saw him, she seized him by the coat, exclaiming : " Husband, listen ; if anyone is to redeem his soul by the alms he gives you, is it not best that it should be your wife rather than such as are not of our household ?"[75] What answer could be made to that ? The husband undoubtedly could have urged good reasons ; but he did not care to prolong a scene that was both ridiculous and painful. Before being allowed to quit the archiepiscopal presence, Waldo was obliged to listen to a homily upon his prodigality, and was formally forbidden, when he was in the city, at least, ever to take food from that day forth anywhere but at his wife's table.[76]

This happened in 1173, under Archbishop Guichard, the third successor of him whom we mentioned at the commencement of this narrative.[77]

Thus far, we have no sign of the Reformer, although we know that the renouncing of this world's goods had become the *sine quâ non* of every popular reform. But our historian has omitted one important fact, which will provide us with a key to what we have already read and to much which follows.

On leaving the theologian, Waldo had resolved to profit more than ever by the very rare opportunities he possessed for listening to the reading of the Gospel which it is true was read only in Latin and in the church. In this he did not fail, but the readings being only occasional, and at times unintelligible, soon tried his patience. The reading was bad, and Waldo was not well versed in Latin,[78] although he understood something of it. He tried to read for himself, and with more profit; but he met with more than one obstacle; nevertheless, that instinct of truth which guides honest souls, told him that he had laid his hand upon a treasure more precious than all earthly possessions. The word of Christ already held his mind under a divine spell; while it bound his conscience, which feared not the chains of obedience. Little by little, its precepts were engraved upon his mind, and he wished to read the whole of it. To attain his purpose, he associated to himself two ecclesiastics, by means of a little of that money which he was happy to get rid of and they to receive.[79] If his riches were sinful, was not that the most excellent means of making friends with them? According to the arrangement made with his co-workers, one of them wrote from the dictation of the other, who translated the Latin into the dialect of the country. The first was Bernard Ydros, the other Stephen of Ansa.[80] They commenced with the Gospels; then they took up a few other books of the Scriptures, neglecting not at the same time to make a little collection of maxims from the writings of the Fathers of the Church. Waldo was never tired of reading that translation; it seemed to be engraved upon the tables of his memory and heart.[81] He was ceaselessly meditating upon it, and soon began to repeat it to others, without giving much thought to furnishing any explanation of it. There were a great many ballad singers about at that time, but none that carried the Gospel with them. Waldo became a sort of walking Bible. He had not to seek far for an audience, as his house was open to the poor. To them it was that he first spoke,[82] teaching them word by word the primary truths which he himself had appropriated. One may easily guess what they were. Did he not find in the Scriptures both the condemnation of his past life and of the general decadence of faith and morals ? " Whether we look at ourselves, or at the time in which we live," he said, " who does not sigh on account of the oblivion into which the precepts of the Gospel have fallen ?[83] Still there remains for us something better to do than merely to complain ; we will practice those precepts, beginning with the very first, which bids us give up earthly possessions and depend only upon God.[84] That will be the means of reviving apostolic life,[85] and with it the Church itself."

Thus spoke Waldo. When his profession of poverty had become well-known and had been imitated by a few disciples, he faced the masses, and we have already seen that he knew how to do that at the proper time. He had noticed that the Apostles were not satisfied with leading a life of poverty, but that they obeyed in a special manner the last command : " Go into all the world, and preach the Gospel to every creature."[86] Without being able to silence the scoffers, he soon gained the confidence of the humble. His disciples became almost as many co-workers for him, no longer hired like the two ecclesiastics, but voluntary. He practised them in reading, and, by assiduous instruction, he strengthened them in their vocation.[87] Then they went out into the public places and the workshops, and visited from house to house, whilst what they had to say, was summed up for the time being, in these words : " Blessed are the poor in spirit, for theirs is the Kingdom of Heaven."

Thus did the Waldensian community come into existence. Rich in promises of a future, by reason of its voluntary poverty, and its fidelity to the meek and gentle Master, whom it was preparing to serve in humility and follow to the end, it was already a living protest against the worldliness of the fallen church. The vow which bound its different members together was not a new one ; it would have alarmed no one if each of its members had not been bound by another vow, more or less tacit, yet real, that of speaking freely. " To become poor," especially when one is rich ; to become poor, no longer after the manner of those who consent to it only on condition of lacking nothing, was rare and beautiful ; but after all it did not accomplish the main object. " To evangelize the poor ; " this was its care, its peculiarity, its ideal, from the beginning ; its wisdom according to some ; according to others its folly.

What will become of the new community ? With humility and unaffected simplicity it marched without fear to encounter danger, perhaps it did not even suspect the danger.

Waldo's friends were beginning to forsake him. If they met him in the street they were careful not to recognise him. At his age, he might, perhaps, have been forgiven had he entered into unprofitable speculations ; but to make. himself poor for the sake of following Christ in a manner different to other people seemed monstrous. There was no doubt amongst his friends that his mind was affected ; upon this point there was a consensus of opinion. As for the ecclesiastics, it is very true that Waldo had estranged them—unintentionally, however. He had disposed of his entire fortune, he had provided for his wife and his daughters ; he had looked after the interests of all sorts of creditors, and of the poor in the street, *and had given nothing to the Church.* This was his offending. Furthermore, what was he doing ? A layman, it was argued, should keep quiet ; even though he may be somewhat of a scholar. A man might be forgiven for giving alms, but not for preaching sermons ! [88] It is true that he did not venture to occupy the pulpit ; he preferred a stone step ; but in one respect that seemed worse, because by that means religion, it was held, was profaned. For one donation which he had was bestowed upon the Church, how many pearls had he not cast before swine ? That smacked of heresy, and the scandal appeared the more lamentable that, in order to go and listen to Waldo, the populace turned its back upon the magnificent preaching to be heard in the Cathedral.

"Ne sutor ultra crepidam," they in the Canon's Chapel sententiously said. A deep, coarse voice would add, " It is time this thing was put a stop to."

Waldo had heard that voice before ; it was that of Archbishop Guichard, whose business occupations, to tell the truth, did not always leave him sufficient leisure to attend to his pastoral cares. He had been worried by a dispute with the house of the Count of Fores which would not relinquish its rights over the city. In consequence of this quarrel, the Chapter had been in a flutter ; it had even been compelled to flee with the Archbishop, while marauders pillaged the houses. But Guichard worked so long and so adroitly that he attained his object. Weary of the struggle and constrained by force of circumstances, Count Guido II. gave up all his privileges to the Archbishop and the Chapter, in exchange for a few castles and the sum of a thousand marks. From that time, the Canons as well as the Archbishop, bore the title of Count. That state of things did not last long, for the people of Lyons did not look with favour upon the transfer of civil power to the hands of the priests, they even rose up against the priests, and forced them to do homage to the king of France. But for the time being, the Chapter was merry, and clerical rule plumed itself to its heart's content. Guichard, now freed from the weighty cares of politics, kept a watchful eye upon the Church. In 1174, he attended the dedication of a chapel at Clairvaux. It has been pretended that two years later he took part in a Synod against the heretic Albigenses; nay, more, that he there pronounced a sentence upon their leader; but that is a mistake.[89] It is more probable that he devoted his attention to the Waldensian mission, and that if he did not lay it under an interdict, he succeeded, at least, in troubling it. If he had interfered in a question pertaining to a private household, what would he not do, now that it concerned, as he believed, the house of God? Thereupon Waldo was undoubtedly summoned again before him,[90] but this time the Prelate found him to be less docile. We may presume that with an accent of conviction, which must necessarily have made a certain amount of impression, he claimed the right to live a life of poverty, to read the Gospel, and to proclaim it after the manner of the Apostles. He did not deviate in the least from the good tradition; on the contrary, he maintained it. But Guichard did not see matters in the light that he did. In his opinion, Waldo was in the wrong, and he took good care to make him feel that he thought so. He filed a suit, and doubtless cited Waldo and some of his brethren to appear before the Synod of the diocese; but that was only as a matter of form. The deliberations were not long pending, and the defendants were called into court. "You are prohibited," said the Archbishop, "from meddling with preaching, even though it be for explaining the Scriptures as you say. You have nothing to do but to obey. Otherwise we shall proceed according to our regulations."[91] Peter rose from his seat and replied, "Judge ye whether it be lawful before God to obey you rather than God: for we cannot refuse to obey him who hath said, ' Go ye into all the world and preach the Gospel to every creature.' "[92]

Upon that Waldo and his friends were banished from the diocese.[93] Little more was wanting to induce Waldo to go and see the Pope.

This took place in the year 1177 on the eve of the third council of the Lateran.[94]

We do not stop at the fact of Waldo's visit to the Eternal City at the time of a great Council. Historians, even those who are most fond of legends, do not pay any attention to this one, or else they doubt it on untenable grounds. But before reaching this point, let us glance briefly at the events that were taking place in the world, and especially in Rome.

The world was then resounding with the news of the brilliant victory of Legnano, won by the free cities of Lombardy against the Emperor Frederick Barbarossa. The Pope, who had had some difficulty with the latter, was as jubilant over it as if it had been the most glorious event of his reign; although he did hardly anything but play the part of a looker-on who watches the game to profit by the issue.[95] Meanwhile Frederick betook himself to Venice, where peace was to be concluded. The Pope announced his intention of meeting him there, and did not fail. A treaty was made, a humiliating one for the chivalric monarch, and it is well-known that in order to obtain its ratification, he condescended to kiss the Pontiff's foot. To this day a flagstone of red porphyry is pointed out in the vestibule of St. Mark's Cathedral, which, the guides say, marks the spot where this ridiculous but imposing ceremony took place. It left a very vivid impression on men's minds. Legend, as well as art, seized upon it ; and, by the order of the Republic of Venice. itself, the scene was represented in a picture which is still to be seen in the ancient palace of the Doges. Frederick is therein represented at the moment when the shoe of Alexander III. rests upon his imperial neck, and when the latter, intoxicated with pride, addresses to himself the famous words : " Super aspidem et basiliscum ambulabis et conculcabis leonem et draconem." Having gained a complete victory, the Pontiff, resplendent as the sun—to which, since the eclipse of Canossa, the successors of Gregory VII. have so often delighted in comparing themselves—thought of employing it for the consolidation of his power, and thereby for the peace of the Church, which was rent by schism. For that purpose, he convened an œcumenical council in Rome, on the first

Sunday in Lent, of the year 1179.[96] Three-hundred-and-two bishops were present, with the Prelates, Senators and Consuls of Rome. The Emperor Frederick was conspicuous by his absence. The Gauls were represented by Archbishop Pons of Narbonne and a few prelates of second rank ; as for their Primate, he had not been able to leave Lyons.

The dominant note at this Council may be easily guessed. The object was to support clericalism. Under Innocent II. it had been proposed to withdraw the election of the Pope from the suffrages of the Princes and the Roman people, and Alexander's successor had been the first to benefit by this change. In fact an attempt was to be made to deprive the laity of their right of electing their bishops. Having gained their independence, the clergy claimed a monopoly, and the movement initiated by Gregory VII. did not fall far short of accomplishing it. The Prelates held high state in luxury and opulence ; the rapacity of the Papal Legates in devouring the revenues of the Church had set public opinion in motion. They were compared to a flight of locusts, and their abuses were justly condemned. When the end of the last session came there remained but one canon to define ; this was aimed against the heretics. The Church, it proceeds to say, has always had a horror of blood ; still it is bound to recognise the fact that the dread of physical pain may have a salutary effect. Therefore, considering that the heretics who go by the name of Cathari, Patarins, Publicans, or whatever they may be called, have become so numerous in Gascony, the territory of the Albigenses of Toulouse and in other places, that they no longer even conceal themselves, as some do, but publicly teach their errors and lead astray the simple-minded, this Council therefore anathematizes them ; both them and those who afford them protection or shelter, and forbids anybody, under pain of excommunication, to receive them either in their houses or on their premises, to protect or have anything to do with them, to perform religious services on their behalf, or to grant them burial among Christians ; and it blesses those who shall take up arms against them. Thereupon, invoking the help of Princes, the Council proceeds to award them, as remuneration, all confiscated properties, besides the general indulgence promised to the faithful.[97]

It is evident that there is nothing in the decrees of the Council concerning the Waldenses. But if the Waldenses did appeal to Rome where they were cited to appear before the Council, [98] it must be admitted at least that their case would have been, under such circumstances, subjected to a preliminary hearing, followed by a resolution of some sort. One writer of the period reports that the Council pronounced a sentence of condemnation against the Waldenses as heretics.[99] But in lieu of anticipating, let us return to Waldo whom we left on the eve of starting for Rome.

Waldo in Rome! The fact seems strange, but the reason is simple. Thus far the various testimony which confirms it has not received the attention it is entitled to, although what it tells us harmonizes with everything that we read on the subject of Waldo.[100] Still, for what purpose did he go? This question will be difficult for those only who are the victims of prejudice. Waldo is dressed up as one of the reformed, and it then becomes impossible to conceive the idea of his going to Rome like a good Catholic. He is dressed almost like a clergyman, and lo, he proposes to have a regular entry made of his vow of poverty! However, it must be confessed that the imagination which could suspect Dante of being " a pastor of the Church of Albigenses of the city of Florence,"[101] was capable of taking still greater liberties on the subject of Waldo. Let us return to facts.

Thus far Waldo had not the slightest visible bond of union with the adversaries of the Church. It was to ministers of the Catholic church that he had first applied for support ; it is out of respect for her that he undertook a journey to Rome. He had taken the vow of poverty like a faithful Catholic, even as one of the old school ; but the validity of his action being disputed, he would go and ask the Pope to sanction it. Nothing could be more logical. The example of Peter of Lyons going to ask the approbation of Alexander III. was followed later on by Francis of Assisi in the days of Innocent III. But in addition to his vow of poverty, Waldo was haunted by a new care. He feared lest the liberty to preach the Gospel, which he claimed by virtue of his vow of poverty, might be contested. He hoped to obtain both from Alexander III. and the third Lateran Council, a permission similar to that which Dominic in his turn invoked from Pope Innocent III. and the fourth Council. Confident of being in the right, he by no means despaired of obtaining justice; for after all, it was quite evident from the Scriptures and the Fathers

that he was introducing no innovation, and he had taken note of
this. This is simplicity,[102] some will say, but whose fault was
that ? We shall soon see, for Waldo has arrived at the gates of
Rome !

The Pope, after ten years' exile, had returned to Rome on the
12th of March, 1178. The unheard of festivities, with which he
had been received, were no longer spoken of ; because the reconcilia-
tions of the Roman people with their Popes were as frequent as
they were insincere, and hence also they were of short duration.
Some new plot was being laid to shake off his tyrannical yoke,
and he knew it perfectly well. What a destiny was that of this
people ! Never free, constantly engaged in revolutions, ever
rolling its stone of Sisyphus ! It was pitiful, especially at that
time, when Italy was witnessing the revival of her civil liberties,
which were dreaded by the very monarch who had sent to the
scaffold Arnaldo da Brescia, the great Tribune of independence.
Between the aspirations of the Romans and those of the Pope
there was, unfortunately, one thing in common, namely, an
incurable and fruitless ambition to rule, or, if nothing more could
be gained, at least to appear to rule *urbi et orbi*. This ambition
was not badly expressed in an inscription, which Waldo may
have read, when he visited the city.

Roma vetusta fuit, sed nunc nova Roma vocabor,
Eruta ruderibus culmen ad alta fero.

Alexander III. lived, if not like a prisoner, at least as if in
an enemy's country.[103] The Eternal City, bristling with 361
towers, 49 fortified castles, and 6,900 ramparts, resembled less
the mystic Zion than a gigantic mouse trap. What may surprise
us is, not that Waldo entered there, but that he ever came out
again. It is true that he entered it with hundreds of Bishops
and thousands of pilgrims, who arrested public attention sufficiently
to permit him to pass in unperceived. In those days there was
nothing going on in Rome of a nature to interest him except the
Council. They were not translating the Bible there, as in Lyons ;
they were attending to quite other labours. The learned
Albinus was about to begin the collection of documents likely
to justify the original rights of the Holy See. Others following
the footsteps of the monk Gratianus were compiling canons—
not without consulting his *Concordia discordantium canonum*,
which had been the rage. Some thought they had made

astounding discoveries on the subject of Virgil. Several were on the point of attributing to him Messianic visions; nay more, some discerned in him the Morning Star that had heralded the sun of the papacy and a new era. Some thought they had discovered that the Apostle Paul had made a pilgrimage to Naples to visit his sepulchre. Finally, he was no longer a magician, but a prophet, and saint in the popular imagination. He was being seized upon as a subject for sacred pictures, and presented to the veneration of the faithful, while his legend was sung before the altars.[104] All this was going on in Rome, and Waldo had not even heard a whisper of it. But if he were unknowing, he was also unknown. Nobody knew who he was, nor what brought him to the Eternal City. His mission, however, they soon heard of in high places, when the time had come for the "Poor of Lyons" to present himself before the conqueror of Barbarossa.

When Waldo arrived in the presence of the Pope he was received as a beloved son of the Church; he had even the good fortune to receive a solemn embrace from His Holiness.[105] Was he surprised at this? Less than we are, undoubtedly. It must be admitted that, after a lapse of seven centuries, the anecdote has become stimulating to the imagination. But why should we look upon that act as a mark of personal benevolence? It was not a question of personal affection, but of sanctioning a vow of poverty.[106] Hence, that kiss did not over-excite the imagination of the Waldenses. No mention is made of it in their writings, nor even in popular tradition. Certainly they do not think of recording it.

The sanction granted by Alexander did not imply, however, liberty to preach—quite the contrary. It is therefore probable that Waldo prolonged his stay in Rome for the purpose of softening the will of the Pontiff.[107] A cardinal who enjoyed his evangelical and artless speech interested himself in Waldo, it seems, and pleaded his cause,[108] so says the chronicle. It adds that on this occasion Waldo engaged not to depart from the doctrine of the Latin Fathers, especially Ambrose, Augustine, Gregory and Jerome, who were deemed the pillars of the Romish Church.[109] Finally, must they not have been convinced, when they listened to him, that he had not the slightest notion of becoming the rival of titled preachers? His mission was more humble. He did not even endeavour to preach, but to talk.[110] One is therefore tempted to believe that, out of regard for Waldo and his defenders, the Pope

may have yielded for a moment, pending a final decision. Indeed,
one chronicle asserts that he did,[111] and another tells us that
Waldo evangelized in Rome, and not without success.[112] But
where did all this dispute take place ?   In the Council, of course.
Let us enter there ; we shall assist at a curious little scene.   We
have a description of it from the hand of the principal actor ; this
was Walter Map, a Welshman, a delegate of Edward II., King
of England.   A passably good scholar, a friend of art, at one time
jester, at another pedant, he concealed under the guise of a truly
conventual humility a courtier's soul, which aimed at effect.   This
will be well seen, for his language soon betrays it.

   " I saw in the Council," says our writer, " some Waldenses,
ignorant and unmannered people, called by the name of Waldo,
their chief, who was formerly a citizen of Lyons on the Rhone.[113]
They presented to the Pope a book written in the dialect of Gaul,
containing the text of and a glossary to the Psalms, together with
several portions of the Old and New Testaments.   These people
insisted that their right to preach should be recognised.   They
considered themselves worthy ; as a matter of fact they were
nothing but fools, like the birds which do not observe the nets and
fancy they can always find a way of escape.   I, poor wretch, who
felt remarkably small in such an imposing assembly, could not
help thinking it ridiculous that their request should be seriously
considered, and that it took so long to arrive at a decision.
Being called upon, I expressed my opinion.   At last, before
several theologians well versed in the Canon law, two Waldenses were brought forward, who were reputed to belong to
the chiefs of the sect.   They were not abashed, for they expected
to silence me.   I took my seat with perturbation.   I have no
hesitation in saying so, for I could not help asking myself whether
for my sins I had not deserved that I should have been refused
permission to speak in so grand a Council.   But the Pontiff
directed me to question them, which I was very ready to do.   I
commenced with the most elementary questions, which everyone
should be capable of answering ; being well aware that a donkey
which can munch oats does not disdain milk diet.

   " ' Do you believe in God the Father ?'
   " ' We do believe in Him.'
   " ' And in His Son ?'
   " ' We believe in Him also.'

" ' And in the Holy Ghost ? '

" ' Equally.'

" ' And in the mother of Christ ? '

" ' Yes.'

" At this the whole assembly burst out laughing.[114]  Our friends retired in confusion and justice was done.  They pretended to be guides and were themselves in want of guides ; resembling in this case Phæton, who did not even know the names of his horses.  These are people without fixed abode. They go about in pairs, bare-footed with a woollen tunic and possessing nothing.  Being poor themselves they follow a Christ who is poor, like the Apostles.  Certainly they cannot take a humbler stand for they have scarcely learned to walk.  But if we admit them, it is we who ought to be turned out."[115]

The end of it all was that the Waldenses lost their cause. The answer of the Council as delivered by the Pope may be summed up in two words :—" You shall not under any circumstances preach, except at the express desire and under the authority of the clergy of your country."[116]

What were they to do ?  There remained nothing for them but to bow their heads submissively and to carry the grave news to Lyons,  Could Waldo return there again ? or would he remain in Italy [117] among the sect of the " Poor of Lombardy," who had also and very justly claimed the right of free speech ?[118]  We cannot tell for certain.  Then occurred that ominous pause which precedes all revolutions, and men hastened to pretend to see in it an indication of wavering.[119]  Not so.  The Waldenses drew themselves back to consult their oracle—that is to say God's own Word. Instinctively they were led to read over again the first acts of the Church of the Apostles, in that book which traces with such truthfulness the relations between them and the ancient Synagogue.  They meditated and compared and were finally able to make out their real position.  They felt as though scales had fallen from their eyes.  Waldo was not far away ; he roused himself like a lion awakening from his sleep, and repeated the apostolic cry, " We must obey God rather than men."  That day a Reformer was born.  The apostolic motto remains ; it forms their Articles of Association.  The choice was made, conscience was saved and with it reason and liberty.  What would be the issue ?  It was well foreseen.  To-morrow rupture ; after that

c 2

persecution.　Meanwhile the mission of the Waldenses took a fresh onward leap.　Like the river which is momentarily interrupted in its course, it advanced with a bound.

Waldo multiplied himself, thanks to the co-operation of his most faithful friends, amongst them perhaps Vivetus, of whom we hear.[121]　With their assistance, if not with them, he taught and evangelized.　The sect of the Waldenses was established.　This was not sufficient; he sent his brethren two by two, into the surrounding countries, and so effectually did the word of Christ spread abroad that, ere long, one could say of the diocese of Lyons what Melanchthon wrote concerning another country at the dawn of the Reformation, " The Gospel resounds in this country—*sonat Evangelium*."

Unfortunately, it was not for long.　Alexander III., driven by the tide of revolution, had quitted his country for the last time and had just died on 30th August, 1181.　Guichard, the aged Archbishop, was also dead and had left his throne a prey to the intrigues which were the ordinary prelude to a new election.　He was succeeded by Jean aux Blanches Mains, heretofore bishop of Poitiers, and the Archbishop designate of Narbonne.[122]　The installation of the new Primate of the Gauls was no sooner decreed at Rome, where Lucius III. had taken the place of Alexander, than it was celebrated by the gay city of Lyons, with the Chapter at its head.[123]　Jean aux Blanches Mains accepted his festive reception with a good grace.　He was said to be a learned and eloquent man;[124] but he had little else than that eloquence which borrows clerical thunders.　When the festivities incident upon his installation were at an end, he turned to business.　The aged counsellors of the Archbishop declared that it was urgently necessary to put an end, once for all, to the preaching which had been carried on in the houses and even in the streets to the prejudice of the sacred ministry.　Moreover, it was the express desire of the Pope.[125]　Nothing remained to be done but to carry it into execution.　John summoned Waldo to appear.　He told him to desist from preaching and enjoined the same upon all his disciples; but he availed nothing.[126]　At last the Waldenses were driven into exile.　It is said that there were about eight thousand of them.[127]

A few years after, a decrepit old man was sighing over his sins in the Convent of Clairvaux.　He read the sacred Scriptures with devotion, and was particularly absorbed in meditating on the Psalms. Every day he celebrated mass for his own soul and that of St. Bernard. When he wrote to friends it was always in these words, " I am doing penance here ; I am atoning for my crimes ; I beseech you intercede for my pardon—*suppliciter exoro quatinus pro reatuum meorum venia intervenire dignemini.*"[128]

This Latin is authentic. It was written by the white hand of John, Archbishop of Lyons, after he had abdicated, previous to doing penance.

Compared with those Primates of the Gauls and their pitiful ideal of shutting themselves up in a convent to mumble over a " *mea culpa,*" Waldo seems to us a grand contrast, owing to the character, simplicity, and logic of his convictions. That which Archbishops muttered at their last hour, he carried written large upon his forehead. He read the same Bible ; but like a free man, surrounded by souls whom he enlightened and saved by means of that book, he found better things to do than to shut himself up in the solitary cell of a cloister, when people were dying of ignorance. He went out and faced the world, bearing the Word of life and followed by a legion of missionaries.

Hunted out of their native town, the Waldenses discovered more than one country suited for their adoption. It must be confessed that up to that time their community had been recruited from none but the poorer classes, and had attracted neither the nobility nor the middle classes. But if the wind had hitherto set always in favour of clericalism, a future was imminent in which it would favour liberty. Hitherto there had been nothing done but preparatory work ; now the mission of Waldo was about to commence in reality. He devoted himself entirely to it, and so thoroughly, that a cloud of silence gathered around him, and it has been supposed that this was the silence of death. Still he was " nel mezzo del cammin di *sua* vita." Only, like the poet he was entering a dark forest, wild and full of dangers. His career was as long as it was laborious. He died full of years about 1217,[129] leaving an ineffaceable impression upon the minds of men, and a vacant place which was more difficult to fill satisfactorily than was the throne of his Archbishop.

But listen ! The forest is filled with sounds. Is that lightning which has just struck ? Yes, it is the greater excommunication pronounced by Pope Lucian III. in the Council of Verone under the

auspices of the Emperor Frederick, towards the end of the year
1183. It runs thus :—" By the present decree we condemn
all heresies; therefore we first anathematize the Cathari and
the Patarins, as well as those who conceal themselves under the
name of Humiliati or Poor of Lyons, the Passagins, Josephites,
and Arnaldists. And as some with a certain appearance of piety,
but denying the real sense of the Apostle's words, arrogate to
themselves the right of preaching, although the very same apostle
says, ' How will they preach if they are not sent ? ' we include
under the same perpetual anathema all those who, in spite of our
interdiction and without being sent by us, shall dare to preach
whether in private or in public, contrary to the authority represented by the Apostolic See and the Bishops."[130]

Evidently this general decree was aimed directly at the Waldenses. They were heretics because they arrogated to themselves
the right of preaching. War was now openly declared ; they were
hunted like wild beasts on the mountains, in the valleys, and along
the roads. What will become of them now ? Will they perish
in the dark glades of the forest ? No, certainly not ; they carried
with them that light which shines in darkness.

# CHAPTER THE THIRD.

## THE DISPERSION.

*The Exodus—The Waldenses enter into Dauphiny after a
protest from Peter of Bruys and Henry of Lausanne—The
reactions in Southern France : why the doctrine of the Cathari
was propagated there ; its progress and influence—Appearance
of the Waldenses : their disputation with the Catholic clergy
at Narbonne and what resulted from it—Diego and the new
tactics of the missionary Legates—Fresh disputations at
Montreal and Pâmiers—Durand of Huesca separates,
capitulates to the Pope, and founds the order of the Catholic
Poor—Bernard I. follows his example—End of the Catholic
Poor; their principle survives—The Waldenses at Metz—
Traces of their mission in Switzerland and the Valley of the
Rhine ; The Brethren of the Free Spirit—Milan the centre
of dissent—The tendency of Arnaldo and the dissent of the
Humiliate—The Poor of Lombardy ; the retrograde party
and that of the conservatives and of the progressists—
The conference of Bergamo and the circular, letter—Mission
in the diocese of Passau and in the rest of Germany—The
Hussite reaction in Bohemia and its relation to the Waldensian
mission : Frederick Reiser—The Unity of Brethren and the
Waldenses' participation in it, through their Bishop Stephen
of Austria—The clue to the dispersion disappears.*

WAS the expulsion of the Waldenses from their native city a
misfortune ? That may be doubted, for it benefited their
mission. One might say of them, as was said of the primitive Christians after the persecution, that " they that were scattered abroad,
went everywhere preaching the word."[129] Who cannot picture to himself the part taken by Waldo in this critical hour ? Was he not the
Moses of this little people which were going out of the land of
bondage ? He it was therefore who must have directed the exodus,

every departing band received from him a parting glance and a watchword.   There is a basis of truth in the legend which multiplies
his presence.   Where are all these exiles going ?   To the field
destined for them.   Their field is the world.   Ploughed up by
discord and famine, harrowed by the most various reactions, it
awaits the new seed.   When the Reformation shall come, the
harvest will be great.

One of the first bands, soon followed by others, took the
direction of Dauphiny.   This can be surmised even without
existing indications. It had been the early home of a number of them,
and it was a possible refuge for all.   The names of Peter of Bruys
and his disciple Henry were still held in veneration and the fire of
their protest was smouldering there.   Peter, a native of
the neighbourhood of Gap,[131] undoubtedly had spread these
principles of liberty and reform, he had learned at school and
found in the Scriptures.   More conservative than his teacher,
Abelard, with regard to dogmas, he had nevertheless aimed
at the uprooting of gross traditional abuses in divine worship, which he wished to see purified.   In his way, he continued the Carlovingian reaction against idolatry, the echo of
which had resounded in Lyons and Turin, during the times of
Agobard and Claude.   After twenty years of labour he finally
succumbed at St. Gilles, a victim to his iconoclastic zeal against
the idolatry of the Cross.   This tragic end, the sinister prelude
to the scenes of the Inquisition, made the greatest sensation.
The monks saw in it the finger of God.   At Cluny, an oracle of
the time declared that his soul had passed from the flames of the
stake to those of Hell.[132]   The reaction revived, thanks to the
appearance of Henry, a disciple of the martyr.   His origin is
unknown.   Whether he came from Lausanne, from some village
of Savoy, or from Italy, it is impossible to state.[133]   At any rate
he was known ; he had been seen by the side of his master, Peter
de Bruys, whose mouth-piece he was, and an eloquent one for the
people.   He was a man of imposing deportment ; his glance and
his powerful voice possessed a singular animation.   Clear, austere
and pliant of speech—now impassioned as the stormy wind, or
striking as the thunderbolt, now gentle as the zephyr that kisses
the flowers of spring—he carried away men of generous impulses and
touched the most hardened hearts.   The people thought that he read
the souls of his hearers ; he even passed for a prophet ;[134] less so,

however, in Lausanne, whence he had been driven, or in Savoy, or Orleans, than in the South of France. At Mans he was for a time the arbiter of public opinion ; but the clergy, seeing their credit more than threatened, collected their forces in time, faced about and constrained him to withdraw. Did he then go into Dauphiny ? Some have been of that opinion. He found there a less excitable and colder population, but yet sufficiently favourable to him to alarm the bishops. They had not the courage to resist him openly. The Cluny monk, shrewd and vulgar under his venerable cowl, scoffed at his fellows, though a little late in the day. " You are petrified with astonishment," he wrote to them,[135] " dazed as the dove charmed by the serpent ; nay, as simple minded as the ox being led to the slaughter.[136] Much cause there is for this indeed ! Had you to defend yourselves against the wisdom of the Greeks, perhaps, the power of the Romans, the cruelty of the Persians, the prodigies of Antichrist, or the rage of a riotous mob ? For shame ! You had only to resist two miserable heretics,[137] and now there you stand with your arms folded as if, because Henry the false apostle and his companions had been compelled to withdraw, there were nothing more to do." Henry had withdrawn then, to go into Provence, it would appear. There he was pursued and summoned before the Council of Pisa, which condemned him to do penance in a cloister. When he came out he went into Languedoc, according to some ; others say to Guyenne, and the chase began once more. St. Bernard had provoked it by his letters to his pupil, Eugene III. ; he in-augurated it by his doleful censures. The Pope delegated Cardinal Alberic to the spot, and Henry who was hiding in the neighbourhood of Toulouse, tracked like a wild beast, was arrested, put in chains, taken to the Council of Rheims, and sentenced to life-long incarceration, under which he soon after died. His adherents, more or less scattered, let the storm pass. There were some yet in Dauphiny, and this knowledge deprived the Abbot of Cluny of his sleep. In his epistle to the Bishops, he examined and refuted the errors of the heretics point by point, whilst he begged the prelates to render his polemics beneficial to those who were led astray. " Rouse yourselves ! " he further wrote, " consider that if the teachers of error are far away, their seed remains ; nay, it abounds, and if you neglect to destroy it, to-morrow the tares will have grown and damaged the harvest.[138]

Let us avert this danger. We do not desire to witness the
resuscitation of that iniquitous brood.[139] Thereupon, from the
depths of his cloister, the Abbot apostrophizes the heretics :—
" Come out in broad daylight, if you dare, heretical outcasts and
schismatic rabble ; come out, ye blind leaders of the blind, from
the darkness that shelters you. I defy you.[140] Truth loves not
dark corners ; light is not made to remain under a bushel ; come,
I say, hasten to the voice of the Church which calls you."[141]

Thus spake the Abbot. There is nothing to indicate that his
voice was listened to. Half-a-century elapsed, and lo ! a new band
of heretics are driven out of Lyons. They lodged in the Valleys of
Dauphiny, and constitute the stock of the Waldenses of the Alps.
We shall have to return again to this point. Let us now follow
their brethren who went down further South, toward the classic
land of the Renaissance and reaction.

Before they reached it, the wind, thus far adverse, changed
and became favourable to them. Let us first form an idea of the
new surroundings by which they were attracted.

" During the second half of the XII. century, protest under
all its forms had a visible tendency to concentrate itself in the
South of France. The principal wandering sectarians—those at
least who left a name in history—are seen to concentrate upon that
point, to found congregations and organize for the struggle.
They were attracted by the superior civilization of the South, by
its light literature, which willingly lent itself to attacks upon the
monks and official prelacy, and by its independent and jesting turn
of fancy. The beautiful country, extending from the Alps to the
Gulf of Gascony, had in truth never thoroughly submitted to
Roman orthodoxy. Arianism had long reigned there under the
Visigoth kings, and the recollections of that form of Christianity
were confounded with the traditions of the glorious independence
of Aquitania. To the eyes of the Southern, Catholicism ever
represented the religion of Northern men, of conquest and of
invasion. Those recollections were still so vivid when the
sectarians first appeared, that the defenders of Rome saw in them
at first only a continuance of Arianism. It was, however, nothing
of the kind. Arianism, whether Visigoth, Burgundian, or Lombard, had truly died under the blows of the Frankish lance."[142]

This could hardly be better expressed. But is the almost
sudden breaking into blossom of the grand reaction of the

Albigenses in those districts now quite clear to us ? Not quite.
Arianism was certainly forgotten; but it is also certain that
" Catharism took deep root in the West, only in those districts
formerly Arian, which Frank conquest had brought back by force
into Catholic unity, namely, Northern Spain, Southern France,
and Northern Italy."[148] From that it has been concluded, on the
one hand, that Arianism had left a leaven of protest against the
ruling Church; on the other, that ancient Manicheism, everywhere repressed and in its turn forgotten, had deposited certain
germs which the superstitions of the Middle Ages relative to
Satan were of a nature to sustain, and which, after having long
been buried, had finally been hatched at the favourable time.
Catharism, making Rome one of the seats of Satan's empire
and attributing the Papal doctrines to the very principle of evil
as their only and necessary source, responded freely to the
antipathy provoked by the scandals of ecclesiastic life, and to a
well-known passionate hostility. The radicalism of its protest
ought not to have been displeasing to men of advanced ideas, and
its manner of explaining the Old Testament anticipated their
doubts, although its metaphysical incumbrances must have caused
thinkers to smile while it left the people indifferent." Are we,
however, hereby made to understand how Oriental Catharism in this
district prevailed over the indigenous reactions ? Why did not our
populations follow rather their own Apostles, Peter of Bruys,
for example, Henry of Lausanne or Waldo? This question,
which continues to be a knotty one, has been answered with a
perfectly just remark,[144] namely, that Catharism, though a leveller
in the field of orthodox dogmatism, nevertheless reserved plenty
of work for the most refined dialectics, and that in another respect,
it was distinguished by its aristocracy of forms. It must be
recognised, for instance, that its episcopalianism was very marked;
to say nothing of the Pope it was said to have, but who does not
seem to be an authentic character. Also the nobility enjoyed
Catharism, and distrusted evangelists sprung from the ranks of
the people, their mission being too democratic for people with
" white hands." As a consequence of these very qualities it was
inevitable that as soon as the nobility should cease to patronize
Catharism it must collapse, and its ruin would be irretrievable.
With that collapse the Waldensian reaction will survive and the
figure of Waldo will grow until it will, as it were, personify
traditional protest.

But we are anticipating. The Cathari were yet preponderant in the South of France, where, however, they were not introduced before the eleventh century. In the year 1119 a Council held at Toulouse had passed a sentence against them, enjoining the Lords of the soil to drive them away. In 1163 a new Council was held at Tours, presided over by Pope Alexander III., and at it the condemnation of the heresy of the Cathari was reiterated; Toulouse, being regarded as its nearest source, was closely watched. In 1165 a third Council passed a third sentence at Lombers; but it was as if the edict had gone forth, "Increase and multiply and fill the whole earth." The heresy invaded the nobility; it was propagated even amongst the ranks of the clergy and pursued its conquest toward the West, " as far as the road goes." There is yet another council; but this time it is a Council of Cathari. It met in 1167, at St. Felix de Caraman, not far from Toulouse, for the manifest purpose of completing the institution of the sect. A Bishop named Nicetas came from Constantinople; he was undoubtedly a delegate of the Eastern Churches of the Cathari, and invested with a sufficiently real power, vividly to impress the popular imagination, which indeed dressed him in its own fashion, and the credulous chronicle presents him to posterity under the magnificent title of *Dominus papa Niquinta*. Besides that of Nicetas the presence of Bishops from Lombardy is noticeable. The Cathari of Toulouse gave a warm welcome to these "good men," as they were accustomed to be called, and actuated by jealousy, they asked that a Bishop should be given to them also.

Toulouse had, therefore, very soon become the principal seat of the reaction of the Çathari. That is explained by the place she occupied in the political world. Her Count of the Raymond lineage was the richest lord of the kingdom; five neighbouring fiefs were juridically dependent on his domain, the most considerable being those of Narbonne and Beziers. Public opinion there favoured independence, both as regards the King of France and the Pope, and hence was favourable to the Cathari called Albigenses. The national spirit became so thoroughly impregnated with the Albigensian protest, that it finally became inseparable from it. The Count of Toulouse, for form's sake, attended Catholic worship, though it was known that the Albigenses held their meetings in his castle, and that he used to attend them.

The Count of Foix adhered to the heresy through his family; as for himself, he was almost a free-thinker. "The Pope has nothing to do with my religion," he would say, "inasmuch as every man must be free to choose his own."[145] The troubadours took a share in the dispute, and certainly the dominant Church was not less ill-used in their *sirventes* than in religious discussions. If the troubadours are to be believed, the Prelates were too fond of "fair women and red wine;" the orthodox are "Romipetes." Nay, more, an outrageous comedy was performed, whose subject was "the heresy of the Priests." The people enjoyed that, and reserved ecclesiastical titles for use in biting sarcasm. "Ameriou miou estre capelan" (I would rather be a chaplain), they often said, "than do that." The clergy, startled and alarmed, dared not always to appear in public. It is said that Priests went so far as to conceal the tonsure, by means of the hair on the back of their heads.[146] Even the great men were not spared, notwithstanding their gravity and accustomed pomp. Thus, when ten years after the Council of the Cathari, the Cardinal Legate, Peter of St. Chrysogone, visited Toulouse, accompanied by Henry of Clairvaux, the latter complained that they were received with jeers. Fingers were pointed at them, and they were called apostates, hypocrites, and heretics,[147] which proved, according to the Abbot, how necessary their visit was. "Had it only been retarded three years," thought he, "it is doubtful whether any worshippers of Christ would have been found in Toulouse."[148] On this occasion he noticed a detail which is interesting to us; namely, that not only did the heretics elect their leaders, but that they sent evangelists as missionaries to inculcate a new Gospel into men's souls.[149]

Such, then, was the state of the atmosphere of the place which welcomed the Waldenses when banished by the Primate of the Gauls. We may surmise how they were received. As for them, whilst inhaling the liberty with which they were surrounded, at first they did not feel quite at ease in the midst of those gross heretics. They were too distrustful of their jesting, virulent and frivolous discussions, to risk being carried along with them. They were fortified by their very stiffness and their own tendencies; above all, by their firm attachment to the Gospel, as well as by the bond of real brotherhood which united them. Nevertheless circumstances exercise an irresistible influence even on granite, and they could not escape altogether. They were about to acquire a grace and freedom of manner that would be of service to them, and also a more impulsive imagination. Their too prosaic minds would yet bring forth the *chanson*, which the people prefer to sermons ; their lessons of morality interwoven with quotations from the Fathers would anon disengage themselves from the latter like a chrysalis, in order to rise nearer the ideal by means of the wings given them by the breath of poetry. Besides, what they gained from their new environment, their own biblical austerity and their moderation had a reacting influence on their new neighbours, by which the latter were civilized. Even the clergy appreciated them—after their own fashion. Says a monk who is not fond of sparing them, " They are wicked, but as compared with the other heretics, they are much less wicked."[150] Hence it is not astonishing that, the opportunity offering, they should be placed in opposition to the Cathari. Nobility, till then inaccessible, half opened its doors to them sufficiently to procure them an influence which soon rivalled that of the Albigenses. They even gained a hold upon general opinion, especially by means of public discussion, which is the ordinary prelude to the conversion of numbers of people and to persecution. But as to the result of their mission, one cannot attempt to define it with precision. Nobody now-a-days asserts that the Albigenses " received the belief of the Waldenses a little while after the departure of Waldo from Lyons,"[151] because the Albigenses and Waldenses must no longer be confounded as they have been heretofore by partisans whose object is very apparent.[152] While waiting for danger to unite them, liberty brought them occasionally into contact ᷄with each other, and sometimes with such success that it is difficult to distinguish the traces of the Waldenses from those of other dissenters. For once that they sided with the Catholics against the Albigenses, they fought a score of times by the side of the latter against their common enemy.

These disputes are furthermore a characteristic sign of the times, and especially of the places here in question. If they are witnesses to the zeal of Romish missionaries, they tell us also how their arrogance must have been humbled to induce them to submit to such discussions ; for, before commencing them, the parties brought face to face were accustomed to choose arbiters by common consent. It was even conceded on both sides that the

Scriptures were to be accepted as a law from which there was no appeal. Generally the arbitrator named was a Romish ecclesiastic, pious, moderate, and weak. In such a case, the sentence was hardly doubtful; but, when neither Popes nor Councils were believed in, was there much risk in being bound by the sentence of a private individual? Good argument was more effective than anything else. If the arbitrators were laymen, then the humiliation of the defenders of Mother Church was overwhelming. " Oh! Shame!" exclaims a chaplain on one such occasion; " the Church and Catholic faith must have fallen into very great contempt if we must submit to abide by the judgment of the laity."[153] Let us attend one of these disputations. It took place between Catholics and Waldenses at Narbonne, and may be reduced to a series of counts of indictment in the shape of accusations and replies; the meeting was under the presidency of the priest Raymond de Daventer. We shall listen to the dialogue.[154]

" This, O, Waldenses! is the principal cause of complaint which we have to present against you; you are in a state of rebellion against the Church of Rome. As a matter of fact you no longer obey either her Priests or her Bishops. By so doing you violate the principles of the Scriptures. Do they not expressly say: ' If any man obey not, note that man and have no company with him.' And again, ' Obey your rulers.' And of him who will not yield obedience what do we read? ' If he neglect to hear the Church, let him be unto thee as a heathen man and a publican.'[155] You see, you are likened to Pagans; so that your portion is with the unbelievers. You are damned, *digni morte eterna.*"

" Gently—you would be right if Bishops and Priests were obedient to the Word of God; but as they are, on the contrary, the very first to disobey, we must choose between two ways—either we must obey God and disobey the Church, or else we must obey the Church and disobey God. Having well considered the matter from all sides, we have concluded that the only path for us to pursue is to decide, as the Apostle Peter did on a similar occasion, when he said: ' We ought to obey God rather than men.' If, therefore, we are not with you, it is only that we may not abandon the path of obedience."

" Error very soon betrays itself by its fruit. Having disobeyed the Church, you are about to usurp the sacred office of preaching;

you have all turned preachers, men and women.  It is scandalous,
for it is well-known that this office  does not become the laity ; it
is even prohibited to them.  It is true that there may be exceptions ; but then, the way to proceed is as follows : the layman
who presents himself for the purpose is examined, in order to
ascertain whether or not he be a good Catholic.  If so, if he leads
an honest life and his words do not lack wisdom, he may upon a
sign from his Bishop or his Curate venture to exhort his neighbour ; at least, this is our opinion.  Even then, there must be
no encumbrance in the shape of a wife, or a business.  Should
the man be a heretic, then, of course, he must not preach under
any circumstances ; it would be a sin to listen to him, even if he
were a cleric.  You are not all clerics ; very far from it ; it is not
knowledge that makes you mad ; but this is your state.  It is
easy enough to understand why you go about saying that neither
Pastors, nor Bishops, nor even holy Mother Church, is entitled to
obedience.  You pretend to obey God !  Nonsense ! that is a
mere pretext.  Indeed, it is clear enough : you teach differently
from the Church,[156] drawing down just wrath upon your heads."

" When we asked the Church to recognise our right to speak,
for the purpose of proclaiming the Gospel, you know how it
answered us.  We have not been convinced of error, and yet we
are far from being agreed.  What you call the exception, is for
us the rule, for it is thus that the Scriptures regard it.  Whoever
is able to spread the Word of God among the people is in duty
bound to do so : such is the Gospel principle, against which all
your fine arguments will fail.  ' To him that knoweth to do
good, and doeth it not, to him it is sin,' says St. James, Chap. iv.,
v. 17.  If therefore, knowing how to evangelise, we were to
abandon that work, we should commit a grievous sin."

" St. James does not say ' him that knoweth to teach,' but
' him that knoweth to do.'  There is a great difference between
teaching and doing."

" Alas ! that is very clear ; but the difference should
not be made so great.  St. James would be astonished to learn,
that, to obey the precept of preaching the Gospel is not to
do good."

" You wish to argue by means of the Scriptures ; very well.
The Gospel of St. Mark, Chap. i., verse 23rd and following
contains something that greatly concerns you.  We read that

there was in the synagogue a man with an unclean spirit. This man on meeting Christ cried out : ' I know thee who thou art, the Holy One of God.' But Jesus rebuked him saying : ' Hold thy peace.' There is the precept for you to follow. The name of Christ should not be proclaimed by your lips, even though you may have learned to know Him. You would soon infuse poison with your fine words."

" Your interpretation is convenient ; but upon what is it founded ? Upon a slanderous judgment you have formed against us. Suppose we should answer that you are the ones, not we, who have the unclean spirit, what would that prove ? But look rather in the same Gospel, Chap. ix., verses 38 and 39 : ' John said to him, Master, we saw one casting out devils in Thy name, and we forbade him because he followeth not us.' What did the Master answer to that ? ' Forbid him not, *nolite prohibere eum*,' do you hear ? ' For,' Christ adds, ' there is no man which shall do a miracle in my name, that can lightly speak evil of me.' There is the precept. If, therefore, we preach in the name of Christ, even when we do not follow the Bishops and the Pastors, they have no right to forbid us."[157]

" Very good, if your preaching were inspired with a spirit of obedience, and you were animated by benevolent dispositions indicating a real vocation. But with your spirit of strife——"

" Very well, we will grant you for the sake of argument, that our disposition is such as you have represented it. Then the case was foreseen by St. Paul in his words to the Philippians, Chap. i., v. 15—18 : ' Some indeed preach Christ even of envy and strife ; and some also of good will ; the one preach Christ of contention, not sincerely, supposing to add affliction to my bonds : but the other of love, knowing that I am set for the defence of the Gospel.' From all this, what conclusion does the Apostle draw ? ' What then ? notwithstanding, every way, whether in pretence, or in truth, Christ is preached ; and I therein do rejoice, yea, and will rejoice.' Cannot you rejoice also ? One would think that you were envious."

" We can only pity you."

" Envy is old, and you would not be the first who have been affected by it. We read in the Old Testament, in the Book of Numbers, Chap. xi., that two men called Eldad and Medad having received the Spirit of God, prophesied in the camp of Israel. This

caused a great commotion. A young man ran to tell Moses;
'Eldad and Medad do prophesy in the camp!' Hearing this,
Joshua, the son of Nun, answered and said: 'My Lord Moses,
forbid them.' But Moses answered: 'Enviest thou for my sake?
Would God that all the Lord's people were prophets, and that the
Lord would put his Spirit upon them!'"

" That has nothing to do with this case, for you are not
true but false prophets."

" So you say, but does that prove anything? He is a false
prophet who speaks not according to the oracles of God."

" You are heretics."

" Again, you cannot be both judge and accuser. The judgment
belongs not to you, but to Him who——"

" To him who presides over us, certainly, to that pious and
venerable ecclesiastic of noble birth and still nobler character——"

" As much as you please—we wished to say just now that
judgment belongs to God, and that it is already pronounced in
His Word. If we were permitted to return to it, it would be for
the purpose of calling your attention to the chief precept of
Christ, to which we were alluding a moment ago. Did he not
say to his disciples, before ascending into Heaven: 'Go ye into
all the world and preach the Gospel to every creature?'"

" That order does not concern you in the least; it was given
to the Church, that is to say, to the Priests. Laymen have
nothing to do with that."

" Of what Church are you speaking? We belong to the
Church of Christ and his Apostles, and we desire to follow the
rule of the Apostolic Church; there is our obedience or our disobedience, according to the way it is looked at. In the time of
St. Gregory, people did not argue as you do, for he said: ' Whoever has heard in his heart the supreme voice of love owes to his
neighbour the voice of exhortation.' And, again, ' As far as it
depends on you, give bountifully of His good word to your neighbour; " proximis vestris boni verbi cyathos date." ' We could
remind you of many other precious maxims, which, alas, are now
a dead letter. But how many practised them before us and are
an example to us?[153] The blessed Honorius and St. Equitius,
for instance, whom the same Gregory mentions in his Dialogues;
and even in our own time Paul Raymond, whose holiness is confirmed by so many miracles. Those, it seems to us, were lay

preachers ; but why should we stop at them ? What men more truly belonged to the laity than the Apostles, the pre-eminent messengers of the Gospel of the Master.[159] It is true that, according to the Synagogue, they were without authority, without vocation, illiterate, incompetent, and above all, very disobedient."

" You are no Apostles ; you are not even laymen provided with the mandate of the Church. St. Raymond had the permission of the Church, but you have not."

" Whose fault is that ? "

" You ought to know. But time presses, and we would like to speak of one more grievance. It bears upon the method and certain already visible results of your illicit mission ; indeed, you go about seducing everybody to some extent. Who are your proselytes ? First, women ; then more women, that is to say, effeminate men.[160] You attract people of unsound judgment, liars, misers ; in short, worthless persons. It is said that you first address yourselves to the women, and reach their husbands through them.[161] Are you not ashamed of yourselves ? You are like a lot of bulls. You know the Scriptures compare heretics to bulls."[162]

" It is repugnant to our feelings to follow you on such ground."

" That is comparatively a small matter. But what is serious and scandalous is that you permit women to preach. Now, we ask, how do you reconcile the taking of such liberties with the precept of the Apostle ? ' Let your women keep silence in the Churches ; for it is not permitted unto them to speak.' "[163]

" You exaggerate. It is less a question of preaching than of teaching ; so that the same Apostle is able to say to his disciple Titus, Chap. ii., v. 3 : ' the aged women should be teachers of good things.' "

" Those women are not called to teach men publicly, but young persons and in private. Notice, if you please, that he speaks of aged women."

" This deserves consideration. But, while recognizing the rule laid down by St. Paul, might not an exception be made of such a prophetess as Anna, for instance, of whom it is written that she ' praised God in the temple ? ' "

" Anna was 84 years old, and by her fasting well deserved the gift of prophecy. Furthermore, we do not read that she

preached or taught; she spoke of Christ, and that was all. Now,
preaching and speaking are very different things."[164]

The Waldenses would have liked nothing better than to leave
the privilege of preaching in the hands of the Priests; provided
always that they were allowed to retain the right of free
speech.

Thus ends the dispute of Narbonne.[165] A few days later a sentence written by the arbitrator, Raymond of Deventer, pronounced
the condemnation of the Waldenses.[166] This sentence had its use
as a local enunciation of that of the Council of Verona. Haste
was made to enforce it, by means of vigorous decrees, like that of
Alfonso II., King of Aragon and Marquis of Provence, and that
of the Bishop of Toul. Both were issued in 1192. The first
especially is of unheard-of virulence, perhaps for the very reason
of its inefficacy. "We order," said the King, "that the Waldenses or *Ensabatés*,[167] who are also called the 'Poor of Lyons,'
and all the other numberless heretics, anathematized by Holy
Mother Church, be expelled from all our States as enemies of the
cross of Christ, violaters of the Christian religion, and public
enemies of our person and Kingdom. Therefore, from this day
forth, whosoever shall dare to receive into his house, or listen to the
preaching of the said Waldenses or such other heretics, wherever
it may be, or to feed or assist them in any way, is warned that he
will thereby incur the wrath of Almighty God, and of ourselves;
and that his possessions will be confiscated without appeal,
according to the penalty provided against those who render themselves guilty of high treason."[168] This decree reminds one of the
Inquisition; but the Dominicans were not yet in existence to carry
it into effect, and it ran the risk of remaining a dead letter. Two
years later it was revived by Don Pedro, Alfonso's successor, and
again renewed in 1197. The other decree emanated from Eudes
of Vaudemont, Bishop of Toul. "With regard to the heretics
called Wadoys," he says, "we order all the faithful, who may
chance to meet with them, to arrest and bring them, bound, to
our See of Toul, in order that they may be punished."[169] These
are the precursory signs of the crusade, which was declared
seventeen years later. In the meantime they seemed to alarm no
one. Fanaticism had been so effectually lulled to sleep by the
songs of the Troubadours, that its awakening was despaired of.
It was no longer a question of driving heresy back within its

intrenchments, but of defending themselves against it. More than
one ecclesiastic, weary of war, joined the ballad singers' chorus.
Witness the monk of Cluny who wrote :—

> " Rome nous suce et nous englot,
> Rome est la doiz de la malice
> Dont sordent tuit li malvès vice ;
> C'est un viviers pleins de vermine,
> Contre l'Escripture divine
> Et contre Deu sont teut lor fet."[170]

And so passed the last years of the XII. century and the
first of the XIII. At that time a pious Bishop, named Diego,
was languishing in his diocese, his soul tormented. Suddenly he came to a grave decision. " What can I do here ? " he
asked himself. " It were better for me to carry my religion to
the heathen." He started for Rome forthwith, for he required the
approbation of the Pope, but this he could not obtain. " The best
thing for you to do," the inexorable Pontiff replied, " is to return
to your diocese." Diego bowed submissively, and made his way
back by short stages, accompanied by a young Canon, whose zeal
indicated the most brilliant prospects. The Pontiff was Innocent III., and the Canon Dominic. These names suggest the
preparation of something new and a change in the times. When
he arrived at Montpellier Diego met the three missionary Legates,
who had just been sent out against the heretics. They were
demoralized, crushed, and on the point of giving up their mission
in despair,[171] " What disheartens us so completely," said they,
" is that whenever we talk with heretics they continually harp on
this string, namely, that we are like physicians who, instead of
thinking about healing others, would do well to cure themselves.
We must admit that the morals of our clergy are abominable. If
no remedy can be found there is an end of the matter ; we shall
be preaching in the desert. We might as well abandon it altogether."[172] The Bishop remained wrapt in deep thought. Suddenly these words came from his lips :—

" Listen ! I have an idea. Be the very first to preach by
your example."

" What then, have we done till now ? "

" Your equipages and this large retinue which accompanies
you, doubtless, solely for the sake of appearances, are not, believe

me, in keeping with your mission, and only contribute to its discredit in this country."

" And then ? "

" You will go on foot ; you will take with you neither gold nor
silver ; in fact, you will act as the Apostles did.[173] That is my
advice. Do that and the wind will change."

Dominic seconded the advice of his aged Bishop, with all the
impetuosity of his thirty-five years.

" Very well, said one of the Legates ; we are of your opinion,
only there is one danger."

" What is that ? "

" Have you thought of this : that we should then ourselves be
innovators."

" But after the manner of the Apostles."

" Ah ! if some one would only lead the way for us ! We would
certainly follow him."

" Well, here I am ! I will lead the way."

Thereupon Diego started upon his course, preceded by
Dominic, that grand greyhound of the chase after heretics, and
the Legates followed in good earnest. The mission was once
more undertaken, and not without some little success.

Here we have one fact among a thousand, showing how useful a protest is, even to the Church which condemns it. The
bare-footed heretics cause the messengers of the Church to step
down from their carriages. A battle is about to be fought, but a
moral victory is already won. The renewed discussions are more
animated and noisy than ever. We shall notice two of them only,
which relate to the dissent of the Waldenses. They are the disputations of Montreal and Pàmiers.

At Montreal the disputation lasted for fifteen days, under the
presidency of two lay arbitrators. The dissenting orator, Arnaud
Hot, spoke at great length, and yet so well as to produce a great
impression upon the audience. " It was a pity that so many good
souls should have heard him," naively remarks the chaplain who
relates the circumstance.[174] However, Hot had a good opportunity :
he showed how the Apostolic ministry had become vitiated in the
Church by becoming a ministry of temporal affairs. This told
in the vernacular, and in the manner one can imagine, must
have made the monks feel as though hail were falling on their
shaven crowns ; so much so that the legates, being unable to

stand it, left abruptly and withdrew with their adherents, a light dwelling in their eyes that was soon to kindle the fires of the Inquisition. The arbitrators on this occasion had no judgment to pronounce. Desertion spoke more eloquently than they could have done, concerning the discomfiture of the Romipètes. The disputations did not, however, usually close in this way.

Diego resumed his journey toward Osma, his diocese. When he reached Pâmiers, in the territory of Toulouse, he made another halt where he was soon surrounded by Bishops and Abbots who had come to implore his support. A disputation with the Waldenses was about to take place in the castle itself, under the auspices of Bernard Roger, Count of Foix, whose wife and sister had joined their society. Another sister, it is believed, had taken the part of the Cathari. As usual, an arbitrator was elected. This honour fell to the lot of a certain master of theology, named Arnaud de Campran. The arguments brought forward by the two parties have not been reported. It appears that the struggle became so lively that Claramonde, the sister who sided with the Waldenses, forgot herself and made some remark. She was immediately snubbed with unheard of rudeness by a monk. " Madam," said he, " go to your distaff ; women have nothing to do with this sort of discussion."[175] Yet she was in her brother's house if not in her own. One might be tempted to believe that the Count of Foix shewed himself more than tolerant on this occasion ; unless, indeed, the monk owed his good fortune, in not feeling the back of some knight's hand, to the regard entertained for the lady of the manor, who, like a good Waldensian, had possibly adopted the maxim that forbids us to return evil for evil. The arbitrator decided against the Waldenses this time, and the dispute seems to have had untoward results for them ; for from this same disputation, held in the castle of Pâmiers in the year 1206, dates a movement of separation which finally brought back a few dissidents within the pale of the Church. It is worth while to follow their history.[176]

Among the adherents of the opposition to the Church who had been present at the dispute of Pâmiers, was a small number of ecclesiastics, among whom a certain Durand was conspicuous. He came from the city of Huesca, not far from the Pyrenees. Shaken in his opinions, and attracted perhaps by Dominic's zeal, he was won over with some others of his colleagues. The few who had separated held a council, and decided to draw up a confession of faith, to be submitted to the Pope, asking him to authorise them to keep the statutes they had thus far observed. Thereupon Durand started for Rome, accompanied by John of Narbonne, Guilliaume of St. Antonin, D. of Naiaque, Bernard and Ermengard of Bêziers, Raymond of St. Paul, Hebrin and several other persons who are not named. Innocent III., who no doubt had been forewarned, welcomed them in a fatherly manner but with shrewdness. He approved of the confession, and authorised the statutes, to both of which they were obliged to bind themselves by oath. The following were their salient points :—

" To the glory of God and of his Church and for the salvation of our souls, we pledge ourselves to believe with our hearts and to confess with our lips the Catholic faith, inviolable and in its integrity, as under the protection and government of the Roman Pontiff. Having renounced the world and given our possessions to the poor, according to God's precept, and having made a vow of poverty, we take no thought for the morrow, and will accept in alms neither gold nor silver, nor anything of that kind, but only enough to eat and wherewithal to clothe ourselves day by day. Our law is to observe the counsels of evangelical perfection as so many precepts. Inasmuch as most of us are clerics and almost all men of letters, we have resolved to devote ourselves to reading, exhortation, teaching, and discussing against all the different kinds of error ; and we intend to propose that those who are the best instructed in the law of God and the maxims of the Fathers be utilised in our school to bring the erring back to the faith and to the pale of the Church, without doing anything that might be prejudicial to episcopal authority. We have agreed to wear the modest religious dress to which we have been accustomed, with shoes cut off at the top and made in such a way that people may know at a glance, and without a doubt, that we have separated ourselves from the Lyonese in body as we are separated in heart, so long as they shall not become reconciled with the Church. If laymen express desire to join us, we shall take care that, with the exception of those who may be capable of talking and disputing with the heretics, they live at home religiously and in good order, working with their hands, and discharging their duties towards the Church with respect to their tithes, first-fruits and offerings."[177]

The statute having been sworn to, the dissidents were granted a few privileges as a recompense for their fidelity ; such as that of not being obliged to take up arms against Christians, nor to take an oath in temporal matters ; so long only as this could be reconciled with the respect due to others, and occasion no annoyance to the secular authority.[178]  They were all banded together under the protection of the Pope, who named them the " Catholic Poor." Before leaving the City of Rome, Durand promised to pay one bezant every year as a token of submission to the Apostolic See.[179]

In a very short time the Pope received complaints from the Archbishop of Narbonne and some of the bishops belonging to his jurisdiction, to the effect that Durand and his associates were becoming unmanageable on account of their boasting.  They had changed nothing in their practices, and Waldenses, who were still unreconciled with the Church, were by them admitted to the participation of the mass.  They opened their doors to unfrocked monks, and by their discourses attracted faithful believers, who were afterwards seen to forsake canonical services ; in which thing the latter only followed the example of their teachers.  Innocent hastened to state these complaints to his protégés, exhorting them to give no more occasion for them, if they did not wish it to be said that the remedy was worse than the disease.[180]  Moreover, he wrote to the Prelates to quiet down their ruffled temper, and to give them a lesson in pastoral prudence after his own style. " Be not alarmed on their account," said he to them.  " If they intend to deceive the Church and to elude its discipline, they will very soon be caught in their own toils.  But if they do nothing worse, for the time being, than retain somewhat of their ancient practices, it may be but pure craftiness, for the purpose of more easily gaining over their former co-religionists, those little foxes which devastate the vineyard of the Lord.  It were better to be patient and to abide results.  So long as they do not wander from the essential principles of truth, it is right that we should deal somewhat indulgently with them.  If they do not break off all at once from their former habits, that is undoubtedly one way of burying them, with a certain decency which spares one's feelings. Let us practice the word of the Apostle : " Being crafty I caught you with guile."[181]

Though the prelates submitted, they were furious with rage, Durand, with his arts of dissimulation and his insolence of

manner, provoked them more than an outright adversary. They
soon renewed their complaints, repeating nearly the same charges.
Innocent also repeated his exhortations to gentleness and prudence.
He even charged them not to permit the poor wretches to be
worried ; he went so far as to guarantee to the latter the right of
electing their own provost, in conjunction with the local Bishop,
for he was vexed to learn that dissidents who were ready to be
readmitted were allowed to remain outside the Church.[182]

Some pretend that in the meantime Durand returned to Rome, [183]
but the truth about this we do not know. It is quite certain that he
had explanations enough to give and new favours to ask. The fact is,
that he never was without the protection of the Pontiff, and by that
means he succeeded in founding more than one refuge for such
unfortunates as age, sickness or privation compelled to seek his
assistance.

With this movement of the Catholic Poor is connected that
of Bernard I., Guillaume, Arnaud, and a few other Waldenses of
Lombardy, who had gone to Rome in the year 1210 and had been
examined before the Pontiff.[184]    They had experienced much
more difficulty than their predecessors in being admitted, and
were compelled to undergo a humiliating interrogation.

" You look to me, with your shoes cut off at the sole, like
tramps," said Innocent ; " that is superstition ! And how
frightful you look with your hooded cloak. It hardly harmonizes
with your uncut hair. You look too much like laymen. And, by
the way, tell me : I am informed that you travel about, men and
women together ; it is even said that you lodge in the same
houses ; I shall not repeat to you all that I hear.[185] What am
I to believe ? "

" We travel with women, it is true, but after the manner of
the Apostles."[186]

" I do not approve of that, nor of certain other usages which
it appears you have not abandoned ; for instance, the mania
several of you manifest for preaching, for administering the
Eucharist, and for hearing confession. There are these women,
too, who meddle with teaching in the Church ; I will not tolerate
anything of that kind, remember."[187]

They were not admitted therefore on that occasion ; but it
seems that they were not long in coming to an agreement. After
all, the Pope had not shown himself very exacting. Bernard in

the following year presented a declaration, in consequence of which his submission was accepted. This is evident from a letter written by Innocent III. to the Bishop of Cremona. He expresses in it the same sentiment he had before formulated, when addressing the Bishops of the Lower Languedoc. "Use gentle means with these people," said he, "for if we are told to invite the lame and the blind to the feast of the Lord, even to compel them to come in; with how much more reason should we beware of thrusting back those who come of their own accord. That is why we commend to you Bernard I. and his colleague. They were, it is true, deeply tainted with heresy; but they have returned to us to take refuge in the bosom of the Church."[188]

On seeing these different companies of "the Poor" returning to the fold of the Church by different ways, we are tempted to ask what difference there was between them. Their origin was the same, and their real object also. One as much as the other, they observed the apostolic rule of life, more especially the vow of poverty. As a matter of fact, they had given their goods to the poor; they did not accept either silver or gold, but food and raiment only. They all followed their itinerant mission, not as in past times, for the purpose of preaching the Gospel freely, but in order to work under the papal shield and to bring back their brethren to the fold.[189] This last trait was more especially the distinguishing characteristic of the followers of Durand; whilst those of Bernard, being less fitted to teach, did not disdain to labour with their hands. The former remind us of the order of Dominican Friars, the latter of the Franciscans.[190] The idea of these orders of Mendicant Friars, which was eminently opposed to the Waldensian idea, is already beginning to shew itself as in a seed. But before it can spring up the seed must die. Did the Poor Catholics succeed in reconciling the statutes of the Waldenses with the authority of the Roman Church? To all appearance they did so, but, as a matter of fact they never did; for, without the liberty to obey God rather than men, the statutes are not Waldensian. Where is the merit of all this? If there be any merit in the whole affair it belongs entirely to the Pope; but of a truth there was very little. Innocent III. has been credited with benevolence, because he was complaisant; just as these "Poor" were submissive because they had flexible backs. If the Pontiff exercised his authority to enforce tolerance on the clergy, to whom

Alexander III. had sacrificed too much, it was because he had no longer to deal with men like Waldo and his first disciples. The capitulation of the Poor Catholics was equivalent to a recantation —if not to suicide—which is always the case, unfortunately, when liberty has to be immolated on the altar of peace.

Such was the fate of this little reaction, which made more noise than work. The Catholic Poor did not long survive their founders. They were finally incorporated in the order of the Hermits of St. Augustine as early as the year 1256.[191] " They became extinct without anyone taking notice of the fact," writes an apologist,[192] and were buried with a decorum against which nothing can be said. The Pope had dreamed of another end, that of the Waldenses properly so-called, and had thought he would obtain it by setting up discord ; but his wish was so far from being realized that the Waldenses do not even seem to have been disturbed by the desertion of the Catholic Poor. One would think they forgot them, for they never mention them ; as far at least as we know. The deserters were not even regretted. They were Priests, mostly, more or less men of letters, but apt to compromise the lay character of the Waldensian mission ; and besides, who knows whether their doctrine was not hiding the old leaven of Manicheism ?[193] They had fallen back too wantonly ; there was too much artifice in their movements, to make us believe that their profession was of a sterling quality. In such a case it is better to separate. Separation purifies more than it weakens.

The Catholic Poor have taken us out of France. Let us in imagination return thither. Before leaving we must take notice of another centre of reaction, away up in the North. This time we shall see a bright ray of Waldensian faith emanate therefrom.

Metz, notwithstanding her bishop, was a city of refuge. She did not even repel the Jews, who were proscribed everywhere. " It was the city of those who had no city of habitation—a mixed city if ever there were one."[194] Hence, it will not be surprising if Waldenses be found there. It is not easy to fix the time of their coming ; but it must have taken place, if not immediately after Waldo was driven into exile, at least close upon the exile of his brethren, under the persecution of Jean aux Blanches Mains. We read that it was during the time of Bertram, who was Bishop of Metz from 1180 to 1212.[195] One day, while in the cathedral, Bertram recognised amongst the congregation two Waldenses whose con-

demnation he had witnessed at Montpellier. As soon as he had
descended from his pulpit he issued the order for their arrest. But
it was not executed. They were protected, we are told, "by some
notable personage belonging to the city."[196] The Waldensian
party had then some adherents there; in fact, they must have
gained a firm footing amongst the citizens of Metz. It must be
remembered, too, that this took place before the year 1199, when the
persecution commenced. "They swarmed," says the chronicle. [197]
The Bishop having learned what was going on, informed Innocent III.
and, thanks to this Pope's letters, it has come to our knowledge.
A translation of the Gospels, of the Epistles of St. Paul, of the
Psalms, and perhaps of some other book of the Scripture, had
been put in circulation; it was eagerly sought after by a large
number of laymen; they met in secret to hear portions explained,
and at these meetings anyone might speak. When Priests intervened to reprove, like true disciples of Waldo they resisted
them face to face, and the Pope took notice of the fact.[198] If their
right were questioned, they appealed to the testimony of the Scriptures. Upon this Innocent III. took the matter in hand; he wrote
both to the people and to the Bishop; to the former for the purpose of instruction and admonition; to the latter to direct him in
his inquiry. "Assuredly there is nothing that is not laudable
in the desire to understand the Scriptures," said the Pope to the
faithful; "but to meet in secret, to usurp the ministry of preaching, to dispense with the ministry of the Priest, to the extent of
scorning it, there lies the evil, and some remedy must be devised.
Who does not know the depth of meaning contained in the
Scriptures? If when endeavouring to penetrate it, learned men
be obliged to recognise their insufficiency, you will be the
more so in that you are simple and illiterate. Hence the Divine
law has wisely decreed that any beast touching the holy mountain
should be stoned to death; this typefies that common people may not
presume by their intellect to attain to the sublime heights of
Revelation and to preach it to others. The Apostle, on the other
hand, exhorts us not to think of ourselves more highly than we
ought to think. We must have knowledge; but not too much.[199]
There remains for you, therefore, but one thing to do, namely, to
obey. Do so voluntarily, and you will not be compelled by
force."[200] To the Bishop the Pope has something more to say:—
"Why do you not tell me whether these people err as regards the

faith, whether they depart from wholesome doctrine ? Inquire
into this without delay ; be in a position to tell me especially, who
is the author of that translation, what is his object in view, what
faith do they who read it profess, and the reason of their teaching.
Do they hold our apostolic See and the Roman Church in veneration ? We desire to be clearly informed concerning these things
for our guidance."[201]

One would say that, finding himself face to face with the
censure and threats of Rome, the Bishop was the one who would
be the most embarassed. Indeed, several of the leading men of
the City refused to submit, protesting that they owed obedience
to God alone.[202] They did not give up their meetings or their
preaching, or the reading of holy books in the vernacular. Let
them prohibit the use of our translation if they like, said they ;
as for us, we shall keep it. It is said by some, that in this affair
the Bishop was even roughly handled.[203] However that may be, he
complained to the Pontiff, especially against a certain " Master
Crespin," a Priest, as we read, and one of his own companions.
This Crespin was possibly one of the authors of the translation ; for,
had he been satisfied with expounding the Scriptures, the Bishop
would not have cried out so loudly against him especially. What
did Innocent III. do ? He charged three Abbots to interfere,
and in concert with the Bishop to proceed to the desired enquiry,
and to the application of ecclesiastical discipline. This mission
had its effect, for the chronicle relates that the Pontifical
Commissioners succeeded in burning " a few books translated from
the Latin into the vernacular," if not in " exterminating the
sect."[204] It is true that more than one copy of the forbidden
translation escaped the flames. As a matter of fact two years
later, at Lieges, people were ordered to place in the hands of the
Bishop any translation of the Scriptures, either French or German,
which they possessed.[205] As for the sect, it was so imperfectly
exterminated that subsequent measures had to be taken for its
persecution. The Crusade had already burst forth ; it raged with
fury in the South, when Innocent III., writing to Bishop Bertram,
invited him to proclaim it against the heretics of his diocese. He
did so, and with such success that the Count of Bat and a goodly
number of knights were enrolled.[206] Yet it does not appear that
the sword had any better success than the sermons of the
Abbotts ; for in 1221 " heresy was not extinct in the City of

Metz,"[207] and the door remained open for new reactions, which invaded Flanders and disseminated themselves to the centre of Europe.

Let us now follow the footsteps of other refugees, who, passing through the upper valleys of the Rhone and Rhine, reached Switzerland and Italy on the one hand, and Germany on the other, and continuing their mission, spread their doctrines in Austria, Hungary, and as far as Transylvania.

Those who went up the valley of the Rhone were, perhaps, about to resuscitate in the mountains of Switzerland the memory of Arnaldo Brescia, and Henry of Lausanne, who had resided there less than fifty years before. At any rate they found they had been preceded by the Cathari, who had penetrated to those heights even as they had almost everywhere else.[208] It is not known where they pitched their tents. Nearly a century had passed away before the presence of heretics was ascertained in Berne.[209] Were these the Waldenses, or did they belong to some other reaction? It is impossible to state. Traces of them may still be found either in Berne itself or in Fribourg.[210] During the year 1400, the magistrates of Berne decreed that no individual holding the creed of the Waldenses should be eligible for civil office or even as a witness before the tribunals. This decree was read thenceforth every year on Easter Monday, that is to say, on the day of the election of the two hundred.[211] Afterwards the storm of persecution arose more furiously than ever, and the Waldenses finally succumbed. If no visible bond united them with their brethren of Italy, they nevertheless heard them spoken of;[212] no doubt by the missionaries, who we shall see joined them from further Germany.

Fribourg is a small city, a thoroughfare between the South and the Valley of the Rhine, which the refugees from Lyons must have reached at an early date. This magnificent valley, thanks to the attractions which it offered, had for a long time been the favourite residence of Prelates.[213] Perched up there in their castles they lived parasitic lives, which their avarice made still more scandalous. In this respect the Rhine had little or no cause to envy the Tiber. What the troubadours of Provence and Italian poets sung at great length in their fruitless invectives, the peasants of the borders of the Rhine whispered low in their simple legends. We can easily guess how the disciples of Waldo, with their passion for voluntary poverty, and especially with the word of Christ, which they came to announce to the poor and destitute, must have made their way in the midst of a population troubled by the worldliness of the clergy and dreaming of an ideal. They made proselytes in Strasburg, a relatively free, commercial and wealthy city—a city in which the Bishop had so often been held in check that he was perhaps the first in Germany to call to his aid the Dominican monks. In 1212 the chase began in earnest; more than five hundred heretics were ferreted out. Were they Waldenses? We are inclined to think so.[214]    They professed articles of faith which correspond more with those of the Waldenses than they do with those of divers sects that, however, in their turn did some missionary work here. Their principal superintendent resided in Milan; to him they forwarded their collections for the poor. But there were two others, one in Bohemia, surnamed the Picard—could it be Waldo?—the other in Strasburg itself. The latter was John the Presbyter, who marched to the stake at the head of a handful of heroes.

"Would'st thou," his judges asked him, "that thy cause be decided by the trial of red hot iron?"

"That would be tempting God."

"Ah! you are afraid of burning even a finger."

"Very well! here is more than a finger; here is my whole body. It is ready to be burnt, if it is a question of rendering homage to the Word of God."

He walked to the stake with a firm step, followed by his seventy-nine companions, among whom were twelve priests and twenty-three women.

Later, in 1216 and again in 1230, the heretics reappeared on the scene of martyrdom, thanks to the persecution proclaimed by Conrad of Marburg. We find always the same tendency, more or less. The Church is for them a synagogue of Satan, the Pope, Bishops and Priests are ministers of the Adversary. They call themselves disciples of the Apostles, and take the Holy Spirit as their guide. They are so numerous that when one of them goes from England or Antwerp to Rome, he is able to lodge every night at the house of one of his brethren. They continue to send their contributions to their chief at Milan.[215]    If these are Waldenses, ought we not to admit that there is here a commingling with the sectarians who are about to appear unexpectedly.

Nothing seems more natural than this.[216]   However that may be, after this date, silence enshrouds them ; of them no more mention is made.   They did not disappear ; but their voice, intimidated by persecution or overpowered by that of other sects, cannot reach us.

What are these other sects ?   We cannot avoid saying a word about them.   First, the Cathari, with whom we are acquainted, and of whom we shall not speak again here ; the more so as they had not in the North that full sway which they had in the South.   There were the Beghards, too, whose principal seat was at Cologne.   These were uneducated Pietists, less careful of the study of the Scriptures than of their vague and mystic speculations. They lived in common, but had taken no vows ; they spent their time in doing penance and in working and caring for the unfortunate. Their first origin dates from the end of the XII. century ; the XIII. was their most flourishing period.[217]   Afterwards, to avoid persecution, they took refuge in the ranks of the Tertiary Friars of the order of Mendicants, especially with the Franciscans, leaving the way open for the entrance of the Brethren of the Free Spirit. These latter were bolder, in thought at least, if not in character. On the one hand they professed the Pantheistic ideas that their master Amaur of Bena seems to have borrowed from the school of Scotus Erigene ; namely, that God is everything, and that man alone of all his creatures is one with him through the Spirit.   On the other hand, they shared the tendency of the hermit Joachim of Floris who had just proclaimed the approaching end of the second epoch of humanity, that of the Son, and the inauguration of the third, that of the Spirit, foretold for the year 1260.   They abandoned the use of sacraments, which in their opinion were losing their importance.   One of their first centres was Paris, where they met at the house of a jeweller named Guillaume.   At Strasburg they had a new master called Ortlieo.   He continued the sect by renewing it ; it was called from that time the sect of the " New Spirit."   To this movement it is that the Strasburg dissent— which we have marked as an offshoot of the Waldenses, whether they be called Ortliebers[218] or Winkelers, which was subsequently given as a nickname—attaches itself.[219]   After considering the matter fully, we find that the principles of this local reaction are sufficiently characteristic.   As a matter of fact, the Ortliebers arrogated to themselves the right of hearing confession, and even

D

that of administering baptism. They rejected the doctrine of purgatory, saying of masses for the dead, and the intercession of Saints; they also abstained from lying, from swearing, and from shedding of blood. We learn from all this that their quarrel with the Romish Church, more especially as regards the sacrament of the Eucharist, the ritual and other ordinances, bore the seal of the mission of the Poor of Lombardy, of whom we shall soon speak. On the other hand, the Ortliebers differed from the Waldenses of France, as well as from those of Lombardy and of Germany, by their allegoric notions, tainted with Pantheism, and by their tendency to spiritualize the dogmas, and even the actions recorded in the life of Jesus,[220] including the sacrament of the Last Supper, which a portion of them set aside as the Quakers do now.[221] From Alsace where they had their centre they spread in different directions, into France, Swabia, and as far as Austria.[222] We find them mentioned for the last time in the XIV. century, and we only hear of them again as the Winkelers, who disappeared in their turn, with other less known divisions, such as the Sifrides, the Tortolans and the Communies. We can understand from this, how it was that the valley of the Rhine became for Germany a nursery of missionaries. An agitation was commenced there which permeated public opinion to a great distance, reacting against the abuses of the Romish Church. Still the principal seat of the Waldenses movement was not here, but in a country which we have still to visit; namely, Milan. We shall go down there, following the tracks of the refugees from Lyons, before proceeding into Germany.

Milan, once the seat of the Western Empire and of the illustrious Bishop Ambrose, had not yet forgiven Rome for casting her into the shade. Resigned though she was, she preserved a leaven of distrust and a remnant of liberal inclinations that showed itself in the morals of the laity. While bowing to the tiara, her Primate had lost the splendour of his ancient prestige and much of his popularity; on the other hand, his servitude had been rewarded. Rome had hastened to confirm the Archiepiscopal authority, which he wielded over eighteen bishops. It extended to the boundaries of Old Lombardy, stretching out on the East, as far as the Venetian territory, and on the West to the Cottian Alps. The Synod of Milan rivalled the Councils in gravity, but hardly anything was heard there beyond the echo of the Roman

oracle, repeated by the Bishops, either of Turin and Asti or of
Brescia and Cremona. Its debates lacked that breath of life which
animated the disputes of the Republican community. Between
the head of the large diocese and the Podesta, harmony did not
invariably exist. They quarrelled more than once, without coming
to blows, however ; this, either because they feared each other,
or because frequent wars with other free cities and ecclesiastical
conflicts had the effect of diverting their attention. Still heresy
was increasing rapidly in the metropolis. The sect of the
Cathari was rooted there, either on the decline or else absorbed
into the indigenous party of the Patarins, who were less a
religious than a political party, and did not draw their recruits, as
at the commencement, from the quarter of Pataria alone, but
were almost as much from the palaces of the nobles.[223] Thanks
to this party, the temporal power formerly wielded by the Bishops
had passed into the hands of the magistrates. The Patarins
protected the smaller dissenting societies, which literally swarmed.
Were there not seventeen in Milan alone ? At least that is what
we are told by one of the Waldenses, who had lived there for a
long time.[224] The refugees from Lyons had hardly arrived[225]
before they found themselves at war with more than one sect,
although on good terms with others, who eventually associated
themselves with them in some numbers. We shall make mention
of the Humiliati, and the disciples of Arnaldo of Brescia.

Arnaldo had filled Italy with his reputation. The voice of the
martyr still echoed in the consciences of the people. Taking
up involuntarily the principal thread of that ancient Puritan movement of the Donatists, which had for a long time been lost sight
of, he reminded the Roman Pontiff that it is not the frock that
makes the monk, and certainly not a successor of the Apostles ;
that the right of apostolic succession is based upon the practical
application of the primitive law, of which the first precept
consists in the vow of poverty.[226] Not only has he no power to
ally himself to the ambition of temporal dominion ; but this vow
absolutely excludes it. Arnaldo said, "A Pope ought to be able
to repeat the words of St. Peter, 'Silver and gold have I none,'
otherwise he is like the salt which has lost its savour."[227] In
speaking thus, the illustrious emulator of Abelard ploughed a broad
furrow, in which since that time the principles of our political
liberty have been sown with a prodigal hand. That Cardinal also,

who recognised in Arnaldo "the prince and the patriarch of political heresy,"[228] had a quick and discerning eye. Was he nothing more than this? We cannot doubt that he was. He did not found a religious sect, but his leanings possessed both a religious and a political character. His religious tendencies opened a way for more than one reaction, and in Lombardy, at least, he seems to have preceded Waldo. This may be a conjecture, yet more than one sign justifies it.[229] At any rate, we shall see the Donatist principle which he had re-lighted making itself pretty plainly visible in the movement of the Poor of Lombardy.

As regards the movement of the Humiliati, it is now an undoubted fact that it brought about, in Milan itself, a distinct association which seems to be linked to that of the Poor of Lyons. We derive our information on this point from the same source as our history. The chronicle of Laon says :—" There lived in the towns of Lombardy a certain number of citizens, who without quitting their own hearths observed a set of rules which they had selected for themselves. Simply clothed, they abstained from lying, from swearing, and all lawsuits which are opposed to the Catholic faith. They addressed themselves to the Pope, asking him to sanction their profession of faith. The Pope replied that he sanctioned all that they did honestly and in humility, " but," he added, " I expressly forbid you to arrogate to yourselves the right of preaching in public." These people made light of the orders of the Pontiff ; they disobeyed and were excommunicated. They called themselves Humiliati," because they were content with plain, uncoloured vestments.[230] This took place under the pontificate of Alexander III. One writer reports that the Humiliati multiplied in Lombardy like the fish of the sea. Those, concerning whom we are writing, constituted undoubtedly a lay branch, if not an offshoot of the general order known by this name.[231] It is they who are referred to in the following verses :—

> " Sunt et in Italia fratres humiliati
> Qui jurare renuunt et sunt uxorati."

Coming into existence about the same time, the Poor of Lyons and the Humiliati made the same appeal to the same Pope, and finished by being condemned by the same Council of Verona which made no effort to distinguish between them ;[232] perhaps because their union was already an accomplished fact, or on the

eve of becoming so. The name which prevailed was that of the
Poor, only they were no longer called the Poor of Lyons, but
the Poor of Lombardy. The principle of the Waldenses was
based upon the authority of Scripture and lay preaching, but
their fusion with the characteristic principles of their associates—
such as their joint duty to support themselves by work in lieu of
by alms, and their independent position with regard to the Catholic
clergy, whom they regarded as unworthy—gave rise to discord,
and this was intensified by persecution. Taking advantage of a
favourable opportunity, they succeeded in obtaining from the town
a site suitable for the erection of a school, which was soon built;
they thereby roused the anger of the Archbishop Philip, who
caused it to be demolished.[233]  Philip died in 1206 and the school
was rebuilt.[234]  His successor, Hubert of Pirovano, followed the
example of Innocent III., just as Philip of Lampugnano had
followed that of Lucius III. Still the young community was
passing through a critical period, as its open way of procedure
terrified the timid ones, who were still seeking some concessions
from Rome. Thereupon Durand of Huesca, the Apostle of the
Catholic Poor, returning from the court of Innocent III. took
these people in hand, for the purpose of bringing them back
within the pale of the Church, and finally succeeded in rallying
around him about one hundred whom he induced to sign the confession sanctioned by the Pope. The perverts signed it on condition that the free use of the above mentioned school building, or of
another suitable for their meetings, should be granted them. Their
petition, transmitted by Durand, was duly approved of and
recommended to the Archbishop Hubert by Innocent III. This
was in April, 1210.[235] We learn that, at the same time, Bernard
Premier was dealing with the Pope for the return of a certain
number of his co-religionists, and we know with what result.[236]
While the perverts were thus returning to the pale of the Church,
those who remained and formed the great majority found themselves
at variance with their former companions. They represent during
this critical period the traditional and Conservative party. They
had up to that time carried everything before them with a high
hand, and unity had been maintained, notwithstanding the distance which separated them and more than one difficulty that had
arisen. This time discord broke out anew and a breach was
inevitable.[237] The rupture was as painful to one party as to the

other, more especially to the original mother community, which could not view without emotion its children thus abandoning the paternal roof; for we must not forget that the poor of Lombardy were an offshoot of the Lyonese stock.[238]   Waldo, who still was at the head of the community,[239] greatly deplored this division. He looked upon it as a misfortune from more than one point of view. He protested and grieved over it for the rest of his days.   After his death an attempt was made at a reconciliation and for this purpose a conference was assembled at Bergamo in May, 1218.[240] There were twelve commissioners chosen, six of whom represented the ultramontane Waldenses and six those of Lombardy.[241] Different questions were there discussed which we shall proceed to note.

The first thing which strikes us as strange is the great importance in which the memory of Waldo was held. It rises above all discussion and seems to make a strangely imposing effect.   We shall see further on what is the reason of this.   In the meantime reciprocal advances were made on more than one point.   The Lombards nominated their superiors for life ; the others chose their rectors *pro tempore*.   It was agreed—in the interests of all and of peace—to refer the nomination to the reunited community and to leave the decision to them, whether in the one sense or the other.   The same conclusion was come to with reference to the ordination of ministers.   As regards the question of manual labour the ultramontane party no longer insisted, as Waldo had done, on its absolute prohibition, while the Lombard party admitted the advantage of subjecting it to a more rigorous control.   A compromise was agreed to.   Let us agree on the other points, they said, we shall be able to come to a solution of the difficulty some way or other.   The points which had caused the disunion seemed to be disposed of.   With regard to matrimony and baptism, there was no conflict to speak of; there was only one isolated fact in dispute.   It was a question concerning Thomas de Jean Francigena and others, who had for special reasons been excluded from the community by the brethren of France. Let their matter, it was said, be thoroughly sifted; they are ready to render satisfaction if necessary and all will be well.   But after all there remained a twofold difficulty—one concerned the memory of Waldo ;   the other had reference to the sacrament of the Eucharist.

" Tell us frankly," said Peter de Relana who was associated with Berenger d'Aquaviva; " do you or do you not admit that Waldo and Vivetus are in paradise ?"

" That is a personal question if ever there was one. Should we do not do better to strike it out ?"

" Well then we may as well separate for good and all."[243]

" Our opinion has not changed. If during their lifetime they have made satisfaction to God for all their sins, they are saved."[2][43]

" Those sins, how are they to be understood ? It is no question of ordinary sins ; the declaration of the Lombards would be too unmeaning for that, and one cannot very well see in what way it could contain anything that was shocking to their co-religionists. It must therefore have reference to some errors with which he had been reproached in his relations with the brethren of Lombardy. In such case one can understand that the French Waldenses would not have been ready to avow them over the scarcely closed grave of him whom they regarded as the founder of the whole sect. Meanwhile the discord became more envenomed on a more serious matter. Unhappily it was the Sacrament of the Eucharist, the symbol of peace, which was destined to re-light the torch of discord without raising any serious point of dogma. The only question was as to the part played by the Priest recognised by the Church. According to the ultramontane Waldenses, if the Priest pronounced the sacramental words the mystery is accomplished, as it is not the virtue of the man which operates, but the word of God.[245] The Poor of Lombardy did not hold that to be sufficient; besides this, according to them the Priest must not be unworthy of his office. Upon that point we will not yield, said they, to those who would subjugate us, even though they be of higher worldly position than ourselves ; for our Saviour did not accept any man's authority. Are they doctors ? Let them meditate on the instruction handed down to us by the fathers. St. Cyprian, for example, says very clearly, that the faithful ought not to receive the sacrament at the hands of heretical, unworthy and profane priests. According to him, it is certain that the Eucharist does not have effect where hope is lost and faith corrupted—where all is a trick and a lie. In arrogating to himself the authority and the verity of the Church the heretic acts like a monkey who, not belonging to our race, is reduced to imitating us. An intruder, cursed of God and dead, he invokes the Saviour and pronounces the words of benediction with blasphemy in his soul. Is not that a sacrilege? He carries audacity even to the point of celebrating the holy sacrament of the Eucharist; but without the presence of the Holy Spirit, how shall his offering be sanctified? God cannot give heed to the prayer of the impious.[245] Jerome teaches us that priests who administer the sacrament of the altar unworthily act in a profane manner. This father says in his Commentaries, that disregarding the law of Christ they imagine that the solemn words of prayer suffice for the celebration, and that neither integrity nor merit are necessary in the celebrant; whereas it is written, as we know, that a Priest who has sinned is not permitted to present an offering. Holy in appearance before the eyes of the faithful, it is not the less tainted with sin in reality, if the soul of the priest be impure.[246] Such as buy or sell holy orders are not legitimate priests, observes Pope Gregory, and it has been said with reason that the curse rests both upon him who gives and him who receives. Such is the case in a matter of simony. Besides which, how can he, who is himself under the ban of anathema, sanctify another? How can he offer or receive the body of Christ if he have no part in it himself?"[247]

"We should prefer to have some proofs taken from Scripture. You lay too much stress upon the man; we prefer to look at the words of benediction which proceed from his mouth."[248]

"The objection is an old one, and if you do not know it, we will repeat the answer made by Pope Innocent. 'Oh! most miserable of the miserable! you forget that which the Lord said to the mercenary priests by the mouth of His prophet Malachi: 'I will curse your blessings.'"[249]

"You no longer agree with yourselves, for you formerly looked upon the matter in the same way as ourselves."

"Yes, formerly, when we were children. It is as St. Paul says: 'When I was a child I spake as a child, I understood as a child, I thought as a child; but when I became a man I put away childish things.'"[250]

"It will be necessary to return to that state, if you still have any wish for unity."

"We cannot believe that which contradicts the evidence of the Scriptures. No, we shall not do that, even though the Waldenses wished to compel us. It is our turn to say: 'We ought to obey God rather than men.' As you know, Paul resisted those who wanted to bring him under the yoke of the law ; and Peter, after he had proclaimed the order which he had received in a vision, touching the conversion of Cornelius, was suffered by the brethren of the circumcision to do as he wished ; they created no opposition or discord ; on the contrary, they glorified the Lord."[251]

The two parties were far from being of one mind. It is clear that the French Waldenses were still afraid of schism; for fear of the Church they hesitated about crossing the Rubicon. Their brethren in Milan, on the contrary, had learned in a good school that conciliation was a snare. They could not consent to a protest without issue, and they were not far from anticipating that separation which was to take place in the days of the Reformation.

After the conference of Bergamo they separated for a long time.[252] The brethren of the diaspora had, moreover, to be officially informed, this being necessary to prevent any misunderstanding. A circular letter was sent addressed "to the brethren and friends residing beyond the Alps," in the name of Otto de Ramezello.[253] The vague address seems to imply that the Lombardy mission was about to be enlarged. Meanwhile the letter could hardly be destined for any others than the missionary brethren of South Germany, and notably for those who were to be found in the district of Passau, which then formed part of the Duchy of Austria. Let us take as our guide the inquisitor who was on duty there, and he will soon put us on the track of the readers.

The inquisitor of Passau unrolls before our eyes a little catalogue, in which are indicated the localities in the diocese of Passau alone visited by our Italian missionaries. There are forty-two, and adherents everywhere. In speaking of twelve of them he adds : "And schools are there also."[254] In one place we even read : "Schools are also there, and the Bishop ;"[255] this is at Einzispach. Elsewhere, at Kematen, there are "several schools," ten it would seem ; but this doleful note is added, "They have killed the Curate there."[256] Why ? Was it perchance as in Styria, where a Curate's barn had been fired, because the Inquisitor had lodged in his house ? These reprisals are surprising in one respect ; they are rare. It would be odious to infer from this that the morals of the dissenters were in unison, especially when the Inquisitor himself eulogizes them. We shall have to refer to these eulogies later on, and we shall see that they are worth more than many apologies. One monk—who loved to account for the movement of reform, into the nature of which his official position had led him to inquire—finds one of the principal causes to be the morals of the heretics, which he praises. In his opinion they present the greatest contrast to those of the clergy, which he criticises with equal frankness. It is true that he did not complete publishing his criticisms. The Jesuit Gretser, who quotes so many pages from the Inquisitor of Passau, omits this one.[257] All the sacraments, it says, the temples, feasts, worship of saints, miracles, relics, the cross, pilgrimages, funeral rites— all are profaned by a frivolous, mercenary, cynical, deceitful clergy; and, as if the testimony of an Inquisitor were not above suspicion, facts are adduced to support it. The most striking part is the final statement, in which our monk reproaches the Priests for asserting, among other impostures, that the Roman See is infallible: "*quod sedes romana non possit errare.*" But, to explain this movement of reform, there are also reasons of a different character, quite external. The schisms which were convulsing the Church; the strifes of the Pontiffs among themselves and against the Empire; the excommunications and persecutions, were opening new doors.[258] For that matter the Emperor was far from protecting them, even though his name was Frederick II. To this very Prince may be traced back the Code which condemns new heresies as political crimes and dissenters as rebellious subjects. For this reason, the fact of the propagation of the Waldenses in Germany is worthy of consideration; the more so as, after the researches now being made, it is of more importance than all that has been said about it till now. As early as the thirteenth century it was increasing rapidly; at the end of the fourteenth it was at its climax, and had then reached every class of society.[259] Adherents multiplied and feared not to call themselves "the friends," in contrast to the Catholic adversaries who, in their estimation were "the enemies" or "the strangers."[260] So there is no cause for astonishment that at that time Waldenses were met with in all the thoroughfares, from Lombardy to the Baltic and from the Rhine to Raab; nor that, in the general opinion, separation from the Church of Rome seemed to be a possibility.[261] But thanks to the assistance of the secular arm, the Inquisition succeeded in charming it away, and it is by the light of the blazing piles that we can distinguish, one after the other, the principal stations belonging to the Waldensian mission. In Bavaria, Ratisbon; in Franconia, Würzburg, Eichstädt, Nuremberg, Bamberg, Heilsbronn; in Swabia, Augsburg, Tischingen, Nordlingen, Donawert, ; in Saxony, Wittemberg, Plauen; in Thuringia, Erfurt; in the Rhenish provinces, Cologne, Mayence, Friedberg, Spires, Bingen, Trèves, Strasburg, Hagenau, Weissemberg, Offenburg, Lahr; in Pomerania and the Margravate of Brandeburg, Stettin and its neighbourhood, Konigsberg in Neunark, Dramburg, Angermunds, Prenzlau; in Austria, Vienna, Steyer, and good number of villages, both in the Duchy of Styria itself and in the Archduchies; in Hungary, Budapest, Oedenburg, Gunz; furthermore, in Transylvania, in Silesia, in Poland;[262] finally, in Switzerland, Basle, Berne, Fribourg, Soleure,[263] as also in the Netherlands[264] were the principal stations. Among the victims, itinerant preachers occupy the first place. Twelve of them were imprisoned in Austria at one and the same time; among them were Hermann of Mistelgau and Nicholas of Plauen.[265] With regard to the persecutors, two of them deserved well of the Church; they were Peter of the Order of Celestins, and Martin of Prague. In the XV. century decadence began. Nevertheless, the Waldenses held their own until the end of that century, as is proved by the persecution which was proclaimed in Brandeburg about the year 1480, and in consequence of which a certain number of fugitives passed into Moravia and Bohemia,[266] where a new centre of reaction was formed, which thenceforth attracted the attention of the Waldenses scattered through Germany. This reaction is well-known, but we must notice it briefly.

Bohemia was its arena, and Conrad Stiekna, an Austrian, was the man who commenced it. He saw, in the errors and scandals of the dominating Church, so many signs of the early coming of Antichrist, for as such he described them. His friend Milicz of Moravia went further; in his opinion Antichrist had come; it was a question of denouncing him. What did he do? He started for Rome, where he posted his thesis on the doors of St. Peter. This audacious act nearly cost him his life. Matthias of Janow, Curate of Prague, in his turn, mounted the breach. He gazed fixedly upon Antichrist, and boldly said what he thought of him. He declared that his name is Legion, for he constitutes the false hurch of the unfaithful, co mposed of monks, prelates and popes.

Finally came John Huss. By his ecclesiastic tendency, he was more nearly associated with Wycliffe—whose writings had just been scattered throughout Bohemia—than with his own predecessors. He learned of him, not only what all dissidents had thought about the original fall of the Church, that it was in consequence of the gift of temporal power by Constantine, but furthermore that in the twelfth century, Satan through the monks of the Inquisition had been let loose in the midst of Christendom for the purpose of establishing the reign of Antichrist, who substitutes for the laws of God " the new bulls, which Jesus Christ did not issue." Excommunicated by the Pope, he appealed directly to Christ, without referring his cause to the Council. The Pope was not so anxious for the reformation of the Church as for the monopoly of the reformation; rather than renounce this, he put the reformer to death. Huss went to the stake on the 6th of July, 1415. Then it was Jerome of Prague's turn. Meanwhile conscience, victorious through martyrdom, was being stirred up; Jacques of Misa, Curate of Prague, celebrated the Holy Communion in both kinds. This was the signal for a long and bloody war. The Hussites were divided into two parties; one national and conservative—that of the Calixtines,[267] had Rokycana for a leader; the other, dissident and radical—that of the Taborites,[226] was directed by Procopus the Greater. After divers vicissitudes the Taborites moderated their excessive zeal, which had sometimes partaken of the nature of frenzy; but they never abandoned their distinctive principles, namely :—

The Bible ; the only rule of faith, independent of the interpretation of the Fathers.

Justification by faith ; " the summary of the Gospel and basis of Christianity."

Two Sacraments only ; Baptism and the Lord's Supper.

From that time the agreement of the parties became impossible, at least upon legal and national grounds. The Taborites were dispersed and several little sects sprang up. One only of them is of interest to us here—that of Peter of Chelcicky. It professed, among other maxims, brotherly equality and separation from the Antichrist—that is to say, the Pope. Moreover, there was to be no armed resistance, and no taking of oaths. The reader perceives that these maxims go further than those of the Waldenses ; indeed, they are an indication of their presence and action.

The beliefs of Chelcicky, according to the national historian of Bohemia, showed him to be as much an offshoot of the Waldensian as of the Hussite tendency.[269] No one denies the presence of the Waldenses,[270] only it is claimed that in Bohemia they were not constituted into distinct communities.[271] If so, which party, then, did they most resemble ? They were more in affinity with the Calaxtines than the Taborites, though retaining some of their tendencies.[272] The latter's austerity of discipline undoubtedly attracted them ; but they were in full sympathy with the former, on account of their hesitancy to separate radically from the Church of Rome. They still exercised a certain influence, and were not reduced to receiving everything without being able to make any return. Wherever there is salt its savour will be felt. Some among the Waldenses of Germany even rose to a place in the general direction of the Hussite mission. This was the case, for instance, with Frederick Reiser, who is worthy of special mention.

He was born in 1401, in the village of Deutach, near Donawert, and was from his infancy instructed by his father, who had made a profession of it in his capacity of a teacher in the doctrine of the Waldenses. At 18 years of age, he, desiring to devote himself to the career of an itinerant preacher, was taken by his father to a friend, a merchant of Nuremberg, called John of Plauen, and placed under his care. This John, of course, belonged to the Waldenses' dissent as did the Reisen family ; he interested himself zealously in their mission, and loved to prepare labourers for it. It was while in Nuremberg that Frederick became acquainted with the Waldensian teachers, who visited the German and Swiss communities. In 1418 he also met a celebrated teacher of Prague, named Peter Payne, who was at that time striving to bring about a union between the Hussites and the Waldenses, and by him the activity of the young Levite was influenced in the same direction. Reiser went forth to visit different localities in Germany and Switzerland. As a preacher he visited the communities of his brethren ; as a merchant the customers of the house of Plauen. Finally, he settled in Heilsbronn, near Ansbach in Franconia, there succeeding in gathering together a certain number of adherents. Soon he underwent strange vicissitudes. The war of the Hussites was going on around him, and he was taken and carried away a captive in their

midst. This was the decisive moment of his life. At Prague
and Tabor, Frederick entered into relations with the ecclesiastics ;
here he found again his old friend Peter Payne, and through his
instrumentality, received priestly ordination at the hands of
Nicholas, Bishop of the Taborites. He then accompanied the
Hussite deputies to the Council of Basle. Returning into
Bohemia, Procop the Great, chief of the Taborites, sent him to
his new destination, the little city of Landscron. His sojourn in
Bohemia was not without advantage to the cause of union. He
was forced to the conclusion that, without the support of the
Taborites, there was no future for the Waldensian mission in
Germany, and that its scattered and isolated communities, almost
strangers to each other, had everything to gain by joining a movement, whose effect was to bring them together and establish a
bond of union between them. He resumed his office of itinerant
preacher that he might again visit his dispersed brethren, feed
them, and bring them to the desired union. He certainly
sojourned at Strasburg, at Basle, at Heilsbronn, and again with
his old friends in Heroldsberg, not far from Nuremberg. If he
did return to Bohemia at this time, it was probably only to obtain
the definite sanction of his plans for organisation. At Tabor
the establishment of a fixed number of itinerant preachers, under
the direction of four Bishops, was determined upon, and the
special superintendence of the Waldensian communities of Germany was put into Reiser's hands. Thenceforth he bore this title
" Frederick, by the grace of God, Bishop of the faithful, who,
in the Romish Church, reject the donation of Constantine."[273]
If union were brought about, the Inquisition was always on
the watch to destroy it, and as early as 1458 Reiser succumbed at
Strasburg. It seems that the torments of the rack extorted
incoherent avowals from him, as they did later from Savonarola.
As Gino Capponi said, in speaking of the latter, one may
have the heart and not the fibres of a martyr.[274] Reiser went to
the stake together with his faithful companion, Anna Weiler, of
Franconia, and their ashes were thrown together into the
Rhine.[275]

During the same year Matthew Hagen, who had been
ordained by Reiser, died at the stake in Berlin, he proving himself more staunch than his Bishop, notwithstanding the threats
and seductions to which his companions had finally yielded.[276]

While the monks of the Inquisition were still bent upon destruction, the Bohemian Brethren built up the edifice of their unity. It was composed of divers elements, both Calixtine and Taborite, cemented by the discipline which Peter of Chelcicky had just elaborated. The plan on which it was arranged was the law of God. The organisation was completed in 1467, by the election of nine ministers, one of whom was called to the office of Bishop. Then a serious question arose as to who was to consecrate him; to decide this the Brethren appealed to the Waldensian fraternity. There were a certain number in the Duchy of Austria, their origin, it was said, dating back to the days of the primitive Church. In one of his writings, Chelcicky tells how Sylvester and Waldo, fleeing from the Imperial Beast, had hidden in the woods ; and how Constantine, having meanwhile embraced the Christian faith, sent an animal for Sylvester to ride and brought him back to Rome, where he received the fatal donation.[277] Waldo did not return ; he kept aloof and protested against Sylvester. " Thou dost not act," said he, " according to the doctrine and example given to us by Christ and our fathers the Apostles."[278] This legend was not contradicted by the Waldenses ; Stephen their Bishop even believed it. Thereupon the Brethren decided to free themselves from the yoke of Romish sacerdotal consecration ; they even laid it solemnly aside and obtained the ordination of one of their Elders at the hands of a venerable Waldensian ecclesiastic. This act generated doubts ; however, it was asked if this were the true priestly consecration, would it not be more surely guaranteed and complete if received from a Bishop, and finally Stephen was asked to intervene. He conferred the laying on of hands upon Matthias of Kunewald, the first Bishop of the Unity of Brethren, who hastened to impart it to two Elders, his colleagues. Thereby the brethren thought they would again become attached to the true Church and accomplish their separation from that of Rome.[279] It has been claimed that Stephen had been consecrated by a Catholic Bishop, but this is a myth. Moreover, it is not a question of finding in Stephen a Bishop in the ordinary sense of the word, but in its primitive and scriptural acceptation.[280] It is to be regretted that he was not supported in Austria by the other Waldensian ecclesiastics. Had he been, their example would have induced their flocks to adhere in a body to the Unity of Brethren, but they had become more jealous for

their Roman consecration and the privileges it conferred than for
their profession of poverty.  Stephen's entreaties were all in vain,.
and, if the truth has been told, his zeal for union betrayed him
to the Inquisitors of heresy, who condemned him to the stake at
Vienna.[281] A few years later Stephen's colleagues passed over to
the Church of Rome and the Waldenses of Austria were no
longer heard of.

If it be true that a few degenerate Waldenses left the Brethren
to themselves, it is not necessarily to be inferred from this that the
Waldensian mission in Bohemia was fruitless.  The Unity owes
it something more than the martyred Bishop's hand of fellow-
ship; she owes to it, partly at least, her very cohesion, and that discipline, which Peter of Chelcicky received from the Waldenses as
much as from his Hussite ancestors.  At any rate, the mission of
the Waldenses has been fruitful for Germany; it there sowed the
first seeds of the Reformation—the Bible—long before Luther's
time.[282] This is now being recognised.  " We acknowledge,"
exclaims a learned man, " that the Waldenses exercised a more
vigorous and wide-spread influence in Germany before the Reformation than has been hitherto believed,"[283] and another writer
adds, " their history is far from having enjoyed among us the consideration it deserves.[284]

We shall not follow the traces of the dispersion of the Waldenses any further; indeed, they cannot be followed.  What
we have said suffices to prove their missionary zeal, which made
them carry out their Master's order, " Go into all the world."[285]
Less than a century after their first banishment, one of their
persecutors confessed that they had spread everywhere.  " Where
is," he exclaimed, " the country to be found, in which their sect
does not exist ?"  Unfortunately, the Inquisition also was
spreading everywhere on their track, putting out, one by one, the
torches that were gleaming in the darkness, and we are assured
that one of the Waldensian martyrs confessed to his judges that
the cause for which he was about to die " was a fire soon to
disappear."[281] With all that a light does still hold on to burn
upon yonder " Alpine-altar."

# CHAPTER THE FOURTH.

### THE ALPINE REFUGE.

*Religious ideas, like birds, have a tendency to build nests for themselves—The retreat of the Waldenses into the Valleys of the Alps was occasioned by two facts: their banishment from Lyons and the Crusade against the Albigenses—The Waldenses reach the Italian side and establish themselves there, thanks to the concurrence of diverse circumstances—The configuration of the country—Uncultivated lands—Is there any reason to admit the existence of traces of ancient local dissent in the Italian Valleys?—Discussion upon this point tends to prove the vicinity, if not the presence, of the sect of the Cathari—The Abbey of St. Mary of Pignerol and the Castle of Lucerna—Thomas I., Count of Savoy and the House of Achaia—New Colonies: that of Calabria—First decrees of persecution against the Waldenses of the Valleys: that of Turin, and that of Pignerol—The Inquisition: its " raison d'étre " and its establishment—The strongholds capitulate: Podesta Oldrado in Milan and the repression in the country towns—First assaults of the Monks at Perosa, Angrogna, Pragelas, and in Dauphiny—Two new decrees, one by Louis XI. and the other by the Duchess Iolante—First Crusade against the Waldenses: Innocent VIII. and his Bull: a check in the Valleys of Piedmont and cruelties in Dauphiny—A Waldensian deputation at Pignerol—An inquiry at Freyssinieres and the letter of Louis XII.—Margaret of Foix and the first glorious return —What was going on within—The Barbes, the Mission and the School—Condition of the Waldenses on the eve of the Reformation.*

A S with primitive tribes, so it is with creeds; after having wandered about for some time they finally settle down on the spot where their native genius can take root. It is a law of

nature. " As soon as a new creed is revealed to mankind it seeks
a new country for its development. As the young birds which,
as soon as hatched, set out all ignorant to find the climate and
shelter most suited to them ; as the hidden stream which flows
by the most direct route to the lake it has never seen ; even
so does a religious idea, hardly conceived in the genius of a people,
go forth to seek in nature the type into which it is to develope."[282]
This was the case with religious ideas in the East until the
appearance of Christianity, and it was also that of the religious
reactions of the Middle Ages down to the Reformation which was
the crown of all. All seek nests for themselves ; the Cathari in
Bosnia, the Albigenses in Toulouse, the Patarins in Milan, the
Joachimists in Calabria, God's Friends in Alsace, the Apostolics
in the mountains of Novara, the Taborites in Tabor. To-day the
homes of all of those ancient forms of dissent are deserted.
Sheltered by the Alps, that of the Waldenses still exists.
It is worth while, therefore, to point out the circumstances in the
midst of which they were led to establish themselves there.

We have already remarked that immediately after their exile
from Lyons, there were some who took refuge in Dauphiny, and
there constituted the stock from which the Waldenses of the Alps
are sprung. This is the well-authenticated report of local
tradition.[283] A chronicle of Malines in the Valley of Queyras says
that " the Waldenses, having been driven out from Lyons, a
number of them took refuge in the country and began to settle in
Pimouzet ; thence they spread into Ginaillaud, Villar, La Pisse,
and Les Pres, the other hamlets of the country being free from
them."[284] Now these names correspond to a number of localities
contained in a little district situated at the junction of the valleys
of Pelvoux and Durance. Pimouzet, which the Waldensian refugees
are said to have made their first stopping place, is situated at the
lower end of Val Louise, on the right, and is now known by the name
of Puy-Saint-Eusebe. Pinaillaud is on the left ; it is now called
Puy-Aillaud. Le Villar is upon the left bank of the Durance,
opposite Puy-Saint-Andre. La Pisse is at the bottom of a small
lateral valley which terminates with the monastery of Briancon.
Lastly, Les Pres are below the Vignaux, another village of Val
Louise, which was inhabited by the Waldenses.[285] From these
different localities, many of the refugees climbed the heights, crossed
the frontier, and reached the valleys on the Italian side,[286] pre-

ceded perhaps by the first scouts, if it be true that any were sent on by Waldo before leaving Lyons. This last supposition is credited by Gilles. "It is thought," he says, "that these persecuted Lyonnais, foreseeing the necessity of a retreat, had before moving them from Lyons, sent some one to reconnoitre and find out beforehand some places where they might put their households in safety." Our historian adds that Waldo "accompanied that band coming toward the Alps of Piedmont, and saw his flock settled there before he left it to return to the other bands, which had started out towards the North, and of whom he led a portion into Bohemia." All this is possible, only we must admit that it is not supported by any fact ; nay, more, there is nothing to indicate the presence of the Waldenses in the Italian Valleys of the Alps before the year 1209, which was the first year of the Crusade against the Albigenses. That event alone would suffice to account for the emigration of which we are speaking; but it is probable that its only effect was to increase the proportions of it.

We do not propose to relate here the history of that famous Crusade. It is well known that Innocent III. was the soul of it, Dominic the Apostle, Simon de Montfort the executioner, and Raymond VI., Count of Toulouse, its most illustrious victim. In the eyes of Rome the latter had become, right or wrong, the personification of the evil genius of Rebellion in religion even more than in politics. Now, let us not forget that this was the time of the most powerful Pontiff that ever lived. It was he who realized the aspirations of the Conqueror of Canossa, and put forth pretensions which were boundless. "The Pope," he himself said, "acknowledges no superior except God. He is the mediator between God and men ; less than God, more than man. He is set over nations and kingdoms. According to the divine law, kings and priests are anointed ; the priest, however, anoints the king, not the king the priest. Now he who anoints holds a higher rank than he who is anointed. Priesthood is as far above royalty in rank as the soul is superior to the body. At the beginning of the world God placed two great lights in the canopy of heaven, one to shine by day and the other by night. As the moon receives its light from the sun, so do princes receive their power from us."[287] Such is the papal doctrine. The rule of action, which Innocent carried out, Jean-sans-Terre knew something of, as did also King

Philip Augustus. Nay, was not the Emperor Frederick compelled to bow his head ? Now, when emperors and kings bowed the head, it was not for an insignificant Count of Toulouse to lift up his. If his predecessors had practised toleration, it was now, thought the great Pontiff, high time to stop. From the very first year of his reign, he had recalled the monks of Citeaux to their office, which was to preach the Crusade. There had been Crusades in Asia ; why not have some in Europe ? People had rushed upon the Saracens ; but were not heretics even more wicked and dangerous ? Hence, death to the heretics ! The Crusade was proclaimed towards the end of 1207. It was a hunting field on a gigantic scale, worthy of Olympus and Tartarus. The king of France was invited to join, together with all the nobility who had willing minds. The Dominicans, those excellent hounds, were set loose, and all monkhood with them. The Count of Toulouse wavered, yielded, and wished to capitulate ; it was in vain. This was not enough, there was another and necessary element in this Crusade. After all, it was not so much a question of bringing him back to obedience as " of catching the little foxes which do not cease from devastating the vineyard of the Lord."[289] Eighteen cities and one hundred and twenty-four villages, with more than 60,000 inhabitants, gave way. It was determined upon to lay the land under an interdict, as in the East. Was this caused by thirst for carnage, or was it a piece of strategy in order to produce a general panic, which should hasten on the victory ? One or the other it must have been, if we are to account for the massacre of Beziers, for instance, where all the inhabitants were slain, including the 7,000 who, mad with terror, crouched down in the Church of St. Magdalen. " Nothing could save them," says a Troubadour, " neither cross, nor crucifix, nor altars ; I do not believe a single one escaped."[290] It was in this terrible hour that the legate Arnaud is said to have spoken the cynical words, " Kill them all ; God knows his own."[291] United in their death or flight, Albigenses and Waldenses crowded the highways ; dazed with fright they rushed pell-mell, mostly toward the East. This new exodus, only to be compared to the one seen afterwards in France after the revocation of the Edict of Nantes, stripped the South of its industrious population. Whither should they flee ? The enemy were everywhere holding the outlets. In the meantime a large number succeeded in reaching Dauphiny, where they were received by their brethren. Soon the country became unable to accommodate so great an influx of people. The valleys of Freyssinieres and Louise were invaded; but the tide of emigration kept flowing in day by day. Finally, the most needy formed a group, and in their turn reached the frontier. The pass of Mont-Genevre unites the valleys of the Durance and the Doire; that of Sestrietres makes a communication between the former and the smaller valleys of Cluson and Pragelas. Now it is unnecessary to demonstrate that natural communications determine the relations between contiguous populations. Habitual, even intimate relations, must have been formed between the inhabitants of those three valleys, and the old Roman road which crosses their territories is a sufficient proof of the antiquity of this intercourse; hence, the refugees had only to follow the established current to enter into relations with the Italian valleys.[292] They descended mostly into the graceful little valley of Pragelas, at that time comprised in the territory of Count Gui of Vienne. According to a certain local tradition, the road of the Traversette, near Viso, did not exist then, as it dates only from 1220; but if the pass were open for the Saracens who had gone up from the valley of the Po into that of Queyras, whence they had finally been driven out after much difficulty, why should it not be open for the fugitives who crossed it in an opposite direction? More than one band ventured into the footpaths of the Croix and Julien passes, leading up to the heights above the central valleys of Luserna, Perosa, and St. Martin, but the bulk of the colony settled in Pragelas, whence it soon overflowed into the neighbouring valleys. " Being once established there," says a Catholic writer, " their own needs compelled them to be so industrious and skilful in cultivating the soil even to the remotest little patches of ground, that, with no other occupation or means of supporting their already numerous families, they gradually cleared enough to supply their wants. Still finding themselves much cramped for room in the Pragelas and the neighbouring mountains, which could only with great difficulty shelter them all—for they were multiplying with great rapidity—they passed thence into the mountains of Piedmont, which are above Périer, and into the valleys of St. Martin and those of Val Lucerne that constitute the upper part of the communities of Angrogna, Villar, and Bobbio."[203]

The Waldenses have arrived. They have earned by the sweat of their brow the places which will be their retreat from one generation to another. The sky is seldom clear over their heads, but further on it unrolls its azure vault. At their feet ravines run down to the valleys of Pelis and Cluson, intersected by dales whose upper end is closed by granite walls, but are bordered lower down with wooded and green hills. Pathways run along the rivers and debouche with them at the little city of Pignerol. There the plain of Piedmont opens out, intersected by the Po. On its north are the snow-clad Alps; on its south the dark mass of the Apennines, almost shrouded in the clouds.

One might be tempted to believe that the fugitives had come there incontinent, like the leaves, blown hither and thither by the storm raging behind them. But it is not so; their emigration was well reasoned. Gilles tells us it was justified by different circumstances, by the simultaneous occurrence of which, the establishment of the Waldensian colony was destined soon to be an accomplished fact.

In the first place, with regard to security, " the situation was favourable to their condition."[294] An individual qualified to judge of this observed, not long ago, that the valleys of Piedmont, made up, as we know they are, of the valley of the Pelis and a part of that of Cluson, which are two affluents of the Po, have as a whole " the form of a quadrilateral, with boundaries clearly marked by ridges of difficult access." " On the Italian side," he goes on to say, " they have extremely steep slopes, and are separated by short and abrupt spurs, whose extremities, formed of granite rock, draw near each other and give to the Alps, when looked at from Turin, the appearance of an immense wall enclosing a garden."[295] Indeed, it has been calculated that the double zone, which comes down from the ridge of the frontier to the plain of the Po on one side and to the Rhone on the other, stretches out seven times further in the direction of France than in that of Italy. Furthermore, it is a fact worthy of notice, that in the case of the latter the valleys are joined together by upper passes, all directed towards a common entrance which can be easily closed; while with the former, the valleys are independent, and open into France through separate roads which afford as many ways of ingress for an enemy. It is easy to see what might result from this. Moreover, history has confirmed the fact that, on the French

side, the Waldensian population hardly succeeded in holding its
own, except in the upper valleys, which communicate with the
more privileged Italian valleys, while on the other side they were
able to face attack ; hence we have a natural explanation of the
fact, which is, however, none the less marvellous, that the Waldenses were preserved in those countries in the midst of enemies.
bent on their destruction. If we compare their situation with
that of their brethren dispersed in so many different lands, we
can easily understand how, elsewhere, they finally disappeared,
nor need their preservation here be—as it has often been—
claimed as due to the intervention of miraculous power. The
hand of Providence was sufficiently apparent in the fact of the
fugitives' arrival, and especially in the circumstances which conduced to their establishment in that lofty retreat ; and it is not
reasonable that we should refuse to recognize that hand till later,
and then only in a few isolated facts, and almost in such a manner
as to give the impression that the God of the Israel of the Alps
is " a God of the hills."[296] Historians " more pious than
erudite "—remarks in this connection a writer who is both—have
attributed to continual Providential intervention that victorious
resistance to the multiplied attacks of the enemy. It is not
necessary to explain their success by means of supernatural
interference ; it is sufficient to examine the configuration of the
country carefully.[297] An instinct almost as sure as that of the
eagle guided the Waldenses to those high valleys, where we find
the cradle of their generations. They were the more easily able
to put their trust in God, in that they sought for safety under the
covert of nature's wings. Such instinct oftentimes makes up for
scientific strategical observation, nor withal renders faith useless.
Faith will, when necessary, of itself perform miracles—who has
not witnessed that ? Meanwhile, it cannot be questioned, as one
of their historians has said, that the situation of the new centre,
in which the Waldensian colony established itself, was favourable
to their condition. With his opinion the following words of the
Catholic chronicle seem to agree :—" The situation of the valleys,
shut in on all sides by high mountains, caused them to be sought
after as retreats by the heretics when driven out of France."[298]
After that there is no need of becoming over-excited or of resorting
to prophecy, after the manner of Leger, who explains the situation
of the country by the purpose of God, " who had prepared it,

according to the prophecy of St. John, for the preservation of the woman clothed with the sun, who holds the moon under her feet against all the floods of persecution which the great red dragon might cast out of his mouth against her."[299]

If we examine facts, we shall find that the locality we are discussing was favourable to the refugees from a second stand-point. There was in the Alpine Valleys, says Gilles, "a considerable amount of unoccupied land suitable for their wants." In other words, half of the country was, when the new settlers arrived, still uncultivated, if not wooded. Its inhabitants, gathered here and there in isolated hamlets, "cultivated hardly any but those spots of more attractive appearance, the tilling of which was easy and profitable; so that the new comers, by means of proper agreements, easily obtained from those who held it, sufficient land in the higher territory of all the valleys, on which to build their homes, with fields to cultivate for a subsistence. There, in the different districts, they built their best and most secure villages.[300] To be convinced of this one has only to glance over some of the most ancient documents belonging to the noble house of Luserna, relating to the valley of that name and the smaller ones of Angrogna and Rora, bordering upon it,[301] or study the act of donation by which Adelaide of Susa granted to the Abbey of Pignerol the right of sovereignty over the small territory which skirts the Cluson. It will be seen that in Val Perosa especially, and even in Val St. Martin, there were uncultivated localities in abundance, whilst the inhabitants were few. The Waldenses established themselves in these regions comfortably, and so as to leave but little room for the Catholic population; this could not be said regarding the valleys nearest the plain. Furthermore, the aspect presented by the entire Italian slope, both as regards cultivation and habitation, points to these conclusions. Indeed, "four habitable zones, one above the other, and clearly distinguished by their produce,"[302] are distinctly visible; so that the most superficial observer is struck by the fact, and asks himself what the cause of this may be. The reason is to be found in movements of the population upwards or downwards, according to the exigencies of the situation; it had to mount upwards under the pressure of persecution by the troops of the Duke of of Savoy and of the outlaws turned loose by the Pope and the monks. The site of the highest hamlets, that of the churches especially, is very significant in this respect. It reveals, at one and the same time, the necessity for security from a surprise by the enemy and the effect of a continuous oppression, sanctioned by law. " It is a remarkable thing,'' someone lately observed, " that, after more than six centuries and a half have elapsed since the Poor of Lyons came with their families to occupy the highest of the Waldensian Valleys of Italy, it would probably not be impossible, even to-day, to draw approximately the line which marked the lower limit of habitation assigned by the natives to their ultramontane brethren; so much difference is there between the patois used in the mountains and in the plain, and even in certain towns, between the patois of the hill and that of the lower valley."[303] But let us return to the soil itself, for it gives us even more information. At the foot of the rocky, bare, and water-bearing snow-capped heights, the ground is covered with fine and sweet-scented grass only, utilized during the summer in the pasturage of cattle. Lower down, the coniferous trees and beeches appear, and among them the first chalets Still lower we find chestnut trees, wheatfields and permanent dwellings. The refugees were undoubtedly obliged to reach this zone to procure their food, and it was only little by little that they mingled with the native population of the hill-sides near the plain, to participate there in the raising of corn, the cultivation of the mulberry and fruit trees and the vine with its waving tendrils. Gradually they brought the vegetation higher up, as it were, and took advantage for their sustenance of all the resources of their limited territory, so that " every undulation of the ground is covered with cultivated fields, meadows, houses, and villages, with their thick frame of fruit trees and high trained vines. No portion has been permitted to lie fallow, and life and vegetation are seen wherever the bare rock does not show above ground. In several places, even the rock itself, is clothed and blooming, thanks to the earth with which it has been artificially covered, and to the little streams of water skilfully directed thereupon."[304] The chestnut tree is the one that towers above this varied vegetation. It is as a king, and it has been named the national tree of the Waldenses. It is found scattered about on all the hills, spreading out its green canopy, and gracefully breaking the line of the horizon. It bears a delicious fruit of a variety called the Lombarda, renowned for its size and sweet flavour, and this fruit serves the Waldensian population in the same manner as the polenta of corn flour does the Piedmontese peasant, and the potato the Irishman. Often during the persecutions no other sustenance was obtainable; hence it is that the Waldenses cultivate with a sort of filial affection that "Saviour tree,"[305] which at an early date covered the ground occupied by their ancestors and grew to a considerable height. It might be concluded that they hastened to plant chestnut trees on their arrival at the lower levels, and that afterwards they took them with them when they retreated to the heights, in order that their necessary bread might be within reach.

So much with regard to the situation of the valleys, from the standpoint of their configuration and conditions of soil. We are thereby afforded good reasons for the arrival of the Waldensian refugees and their attempt to settle there; without, perhaps, sufficient explanation of the stability and permanence of their establishment. In order to understand this, one must take into account, not only the natural surroundings, but also the inducements offered by the existing society with its more or less unsettled ideas. Now, on this point we must hear what Gilles says. "The natives and their neighbours," he writes, "were not far from having the same feelings and knowledge, with regard to religion, and they gave evidence of this by the promptness with which a great number of them joined the Lyonnais and professed the same religion."[306] Thereupon he invokes—rather *mal apropos*—the testimony of a Catholic writer of his time, in order to show that upon their arrival in the valleys "the Waldenses found there the true seed of religion."[307] This conclusion goes too far; it overleaps the facts. As yet there had been nothing that could positively justify such a conclusion, so that whatever value it may have is only that due to *à priori* reasoning; in any case, in order to arrive at this conclusion facts should not be forced. Now what may be the meaning of this phrase—"true seed of religion?" According to some, it refers to a certain more or less evangelic and anti-Roman tendency in a latent state; according to others it means "Biblical principles," properly so-called, which already flourished before the Waldensian immigration. In our opinion, the first interpretation does not give perhaps the full meaning of Gilles' words; but, if it weakens them, it is in order to make them agree with the facts. The second, on the contrary, strains the words of Gilles and invents freely. It expresses an absolutely gratuitous opinion, which is on that account unsustainable.[308]

Is then the conventional belief to be repudiated ? We think that it necessarily must be. But it may be said by the reader that he has not yet been made able to form definite opinions on that point, and he may wish to know more about the matter. He may wish to know still more about the actual origin; he may say that at the beginning of the book that was discussed from a general standpoint only. We shall, therefore, succinctly restate the arguments. Some have contended that the Apostles Paul and James may well have sown the true seed of religion in Waldensian soil when on their way to Spain; but this theory cannot be seriously maintained. Even were it the case, as has been asserted, that the Gospel penetrated to these valleys in the early days of the Church, when the persecutions of the Cæsars were being carried on, this would not require us to admit that Christian faith took root there and maintained itself continuous and unchangeable. Such a conclusion could only be tenable on the assumption that the ancestors of the Waldenses had been more successful in escaping from the influence of the world than were the monks who retired into the desert. It is upon such an hypothesis, however, that it is possible to imagine that the Waldenses dispensed with the Reformation. It is true that Gilles does not venture thus far, but Leger and Rizzi go if possible further, and indeed reproach Gilles with having accepted the name of "reformed." It is stoutly asserted by them that the Waldenses obtained their belief from the Apostles or their immediate successors, and that from that time "it has never changed in the valleys," and that, therefore, the Waldenses "have never undergone any reformation." Were these things indeed so, the question would arise : Have the Waldenses been a race of living beings or a collection of immobile mummies ? Is there nothing for the Waldenses to repeat but the "apology of their evangelical immobility ?"

The principal champion of the Waldensian legend is himself compelled to admit that "it would be absurd to ask for proofs of the apostolic succession of the Waldensian Church in times anterior to the seventh century."[312] Up to that time—indeed up to the time of Claudius, Bishop of Turin—there is no reason to suspect the existence of Christian doctrines, other than Roman, in Waldensian Valleys. Murton does indeed conjecture that Claudius, being a Spaniard, may have visited the Waldenses on his way to Italy, and he—the wish being father to the thought—goes on to say that he may there have imbibed Waldensian opinions.[313] Of course this is but a conjecture on which Murton laid no emphasis, for he elsewhere states that "the doctrine of Claudius spread from Turin even to the valleys."[314]

Claudius presumably imbibed his opinions at the seat of the Carlovingians—whose mouthpiece he became on the Italian side of the Alps—and from direct study of the Scriptures. It has been stated by Leger that with the population of the valleys, he " openly separated from the communion of the Romish Church and from the Pope." But Leger could not of his own knowledge know anything of this, for he is separated from Claudius by an interval of time as wide as that which separates the period of Claudius from that of the Apostles. Claudius, as a matter of strict fact, never did separate from the Church of Rome; when living he protested with emphasis that he " was preserving unity and desired neither schism, sect, nor heresy," and he ever struggled against them[316] as becomes what he was—a Bishop. He himself states that while protesting against the errors in his church he stood alone in the breach;[317] and it seems likely that his protests perished with him, for unlike Fra Dolcino, of whose retreat in the mountains of Novara local tradition[318] still tells, no record of any kind remains in the valley that commemorates his protest.[319] It is true that Leger states that the doctrine of the Waldenses differs in nothing from that of Claudius; and other writers have repeated his statement, though it will bear no investigation.[320] Brezzi, on the other hand, asserts that the original articles of faith of the Waldenses were identical with those of Bruys.

Those conjectures are wide of the mark, and on careful examination of the matter a different conclusion is reached. The Waldensian re-action has its own distinctive character, and the settlement in the valleys of those who took part in it cannot be doubted and sufficiently explains the origin of the dissenting population there. Their establishment is possible under the conditions heretofore pointed out; political circumstances favoured it as well. It has sometimes been claimed that there was in the Italian Alpine Valleys, or in their vicinity, before the time of the arrival of the refugees from Lyons, a distinct anti-Roman tendency. It has been claimed that a search in the archives of such houses as those of Lucerne and Pignol, and neighbouring monasteries would reveal secrets which would establish this view. It was said by Leger himself that but for a fire which consumed his memoirs this theory would have been established, and Meytre seems to credit this.[321] So much does imagination rule in questions of this kind that there be many who imagine that the archives hold secrets that would establish their views about the apostolic origin of the Waldenses. Such forget the fact that the archives *have* been searched, and that nothing has been found which can be cited in support of the opinion that an evangelical population existed in the valleys before the arrival of Waldo's disciples. Baron Manueli di S. Giovani testifies to this. He says :—" The first germs of the Waldensian heresy, in the valleys of Piedmont were brought there from neighbouring French provinces, at the end of the 12th century." Before that time they did not exist there, and he adds the following proof, to those alleged by the most creditable writers, Protestant as well as Catholic :— " No mention of them is found in any authenticated document; neither in foundation deeds nor other documents concerning monasteries and churches, erected not long before in these very territories and in neighbouring ones. They contain no allusion to the existence of heretics in their vicinity. Had heretics existed allusions to them would have been sure to occur and the expediency of making these foundations with a view to combatting their errors and defending the Catholic faith would have been demonstrated in the deeds.[322] It has been claimed by some that as early as the eleventh century some glimmerings of evangelical light are discernible in the Waldensian valleys. Monastier is cited as saying that Pietro Damiani complained in a letter to the Duchess Adelaide of Susa that the clergy of her States " did not observe the ordinances of the Church."[323]

Monastier is mistaken, however. Damiani does not say that the law of celibacy, sanctioned by Pope Gregory VII., met with strong opposition everywhere, even in the States of the Duchess. On this account, Damiani wrote to Adelaide concerning the incontinence of his clergy—*de clericorum in continentia*.[324] On the other hand he found fault with Bishop Cunibert of Turin for permitting priests to marry.[325] The question, therefore, was that of the marriage of priests, which the Pope wanted to put a stop to, and which he called incontinence. This had not anything to do with the Waldenses, who were chaste, even in the Roman sense of the word and upon the testimony of their enemies.

Then the bull of Pope Victor II. to Viniman, Archbishop of Embrun is cited. It is dated in the year 1057, and according to Hudry-Ménos, it states that Archbishop Viniman was invited " to take measures against heresy," and warned that his diocese " was wonderfully corrupted thereby."[326]

But the bull itself reads thus :—" The Church of Embrun, formerly so remarkable for its piety and wealth, has been plunged into misery and corruption—first, by the Saracen invasion and cruelties ; then by the arrival and sojourn of fugitives and people without discipline ; and finally, by the long oppression undergone by its pastors."[327]  There is in this allusion to heresy, and if there be taken into account the political troubles of that epoch, the anarchy and disorder caused by the Saracens and Hungarians in Embrun as much as in the surrounding country, the words of the bull are capable of a perfectly natural explanation. Again it is stated, on the authority of Murton that Urbanus II., in the year 1026, denounced Val Louise as " tainted with heresy."[328]

The text, however, contains no such statement.[329]

Then Monastier, quoting the so-called chronicle of St. Throu, in Belgium, states that a monk, called Radulphus, about to start for Italy, complained how, on crossing the Alps, he had to traverse " a territory contaminated by an inveterate heresy touching the body and blood of the Lord·"[330]  This chronicle dates apparently from the beginning of the twelfth century. It is claimed that the territory mentioned is in the Valleys of the Alps. These words are put forth as " an indication of evangelical and anti-Romish tendencies among the inhabitants of the valleys, before the arrival of Waldo or of his followers."[331]

But the quotation is unfortunate. The chronicle of St. Thron does not speak of a territory at the crossing of the Alps. Radalphus went to Rome, it says, and reached that city after having been robbed by marauders. He stopped a few days there, and hardly knew how to decide with reference to the rest of his journey. He had just been told that one of the territories he intended to traverse " was contaminated by an inveterate heresy touching the body and blood of the Lord." What still further augmented his uneasiness "was a pain in his hip which had troubled him for some time. It prevented his walking, and did not even permit him to ride on horseback." He therefore abandoned his plan and returned by the way of the St. Bernard.[332] There is, therefore, no occasion to look for a nest of heresy at the crossing of the Alps, and it must be admitted that, with his lame hip, Radulphus would have been in a bad condition to visit the valleys. Furthermore, the heresy alluded to by him was precisely at that time professed by the Cathari in Italy and elsewhere, while it was far from characterizing the first Waldenses.

The quotations cited to defend a view should, if possible, be obtained direct and not at second hand. Major Rochas d'Aiglun said not long ago, " so many books have been lightly written on the authority of second-hand documents that now-a-days a reader, anxious to get to the bottom of things, cannot rely upon simple statements."[333] An author should certainly be no less scrupulous than his reader, and it is for this reason that so many quotations are cited and examined here.

There remain to be examined the arguments advanced in support of the proposition that the early Waldensian protest was derived from the reaction of Claudius, or from that of Peter of Bruys. The validity of this conclusion has been strongly denied.[334]

In speaking of the hypothesis of the Waldenses' antiquity, Hudry-Ménos confesses that he knows not how to prop it up. " In order to give an historical basis to this hypothesis," says he, "there is need of documents that are wanting."[335]

In summing up the arguments that have been advanced in proof of the antiquity of the Waldensian faith, we need not arrive at a directly negative conclusion. We may believe that the point of contact between the Waldensian refugees and the anti-Romish re-action, which stirred the minds of northern Italy, is supplied by the Cathari, and the following reasons that support such an opinion may be stated.

The Cathari had spread over the north of Italy before the twelfth century. As early as 1028 we have unequivocal indications of their presence in the village of Montfort, in the diocese of Asti.[336] Afterwards they are found swarming in Susa, Coni, Saluzzio, Bagnolo, and other localities in the vicinity of the Valleys of Luserna and Pragelas. This being so, the refugees on their arrival could count upon their neighbourliness. If before the Crusade, Waldenses and Cathari were able to approach each other in a brotherly fashion, to the extent of living in harmony under the same roof, as we have seen in one instance,[337] it would not be extraordinary if the same thing should happen again, when in the face of such dangers as threatened all now brought near together under the shelter of the Alps. Now this is precisely what happened, and we notice without the least surprise that the first inquiries of the Inquisition reveal the presence of Cathari in the very valleys. In the fourteenth century they lived there, and there in the following century they as a sect died. Pope John XXII. mentions, in 1332, a certain Martin Pastre as having preached in those parts " against the incarnation of the Son of God and the presence of Christ's body in the sacrament of the altar."[338] If this accusation be correct, it can only refer to some of the Cathari. In 1387, Father Septo of Savigliano came to establish his tribunal in the Church of St. Dona in Pignerol, where he summoned before him a large number of inhabitants of the surrounding places, both from the mountains and from the plain, and very thoroughly indeed did he do his work of prosecution in the valleys. The fact that becomes most incontestably evident is the intimate and intertwined co-existence of Waldenses and Cathari. What brought them thus together? Was it a mis-understanding, or a comprise? The fact is that the Inquisitors were puzzled to distinguish between them.[339] In 1403 the monk Vincent Ferreri visited the valleys of the Alps, and there he too remarked upon the co-existence of the Waldensian refugees with "the Gazari."[340] Finally, in 1451, a man named Philip Regis came down from Val St. Martin to Pignerol, on account of a charge of heresy brought against him by the Judges. His cross-examination shows that he himself was no longer able to dis-tinguish between the doctrine of the Waldenses and that of the Cathari ; and yet this is the man who, in the absence of the Elders, would have been obliged to fill their place.[341] It is, there-fore, evident that a mingling had taken place between the Wal-denses and the Cathari in the very bosom of the valleys. The question of the date at which this happened is an important one. Does it suffice to conclude with the historian of the Cathari, that their sect took shelter in those valleys " as early as the beginning of the fourteenth century ?"[342] We are inclined to believe that they did not wait till that time ; we think that the Cathari may just as well have preceded the Waldenses in their retreat or have accompanied them thither.[343] This would not prevent us from recognising the fact that others may afterwards have joined them, during the time that they were established there, arriving either from France[344] or from the upper regions of Italy.[345] We thus see that even religious circumstances conduced to facilitating the establishment of the Waldensian colony in the valleys of Piedmont; nor must we lose sight of political circumstances as well.

At the moment of the Waldenses' arrival, anarchy threatened everywhere. The Pope reigned almost absolute; he was the " roi-soleil" of nations. The Emperor, with his train of vassals, —a more or less luminous, but frequently eclipsed satellite circled around him. The feudal edifice was shaken; it threatened to tumble down at the people's call for liberty. The Church, ever encroaching, was taking possession of kingdoms, dukedoms, and lesser manors. Its power penetrated with that of the Empire, even into the little valleys of the Cottian Alps. In 1032 the royal dynasty of Burgundy ceased to exist. On account of their strategic and commercial importance of the passes over the frontier, the feudal lords struggled for their possession as they had done under King Cottius, the Longobards, the Saracens, and the Hungarians, and this struggle they carried on, notwithstanding Imperial intervention. The French slope belonged to the county of the Dauphin, as did also Val Pragelas; the Italian slope formed a part of the domain of Savoy. Sometimes one Prince, sometimes the other, was dominant; both had to deal with bishops, to whom were confided certain privileges and the charge of Abbeys which were being enlarged. Among the latter was the Abbey of St. Mary of Pignerol, of the Benedictine order, whose foundation dates back to a very early period. In 1064 it received from the Duchess Adelaide a rich grant of territory. Twelve years later, this princess ceded to it all her rights over the valleys of the Perosa and St. Martin, and finally she presented to the Abbey the Castle of Pignerol and its dependencies.[346] All these gifts were confirmed by the Popes Calixtus II., Victor II., and Urbanus II., together with the grants of new privileges.[347] While the Abbey of Pignerol was flourishing, that of Villar in Val Pelis was in ruin. The lord of those places had chosen for his residence the hill that rises on the right bank of the river, at the point where the little valley of Rora opens. He was placed there, it is believed, by the Marquis of Susa, to keep the passage of the Alps.[348] It would be difficult to say from whence this lord sprung. It has been supposed that he had Longobard blood in his veins, and was related to his sovereign ; a family tradition states that the head of the house of Luserna was a monk.[349] If this be so, the monk did better service to the Church by breaking his vow of celibacy than by keeping it, for the house of Luserna furnished more than one Prior to the abbeys of St. Justus, Novalese, St. Michael, Staffarde, Cavour, and Pignerol. The genealogical tree begins with Henry of Luserna. His son William exercised full right of seigniory in the valley. In 1154, he granted some lands in the Alps to the Abbot of Staffarde. He had three sons—Henry, whose line soon died out; Hubert, from whom the Manfredi and Billours are sprung ; and, finally, Peter of Angrogna, father of Richard, Podestat of Pignerol, and of Berenger from whom the Rorengs were descended. The three families of the Manfredi, Billours, and Rorengs, were perpetuated to modern times; the last two have now disappeared ; that of the Manfredi still exists.[350] On the arrival of the Waldenses, the seigniory of the valley was divided between William's sons. The prestige of the house of Luserna was on the increase; and although there are no traces of their having used a coat of arms down to the thirteenth century, this is not very strange, for the same thing obtains with the house of Savoy, and every one knows that coats of arms are the result of gradual development. At first they have a personal and therefore unnoticed origin ; then they appear in public, after which they flourish and bloom with the name they adorn and symbolize, when, in consequence of the alliances and privileges which are successively entered upon from time to time, fresh quarterings and additions are made. During the thirteenth century, the seal of the lord of Luserna was a little star, surrounded by thick darkness.[351] Later, it bore the well-known inscription, " *Lux in tenebris lucet*," and the addition, " *Verbum tuum, O Domine, lucerna pedum meorum.*" This religious symbol, its origin easily explainable by the monkish origin of the house of Luserna, contains nothing which would indicate the existence of any protest in the bosom of the Church.[352] That motto, like so many others of its kind, was, after all, and notwithstanding all embellishments, but a lamp without oil.[353] With the coming of the Waldenses came the oil to fill that lamp which then was kindled, and continues to burn even unto this day.[354]

By crossing the frontier and descending into the valleys, the Waldenses escaped from the power of Gui VI., Count of Vienne. This at first they may have regretted, but it seems highly improbable that at that critical time, and in the face of an uncertain future, they should have thought of soliciting from him the annexation of the higher localities of Angrogna which they had just invaded. A chronicle, but one too modern to deserve absolute credit upon so special a point, goes so far as to state that they obtained this privilege.[355] Even if credence be given to the chronicle, it only indicates that, under the reign of that prince, settlements were possible, and some measure of liberty was enjoyed at a time when, on the other side of the frontier, all was anarchy and disorder. About this time there arose upon Italian soil another prince, whose valour and liberal-minded dealings caused him to be beloved by his new subjects.

Count Thomas I. of Savoy, born in 1178, the son of Humbert III. and Beatrix of Burgundy, came of age in 1192, and from the beginning strove to bring about the union of his hereditary estates, divided by recent revolutions. The difficulties he had to encounter in his task were due to clerical reaction and small vassals. At Pignerol the people groaned under the yoke of the monks, and as early as 1198, Count Thomas had been called thither by the inhabitants, to support their complaints against the jurisdiction of the Abbot of St. Mary. " This is the first time," writes a Canon of that town, " that there has ever been seen princely authority disputing with the abbots concerning the exercise of their temporal power, without, however, daring to contest it or call it in question."[356] The Bishop of Turin also had provoked disorders owing to his grievous exactions; but he had been obliged to yield. Jacques Carisio, Abbot of the Benedictine order, who succeeded him in 1206, acted as if he meant to hinder the prince in his purpose. Tired of his intrigues, and those of the Prior of the Pignerol Abbey and a few other lords, Thomas took up arms and carried war into Piedmont. When he arrived under the walls of Pignerol, the citizens opened the gates to him, put the city in his power, to the Abbot's great displeasure, and proclaimed him sovereign.[357] The times were favourable to emancipation; the question for the districts was the shaking off of the old feudal yoke,

E 2

which had now become intolerable.  Pignerol was among the first
to claim the restoration of her franchise, which dates from the
year 1220.  From that time she continued, day by day, to increase
in importance, and became the principal city of the still very
limited territory which constituted the province of Piedmont.  In
the meantime Thomas was raised to the dignity of Vicar of the
Empire, and the credit of his policy was only increased thereby.
The Waldenses who had settled upon the heights above the valleys
were beginning to come down, bringing with them the light of the
Gospel.  The monks of the Abbey were alarmed ;[358] the Bishop
of Turin, indeed, bethought himself of driving them back, and
even out of his diocese ; but he troubled himself without taking
action, for Prince Thomas, busy in conjuring up still more threatening storms, needed all his thunderbolts, and thus his attention
was called elsewhere.  There is no necessity, in order to account
for Thomas' moderation, to make it appear that he, followed
by all his vassals, had set off on the Crusade against the Albigenses.[359]  He had, in fact, something better to do than to mount
guard over blaspheming and troublesome monks, while the Waldenses were there to hold them in check at the least sign.  As for
his nobles, they, of course, observed the same attitude, both dis-
creet and judicious.[360]  The chronicle, therefore, speaks the truth
when it says that while the Prince was " so busy elsewhere, these
poor Waldenses, who were hardly known, or were looked down
upon as miserable wretches, were not hindered in the least, either
by Thomas or the Lords of the Valleys of Piedmont, from settling
in those mountains, almost by the same means and under the same
conditions as in those of Pragelas in Dauphiny."[361]

In 1226, Frederick II. descended into Lombardy, and there
organized the Ghibelline party.  The following year, Turin and
Pignerol, with Count Gui VII. of Vienne, together joined the
Lombard alliance.  Pope Gregory IX. hurled a sentence of
excommunication against the Emperor, whilst an army went up
from Milan into Piedmont, and was there defeated by Count
Thomas.  Overpowered by new complications, Count Thomas was
afterward persuaded to grant the franchise to the city of Chambéri ;
then he betook himself to the siege of Turin, where he was over-
taken by death on the 1st of March, 1233.  Amadeus IV., his
successor, was also obliged both on the north and south side of
the Alps, with sword in hand, to stand for his rights.  On the

south side his sovereignty had not taken deep root. The city of Pignerol, like Turin, professed to be loyal, but the profession was all; Amadeus, therefore, surrendered his claims upon Piedmont to his brother, Thomas II., and constituted him his representative. The latter repaired to the spot; he negotiated with Alboin, Abbot of Pignerol, and he obtained the rights and privileges which the latter had quietly re-appropriated, and, by an agreement concluded on the 31st of January, 1246, he founded in this city the house of Achaia.[362]  The treaty concluded with the Abbot, who guaranteed him all rights over the castle, the city, and territory of Pignerol, as also over the valley of Cluson, in short, the entire sovereignty. On his side, Thomas II. agreed to defend the rights of the monastery against all comers. This alliance seemed to forebode no good to the Waldenses; but it does not appear to have at once produced those evils which subsequently grew out of it.

The Waldenses dwelt a long time in the valleys before they were molested by persecution. The first colonists had sufficient time to establish themselves; they increased and prospered, and many of them died full of years, leaving to their children a safe asylum. With every returning spring came seed-time, with every autumn came the increase, and in the villages the sounds of the flail on the threshing-floor were mingled with the voices of children at happy play.

The colony visibly prospered, nor lacked the observance of country festivals and recurring public rejoicing. Here, as in Pragelas, the Waldenses are said to have "multiplied furiously."[363] Their increase beyond the power of the land to sustain them caused new swarms to leave the Alpine bee-hive. Some bands once more crossed the frontier to colonize the banks of the Durance, between Cisteron and the county of Avignon. Their activity was soon crowned with unparalleled prosperity, as is evident from the foundation of the villages of Cabrières, Mérindol, and Lormaret,[364] and the enlargement of the hamlets which already existed. Other bands spread abroad in Piedmont, especially toward Saluzzo, in the valleys of Paesano, Crussol, and Onvino; and also toward Meane and Susa. Many of the Waldenses ventured further away into the plain; but, of all those attempts at colonization, the most celebrated is unquestionably that of the Calabris.

The kingdom of Naples, subjugated by the house of Anjou, was in course of consolidation under the sceptre of King Robert. This Prince lavished upon his subjects grand promises of peace and protection, and they, unmindful of the proverbial untrustworthiness of princes' promises, credited them. Robert had certain rights in Piedmont, and seneschals in his service were busy bringing back to obedience the rebel communities of Coni, Fossano, and Cherasco. Their soldiery, consisting entirely of adventurers and plunderers, were, from Saluzzo to Turin, carrying desolation into the adjoining neighbourhood, causing more than one Waldensian family to withdraw to the shelter of the mountains. With or against their will the territories submitted ; but peace did not seem to be established.[365] Meantime while the tide of Waldensian population was at its flood and ready to overflow, and when the young and impatient were anxious to emigrate, opportunely enough, some of the Waldenses happened at an inn to meet a nobleman of Calabria, who was then staying in Turin.[366] Some have thought, and it seems highly probable, that this personage was in the service of one of the king's seneschals, whose duty it was to enrol emigrants.

The venerable Gilles relates that in the course of the conversation which took place between the Calabrian nobleman and the Waldenses, the former, "having heard from them that they had need of new habitations, offered to procure for them vacant and fertile lands in Calabria, as much as they might want, on the condition that they should in the future pay a reasonable revenue to those to whom they might become subject. These things were promised on the condition that they should demean themselves well and virtuously. Thereupon the Waldenses sent capable men to examine the place, and they, having found it a pleasant one, were granted a great stretch of country, producing abundantly, as the fruit which there grew uncultivated (and was wasted for want of hands to gather it) amply testified. There were plains and hills covered with all sorts of fruit trees, growing in utter confusion ; among them chestnuts, walnuts, olives, oranges, larches, and firs ; there were good pastures and also good fields for arable tillage. The bargain which was concluded was that, in exchange for a rent for the land occupied, the Waldenses should have the privilege of forming among themselves one or more communities, and should be allowed to establish the necessary leaders of their people, and impose and exact taxes without permission asked or obtained, or the rendering of any account to any but their own people. An agreement with the lords and magistrates, concerning all ordinary and casual rights, was also made; and an authentic deed embodying all these matters was obtained. This deed was subsequently confirmed by Ferdinand of Arragon, King of Naples. The deputies having returned to the valleys, and having reported the above, a large number of people prepared for the journey, selling their claims to their relatives who remained behind. Young people got married before their departure, then, taking leave and commending themselves to God's keeping, they set out on their five and twenty days' journey to their new home, near the town of Montalto in Calabria. In the immediate vicinity of Montalto, they first erected and peopled the village called Borgo d'Oltremontani, so called from the Apennines which lie between the valleys and the new territory. About fifty years later, their number having multiplied and increased, by the addition from the valleys of new comers, who joined them from time to time, they built another village about a mile distant from the first, and named it St. Sixtus; it was here that one of their most famous churches was afterward placed. Subsequently, in consequence of their rapid increase and new arrivals from the valleys, they built and populated Vacarisso, Argentine, and St. Vincent. Finally, Marquis Spinello allowed them to build on his estate the walled city of Guardia, which stood on elevated ground near the Mediterranean, he granting to the inhabitants important privileges, which in time caused it to become a rich and notable city. In all these places those Waldenses, or Ultramontanes, multiplied greatly. About the year 1400, several of the Waldenses of Provence, being persecuted at the instigation of the Pope reigning at Avignon, returned to the Valleys, whence their fathers had gone forth, and thence again, accompanied by dwellers in the Valleys, they went to live within the boundaries of "l'Apouille," toward the city of Naples, in time building there five small walled cities, namely, Monlione, Montalto, Faito, La Cella, and La Motta. Finally, about the year 1500, a few from Fraissiniére and other Waldensian Valleys went to live in the town of Voltura, near the five small cities, founded by their predecessors. After this exodus in 1500, the Waldenses of the Valleys did not to any great extent go forth colonizing, though it is true that in time they spread to the other parts of the Kingdom of Naples, and as far as Sicily, as well as to other places.[367]

Thus did the population of Calabria gradually increase. In the days of the Reformation it numbered nearly four thousand souls.[374] We shall later recount how the colony came to an end. Far from its sheltering mountains, isolated in a Roman territory, exposed to political storms, it is a miracle that it lived at all; but it was destined to succumb to the first persecution instituted against it. What astonishes us at first is that this should have been so long in bursting out, when we consider that it had already been ordered, by the head of the house of Anjou, against heretics, undoubtedly for the most part Cathari, who more than fifty years before had scattered themselves throughout the Southern countries of Italy.[375] There are, however, two circumstances which will aid us in understanding the matter. On the one hand, the lords of Puglia and Calabria, as well as their King, were evidently interested in fostering the establishment of the colony; on the other, although denounced in open council, the schism of the Waldenses was not an accomplished fact. They went to mass now and then, and still had their children baptized by Catholic priests. It is true that missionaries visited them occasionally, for the purpose of instructing them in the Holy Scriptures, hearing their secret confession, and keeping up their relations with their brethren in the North; but all this was carried on without any noise and with all the precautions rendered necessary by danger. Nevertheless, persecution began to trouble the Waldenses in their Alpine retreat.

We saw that the monks of the Abbey of Pignerol were not ill-situated for spying out the arrival of the Waldenses. The first to take alarm, they naturally denounced them to the Abbot of their order, Carisio, Bishop of Turin. He meditated an appeal to the Emperor Otho IV., who had just overcome his rival in Germany, and had gone down into Italy to receive the Imperial crown at the hands of the Pontiff. To that end the Prelate prepared an edict of persecution and waited for a favourable moment to have it sanctioned by the monarch; but just as the opportunity seemed to present itself, it suddenly disappeared. The Emperor, who had granted the clergy of Turin certain privileges,[376] was excommunicated by the Pope for invading the States of Frederick II., King of Sicily. Thereupon he hastened once more to cross the mountains, and the edict was not signed ; but the draft remains, and it has its value, for the Waldenses are there mentioned, for the first time since their arrival in Piedmont. It was drawn up about the year 1210, and this is its tenor :—

"Otho, by the grace of God, an ever-august Emperor, to his well-beloved son, the Bishop of Turin.   Grace be unto you and good-will.   God's clemency is manifestly visible in this, that, actuated by the error of incredulity, he reveals to his faithful ones the truth of faith.   Indeed, the just live by faith, and whoever believes not is already condemned.   Therefore, not having received the grace of faith in vain, we desire that those who endeavour, by means of the wickedness of heresy, to extinguish in our Empire the light of the Catholic faith, be punished with severity and be everywhere separated from the body of the faithful.   We send you, therefore, upon the authority of these presents, an order to expel from the entire diocese of Turin the Waldensian heretics, and whomsoever there may be who are sowing the tares of false doctrine and opposing themselves to the Catholic faith, no matter what the error be founded upon, conferring upon thee at the same time permission, complete authority and full power, in order that by thy diligent care the garner of the diocese of Turin may be thoroughly cleansed from all wickedness, which raises its head against the Catholic faith." [377]

This decree remained a dead letter.   There remained nothing for Carisio to do but to place the matter either in the hands of Prince Thomas, or before the Apostolic See.   The Prince was hardly in the proper humour to gratify his wishes ; but when, a few years later, he received the keys of the Castle of Pignerol from the hands of the prior of St. Mary's, in compliance with the entreaties of the latter, it is possible that he may have authorised the following decree, which we read, under an uncertain date, among the first statutes of that city : "Whoever shall knowingly harbour a Waldensian man or woman shall pay ten sols for every offence." [378]   This fine seems insignificant, but it is estimated that it was equivalent to about 280 francs. [379]   The decree this time is really authentic.   It is nevertheless possible that the sanction of one of Thomas's successors ought to be recognized here and not his own. [380]

This much had to be said concerning the Prince.   The Roman Pontiff naturally listened intently to the statements of the

Bishop who had been outwitted, owing to the unexpected departure of the Emperor Otho, whose coveted signature he had hoped to obtain. The anathema was hurled, and there was no thought of stopping it for so small a matter as the want of a signature. The Waldenses of the Alps, unlike the Albigenses, did not constitute a danger or obstacle to the establishment of papal supremacy. Innocent III. had just then received the backsliding Waldenses into the fold. He was out of patience with the recusant and did not feel inclined to spare them any more than their brethren the Cathari, but his power was limited. Although let loose against heresy, the Albigensian crusade was confined by political circumstances to certain localities. Had he but been able to double it, so as to strike Lombardy also and cleanse it of its inveterate and manifold heresies, then would certainly have been seen fire and sword spreading terror abroad, and the fate of the Alpine refugees might well have been an evil one. However, even under such circumstances, the Pope could not have flattered himself that he would certainly witness the disappearance of all the little foxes, so much was his entire vineyard infested by them. To destroy them there would have been need of an ideal, a universal, Crusade—that is to say, one which it would have been impossible to carry out. Nevertheless, this ideal and regular Crusade, which realized the dreams of priestly tyranny was in another way instituted. Every one recognizes it in the Inquisition. Instead of rushing like wolves upon the heretics, the priests seemed to say to themselves, "Let us like the spider lie in wait for them in the dark; or in the garb of the shepherd, let us kill them after the manner of Agnelet, ' to keep them from dying.' " Did Innocent foresee how profitable this change of tactics would be to the Church? Perhaps not. He had foreseen, however, that the Church might look to the armed bands of the Mendicant Orders for powerful assistance. It is even said that towards the close of his life he became a monomaniac on this subject. The Basilica of St. John of the Lateran appeared to him in a vision to be on the point of falling down, when two unknown men stepped out of the darkness and rushed forth to support it; they were Dominic and Francis of Assise. However that may be, at the fourth Lateran Council, held in Rome in 1215, he confirmed to the letter the condemnation of the Waldenses pronounced more than thirty years before at the Council of

Verona, not however, without adding special prescripts, conceived with the purpose of enclosing the ecclesiastical world in the meshes of the Inquisition. Each Bishop was ordered to establish in every parish a lay committee of informers against heresy.[381] Yet, after the idea had been started, it was soon discovered that it would not succeed in that way. The machine was perfect, but one wheel would not work, and this was the part assigned to the laity. The fact is that they had not the instincts of the hound, which, with keenness of scent, are only to be acquired in the seminary. Gregory IX. knew this very well, and he let the monks loose. He had the choice between two orders—the Franciscans and the Dominicans. It is known that, in order better to overcome the Waldensian protest, both brotherhoods had begun to imitate it ; the former by leading a life of poverty, the latter by filling the office of preachers. The vocation of the Dominicans was particularly obvious. They had made their first sortie before the Crusade, and were upon the heretics' tracks ; they had also gained the confidence of the Bishops, by their self-denial, zeal, and dialectic skill. Briefly, they had become the monks of ready help ; it was to them, therefore, that the Pope applied. He succeeded by their means in disciplining the Inquisition, and in urging it to action of a resolute kind ; that was not done in a day, but still sufficiently speedy. What was needed to establish the Inquisition was a solid and legal foundation, namely, dogma, law, a code, and the support of the secular power. Now, none of these elements were lacking. Dogma was there, within reach of all, saying by the mouth of every priest, that heresy is the greatest of crimes, because it offends against the Divine Majesty. If anyone, therefore, be guilty of it, he must be dealt with by the Vicar of God, the Supreme Judge, the Emperor who does not bear the sword of Justice in vain. Of course the heretic deserves, at least, the penalty incurred for high treason, namely, the loss of all property, and death ; yet the Church desires not the death of the sinner, but rather that he should turn from his wickedness and live. If he be converted he shall live ; but for this clemency he must recant and do penance. If he refuse to be converted, then shall no mercy be granted to him. It will not suffice that he be excommunicated ; he must be delivered up to the secular arm and die ; it will be but justice.[383] Thus heresy was made to become a public crime—even the greatest. The law which made it so, being once obtained and formulated, the anvil was at last found upon which were successively hammered out the codes of inquisitorial procedure. The Dominican Code was sanctioned in 1232 for Aragon, Germany, and Austria; the following year, thanks to the decrees of the Princes, who seem to have been as zealous as was Gregory IX. on this point, it was authorized in the South of France and Lombardy. Among all these decrees, we easily understand the decision of tone of the Emperor's; yet it is surprising, and justly so, that Frederick, the old heretic, should have been the promulgator, and that he should have devoted all his Teutonic fury to such a villainous enterprise. At the time of his coronation in Rome, on the 22nd of November, 1220, he assumed an Olympian attitude, and hurled his first thunderbolts in the shape of a decree against the heretics. Nor did it strike the air only, for that decree was only the first of a whole series of legislative edicts. When he arrived at Padua he reiterated his edict more than once, aiming at Lombardy. Then he entirely dropped the mask; his religious intolerance was evidently made to subserve his fierce political ambition, and this led him to sacrifice whatever principles he may have had, and to ape the Pope, at the very time, perhaps, when he flattered himself that he was deceiving him. When he writes from Catania to the Bishop of Madgeburg, his legate in Lombardy, concerning heresy which was springing up, it might well be thought from his language that he was quite disconsolate. He sighs over the hostile heretics.[384] He complains of them to Pope Honorius III., and impeaches those free—nay, too free—cities which are so ungrateful to him for his zeal.[385] Meanwhile, his decrees are enacted into constitutions, and he goes on adding to their number. Yesterday, the thunderbolts; to-day, hail. He took measures for having his decrees well posted up, and above all, observed by all his officers, podestas, consuls, and rectors.[386] Nay, more, like a good successor of Barbarossa, he took the trouble to urge even the priests to hunt up heretics[387] and to revive the zeal of the Pope,[388] which was hardly necessary, as it had not grown cold. Meanwhile, his cunning and angry glance had turned toward the North of Italy, for there the heart of Italy was still beating; there was yet a remnant of liberty, which upon him had the effect of a pestilence. It might be thought from his words that he was alarmed. If the North were to defile the Mecca of the West, he would be grieved, and he would not like to have his sainted island contaminated by it.[389] Was he in earnest, or was he laughing behind his political mask ? At any rate, liberty of thought, which he misused so badly, had in him a deadly enemy, and the tribunal of the Inquisition could not have been set up under better auspices. Undoubtedly, if the infernal machine had worked according to the wishes of its sponsors, it would have anticipated a certain steam guillotine imagined by a modern satirical poet, which in three hours

> fa la testa a centomila
> messi in fila.[390]

But the heretics were a stirring folk, who did not allow themselves to be thus dressed in line. Theoretically, it could be very quickly done. Cathari, Poor of Lyons, Patarins, Passagins, Josephites, Arnaldists, Speronists, etc., all would be aimed at, riddled with bullets, and sent to the gibbet. A stroke of the pen : the signature : and the decree would be enacted. Practically, it was another thing; here is a case of art being difficult. The opposition was strong. The executioners had their martyrs. Victory in the Crusade soon smiled upon them in the South of France ; but two Inquisitors of the province of Alby were massacred, and those of Toulouse and Narbonne escaped the same fate, but not without difficulty. Finally, heresy disappeared. Thousands of fugitives had reached the sea or the mountains to take refuge in Lombardy. It was there that resistance centred, but in vain, for it had to be broken. Honorius III. first sought to apply to that resistance the decrees of the last Lateran Council. The podestas were slow to obey, for they feared to cause an uprising; they contented themselves for a while with slight vexations. Here, a house where the heretics held their meetings was pulled down ; there, the castle of a Patarin lord was razed to the ground. Nor did the Waldenses' house in Milan—no doubt well known, as the Pope had heard it spoken of—escape these first severities. Once before it had been destroyed and again rebuilt.[391] Its days were now surely numbered. One more message from the Pope, and then the repression began in earnest. Until the monks of the Inquisition arrived or set about their work, the Archbishop took charge of heresy ;[392] but he was driven out of the city. Quiet was re-established; then, suddenly, a loud alarm bell was heard; the Emperor Frederick has sent out a decree which concerned the civil power, and, therefore, the communes. The clergy, hardly secure, attempted a decisive step with the podesta; the latter still hesitated, and convened the assembly of the people. It met on the 13th of January, 1228, and decreed that: Heretics should be forbidden to reside either in Milan or in the villages under its jurisdiction; their houses should be demolished; their property confiscated; whosoever should harbour them should pay twenty-five pounds; whoever should rent them a lodging, fifteen pounds; finally, an inquisitorial commission should be elected to seek out the guilty, it should be composed of twelve citizens and four mendicant monks. This was a mark of deference to the Pope, but he clamoured for decrees. The following year a Legate made the podesta and the assembly of the people swear to observe that law without mercy.[393] Everything was sworn to; still, somebody had to be found who would bell the cat. The Cathari and Patarin party had adherents among the leading citizens; the wealthiest belonged to them, and sheltered the " perfect" in their castles, just as their co-religionists had done in the South of France. Robert Pacta and Lantelmi received them in their domains; the latter even put them in possession of one of his castles. Still the clerical tide was rising. The podesta looked to see which way the wind was blowing, and said to himself that it was favourable to clerical reaction, and that he was ready for anything. Thereupon he started and began to incite people to fall upon the heretics. He enforced the decrees of the Council, of the Emperor, and of the Archbishop. He even issued one after his own taste, which reads as follows:—

"In the name of the Lord and in this year 1233, of the Incarnation, on a Friday, the 15th of September, the seventh convocation under the administration of Oldrad of Tresseno, Podesta of Milan, the Dominican friar, Peter of Verona, by virtue of the authority in him vested by the Pontiff against the heretics, as set forth in a charter attested and drawn up by Obizzon Scazzago, a notary of Milan, in 1232; by virtue also of the authority in him vested by the commune of Milan, and bestowed in the general assembly against the above mentioned heretics, as stated in another charter extracted and translated by Singhimbaldo della

Torre, notary and knight of this community, the said Peter has decreed and ordained that the chapters, hereinafter set forth, be numbered among the other statutes of this republic, which chapters are contained in the letters of the sovereign Pontiff, addressed to the friar Peter of Verona, by virtue of which all heretics are anathematized ; Cathari, Patarins, Poor of Lyons, Passagins, Josephites, Arnaldists, Speronists, and others of divers names, having different faces but united together by the tail, which heretics, being condemned by the Church of God, must be in like manner condemned by the secular arm."

The decree does not end here, but it goes no further than to transcribe the dispositions already issued by the Pope as well as the Emperor. These state that the impenitent heretics render themselves liable to the penalty of imprisonment for life ; those who conceal or uphold them, to excommunication first, which involves the forfeiture of civil rights, then, in case of impenitence, the penalty inflicted upon the heretics themselves. Finally, the decree concludes :—

" No layman is allowed to discuss, either in public or in private, the subject of the Catholic faith, under penalty of excommunication. Anyone who may hear of heretics gathering in secret conventicles, or celebrating rites and usages apart from the communion of the faithful, shall hasten to report to his confessor or other person, who shall also surely inform the prelate, this again under pain of excommunication. Children of heretics, and those who conceal or defend them shall, until the second generation, be incapable of holding ecclesiastic offices and benefices. Furthermore, the houses of those who shall rashly receive such heretics into the city shall be demolished without delay or appeal. If anyone knows a heretic, and does not denounce him, he shall be fined twenty pounds ; and in default of payment he shall be banished. Moreover, the sentence shall not be remitted without payment of the said sum. Finally, those who conceal and defend heretics shall be deprived of the third part of their possessions, for the benefit of the commune of Milan ; and in the case of a second offence they shall be driven out of the city and jurisdiction, and shall not be permitted to return within a certain time, without having dreed the aforesaid penalty."[394]

The podesta kept his word, and the proof is that an equestrian statue was awarded him as " the defender of the faith." It was placed on the facade of the ancient palace of the commune, in the Broletto Nuovo, now called the Merchants' Square, and there it stands unto this day.   Upon it is the following inscription :—

Atria qui grandis solii regalia scandis
Civis laudensis fidei tutoris et ensis
Presidis hic memores Oldradi semper honores
Qui solium struxit Catharos ut debuit *uxit*.[395]

But all these things did not happen in a day, though Peter of Verona, the invincible, of Moneta, Rhenarius Saccho, and many others co-operated and gave themselves heart and soul to the work of repression.   When the persecution began to rage Frederick accused the Pope of growing slack—nay, he accused Gregory IX. of actual complicity.[396]   It was, thanks to that perfidious monarch, who, with a light heart, sacrificed the holiest of liberties on the altar of his human ambition that the Inquisition worked prodigies ; Milan purged itself with the blood of heretics of the offence given to Frederick II. to such an extent as to earn the praise of Gregory IX. [397]   Even after all these things heresy still existed. Several of the principal lords of the city continued to protect it ; meetings were held, sometimes at the house of the chief standard bearer, d'Allia, sometimes at the castles of La Gatta, or Mongano.   The rage of the Inquisitors urged them to such unheard of excesses, that at last the indignation of the people burst forth. Peter of Verona was killed ; Rhenarius Saccho fled ; Moneta only escaped death by, crucifix in hand, arresting and sending to the stake those who had sworn to do away with him.   The monks were again hindered in their work of repression by the influence of Ezzelino da Romano, a satellite of Frederick II.   In 1280, the famous Guillelmina, with her dreamy ideas concerning the Holy Spirit, of which she believed herself to be the mouthpiece, had a whole people for her admirers.   The Inquisition had now paused in its work, and by degrees quiet was restored.   At the same time the other communes of Lombardy submitted in their turn, each one reading in its own fashion the decrees issued by the authority of the Church and backed by that of the Empire, though this also was gained only at the price of sanguinary struggles.   At Brescia resistance had even got the upper hand.   Pope Honorius III. tells us that the heretics burned the churches and that, from the top of the towers, they threw firebrands down upon the city as a symbol of anathema against the Church of Rome and its adherents. He commanded the Bishop of Rimini to repair thither, and to raze to the ground the castles of the most guilty lords, such as the Gambara, Ugoni, Orani, and Bottazzi, but only to half pull down the towers of those who were less compromised, It may be doubted whether this order was literally carried out. At Monza, Bergamo, Plaisance, Modena, as far as Liguria in Tuscany, and in the cities of Umbria, fighting everywhere took place at the approach of the monks, but they were eventually obliged to succumb. Notwithstanding all her shrewdness and prestige, the Queen of the Adriatic herself became resigned to the intrusion of the abhorred tribunal; she insisted, however, that her three "wise men in matters of heresy" should be admitted to seats that they might watch over its proceedings.

Thus fell the strongholds of the dissident reaction. The Waldenses are hardly mentioned, for the Patarins had the same precedence here as the Albigenses in the South of France. It is, however, certain that they met with more than one check. In spite of all this, their school at Milan was still standing; whence a constant stream of missionaries proceeded to reap a harvest at a distance; and from all quarters of Germany loving eyes were turned toward her as the "Alma Mater." Several, up to the year 1325, still went there; some from the depths of Bohemia, to receive instruction from the lips of their venerated masters; others to do homage to the Bishops, and to deliver up the amount of the collections made in their churches.[398] In the year 1368, the Waldenses gave the last sign of life that we know of, by sending out a circular letter addressed to the Brethren in Austria, who had become alarmed at the news of the recent defections. The ebb tide had set in with full force, but in the midst of this raging sea, where everything was being lost, a pale ray of light still shone. It came from the lighthouse fixed upon the rocky summits of the Alps. Let us return there. Rome had already cast angry glances in that direction, and now began to bellow forth Anathemas.

While the tribunal of heresy triumphed everywhere, thanks to the odious complicity of papacy and the empire, it has been said that the Lord of Luserna demanded a certain tolerance in favour of the Waldenses. Such is the assertion made, and furthermore, it is added that this act of magnanimity is connected

with the treaty of submission to the house of Savoy, made or
ratified in the year 1233.[399] If this be so, the escutcheon of
Luserna did momentarily shine with a pure light, too soon, alas!
obscured by the darkness of intolerance. It must be granted that,
with the Abbot of St. Mary on the *qui vive*, and the Bishop of
Turin on the watch, the Mendicant friars were early invited to
come and spy out the Waldenses' retreat. They were, however,
hardly bold enough to venture in there—and indeed they had good
cause for their temerity—but were obliged to stay for some time
in Pignerol. At last a station was established in Perosa. It is
mentioned in the reign of Amadeus V., under the following circumstances : Amadeus' grand-nephew, Philip, having received Piedmont in appanage, had gone thither to receive the oath of fidelity
of his vassals of Luserna, Piossasque, and other localities. His
jurisdiction extended to the far end of the Val Perosa, and we
read that he maintained an Inquisitor there at his own expense.[400]
In 1301, he married the Crown Princess of the house of Achaia.
It has been ascertained that, on this same date, a monk of
Bergamo was residing in Perosa, invested with full power to
" seize heretics of whatever sect, condemned by the Church of
Rome."[401] Later, toward the year 1312, allusion is made to a case
of death by fire for the crime of " valdesie."[402] The Inquisition
did not stop there ; it succeeded in planting a garrison in the chief
town of the valley of Luserna, under the protection of her Lord.
Thence, slinking into the neighbouring places, the monks made
their way into the valley of Angrogna, as far as the pastor's
house, and there hatched their plots. Once they are said to have
paid dearly for their audacity. One Pope tells us that the
Inquisitor, John Albert of Castellazzo, having displayed an
intention to exercise his office, the inhabitants of Angrogna
hastily armed themselves and assembled upon the public square.
Their angry eyes were turned in every direction to find the Priest
Guillaume.[403] He appeared after celebrating the mass, deprecatory
and paternal, as to his air. A cry was raised, " Down with the spy
and traitor !" and he was stricken down. Then the people rushed
tumultuously down the valley and besieged the Inquisitor's
residence. The place had to be abandoned, of course.[404] Castallazzo,
no doubt, carried his complaint to Pignerol, to the Prince of
Achaia, and further still. The Lord of Luserna had his mandate
and he was ordered, not for the last time,[405] to lend assistance to

the judges of heresy. The monks retraced their footsteps, but noiselessly. It might be thought that they profited by their lesson. In one sense there is no doubt they did; but if their caution increased, their zeal did not diminish. We can now only surmise what went on for some time after these events. In 1374, an Inquisitor fell at Briquéras, at the entrance of the valley; it was Father Antonio Pavo of Savigliano.[406] Some time before this happened there had been a disturbance at Susa; the monastery had been broken into, and the famous Pietro di Ruffia, Inquisitor-General of Piedmont, had been despatched.[407] Thereupon Pope Gregory complained to Amadeus VI., of Savoy, and took advantage of this opportunity to exhort him not to permit the thorns of error to grow in his States, but to fight valiantly against heretics; " as valiantly," he added, " as thou didst against the Turks."[408] At the same time the Bishop of Turin received positive instructions; as a consequence there succeeded some acts of repression. But now there was heard a sharp cry of despair, which no iron hand could smother. We hear it still re-echoed, as from age to age it has been, in the mountains and huts of Pragelas. It was at Christmastide of the year 1400 that Borrelli, a Franciscan monk, accompanied by a band of hired assassins, intent only on violence and carnage, fell upon the villages occupied by heretics. Fathers and mothers rushed out of their dwellings, and fled toward the mountains, carrying their children with them; the snow covered the ground, and there was none to succour. Without shelter, famished, dying of fatigue, the fugitives fell one by one. Men, women, and children, they fell asleep upon nature's breast, never more to wake. It is said that a band of these unfortunates were lost in the ravines of Alberjean. When daylight dawned, the mothers held in their arms nothing but dead bodies, and they numbered upwards of fifty. For once, pity was not dumb; its voice reached the ears of the Pope, who, it is said, now begged the Inquisitor to use moderation.[409] It may be supposed that on the other side of the frontier, times were no less hard.

In France, the Crusade had mown down its victims by thousands. Monks and prelates followed the reapers to glean what might have been left. The Inquisitor Pelisson mentions in his chronicle more than one execution; for instance, that of the woman burned on the day of the canonization of St. Dominic. The learned and voluminous reports of Bernard de Caux and Jean

de St. Pierre deal with 106 localities, and are well worth
reading. That of Bernard Gui is no less eloquent; he is respon-
sible for the death of 630 persons. "The exact truth," observes
M. Donais, "is that he knew of 930 cases of heresy, and 42
persons were handed over to the secular arm between 3rd March,
1308, and 12th September, 1322."[410] For his services Gui was
promoted to a bishopric. The victims of this Crusade were, however, mostly Cathari, rarely Waldenses. There were many, as
may be inferred from the names we find, who, Cathari at that
time, afterwards became Waldenses.[411] Heretics of any kind were
accused of "Vaudoisie."[412] A nun of Lespinasse, of the order of
Fontevrault, was accused of having given alms to Waldenses.
Hers was a serious case, so she was condemned to go in peace,
which meant that she was to be confined in a solitary cell, to see
no one, not even the person from whom she received her food, as
it was to be handed to her through a little window.[413] In these
actions we recognise the relations which existed between the
South of France and Lombardy; but as they refer almost altogether to the Albigenses, their history may be left to that body's
historians.[414] The Waldenses being less numerous than the Albigenses, scattered less; they endeavoured to keep together, and
their tracks did not remain unknown to the "Hounds of the
Lord,"[415] who voiced the Bishop to the chase. But the Bishops
were slow to move, and had to be urged on by the Pope, as we
see by the admonitions addressed to the Bishops of Vienne and
Valencia by Benedict XII.[416] The number of Waldenses had been
diminished; but again, by reason of the increase in the population
of the higher valleys, and above all, by the return to Dauphiny
about the year 1350 of those who had fled into Italy, it increased
sensibly. Dauphiny, and even certain localities of Provence and
Savoy, were again full to overflowing with heretics, so much so
that the clergy hardly dared to molest them, or lend assistance to
the Inquisition, whilst the civil authorities resisted prosecutions.
Gregory XI. was obliged to interfere. His remonstrances to
Charles V., King of France, were earnest and oft-repeated.[417]
He was particalarly vexed with the Governor of Dauphiny. His
most pressing appeals were directed to the Archbishops of Vienne,
Arles, and Embrun. His complaints singularly resemble those
of the Abbot of Cluny, of venerable memory. "We are informed," he tells those too peaceful prelates, "that your terri-

tories have, for a long time past, become a den of heretics. Your predecessors neglected to deal as they should have done with such a state of things, and you follow their example only too closely. When such is the case, is it surprising if heretics swarm and spread around you?"[418] That was in 1375. Five years later, from his see at Avignon, Clement VII. gave the signal for new reprisals.[419] Then the fierce Franciscan monk, Borelli, who had acquired such an unenviable reputation in the valley of the Pragelas, appeared on the scene. First, he summoned the inhabitants of Freyssinières, Argentière, and Val Louise before him. That was to satisfy a mere form. As they did not appear, he had them condemned in default, and several were burned at the stake, the victims being mostly from Val Louise. Perin says that "as many as one hundred and fifty men, several women and a number of their grown-up sons and daughters perished." He mentions as being amongst that number, Guillaume Marie of Vilar, Pierre and Jean Long, Albert and Jeanne Vincent. The victims of this slow persecution were less numerous in the other two valleys; says the same historian, they were "to the number of eighty," and he names in that number three women, viz.: Astrue Berarde, Agresonne Bresson, and Barthélemie Porte. This general sentence was pronounced in the Cathedral of Embrun, in 1393, and was executed at Grenoble.[420] Borelli had undoubtedly undertaken to prove that the order of St. Francis could be as useful to the Holy Office as that of St. Dominic. The proof was, as we have seen, only too conclusive for a leaden silence, doleful and cold, he left in the places through which he had passed. It might be compared to that which makes itself felt in the mountain hut when a vulture has been hanging over it. Half-a-century elapsed, and danger seemed to have again drawn off to a distance, when once more it approached, and this time very ominously. It was in the year 1460 that a Franciscan monk named Jean Veylet, provided with the authority of the Archbishop of Embrun, took up against the Waldenses of the valleys of Freyssinères, Argentière, and Louise, the indictment of Borelli, of bloody memory. Peace, life, and property—especially property—were threatened; the Inquisition, with its villainous mode of procedure, "bled and swallowed." The Waldenses' distress was great; compassion was aroused for them, and they were advised to carry their complaint direct to the sovereign. They therefore appealed to Louis XI., who ordered an inquiry to be made, which was slow, of course, but advantageous to them. It established two points—first, that the Waldenses were not such as the judges of heresy had been pleased to represent them, but faithful subjects, neither wicked nor heretics; second, that the persecution which they were made to undergo was too much fomented by the avarice and cupidity of judges whose proceedings were most venal. Thereupon King Louis issued the memorable decree, dated Arras, May 18th, 1478, which began as follows :--

" On the part of the villeins and inhabitants of Val Loyse Fraissiniére, Argentiére and others of our land of Dauphiny, it has been made clear to us that whereas they have lived, and desire to live like good Catholic Christians without holding, believing, or maintaining any superstition, not in accordance with the observance and discipline of our Holy Mother Church, nevertheless certain Mendicant Monks, calling themselves Inquisitors of the Faith, and others, believing that by means of vexation and molestation they might unduly extort possessions from them, and otherwise personally ill-use them, have attempted and do attempt falsely to impute to them the holding and believing of certain heresies and superstitions against the Catholic Faith, and under cover of this have involved and do involve them in great complications of suits, as much in our Court of Parliament of Dauphiny, as in various other countries and jurisdictions. And in order to bring about the confiscation of the property of those whom they charge with the said accusations, several of the judges and likewise the said Inquisitors of the Faith, who are usually Mendicant Monks, have instituted, and do daily institute, proceedings against many poor people, without reasonable cause, under the cover of the office of Inquisitor, and have also tortured some and put them to the rack without preceding inquiry, and condemned them for crimes they had never committed, as has been afterward found; and have taken others and exacted large sums of money to set them at liberty, and have by various means unjustly vexed and molested them, to the great prejudice and damage, not only of the said petitioners, but of us and of the entire common weal of our estate of Dauphiny. Therefore, desiring to provide for this, and not to suffer our poor people to be vexed and molested by such unjust means, inasmuch as the inhabitants of the said localities say that they have ever lived, and desire to live like good Christians and Catholics, without having ever believed, or held any other belief but that of our Holy Mother Church ; nor maintained or desired to maintain or believe anything contrary to the sincerity of our faith, and as by right, no one should be condemned for the crime of heresy except those who, by continuous obstinacy, would persistently maintain and affirm things contrary to the sincerity of our faith—We, after long and mature deliberation, and in order to obviate such frauds and abuses, vexations and undue exactions, have granted to those suppliants, and do hereby grant, and of our own certain knowledge, special pleasure, full Royal and Dauphinal power and authority, have desired and decreed, and do desire and decree by these presents, that those suppliants and all others of our country of Dauphiny be relieved from all proceedings ; and all the suits which some of them may have been obliged to institute because of the above-mentioned matters, we have of our certain knowledge full Royal and Dauphinal power and authority abolished and do abolish, have put and do put to naught, by these presents, and desire that never, for all past time to the present shall anything be expected of them, on account of these matters in person or estate ; nor shall they be even reproached therefor, except, however, there be some who obstinately, and with hardened courage, maintain and affirm anything against the Holy Catholic faith."

In consequence of this decree, restitution was to be made of confiscated goods, without appeal or delay, and the will of the King would protect the owners in the future against the rapacity of the judges. For, says the decree, " in order to obviate the frauds and abuses perpetrated by the said Inquisitors of the Faith, we have forbidden and do forbid the said Inquisitors of the Faith to be henceforth permitted to proceed against any of the said inhabitants of our country of Dauphiny, or to maintain any suit in court against them, for the above mentioned or similar causes, without having previously obtained for that purpose letters patent from us."[421]

One sighs with relief on reading this decree, which would appear to have been dictated by a heart that felt for the " poor." At all events it is worthy of a prudent king, who was slower than the priests to shed blood. It is true that upon one point it sur-

prises us, especially if there lurk in our mind any prejudice with
respect to the creed of the Waldenses before the Reformation.
According to the letter of the decree those who were protected by
the King had represented themselves as a body of "good Christian Catholics." Did this denote cowardice on their part in
order to avoid ruin, or did the king allow himself to be ill-
informed by benevolent agents, who were filled with compassion
for those unfortunate and oppressed people? The reason may be
found elsewhere. The Waldenses had the right to call themselves
Christians—nay, even good Catholics, especially as compared with
their persecutors, who really were neither the one nor the other.
Besides the king was not then in the humour to suffer their protest to be scrupulously examined by the light of theology; for it
is evident that, if he had left things to take their course, he would
have lost the opportunity of re-establishing peace. Let us not
forget that "Louis by the grace of God, king of France," was,
even according to the address of the decree, "Dauphin of
Vienne," and not long before, in writing to the "faithful governor
of his estates of Dauphiny," he had been interested in doing an
act of wise policy. The inquiry must have proved to him that
public conscience, in Dauphiny, revolted against the iniquities of
the Inquisitor monks. It became important, therefore, to satisfy
public conscience and run no risk of alienating from himself the
affection of those living on the frontier. After all, that would
always have been the sentiment which would have prevailed in
the policy of the Princes of the house of France, as well as in
that of the house of Savoy, had it not been so resisted by the
corrupt and fatal action of the clergy. Alas! Princes yield but
too easily, though sometimes with but an ill-grace. In this case,
it might be thought that a word would have sufficed to stop the
persecution, and that the decree having been issued, the appeal of
the Waldenses would have been satisfied; but the use that was
made of the decree by the Archbishop was to cling to the exception it contained, and to hold that there existed indeed in the Valleys
of Dauphiny "some who obstinately maintain things contrary to
the Catholic faith." In support of this he produced the testimony
rendered by curates and other agents interested in his cause; so
that the case had to be begun over again. "For lack of means
to defray the expenses of such a long suit," says Perrin, "most
resorted simply to flight, there being only one among the perse-

cuted, a certain Jacques Paliveri, who protested against the undue vexation, to the prejudice of the letters obtained from His Majesty, and demanded a copy of their proceedings that he might have recourse to those whom it concerned. The Archbishop left him in peace, persecuting those who had not sufficient courage to resist his violent measures." It appears that even some of the boldest paid dearly for opposition. Thus "the consuls of Fraissiniéres, Michel Ruffi, and Jean Giraud did not get off so easily," adds our historian, "for being summoned to appear before the said Archbishop, to answer in their own name and in that of the inhabitants of the valley, they answered that they had nothing to say before the said Archbishop, inasmuch as their suit was pending before the King and his Council, that therefore they protested and asked for a copy. Being urged to answer, notwithstanding all protestation to the contrary, Michel Ruffi, tossing his head, answered in his language : *Veici rages ;* and upon renewal of entreaties : *Veici una bella raison.* The Archbishop, irritated against the said consuls for such contempt, sent them to the stake without more ado."[402]

While the clergy of Dauphiny rendered the just edict of Louis XI. useless, those of Turin obtained an iniquitous decree from the Duchess Iolante, elder sister of the King of France, and widow of the most easy-tempered of the Dukes of Savoy.

The Inquisition had never really withdrawn from the attack ; on the contrary it was ever on the watch, and took advantage of every opportunity to oppress, still further, the peaceful inhabitants of the valleys. An Inquisitor, named Jacques, of Buronzo, near Novara, weary of preaching in the desert, and not knowing how to proceed against an entire population, had obtained an interdict against the valley of Luserna. By this means, which was never without result in the Middle Ages, he had been only too successful in bringing back more than one Waldensian to the fold of the Church. Yet, as the rope will break if it be stretched too much, he stopped in time, and in 1453 [423] invoked the suspension of the interdict by means of a decree from Nicolas V., holding himself at liberty to take up again at any time, with renewed zeal, the course of his inquisitorial proceedings. Twenty years later, the Waldenses had to deal with a new Inquisitor called Jean Andre, of Aquapendente. We gather from the decree hurled by him against the Lord of Luserna, that the Waldenses who had yielded to the threats of his predecessor Jacques, had not not become Catholics, but had lived and died impenitent; whence he is careful to conclude that their possessions had thereby been forfeited. His object was to gather this inheritance, to take it away from those who held it, in order to divide it between the Lord of the Manor, the Bishop, and the Holy Office. On the very first Sunday following the communication of the decree, officials who were recommended to read the proclamation very distinctly,[424] made it known to the inhabitants of the valley after mass. The house of Luserna had then a woman at its head. She decided to submit to the decree, but held herself at liberty to do as she pleased about carrying it into execution. She regretted, perhaps, that she could not appeal to the clemency of a prince, like Amadeus IX., of blessed memory, for he had died three years previous. Under his reign the oppressed could indeed breathe, and the Jews of Chamberi knew something of this. A Dominican monk having preached there to incite the people against them and drive them out, the crowd was about to rush upon them, thanks to the countenance of an impetuous and brutal nobleman called Aimar de Varax, when the Ducal Commissioner appeared on the scene, threatening the fanatics with the indignation of the Prince. But the times had changed. The regency had just been thrust into the hands of the Duchess Iolante, and the moment was favourable to the judges of heresy. In the towns several Waldenses were seized; more than one promised to change his religion, but for them it was a mere change of torture, for they could not avoid the burning fire of remorse. To some it appeared that there was but one way of escape, namely, by flight; some fled in the direction of Provence, others towards Calabria. However, the Inquisition got wind of their project, laid its snares, and recaptured some of its victims. Their fate was no longer doubtful. The martyrdom of Jordan Tertian, burned at Susa, and of Hyppolite Roussier and Hugon Chiamp of Fenestrelles, executed at Turin, are cases in point; furthermore, there are those of Ambroise Villermin and Antoine Hiun, who were hung upon the Col de Meane.[425] Besides these there were many others; but their names are lost. Still the grand Inquisitor was meditating a radical repression. The decree issued not long before in the name of the Bishop of Turin had not produced the desired result. It was true that it could not be expected that the heretics of the valleys would be in the humour to permit their rights of property to be violated, now that they were settled there; but the Lords of Pignerol and Cavour, and he of Luserna especially, were not over-devoted to Mother Church. The fact is that they did not afford the support which was demanded of them, so something had to be thought of which would be effective in making them yield it. In the days of the blessed Amadeus "those people did not care a bit about us," said the monk, "but under the regent we shall see whether they will long turn a deaf ear." Thereupon, André of Aquapendente went to the Bishop Campesio; they conferred together for a time; a clerical messenger started for the country residence of Iolante at Rivoli, and a short decree soon appeared, reading as follows:—

" Iolante, elder sister to the King of France, Guardian and Regent of our very illustrious son Charles, by the grace of God Duke of Savoy.

" To the beloved and faithful Lords of Pignerol, and Cavour, and to the Lord of Luserna, and to all other officers or lieutenants, and to the mediate and immediate subjects of our son, to whom these presents shall come, Greeting:—Having looked into the request and the letter of the Inquisitor of heresy, a copy of which is herewith attached, and after examination has been made of them by our Council, in our residence, we enjoin you so to act, that more especially the people of the valley of Luserna may enter within the fold of Holy Mother Church.[426] And we enjoin you all, as many as you may be, under penalty of a fine of one hundred marks of silver each, and, with regard to officers, under penalty of being deprived of their charge, that the said letter of the Inquisitor in its form, spirit, and tenor, and in conformity with the requirements of justice, be by you received, considered, and observed, and that ye may cause it to be received, considered, and observed in its integrity, by all whom it may concern, and that you insist upon the full and entire execution of it, without permitting yourselves to be hindered by any opposition, excuse, or frivolous exception whatsoever, and without waiting for any further order; and let every one of you fear lest he may incur the penalties here above imposed. And since thou, Lord of Luserna, here above mentioned, hast refused to carry out the said request, and, furthermore, hast retained that letter in thy possession, at the instance of the Fiscal Attorney-General of Savoy, and through the above-mentioned Ducal officers, we summon and

enjoin thee to appear on the 10th of the month of February before
our Council, in our residence, where thou shalt be present and
appear, under the pains and penalties as aforesaid, in order to
answer before the Fiscal Attorney concerning the charges brought,
and to be brought, against thee. Failing in which, on that same
day, through the Council, thou shalt be made to see and hear the
declaration of the penalties imposed, and the consequences which
may result from them.

" Given at Rivoli, this 23rd day of January, in the year of the
Lord, 1476."[427]

According to what we have just read, the refusal of the Lord
of Luserna seems to have been explicit.[428] That does him honour.
Still, there is no reason for suspecting him of siding with the
Waldenses in attempt to break the union of the Catholic Church.
All his merit lies in his not responding with warmth to the more
or less arrogant requirements of the Holy Office.[429] His predecessors had protested quite sufficiently concerning their orthodoxy,
their faithfulness, and the sincerity of their efforts towards the
extirpation of heresy at Angrogna and St. Jean, as well as at Bobi
and Villar. Nor was it their fault if, when they lent themselves
to be the instruments of inquisitorial intrigues, the population
rose against them ; but that was what did happen.[430] However,
the Regent of Savoy had hardly signed the decree when her attention was called off elsewhere by changes in her Kingdom. The
clerical party, however, who watched so carefully to prevent the
execution of Louis XI.'s decree, worked just as hard to ensure that
the one issued by his sister Iolante should not remain a dead letter.
They endeavoured to enforce it, but at first, almost without result.
When Charles I. came into power, after the premature death of
his brother Philibert, he sent delegates to the spot to enquire into
the state of affairs,[431] and finally left the decision with the court
at Rome. That was the match which exploded the mine of the
Crusade.

Innocent III. had proclaimed the Crusade against the Albigenses ; Innocent VIII., of bad eminence,[432] was to proclaim the
Crusade against the Waldenses. John Baptist Cibo, for that was
his name, had attained the apostolic chair, thanks to the venality
of his electors. He had nothing to recommend him. Just as
the other Innocent had been powerful in character, the present

one was weak and violent. The Romans hailed his accession humming the lines :—

> Octo nocens pueros genuit, totidemque puellas :
> Hunc merito poterit dicere Roma patrem.[433]

If Innocent VIII. had not a soul of steel, he had a face of brass. Far from being ashamed, he married off his sons in the face of the world, and with every wedding there was a feast at the Holy Father's. We do not wish to recall certain wanton scenes, which, moreover, were hardly noticed in those days ; but there was much talk concerning a mysterious personage, a prisoner in the Vatican. His name was Djem. Fleeing from his brother, the Sultan Bajazet II. Djem had thrown himself into the arms of the great Prior of the Order of Malta. The Pope, seeing in this a possibility of gain, made an agreement with Bajazet. " I will hold your brother Djem behind the bolts of St. Peter," said he to him, " if you pay me 40,000 ducats per annum for the service," and the bargain was struck, for Innocent was ever ready to turn a penny. The curia fixed a tariff upon sins. A crime could be expiated for a specified charge, and those able to pay indulged in sin at the market price. The Roman chronicle relates a villainous anecdote on that subject. Someone chatting one day with the Chamberlain of His Holiness, asked why penance was no longer obligatory. " It is," said the Chamberlain, "because God desireth not the death of a sinner, but rather that he should live and pay." They had gone to that extent. The holy city, a prey to anarchy and every vice, was imprecating fire from Heaven upon herself. The Pontiff, instead of dressing in sackcloth and ashes, in order to avert such a calamity, set himself up as censor of the universe, and began to bring about a rain of fire and brimstone. He commenced with the heretics, and appointed the most ferocious Inquisitors ; in Spain he appointed Torquemada ; in Germany, Kraemer and Sprenger, whom he provided with a special bull, in which Germany is designated a country inhabited by sorcerers, male and female, " who had made an impious compact with the devil."[434] Finally, he proclaimed the Crusade against the Turks, and that, too, while he himself was the Sultan's deputy gaol keeper. It need not surprise us, if, in the estimation of such an Innocent, the Waldenses were nothing but " sons of iniquity," worthy of the Papal Gehenna.

Charles VIII. had succeeded Louis XI. upon the throne of France and Charles I., the warrior, had followed his mother Iolante and his brother Philibert, the Hunter. The Pontiff, as early as 1485, for the repression of the Waldenses of Piedmont and Dauphiny, accredited a nuncio and a general inquisitor to those two Princes. When the moment had arrived, he addressed the bull which was to be the signal for the Crusade to the Nuncio. It bears the date of May 5th, 1487,[435] and begins thus :—

"Innocent, Bishop, servant of the servants of God, to our beloved son, Albert Catanée, Archdeacon of the Church of Cremona, our Nuncio and Commissary of the Apostolic See for the Seigniories of our dear Son, the noble Charles, Duke of Savoy, both on this and the other side of the mountains, and Vienne in Dauphiny, and the City of Zion, comprising the diocese and neighbouring localities, greeting and apostolic benediction.

"The desires of our heart induce us, with vigilant solicitude, to look for some means of extricating from the abyss of error, those for the salvation of whom the Sovereign Creator of all things was himself pleased to endure the sufferings of human nature, and to seek their salvation by the help of Divine grace ; we, to whom he has committed the charge and government of his flock, have at heart the triumph of the Catholic faith during our reign, and the extirpation of the wickedness of heresy from the midst of the faithful. Now we have been informed, greatly to our displeasure, that several sons of iniquity, inhabitants of the province of Embrun, adherents of that very pernicious and abominable sect of wicked men, called Poor of Lyons or Waldenses, which has unfortunately raised itself up for a long time in Piedmont and in the neighbouring places[436] by virtue of the evil one, who endeavours with fatal sagacity to ensnare by artful and circuitous ways, and in the darkness of precipices the sheep consecrated to the Lord, and to lead them finally to the perdition of their souls, causing them to wander, under a certain false appearance of sanctity, rejected by their own sense, hold the following of the path of truth in great abhorence, and observe superstitious and heretical practices, say, do, and commit many things contrary to the orthodox faith, offensive in the eyes of his Divine Majesty, and very dangerous in themselves to the salvation of souls. Our beloved Son, Blaise de Mont-Royal, of the Order of Preachers, Professor of Theology and General Inquisitor of those localities, has therefore betaken himself there to induce them to abjure the above-mentioned errors and profess the true faith in Christ, and to extirpate from among them all sorts of evil, having been previously destined for that purpose by the Master-General of the said Order, and afterwards by our beloved Son, Dominic, Cardinal Priest of the title of St. Clement, Legate of the Apostolic See in those regions, and finally by Pope Sixtus IV. of blessed memory, our immediate predecessor. These people, far from abandoning their very wicked and perverse errors, stopping their ears like the deaf adder, and adding to the evils already committed, still greater ones, have not feared to preach them publicly, and have drawn by this means to these same errors, others of Christ's faithful, to vilify excommunications, interdicts and other censures of this same Inquisitor ; to throw down his house and to take away or alienate his goods, as also those of several other faithful men ; to kill his servant, to make open war, to resist their temporal Lords, to ravage their properties, to drive them with their families out of their parishes, to burn or destroy their houses, to prevent them from receiving their revenues, and to do them all possible harm ; as also to commit an infinite number of other iniquities likewise execrable and abominable."

These things being so, there is nothing for it but the extirpation of this accursed sect, and the devotion thereto of all possible energy. Consequently, the Nuncio is authorized to call for the co-operation of the Archbishops, and to invoke the support of the secular arm from the King of France, the Duke of Savoy and the Lords, as they shall judge expedient, " in order to proceed with armed hand against the said Waldenses and all other heretics, and to crush them like venomous serpents," neglecting everything, whether threats or promises, for " so holy and so necessary an extermination."[437] To all those who shall obey is granted plenary indulgence, together with permission to seize the heretics' possessions. Their neighbours and servants, debtors included, are loosed from all obligations, but they must withdraw from their company at the earliest opportunity. Woe to the refractory ! Princes and Plebians, Lords and Slaves, all are struck at by the interdict.

Such was the signal for the Crusade. What the Waldenses had endured thus far in the shape of bloody molestations was but " roses and flowers," says Leger, as compared with what was about to follow. The threatened region was divided among three Sovereigns : the King of France, the Duke of Savoy, and the Marquis of Saluces. It has been remarked that they took no part in the Crusade. That is untrue. They authorised it. Even had they been satisfied to remain passive, their attitude would have resembled that of the shepherd who permits the wolf to enter the sheepfold, but their asistance was not of this negative kind. Charles VIII., King of France, hastened to respond to the Pontiff's appeal, with express orders ; he enjoined the authorities to lend their support to the Nuncio Catanée.[438] It is true that these orders can refer only to the district of Dauphiny ; but when the King of France set the example, the Duke of Savoy was, of course, obliged to bow his head. Charles I., the warrior, was therefore, though somewhat against his will, submissive. He himself declared his unwillingness, and we must believe him. As for the Lord of Saluces he was of no importance, and moreover he was not primarily concerned. Albert of Catanée had only to follow the path marked out for him. Whilst a few bands of soldiers were recruited for him, he reached Pignerol, and stopped at the convent of St. Laurent, belonging to the order of the Humiliati. From there he sent out a few preaching monks towards the valleys, to invite the Waldenses to repentance ; but it was of no avail. Seeing this the Nuncio allowed the time of grace to elapse; for he tells us everything was done according to law and order ;[439] after which operations commenced. The Legate's strategy does not seem to have roused the enthusiasm of experts in such work. It is beyond our comprehension ; it seems to have been a chase in the dark. Instead of directing his forces against a given point, he scattered them in order to let not one escape ; but the net of his militia was so much stretched that the meshes broke, and the haul seems to have been but inconsiderable. It is a matter somewhat surprising that the Legate's writings include no mention of the double attack directed against the valley of the Angrogna. Perhaps he was not present ; besides the check received by his men there does not constitute an element necessary to his narrative, which is essentially apologetic. Let us pause a little before taking up again the thread of his blood-besprinkled journey across the frontier, while we hear of the attack from other sources.

If we believe the Waldensian tradition, which, as will be seen is borne out by witnesses, that against the valley of Angrogna, deserves to be mentioned among the principal attacks. The reader knows that at the summit of this valley is the Waldenses' sacred refuge, "their last earthly refuge," called Prè du Tour. Protected as it is on the north by the bare ridges of Infernet, on the south by the rampart of Vandalin, on the west by the heights of Sella Veglia and Mount Roux, it is almost inaccessible, except from the east; that is to say, to reach it one must enter by the door. Now the door is overhung on the left of the stream by rocks, which command it like the bastions of a gigantic fortress, and these natural bastions are guarded by all the force available, for behind the front ranks were sheltered the old people and the women and little children. So good was the guard that the enemy never succeeded in penetrating there during all the days of the persecution. Once they almost succeeded, however, but before reaching the spot they had already received a check. A band of Crusaders had just climbed the border line of St. Joan, the name given to the hills which, at the approaches of the Valley of Angrogna, overlook this locality. They had hoped to force a passage at the village of Rocciamanéout, but were suddenly brought to a standstill by the advanced guard of the Waldenses. The mountaineers, well stationed, had provided themselves with cuirasses and targets made of hides or chestnut bark, and these protected them against the arrows of the enemy. The latter, greatly superior in number, were obliged to shoot upwards, and were therefore at some disadvantage, but the assault was a severe one nevertheless, and the position seemed for a moment to be in jeopardy. More than one of the Waldenses fell, but the ranks were maintained close. The irritated assailants renewed the attacks with greater fury. One of the leaders, followed by a band of soldiers advanced, breathing out threatenings and violence.[440] All eyes turned towards him. " God, help us "—the women's voices cried—*Dio aintaci*.[441] Tradition describes the leader of the assailants as a giant of swarthy complexion—a Goliath, full as to his mouth of curses and blasphemies, and called by the name of the Black One of Mondovi. As he advanced suddenly, whether from bravado or because of the heat, he raised his vizor, and quickly a swift arrow, sped by Pierre Revel, stretched him on the dust. Then terror seized upon the enemy,

F

and they fell back in disorder, only to return to the assault by
another way.   The Waldenses now hastened to reach the heights
of the valley while the Crusaders reascended, and drew out their
bands in *echelon* on the left of the stream.   Having reached
Serre, they disappeared in the lowlands beyond the hill and
entered into the pass of the Rodraille, at the approaches of Pré du
Tour.   At that instant a dense fog unexpectedly fell upon and
surrounded them, and the path which winds along the Angrogna,
was lost in darkness.   Suddenly, some Waldenses posted in that
vicinity came out of their retreat ; arrows flew through the fog ;
rocks were hurled down from the mountain sides ; and with their
noise the earth trembled and shook.   Heaven and earth and the
inhabitants thereof seemed to have formed a holy alliance against
the redressers of heresy.   The Crusaders, confounded and amazed,
tried to beat a retreat ; but the narrow path was obstructed by the
troops behind.   Confusion and panic in such a situation was fatal,
many, looking for a means of escape, slipped and fell from the
rocks into the torrent below ; many threw themselves down head-
long, as eager to anticipate their fate.   Amongst the number of those
who perished was Captain Saquet of Polonghera, of the province
of Coni.   It is said that he had just threatened the heretics with
certain ruin.   Tradition says, " This man having fallen from a
rock into the stream, which is called the Angrogna, was carried
away, and thrown by it into a large and deep hole, formed among
the rocks."   The pool received thereafter the name of " Gouffre
de Saquet," and its name ever since has helped to preserve the
memory of that signal victory sent by heaven to its people.[442]

The rout was complete and disastrous, and little likely to
appease the wrath of the Nuncio against those who had brought it
about.   According to his account, the case was very different in
the territory of Dauphiny, which comprised, as will be remembered,
the valley of Pragelas, where Catanée caused twenty-two
Waldenses of Briancon and Césane to be arrested and brought
into his presence ; they were, if he is to be believed, among the
principal people of those localities.   He adds that the heretics, not
satisfied with assaulting the Inquisitor, Veyleti, and covering him
with wounds, had caused much grief and apprehension to certain
magistrates and to the good souls in general who had been
interested in their safety ; and now they wished to drive him from
amongst them, for when they should have done with the Nuncio,

they thought they would be left in peace. In short, they had stirred up the water; moreover, Catanée was there to testify to the fact, and to re-establish order; they were, therefore, put to torture and forced to confess their faith. Two of their number having refused to recant, were handed over to the executioner; as for the others they re-entered the bosom of the Church, safe if not sound.[443] The report of this was sedulously disseminated, and the preaching monks called upon the people to seize the golden opportunity and obtain pardon. Several of the inhabitants of Val Pragelas, and of the neighbouring places, took advantage of the occasion, and their return to the faith was celebrated with solemnity in Briancon.[444] But not all bowed the knee, for many belonging to Mentoules, Usseaux, Fenestrelles, and several villages in Val Cluson, wishing to avoid this, withdrew to the summits of the mountains, and there prepared for resistance. When the attack was about to commence, the Waldenses sent two men to parley; they were Jean Camp and Jean Désidère. This is what they had to say :—

" The true faithful of Val Cluson entreat you, reverend and magnificent Lords, not to be led by the speeches of our enemies to condemn us without hearing our defence. We are the king's faithful subjects, and hold it an honour to bear the name of Christians. Our Barbes, who are educated and respectable persons, declare themselves ready to prove to you in a manner as clear as day, and in open conference, either on the testimony of the Old or New Testament, that we are orthodox with regard to the articles of our faith, and deserve not abuse but praise; for we will not follow the transgressors of evangelic law, and those who turn away from the tradition of the Apostles, nor obey their wicked institutions. We delight in the poverty and innocence which marked the origin and development of orthodox faith. We despise wealth, luxury, and lust for power, and all these things which are, alas! too truly the characteristics of our persecutors. Now you say that the destruction of what you call our sect, has been ordered. Beware, lest you make war against God, and draw down His wrath upon your heads, and lest, believing you are doing right, you be guilty of a great crime, as was the case with St. Paul. We have put our trust in God, for we are endeavouring to be acceptable unto Him rather than unto men. We fear not those who kill the body, but cannot kill the soul.

Know ye, therefore, that if it be not God's will, the forces you have gathered together against us will avail nothing."[445]

The Nuncio Catanée answered, and it is unnecessary to say how ; that can be easily imagined. He pretended that his answer terrified the Waldenses to such an extent as to induce them to ask for eight days' grace for reflection, declaring themselves ready to abjure, if convinced of error. Aymar de la Roche, Prior of Mentoules, with some few preachers, went to visit them, in the hope of touching the heart of this people ; but they were not received in the manner they had hoped for and desired. "We are in the right ; it is you who are the leaders into evil," the people cried to them,[446] and the messengers were obliged to return without having concluded anything. Then the Nuncio, having exhausted all his legal proceedings,[447] gave the signal for the combat to commence. The Waldenses, who had withdrawn to almost inaccessible heights, armed with arrows and short javelins, made a fierce resistance ; nevertheless, a number of them perished, especially at the defence of the Mont Fraisse cave. Fifteen of the most prominent heretics were sent to the stake. The next day the Crusaders attacked another refuge, steeper and more formidable : that above the rock of Roderie. They combined all their forces for this assault, but the Waldenses were protected by the nature of their position, and the soldiers were obliged to fall back before an avalanche of stones. Several were killed, and a still larger number were wounded, being then precipitated over the rocks. The battle raged with much fury from daybreak till evening.[448] In this case, however, the persecuted folk were dealing with much more skilful adversaries than the Black One of Mondovi and Captain Saquet. King Charles VIII. had sent for his lieutenant, Hugues de la Palu, who, assisted by the Councillor Jean Ribot, went straight at his work. The very next day the Crusaders returned to the assault with engines of war, and the Waldenses were obliged to surrender. "Prostrate upon the earth," says Catanée, they promised to abjure if they were pardoned. Peace was granted them, and by the order of the Nuncio, all that multitude set out for Mentoules ; there, after a solemn celebration of the ordinary rite, leaving their old leaven, and having been made into a new lump, according to the word of the Apostle, they re-entered the Catholic union."[449]

Then the Nuncio Catanée crossed Mount Genèvre, and went
to Embrun, for the purpose of directing the Crusade in the
direction of the valleys of Louise and Freyssinières.    There he
repeated the menaces and promises contained in the Pope's Bull,
and, with burning words, stirred up the zeal of the faithful, who
had hastened to him from several localities of Dauphiny.    After
this prelude, Hugues de la Palu arose, and, at the head of his
army, invaded first the narrow valley of Freyssinières.    At the
sight of the soldiery, the inhabitants scaled the heights, and concentrated themselves upon four different points, especially on the
rock called the " Church Rock."  Hugues, by taking a cross-road, got
at this last-named vantage ground, and compelled the defenders to
surrender, the rest soon following their example.    Almost
all went down to perform the act of submission.    " You ask for
mercy, come and ask it at Embrun," answered the Nuncio.[450]
They went, but we do not know to what number.

In Val Louise, the rage of the Crusaders had freer scope, and
their irritation at the care the persecuted people displayed for
their lives and their faith rendered them furious.    The refugees
for the most part betook themselves to a cave, which owes almost
all its celebrity to this Crusade.    It is situated on the slopes of
Pelvoux, the Viso of the Briançonnais.    Almost half-way up that
mountain is a narrow gorge, which leads to the cave called Aigue
Fraide, because of the spring which there issues from under the
glaciers.    In front of the opening, stretching out on a projection
of the mountain is a platform, from which the eye looks down
upon the surrounding ravines.    This can only be reached by a
frightful path, overhanging the precipices.    Such is the spot
where the Waldenses awaited their persecutors.    They had pro-
visioned themselves for two years, says the Nuncio, who was
present at the assault.    At first messengers were sent to summon
them to perform the act of obedience.    That was of no avail.
Measure the height of those rocks, answered they, and go
and tell him who sent you that we are resolved, if necessary, to
die for our faith.[451]  Catanée harangued the devout troops before
they mounted to the assault ; but the stones began to roll down,
and all attempts to reach the platform by a direct ascent had to
be abandoned.    At night Hugues de la Palu bethought him of a
stratagem, and he conceived the idea of putting it into execution
the very next day—a Sunday.    He managed to get a number of

young men to climb from behind, and unperceived to the summit.
From this point they, by means of ropes, lowered one another to
a rock that overlooked the entrance to the cave. The Waldenses
could not see them, nor had they any suspicion of their presence,
as their attention was taken up by a feint attack, which was
renewed in order to effect a diversion.[452] At the proper moment, a
simultaneous rush was made upon the besieged from above and
below, when, taken by surprise, and disconcerted, they were
vanquished. They were possessed with such terror that more
than ninety precipitated themselves from the rock. The Nuncio
says that the survivors were pardoned,[453] but tradition says differently. It alleges that the soldiers piled up green wood at the
entrance to the cave, set fire to it, and transformed that refuge
into a tomb.[454] When an entrance was afterwards made, 3,000
victims were found, it is said, among whom were 400 children,
who died in their cradles or in their mother's arms.[455] According
to another version, which perhaps falsifies in a different direction, there were "thirty families only, numbering in all 70
persons—men, women, and children."[456] It is to be believed that
"had the Waldenses been in such small numbers, it would not
have been necessary to send the lieutenant-governor of the province with a miniature army against them."[451] The cave is still
there : a place of horrors. It is called the Balme des Vaudois, or
the Balme Chapelne.

The city of Embrun also witnessed the arrival of the poor
inhabitants of the valley of Argentiére, seeking for pardon. The
goods of the heretics were confiscated, especially in Val Louise,
which it was intended to re-people with Catholics. "Never since
that time," says Muston, "has the Waldensian Church risen again
in those valleys."[458] On quitting these desolated spots the
Nuncio left the care of fulfilling his mission to a Franciscan
monk, named Francois Ploireri, who immediately went to work.
He summoned to Embrun those Waldenses who had not re-
entered the pale of the Church, or were backsliders. He instituted a number of proceedings against them, and, in order
that no appeal might be had from his decision, condemned them,
with the assistance of a Councillor of the Parliament of Dauphiny,
called Pons. The general sentence having been once pronounced,
it was posted up on the door, "and at the foot of it were the 32
articles of the creed of the said Waldenses."[459]

The account of this Crusade may be closed with one more incident, for which we are indebted to tradition, narrated by Gilles. A battalion 700 strong, climbing over the pass of Abriès, reached the heights of Val St. Martin more or less unexpectedly, and fell upon the village of Pommiers in the township of Prali.[460] The advent of the soldiers was discovered in time, so that while the Crusaders were scattering for the purposes of plunder, the "Pralins" fell upon them. All, except the colour-bearer, were killed, according to Gilles; or, "killed and put to flight," according to Muston. The colour-bearer had, during the flight, hidden himself in a ravine under the snow. Cold and hunger drove him out at last, and his life was spared. "Having cooled down a little, the 'Pralins' let him go unharmed, to carry the news of the total defeat of his companions."[461]

Thus ended the Crusade, the date of which is not yet fixed. According to Waldensian historians, it took place in 1488;[462] but the accuracy of this date may be doubted, as it does not agree very well with the circumstances which accompanied the event. Indeed, we know that the bull of Innocent VIII., first proclaimed at Rome, May 5th, 1487, in the third year of his pontificate, was less than two months afterwards (June 26th) repeated "in the convent of St. Laurent, without the walls of Pignerol."[463] The season was propitious for its execution, and there is nothing that indicates delay. The Crusade, therefore, probably commenced in the year 1487.[464]

Charles I., Duke of Savoy, had not been indifferent to the vicissitudes undergone by his subjects in the valleys.[465] Their sufferings, as well as their courage, had touched his heart. He delegated a Bishop to confer with, and assure them as to his true feelings. The prelate went up to Angrogna, and delivered his message of sympathy at the village of Prassint. It was agreed that the Waldenses should send a deputation, composed of twelve of their principal men, to do homage to the Duke. Charles awaited them at his castle of Pignerol. He had doubtless heard much about the heretics, and what he had heard seems to have whetted his curiosity. The deputies arrived. The Duke received them with the courtesy and breeding due from one of the house of Savoy; his youth—he was then only twenty—rendering it the more charming. According to some, he excused himself for having tolerated such a cruel war; according to

others, " he granted pardon on receipt of such a sum of money
as should defray the expenses of it."[466]    These two versions certainly differ materially, but one does not necessarily exclude the
other ; still, whatever the means, peace was re-established, and the
Waldenses had the opportunity of becoming convinced that, but
for clerical interference, they might have enjoyed some little
liberty.    The audience ended in familiar conversation, during
which children were mentioned.    The Duke, who could hardly
overcome his surprise at the nursery tales which had been palmed
off upon him, asked with a smile : " Is it true that your children
are born with a black throat, four rows of hairy teeth, and one
eye in the middle of the forehead ? "    Some were presented to
him, and they took it upon themselves to answer.    The Duke
blushed for having been so credulous, and was indignant with the
slanderers.    This is an anecdote worthy of being chronicled, as
showing what fanaticism could invent.

    The most advantageous result of the conference at Pignerol
was peace—a lasting peace which, in the valleys subject to the
house of Savoy, was not again interrupted until after the Reformation.    The comments made upon the Prince by the deputies as,
with light and joyful hearts, they returned to their firesides, may
be surmised, and are undoubtedly reflected in those of Waldensian
writers.    " God has touched the heart of the Prince," some said ;
" God be praised," others added, " our young Duke has harked back
upon the natural kind ways of his race."[467]    They were jubilant in
the valleys, and bonfires were kindled on the mountain-tops as a
sign of rejoicing ; but a mysterious, unexpected, and unforeseen
grief soon quenched the joy in every heart.    The young Duke
died in that very Pignerol on March 13th, 1490.    It has been
suspected by some that he was poisoned.[468]    Nothing, however,
is known for certain ; still, one thing we do know, namely, that
suspicion did not fall upon the Waldenses, and that none mourned
his death more sincerely than they : indeed, it came near being
fatal to them, for its effect was to place the power once more in
the hands of a regent.    Only two years later another death took
place, which, however, did not cause any regret—that of the
author of the Crusade.    Innocent VIII. had just received a singular present from the Sultan ; it was a portion of the lance
which had pierced the side of our Saviour.    He rejoiced so much
over this, that he ordered a procession to go out and meet

Bajazet's messenger, in order to receive and instal with suitable ceremony the relic, which might indeed, as a symbol, have suggested some serious reflections to him. As he was about to die, a Jewish physician suggested, as a last remedy, a draught of human blood. Three apparently motherless young boys were brought; they permitted their veins to be opened, for money which other hands received; but the innocent blood did not help the Pontiff, who had already drunk too much of it. He went to his grave on the 15th of July, 1492.

Still, the peace granted by the Duke of Savoy had not put an end to all the effects of the Crusade. In Piedmont it left a door open for the molestation of inquisitorial procedure, both regular and secret; clerical reaction, however, had at least been checked. In Dauphiny people envied the fate of the subjects of the house of Savoy, and not without cause. After the Crusade there happened that which always followed war in those barbarous days; the vultures and crows came down upon their prey. In this case the vultures were represented by the officials of the Royal Treasury, and this is shown by the following decree, issued March 4th, 1488 :—

" Charles * * * We, having received a humble petition from our friends and faithful counsellors, Hugues de la Palu, Lord of Varas, Lieutenant-Governor of our country of Dauphiny, Sire Pons, Counsellor in our Court of Parliament at Grenoble, and Charles Baron, our Counsellor and Chamberlain, setting forth that, by our other letters-patent given at Angers, in the month of June past, we appointed and delegated them to take, seize, and put into our hands all estates and property whatever of certain inhabitants of the said country of Dauphiny, called Waldenses, who, by sentence of our dear and beloved master, Albert de Cappitaneys, learned in every law, appointed by our Holy Father the Pope for that purpose, had been declared confiscated and belonging to us, because of the evil schisms and heresies which they had heretofore held and were holding against the Holy Apostolic Faith."[469]

Another share of the confiscated property had fallen to Jean Baile, Archbishop of Embrun, and it increased day by day, in consequence of new confiscations. On the arrival of his successor, Rastain, in 1497, the patrimony of the Archbishopric had attained very goodly proportions. The latter prelate examined it carefully, and compared it with the documentary titles. He ascer-

tained, also, that the people of Freyssinières were still under the
burden of excommunication ; therefore, he said to himself, " I
shall not go to visit their accursed valley." One day he was
approached by a certain Fazy Gay of Freyssinières, who said
to him :—

" We are expecting you up yonder," your Grace.  " Shall you
not come up and see us ? "

" No, indeed."

" Why, pray ? "

" The excommunication which was hurled against you has not
been taken away."

" I beg pardon, your Grace ; it is a long time since we were
freed from it.  You must forget that we obtained absolution by
the decree of Louis XI."

" Nonsense.  You are under condemnation by the authority
of the Pontiff : *authoritate pontificis romani.*  I believe that's
clear."

" So that we shall be deprived of your visit."

" You will not see me in Freyssinières, so long as you are not
reconciled with the Pope."

" But then, of what use was our promise to live like good
Catholics ? "

" I have nothing to say in the matter, I tell you.  That is to
say, I am quite willing to send you Sire Jean Colombi ; he will
find out all about the rights of things.  Moreover, I will write to
Rome."

It was found afterwards that the Pope never sent any reply to
that communication.  Alexander VI. had his hands full elsewhere ;
he was just then stirring up the fire which burned Savanarola.
Meanwhile, Charles VIII. having died, Rostain went to attend the
coronation of Louis XII., and the people of Freyssinières sent their
delegates to the new king, charging them to present to him their
everlasting request.  It was the old question of recovering their
property, unjustly withheld by the Archbishop.  The king referred
the matter to his Chancellor, who questioned Rostain.  He,
shrugging his shoulders, answered, " What can I tell you ? it is
none of my business.  The goods that are claimed were confiscated before my installation.  In Paris you will find members
of the Parliament of Grenoble, Counsellor Rabot among others.
Ask them ; they will give you information."  The Waldensian

deputies were heard in their turn; they said: "We ask that the decree of Louis XI., of blessed memory, be observed. Our best property is annexed to the patrimony of the Archbishopric. All our complaints have been in vain. After the king has decided, we to the prejudice of his legitimate authority, are referred to the Pope."

Thereupon the Royal Council decided upon an inquiry. The commissioners delegated for the purpose arrived in Embrun, on July 4, 1501, and Rostain, out of deference to his rank, was permitted to take part in the inquiry. He soon, however, got into a very bad humour, because the royal officers, from a feeling of delicacy, refused his interested attentions, and he showed his displeasure very plainly—first, by disputing their right to examine the papers in the case; afterwards, by fuming during the whole inquiry; and finally, by spreading annoying reports of the procedure. What made the Prelate most bitter was that the commissioners should, although with reserve, have granted the Waldenses absolution as regards contumacy.[470] He at once protested, and began to aver that his colleagues showed too clearly by their remarks that they had espoused the cause of the heretics.

"We wish to be just, first of all. If our remarks are at fault, let your Grace denounce them," said the commissioners.

"Well, Monsieur d'Orleans, since you invite me to do so, I will tell you that I was pained to hear what you said at the Inn of the Angel."

"What was that?"

"Oh! What you said there goes beyond anything I could have imagined, and I am so deeply grieved at it, that I still wonder whether you really spoke the words which are attributed to you."

"May I ask what they are?"

"It is affirmed that you said, 'I would that I were as good a Christian as are the worst inhabitants of Freyssinières.'"

"And that distresses you."

"It seems to me there is good reason why it should."

Malicious people averred that what most distressed the Archbishop was the fear of having to restore to the Waldenses the beautiful vineyards of St. Clement, St. Crespin, and Chanteloube, as well as the estates of Chateau Roux.[471]

Upon receipt of the Commissioners' report, Louis XII. issued the following decree :—

" Louis, by the grace of God, king of France, etc.

" It having come to our notice that the inhabitants of Freyssinières have suffered great wrongs and vexations, difficulties and labour, desiring to relieve them, and that they may be reinstated in the possession of their property, chattels, and estates, we order by these presents to all those who are with-holding the said properties, incontinently and without delay to dispossess themselves of them, and hand over the said properties, and return and restore them to the said suppliants or their pro-curators, each one in his place, and in case of opposition, refusal, or delay, we, having regard to their poverty and misery, in the which they have long been and still are detained, without being able to obtain justice—WE desiring with all our heart that right shall be done to them, will our own selves know the reason thereof, &c., &c.

" Given at Lyons on the 12th of October, 1501." [472]

After this new decree, nothing, it would seem, remained but to obey. However, the Archbishop did not see matters in that light. He drew a distinction. " I am not indebted to the inhabitants of Freyssinières for my property," he said, " I received that from my predecessor. I am quite willing," he added, " to conform to the orders of His Majesty; let us return confiscated property to the Waldenses; I wait but for one thing, namely, that the Lords of Dauphiny set me the example."

The reader will not have forgotten that, as the representatives of the civil power, these latter had had their bountiful share. Besides which, on this matter, Lords and Prelates always went hand and glove. Several personages were summoned before the king. They excused themselves without much ceremony, and actually went so far as to say that in order to carry out the desired restoration, they required, as did the Archbishop, the absolution of the Pope. Perhaps the Papal Bull which followed was obtained, if not directly by the Archbishop, at least by one of his dignitaries on a mission to the the Court of France. Such is with fair probability affirmed.[473] If this be so, it must be confessed that when hope was lost, the Waldenses found an unexpected protector, whose favour, however, was more venal than efficient:

venal, for we are speaking of the Pope, whose conduct suggested the well known distich:—

Vendit Alexander cruces, altaria Christum.
Emerat ille prius, vendere jure potest.

The protection was insufficient, because Archbishop Rostain laughed at the Bull, and did not consider it obligatory. In order to be so, he replied, it must proceed directly from the Holy Father. In short, we learn here that nothing availed against his sacerdotal avarice, and the Poor of Lyons, or rather the faithful amongst them, would have lost less time, and perhaps less credit, had they kept Waldo's ideal in sight, and had ceased to protest against it.

The narrative thus far has not led us to the valley of the Po, into which, however, we know that the Waldenses had a long time before penetrated, either from France or from the valley bordering upon that of Luserna. Had the valley escaped the storm of the Crusade? Judging from his memoirs, Albert de Catanée would not seem to have betaken himself thither; no known fact indicates the presence in those parts of his soldiers, renowned as they were for their fanaticism.[475] The conclusion that may be drawn from this is, that the Waldenses had not yet collected there in sufficiently large numbers to draw upon themselves general attention; or, as we prefer to believe, that during the raging of the Crusade there was no need of Romish thunderbolts to reduce the heretics to silence, and that the mild inquisitorial hail alone was sufficient. After the Crusade, those who fled from Val Luserna, and particularly from the localities of Bobi and Rora, seem to have contributed to swell their number, but, at the same time also, the danger which threatened them. Be that as it may, persecution did later fall upon them, and our business is to relate the facts, but before doing so we must go back a little.

It will be remembered that the valley of the Po had received the refugees from France, after the famous Crusade against the Albigenses. They had reached it—a part of them at least— by the more or less frequented paths in the vicinity of Viso. The whole frontier, as far as the Maritime Alps, was traversed by the stream of emigration; divers points of the territory now comprised in the province of Coni being repeatedly attained. This city witnessed the rapid increase of heretics, either within its

walls or in its neighbourhood, as far as Dronero, Busca, Savigliano, Saluzzo, up toward the Alpine frontier, from the valley of
the Po to that of Maira, and the pass of Tende.    Yet it was
further on, into the free cities of Lombardy, that the stream of
emigration finally flowed.    Coni was for the Albigenses hardly
more than a city of passage.[476]  In the XV. century, heresy had
by no means disappeared from it.    In 1417, the Inquisition asked
to be permitted free entrance and assistance, as it had learned on
good authority that in more. than one locality heretics abounded,
and that they even enjoyed sufficient favour to dare to hold meetings, and to teach their doctrines by means of which they out-
rageously lacerated the bosom of Mother Church, and precipitated
souls into the abyss of perdition.[477]  It has been doubted whether
at that time the Inquisition obtained the des ired support.[478]
Thirty years later, its action was only too manifest.    This was in
the time of Duke Louis of Savoy.[479]  A local chronicle says that
in 1445, some thirty houses were destroyed by fire in one of the
streets of Coni, and that this accident seemed to herald the
avenging flames of the Catholic faith.    With the assistance of
monkish zeal, the omen was realised.    Twenty-two inhabitants of
the village of Bernezzo were summoned to Coni and burned.  The
chronicle is ambiguous as to whom they were.    It says : " They
profess the heresy of the Poor of Lyons whom some call Gazares
and others Waldenses.[480]  But it was in the domain of the Marquis
of Saluzzo mainly that the heretics succeeded in settling.    It is
the opinion of more than one writer, that Bagnolo was one of the
most renowned centres of the Cathari,[481] and some Waldenses
may have intermingled with them.    Still the latter shewed a
tendency to settle more to the west, towards the sources of the
Po, in the villages of Pravillelm, Biolet, and Bietonet, notwithstanding the Inquisition that aimed at their destruction.

      We have now arrived at the year 1509, in the month of
November.[482]  Margaret of Foix, for the last five years widow of
the Marquis Louis II. of Saluzzo, still young, but morose and
bigoted,[483] " was free as respects her own power, but a slave to
her confessor."[484]  There is little doubt that her zeal alarmed the
lesser Lords of Paesane, and that would explain the conflict of
jurisdiction which we find arose between the Marchioness and her
vassals.   The latter, jealous of their rights, claimed to manage
the inquisition of heresy in concert with the monks and the bishop

and without the intervention of the Princess. Margaret thereupon bought up the rights of the monks and of the bishop, though without relinquishing her own, and intimated to her feudatories that she freed them from all care as regards the necessary expenses, including the cost of wood for the piles.[485] Then Angelo Ricciardino, a Dominican monk, Inquisitor at Saluzzo, betook himself to Paesane, and caused it to be proclaimed in the public market place, that the inhabitants of Pravellelm, Biolet, and Bietonet, and of the Serre of Momian should come down to him and do penance. No one went down. In the meantime an unknown man from the borough of Saint Frout was arrested. His name was Pierre Faro Julian.[486]

" Tell me what you know about the Waldenses of your village," said the inquisitor to him ; " I promise you that you shall thereby save your life and property."

" Well, they are all heretics, from the first to the last."

The Inquisitor desired nothing more. A second witness was examined, and the same confession obtained, with respect to all the neighbouring villages. Thereupon, on the 25th of November, St. Catherine's Day, the monk sent out myrmidons with orders to arrest the principal heretics of Pravillelm and Oncino in church and during Mass. They were able to seize two only, Francois Maria and Balangier Lanfré.

" Are you Waldenses ? "

" We are.[487] "

On hearing this the Marchioness sent out 200 soldiers, with orders to assist the monk Ricciardino. The latter directed them toward the villages of Pravillelm, Bietonet, and Oncino. Go, said he to them, and bring all those heretics to me. Warned betimes, most of the intended victims fled to Barge, with their cattle ; but some were arrested and thrown into prison, and the deserted homes were pillaged. The inquiry began, not without the aid of torture, and on the 24th of March, 1510, Jacques, Mainero, Antoine Lanfré, Francois Luchino, and Guillaume Maria were sentenced to be burned at the stake the very next day. That day had been chosen for the execution on account of its solemnity, it being the feast of the Annunciation and Palm Sunday, and the execution was to take place at Croès, in the territory of Paesane, in a meadow opposite the house of the said Mainero. The pile was ready awaiting its five victims ; but snow and rain fell in such quantities, that the execution had to be postponed till the morrow. At night, the prisoners broke the bars of their window, and escaped with great difficulty, dragging their chains as far as Bosco Piano. There a friend came to their assistance, their chains were taken off, and they were free to go where they pleased; they reached Barge safe and sound. After this the rage of the Inquisitor may be imagined. He insisted that the spectacle should take place just the same. To be sure there were no condemned culprits available, but that could be managed. In the prisons of Saint Front were three Waldenses, who had been promised their pardon, because they had, without any need for the application of the torture, confessed everything. We have already named one of them, Belangier Lanfré; the others were Julian and Maria.[488] To break promise to heretics could be no sin; moreover, in some way or other, justice must be satisfied,[489] so these men were burned alive on the banks of the Po, on May 12th of the same year. Many others of their co-religionists were arrested, and after being cudgelled, were sent out of the country.[490] Among the number was a man of the Bianchi family and his mother, Antoine, George Mainero of Serre Oncino, and Luchino Verminella of Pravillelm. Nicolas Rosso of Mombracco and his brother went to the stake a few days later at Saint Front. Finally, on the 18th of July, the house where the Waldenses were holding their meetings was demolished. Externally it had, we read, a pretty appearance; within it looked like a labyrinth.[491] Even the name of the village of Pravillelm was by order changed to that of St. Laurent; tradition, however, laughed at the ceremony, and the former name continued to be used. All the property of the heretics was confiscated; one third went to the Lords of Paesane and Oncino, and the rest to the Marchioness.[491]

Nevertheless, the fugitives had reached the valley of Luserna, and had scattered through the localities of Rora, Angrogna, and Bobi. They were not satisfied with the cordial reception given them by their co-religionists. In vain more than once did they send up petitions to Margaret to be permitted to return to their firesides. Finally they resolved upon an heroic course. "A valiant and courageous man among them—having been promised by other exiles that they would follow him and imitate his example—went, well attended and unexpectedly, to visit the houses and properties they had abandoned, then occupied by the neighbouring papists. With his two-handed sword he cut in pieces all whom he met with on the properties, both men and beasts ; then, having done this in one district, and having carried away the goods found in their houses, in order to defray the expenses of the journey, the party withdrew to another district. Continuing in like manner, they so frightened the papists of the surrounding country, that not only did they no longer dare to be found in Pravillelm, Bioletz, or Bietoné, but even trembled in their own houses, so that they themselves prevailed upon the Marchioness to permit the Waldenses to return and occupy their dwellings in peace, with the enjoyment of their liberties."[493]

Such, in brief, is the account of the return into their homes of the Waldenses of the Valley of the Po.[494] This took place in 1512. The local chronicle, which, as we note in passing, does not agree with Gilles' History, says not a word of the individual who directed the return ; on the other hand, it furnishes new details concerning the compromises stipulated for between the Lords of the place and Margaret, and we are surprised to have to note the intervention of the Pope. " In the year 1513," says the chronicle, " about the 8th of July, Madame having seen the pardon and absolution granted by Pope Leo to the men of Pravillelm, Biolet, Bietonet, and Serre of Momian, her ladyship, in her turn, pardoned the aforesaid, that is to say, as far as her jurisdiction extended. Madame furthermore remitted to them two-thirds of their goods, which had not yet been sold, and authorized them to re-establish themselves in their homes on payment of 4,400 ducats, which they agreed to pay within a certain time."[495] All this property put together did not amount, however, to even one-third of the required sum, so that when the period had elapsed, as the Marchioness did not receive her money, she issued a decree, dated April 24th, 1514, ordering the Waldenses to leave the country within three days, under penalty of death. This decree appeared so cruel that the public conscience was shocked. A remonstrance was addressed to the Marchioness, who finally agreed that the Waldenses should pay down 600 ducats, and the rest of the sum at the rate of 40 ducats per year. The Lords of Paesane, to whom had fallen a third part of the confiscated property, gave it up in their turn, under the following conditions :—

The Waldenses were to pay the sum of ten golden ducats
yearly on St. Martin's Day ; they should see to it that the mill was
kept in good order, and they should be expected to bring in to
the Castellan of Paesane partridges, hares, and nests of hawks at
the price of three drachms.[496]   After that, we learn that the Waldenses of the Valley of the Po began to lead, if not a peaceful
life, one that was much more free from torment.   Margaret of
Foix, more papist than the Pope, never became reconciled to
them ; and yet they had one thing in common with her, namely,
the Gospel text : " Si Deus pro nobis quis contra nos ? "[497] —with
this difference, however, that the Marchioness carried the motto
engraved upon her shield, whilst the Waldenses bore it in their
hearts.   Were it not for their faith, one could hardly account for their
return being so obscure (and yet so glorious) or even for its taking
place at all.   It was indeed a glorious return, for it proved something better than their attachment to legitimate but material
property, which was, moreover, assured to them neither by
right of conquest nor by that of re-purchase, nor yet by right of
birth.   What the return of the Waldenses does prove, is fondness
for their homes, and also love, a holy love, for their country.
From this point of view, so limited an undertaking, hidden in the
darkness that surrounds the name, the figure, and the memory of
its hero, is far from being insignificant.   Some have attempted to
throw ridicule upon it,[498] but the ridicule has recoiled upon the
traducers.   Who knows, after all, whether this first glorious
return did not suggest the idea of the second, the splendour of
which had the effect on the other hand of relegating the patriots
of the Valley of the Po more than ever to oblivion ?

Let us pause a moment to throw a final glance upon the
mother-colony of the Alps.   We may, without circumlocution,
confess that it is impossible to ascertain with any certainty what
went on there.   Persecution compelled the Church of the valleys
to sink into a silence which too often conceals her from our sight ;
her history, like the lofty mountain-tops, is enveloped in the
mists of obscurity.   We have noticed in the people certain movements in diverse directions.   These movements cannot be altogether
accounted for by the numerical increase of the inhabitants ; it was
largely due to the inquisitorial repression, which enclosed the
settlers within ever-narrowing limits, and contended with them
for their property and the soil consecrated by their labour ; hence

emigration became necessary to the people, and it served, too, for the development of spiritual life. The emigration, too, especially where the least danger threatened, as between the two slopes of the Alps, was continuous. But even there a danger was to be apprehended : viz., the ruin of the community through dispersion, unless indeed the Waldenses were careful to anticipate the danger by pastoral action among their missionaries.

Who has not heard of the Barbes ? They are the most legitimate representatives of the early Waldenses, so much so that the latter derive from them the nick-name of *Barbets*. The name of Barbes was not invented, but borrowed from popular use. It meant " Uncle."[499] We know that in ancient times—even now it may still be observed—the uncle was a conspicuous character in the family, especially when, renouncing matrimony, he gave himself wholly to family life. He was the jealous guardian of the family traditions, the tutor or pedagogue.[500] The children had as much veneration for him as for their father, nay, even more when the latter was neglectful of his office. By degrees, the name of Uncle became a title of respect, which was applied to every man who was venerable either by age or character. The Waldensian Barbe may therefore be compared to the Elders in Israel and in the primitive Church.[501] He was not a Priest, nor did he aspire to become one ; he did better—he threw the priest into the shade.[502] His essentially moral authority was fed by the decadence of official priesthood, and became the more real as the ecclesiastic consecration became more illusive. The Barbe did not desire schism in God's family, he wished to see discipline ; he did not assume, as a rule, the privilege of administering the sacraments. He aimed, first of all, at preaching the good lessons of the Scriptures when on his visits, and in hearing the confessions of the faithful ; hence the title of teacher, applied to the Barbes by their disciples as well as by their adversaries,[503] and hence, too, the usage which gives the name of schools to the places of worship and the meetings at which they presided.

Attempts have been made to draw up a list of the Barbes, that is to say, of the leaders of dissidence in the valleys of the Alps before the Reformation ;[504] but these attempts must be renounced. The following are the names of some of the principal Barbes :—

Barbe Paul Gignoso of Bobi.
,,     Pierre of Piedmont.
,,     Antoine of Val de Suse.
,,     Jean Martin of Val St. Martin.
,,     Mauhien of Bobi.
,,     Philippe of Luserna.
,,     George of Piedmont.
,,     Etienne Laurens of Val St. Martin.
,,     Martin of Méane.

These, according to Léger, dwelt in the valleys.[505]

Barbe Barthèlemi Tertian of Méane may have been of the same family as Jordan Tertian, the martyr. Léger says he was called " the large-handed Barbe."

Barbe Jean Girard of Méane.
,,     Tomasin Bastia of Angrogna.
,,     Barthèlemi ,,    ,,      ,,

The first withdrew to Geneva, and became a printer; the second died in Puglia, and the third in Calabria.

Barbe Jacques Bellonato of Angrogna.
,,     Jacques Germano of Val Perosa.
,,     Jean Benedetto.
,,     Jean Romaguolo of Sienna.
,,     Francesquin of Val Freyssinières.
,,     Michel Porta of Vallouise, or of Pragelas.
,.     Pierre Flot of Pragelas,
,,     Jacques of Legero.[506]

There is no attempt here at specifying the time at which they lived, or even at uniting them in the same epoch. The well-known names of four contemporaries of the Reformation may be set down here : they are

Barbe Pierre Masson of Burgogne.
,,     George Morel of Freyssinières, or of
           Chauteloube.
,,     Jean of Molines.
,,     Daniel of Valence.

The Barbes have also been called pastors : they were so indeed, but their parishes consisted of the dispersed tribe of the Israel of the

Alps.  Anyone of them might have said, as Wesley did later, " My parish is the world."  They were both the messengers of God and of their brethren, having their heart set on replacing the light of the Gospel upon the hill-top, strengthening the bonds which united the communities, and reviving languishing faith everywhere.  Their task was so vast that they were insufficient for it, and oftentimes their grave and sober pastoral epistles had to supply their places, as well as might be, during enforced absences. The letter of Tertian, *aux grands mains*, is a characteristic one.[567]

The Barbes carried on with very special solicitude the intercourse between the mother colony of the Alpine Valleys and the daughter colony of Calabria.  So great was their zeal for the latter, that it might almost seem at times as if the ecclesiastic centre had been established there at the end of the XIV. century. According to a popular idea, based on the inquisitorial proceedings, the leader of the Waldenses resided in Puglia.[508]  A monk states, after an inquiry had been held, that it was thence that preaching in the valleys was provided for.[509] The reason for this probably was that the Barbes journeyed ceaselessly to and fro, between those two poles of the Waldensian mission in Italy.  On the way they visited individual brethren or scattered communities who awaited their arrival, in order that the members might together receive absolution from their sins.  It has been claimed that in almost every principal city there was some house used as a conventicle.  It is true that, with the exception of the room at Milan, which has been mentioned before, there is no certain information on this point; but traditions, vague though they be, are unanimous on the subject.  On this matter Gilles says :—

" The Barbes had in Florence a house belonging to them, with moneys for their various needs, in going and coming through Italy.  They had another in Genoa, and several disciples there, as also in Venice, where the minister informed Gilles, on the occasion of a visit made by him to this place, that the faithful numbered six thousand.  There were also a great number of disciples at Rome, and almost everywhere else."[510]  It is possible that the statements are exaggerated, nay, it is quite probable.[511]  We certainly know that the presence of a mission house was rather the exception, and its absence a rule.  Whether by preference, or of necessity, the Waldensian missionaries followed the example of the Apostles, and accepted from their co-religionists hospitality for themselves, and accommodation for their meetings.[512]  We may notice too, the general assemblies in which unity of faith and action was declared; they were convened with such circumspection that for the most part they were unknown to the Church police.  They are only mentioned once or twice in the chronicles of that age.  Here is an allusion to an assembly of that character.  Pope John XXII. in his brief of the year 1332, says :—" We have heard that in the valleys of Luserna and in the territory of Perosa, the heretics, and the sect of the Waldenses especially, have multiplied to such an extent, that they permit themselves to assemble frequently in the form of a chapter, and their meetings number at times as many as five hundred persons."

This was in the time of Aimon le Pacifique, and of Prince Philip of Achaia.  If the number seem a large one, it can after all be accounted for without any need of asking whether Waldenses only were there spoken of.  It only requires to be admitte1, what is very obvious, namely, that the assembly was composed not only of Barbes, but also of those faithful to the example of the primitive Church, which class might include the Cathari.  These general assemblies were essentially missionary in character, as proved by the assembly's management of the Waldensian mission interests, and by their connection with the propaganda of their brethren in Italy and elsewhere, and above all, in Germany.  More than once a collection of contributions of money for transmission to the leaders of the Hussite dissidence was decreed.[513]  There were periodical regular assemblies for the transaction of current and extraordinary business, as the needs of the day demanded.  They always aimed at the " preservation of unity and the maintenance of uniformity in the churches."  At times, " delegates from all quarters of Europe in which there were Waldensian churches " in a condition to send them, hastened to be present at such meetings. " Such was," says Gilles, " the character of the Synod held at Laus of Valcluson in la ter times, when there were present 140 Waldensian pastors, who had come from different countries.  At other times they kept up communication by letter, as far as they were able."[514]

The character of the Barbes is of primary importance; they were the Levites and the Judges of the Israel of the Alps.  The question whence they came may, however, still be asked.  A man did not become a Barbe in the same way as he became an uncle ; there was, it is said, a school of Barbes. What do we know about this school ?

First, let us get rid of any ambiguity of expression, for words are sometimes deceptive. There are schools and schools. It was remarked before that this name was given to more or less public meetings presided over by the " teachers," that is to say, by the ministers of the community. This usage, as has just been said, [515] betrays the spirit of dissidence. Let it be added that, when coming from the pen of the Inquisitors, the expression is capable of still further explanation, as Roman Catholic custom is against the employment of ecclesiastic terminology, when speaking of the usages of a sect. We must keep these distinctions in mind, though it is to be confessed that, in certain cases, to do so is not an easy task. Thus, when the monk, Vincent Ferreri, informs his superiors that the Waldensian schools found by him in the valley of Angrogna were destroyed,[516] what does he mean ? Does he refer to forbidden meetings, or to the pulling down of some house used for purposes of meeting, or to the school of the Barbes ? All these hypotheses are possible, the more so that if the school of the Barbes had a house of its own, it was according to the tradition, at Pré du Tour. Yet Pré du Tour hardly suffered any devastation but that effected by time, as before the Reformation at least, persecution did not penetrate there. Another Protestant author, Flacius, surnamed Illyricus, whose testimony is often quoted upon the point in question, relates that, according to the official records of the Inquisition, there existed in Lombardy, in the middle of the XIV. century, schools—that is to say, a species of academies—where " sound Christian theology " was taught ; thither contributions from Bohemia and Poland were sent, and more than one student left Bohemia to go and attend the lessons of his " Waldensian teachers."[517] This time we have to do with a school, above all a Waldensian school.[518] But where was it ? At Pré du Tour, Waldensian historians have until quite lately unanimously answered.[519] It would seem that they are mistaken ; not because Pré du Tour may not be comprised within the limits then assigned to the territory of Lombardy ; but because Milan is specified by the writer quoted as the place of residence of the teachers of the theology spoken of, and consequently the seat of the Waldensian school. Indeed, he adds that, as early as 1212, there were at Milan adherents to the Waldensian doctrine, and that some Alsatians had sent collections to those Milanese " as to their teachers."[520]   This agrees perfectly with the testimony already gathered concerning that epoch.   In fact, the school of Milan was mentioned by Stephanus de Borbone. This Inquisitor tells us that a Waldensian, arrested at Jonvelle, on the Sâone, near Jussey, confessed to him that he had quitted his country more than 18 years before to go to Milan and study the doctrine he was now propagating.   Moreover, Flacius[521] does not ignore the existence of Waldenses in the valleys of the Alps ; on the contrary, he shows that they there survived persecution ; but he finds no mention of their school in the reports of the Inquisition.   That leads us to think that the school of Pré du Tour was not so famous as has been thought, and that it has been confounded with the school at Milan.   The impression becomes stronger when we find that " the college of Barbes furnished so many pastors and so many evangelists to all regions of Italy, and even to Bohemia, Moravia, Hungary, &c."[522]   Still, the school of the Barbes did exist, and although a very modest one, it had its mission and its merit, which need not be ignored.   If thunderbolts of eloquence were not forged there, the students were taught to become something better than " riders of hobbies."[523] There, far from the noise of large cities, under the shadow of the Alps, there might be inhaled the peaceful calm necessary for meditating upon the Scriptures.   Faith might grow in that austere solitude, and character might be formed strong as the native granite.

The college of Barbes is known to date back to the time of Waldo himself.[524]   After his time it simply multiplied.   The Waldenses of the Alps were not long in organizing it for their own uses ; their tendencies, being both biblical and didactic, made such a school a necessity.   If, in addition to this, we consider the circumstances of their new condition, and the wants necessarily created by emigration, we shall at once recognise the fact, that if a college had not previously existed, they certainly would have had to invent one.   It appears to have had, for a certain time at least, a fixed domicile, which everything tends to locate at Pré du Tour, where, moreover, a vague recollection of it is preserved.   Its name exists as that of a small hamlet situated on the left bank of the river, and overhanging the little valley.[525]   A house, which may be seen at the upper end of the hamlet, contained until lately a singular relic. It was a large stone table, more than two metres square, by ten centimetres in thickness, and weighing upwards of 80 tons. "It is generally believed," remarks the pastor of that locality in connection with this subject, "that around this table were gathered the pupils who attended the ancient school of the Barbes. More than a dozen can be accommodated very comfortably." "Formerly," he adds, "inscriptions might have been read upon it ; but now there is to be seen nothing but a cross, which might well be an argument in favour of the antiquity of the relic." The work necessary to reduce that enormous block of stone to the shape of a table, and the almost Cyclopean efforts necessary to transport it, and introduce it into the narrow room, wherein he found it, "show," says he, "very plainly that such labours were rather the work of an association of men, than of a single family."[526] Be that as it may, the name of college, fixed by local tradition, has survived, and it will be difficult to explain it without admitting the existence at Pré du Tour of the school of the Barbes. It would be interesting to know exactly what was taught at the Waldensian school. On this subject the Barbe Morel speaks as follows[527] :—

"All those who are to be received among us seek admission on their knees,[528] with the sole object of performing an act of humility, doing this while as yet they live with their parents. They ask, I say, those of us whom they meet, that we should be pleased to admit them to the ministry, and they ask us to pray to God for them that they may be rendered worthy of so high an office. When we assemble, we communicate their request to the brethren present, and if the applicants be well thought of, they are admitted by general consent to receive instruction. As almost all our new members come to us from the class of shepherds or husbandmen, they are mostly from 25 to 30 years of age, and quite illiterate. We keep them on trial for three or four years at most, and only during two or three months in winter, in order that we may be satisfied that their conduct is irreproachable.[529] This time is spent in teaching them to spell and read, and in making them learn by heart the Gospels of Matthew and John, the so-called canonical epistles, and a good portion of those written by St. Paul ; after which our new members are taken to a certain place, where several of our women, called sisters, live a single life. They live here for one, and sometimes two, years,

ordinarily attending to mundane duties, if I must so describe any.
Finally, the aforesaid pupils are admitted to the pastoral office,
and to preaching, through the ceremonies of laying on of hands and
the sacrament of the Eucharist; then duly instructed, they are
sent out in pairs to the work of evangelizing.[530]

According to this report, the school curriculum was very
elementary. It is difficult to find in it such elements of a complete preparation as have often been enumerated, viz., Latin
and the living languages, arithmetic, moral philosophy, and
the history of philosophy, medicine, surgery, and a technical and
professional education, besides fourfold theology.[531]  Again, if
Morel's words be authentic, it does not follow that they must be
literally applied to all the phases passed through by the School of
the Barbes, then in decadence and apparently dispersed, nor in a
special manner to the College of Pré du Tour, which he does not
mention.  During its flourishing period, that school might well
have been a focus of light without enforcing such a curriculum as
that to which we have just alluded.  Now it is this period that
seems to be reflected in the current tradition, and especially in a
page of Gilles, which may be worth while quoting :—

"This Waldensian people has had very learned pastors, as
appears from their writings, well versed in science, and languages,
and in understanding of the Holy Scriptures, and of the writings
of the doctors of the ancient church.  Above all, these Barbes
have been very laborious and watchful, both in instructing their
disciples properly in the love and fear of God, and in the
exercise of deeds of charity, and especially in transcribing for
the use of their disciples, before they had the conveniences of
printing, as much as possible the books of the Holy Scripture ; for, as they were themselves marvellously well versed
and assiduous in the reading of it, so did they carefully
recommend the perusal of it to their hearers.  They were very
careful in instructing the young, and especially the hopeful
students sent to them to be trained in true piety and the sciences.
From amongst these they selected such as in due time they
recognised to be fitted to enter the holy ministry, always retaining
them near themselves, and exercising them in all needful things,
until they could be usefully employed ; the others they sent back
to their parents, or taught them some honest trade.  Every one
of these Barbes, besides the knowledge and exercise of the

ministry, was acquainted with some trade, especially with medicine and surgery, in which they were very expert, and their skill was held in great esteem. They practised their art both with a view to render succour to their disciples, if need be, and to serve as a pretext for, and aid in defraying the expenses of their distant and dangerous travels." [532]

On reading those words, one understands how, under their modest name, the Barbes were, after Waldo, the fathers of the Waldensian Church. Every institution has its vicissitudes, and after progress comes decline. On the eve of the Reformation everything was on the decline—faith : light : life. But for the lantern of Morel, the school itself which represented these virtues, would have escaped our notice. It might be thought that the Waldensian people had disappeared. However, matters were not so bad as that, though after the Crusade, there was retrogression ; they hid ; they dissembled ; they kept silence. The Brethren of Bohemia were so startled by these signs of decay, that they demanded to know whether they were the only ones left to raise a protest. They determined upon an enquiry, and a deputation started for the East. After having visited Constantinople, Thrace, Palestine, and Egypt, it returned and related to the assembled brethren the result of its mission. It was pitiful and without fruit, they said ; their journey had been a useless undertaking. False doctrine, evil customs, superstition, and relaxed discipline, had become the general plague ; the world was sunken in iniquity. Some time after this enquiry—viz., in 1497—a new deputation composed of two men, the Bishop Lucas of Prague, who had led the first mission, and Thomas, the German, started for Italy and France. [533] This time the result was more encouraging, for in several localities throughout Italy, the deputies found hidden a remnant that still feared God. There was such in Rome, for instance, that avoided superstition and worldliness, thanks to its clandestine meetings, though it escaped death only through dissimulation. [534] One day the Brethren went to visit a Waldensian, and to him they spoke of Rome, of the Beast of the Apocalypse, and of the pomp and general corruption which then existed under the reign of the Borgias. The Waldensian deplored what he saw as much as they did, and waxed indignant.

" But why," he was asked, " do you not make a public protest ? "

That, he said, would be of much use, forsooth; he had known a man who had protested, and his fate was not such as to encourage others to follow him. This man dared to say quite loudly that Peter did not act as now did his successor. They took him, sewed him in a sack, and now he was drinking the water of the Tiber.[535] That was an instance of how it was free for some to sin to their heart's content, to perjure themselves, to lie, to wallow in all the vices; but as for telling the truth, that must be very circumspectly gone about, for the truth-teller's life was at stake. As for the speaker, he believed that it was better to eat the beast than to be devoured by it. He held to that.[536] He might be asked as to his duty to bear witness to the truth, but certainly he did not see why, in such times as these, it could be wrong to act as did Nicodemus, Joseph of Arimathea, and so many others.[537]

The good brethren were much displeased at all this.[538] On their homeward way it is conjectured that they may have been witnesses of the death of Savanarola in Florence. The purpose of their mission brought them—whether before or after their visit to Rome we cannot say—to the valleys of the Alps.[539] Here they were given a cordial reception and perfect unanimity.[540] They were impressed by the number of the Waldenses, and greatly rejoiced to see the spirit which animated them.[541] After having conferred with them to their hearts' content, and not without profit to both parties,[542] they departed, carrying away with them two letters in Latin, of which one was addressed by the Waldenses to King Ladislas the Clement, for the defence of their brethren who had taken refuge in Bohemia; the other from the pen of a certain Thomas " de fonte Citiculae," and destined for the missionary priests. The letter to Ladislas testifies not only to the survival of the Waldensian dissidence in the valleys of Piedmont, but also to the ardour of their polemics.[543] Oppression had only succeeded in arousing it still more. Being obliged to dissemble, it became concentrated, and was the more to be feared. It is not surprising that such as be oppressed lose patience. Let it be remembered, moreover, that this time they were subjected to a trial that threatened something more precious than life, for their morals were calumniated, and their wrath broke out at this. They protest that so far from its being true, as has been said, that in meetings they gave themselves up to acts of the most revolting immorality,[544] it is a notorious fact that for more than forty years not one among them had with impunity violated the rule of good morals.[545] Everything was allowable to the accusers, because the calumniated passed for heretics; but their adversaries, and not they, were the heretics.   By slander of that kind, their enemies had tried to persuade the King to drive them out of his kingdom as though they were plague-stricken.[546] Their reply to all calumnies and accusations was to ask that their lives might be equitably examined,[547] and their great hope was to be found worthy to suffer in the cause of justice.   Whatever might be done, they would never be shaken.   Who, they asked with the Apostle, should separate them from the love of Christ? Never should that plant, by God planted and watered with their own blood, be rooted up.   They asked the king to be sure of this: that rather than abandon the truth and follow the path of falsehood, they would, with Divine help, endure chains, prison, and exile, for a long time, and in all patience.[548] The reason that the Priests hated them was that their own deeds were evil, and the lives of those they hated condemned them.   They were hypocrites, given to all kinds of vice; they desecrated the temple of God, and drew down his just wrath upon themselves.   They were suffocated with their own fat, and inculcated the duty of fasting; they wallowed in debauchery and extolled chastity; they forbade people to enter inns, and when evening came they became drunk; it was when they were full of lust and iniquity that they dared to present themselves before God on behalf of sinners, though then their prayers might ascend no higher than the roof of the church.[549] The clergy thought only of wielding power and heaping up treasures, and by their means the church was being peopled with such as were as horses and mules, in despite of the Holy Spirit, who said by the mouth of the prophet: "Be ye not as the horse or as the mule, which have no understanding."

The analogy between mules and monks was drawn, and it was sought to be shown that as the mule is neither a horse nor an ass, so is the monk neither man nor devil.[550]   To go to church where such men officiated was a crime.[551]   The monks and priests were become as filth, like the smoke of the lamp that goes out, leaving only darkness and a mortal stench.[552]

The boldness of this language betrays the influence of the Bohemian Brethren, who had sufficiently reproached the Waldenses for their indecision.   This influence is furthermore acknowledged in another writing, only a few years later, in which the Waldenses explained the reason for their separation from the Romish Church.[553] We shall have to return to this. It is impossible after these events to follow the circumstances of that revival of Waldensian independence which preceded the Reformation, with its vicissitudes, the power it exerted, and the reactions it underwent. After a virulent protest, came compromises. To speak of hating the Church and having no part with the Priests, was very easy ; but it provoked annoyances of all kinds ; it was a step on the road to martyrdom, especially when every move was spied upon ;[554] for among those imitators of the Apostles, Judases were found. There is nothing surprising in this, but it is none the less distressing to be compelled to admit that it is true. " Among the people of the lower class "—we are quoting the words of Barbe Morel of Freyssinières—" we have false brethren, who go secretly to the monks, bishops, magistrates, or other agents of Antichrist, and say to them, ' What will you give us if we deliver the doctors of the Waldenses into your hands ? We know where they are hiding.' " " As a matter of fact, we do not dare to show ourselves everywhere publicly. When we do, they consult together, after which these agents come in the night time, often without our knowledge armed to arrest us. Thus does persecution begin anew ; it ordinarily happens that one among us is led to the stake, sometimes followed to his execution by several of our people ; sometimes instead he is forced to pay a large sum of money."[555] Under such circumstances one understands how, in order to avoid danger, more than one Waldensian would still attend mass,[556] and, instead of the Ave Maria, say, perhaps, in an undertone : " Den of bandits, may God confound thee ! "[557] words which clash somewhat with the Liturgy. All this was possible, even before the revival ; it is the shade in the picture. According to the allusions of Claude of Sayssel, Archbishop of Turin, in the first days of Luther's protest[558] the revival continued, and the small people he despised was still to be feared in its profound retreat. He ascertained, indeed, the existence of a state not far removed from schism, for the Waldenses professed that the sacraments were not to be received save from the hands of a priest ;[559] he deplores the fact that certain people should believe the words of their heretical Barbes ;[56ᴶ] he believed it opportune to write a book to refute their tenets, and, before laying down the pen, he entreats his flock not to give heed to " those false prophets who come to them in sheep's clothing, but inwardly are ravening wolves."[561]  The Prelate had not finished writing his polemic, when the world resounded with the cry of alarm sent out from Wittemberg, and beyond any doubt, more than one echo reverberated through the Alpine Valleys.  The following year Luther appeared before the Diet of Worms, only to disappear immediately from the public stage into his retreat at Wartburg.  When he was thought to be dead he descended from the mountain, like Moses, with the book of God; and the Reformation spread from city to city.  At the same time it had sprung up in Zurich and Basle, whilst it permeated the surrounding country, thanks to the preaching of Zwingle and Œcolampadus.  A son of Dauphiny then came to Geneva and found the lamp of faith, at the point of extinction.  Upon it could still be read the inscription : " *Post tenebras spero lucem.*"  Farel relighted it, and its first beams came to meet the little taper that had shone alone from the candlestick of the Alps.  Three generations before, it is said that Bishop Reiser, on the point of death, had declared that the Waldensian reaction was about to disappear in Germany. It did disappear indeed, like the morning star, which is lost in the full light of day.  When the sun of the Reformation arose, the Waldensian light was shining still, if not as brightly, at least as purely as in the past ; but in the presence of the new sun, it might well appear to have grown paler.  Morel testifies to this with childlike simplicity, and an ingenuous joyful expectation, which recalls that of the prophets of old : " Welcome ! blessed be thou, my Lord," he writes to the Basle reformer ; " we come to thee from a far off country, with hearts full of joy, in the hope and assurance that, through thee, the Spirit of the Almighty will enlighten us."[562]

That is the last word of the history of the Waldenses before the Reformation. The cry of the navigator, who, at the early dawn, saw the New World appear, was neither more sincere, nor more joyous, nor yet of better omen.  It was as if, from the valleys there re-echoed the voice of Simeon, welcoming again the Saviour of the Israel of the Alps.

# CHAPTER THE FIFTH.

## LITERATURE.

*Preliminary remarks.—The Waldensian dialect and a general view of materials.—*VERSIONS OF THE SCRIPTURES*—Early versions which have disappeared—Those of Waldo and the Waldenses of Metz—Ancient versions that have survived, but which are contested—Manuscript versions of Lyons and Paris—More recent but recognised versions—MSS. of Cambridge, Grenoble, Dublin, and Zurich—Comparative specimens —Connection between these versions and what is inferred therefrom with respect to their origin—A version in a foreign tongue—MS. of Tepl.—*PROSE WRITINGS*—Those which have perished—Gleanings of original writings—Compilations from a Catholic source—The Doctor and the Orchard—Brainless treatise—The commentary on the Lord's Prayer—The Virtues, the Canticles—Compilations from a Hussite source— The epistle to King Ladislas—The treatise upon the cause of breaking with the Romish Church—The collection of the Treasure and the Light of Faith, containing The Ten Commandments, the Seven Sacraments, Purgatory, the Invocation of Saints—The Power granted to the Vicars of Christ, Antichrist, and the Minor Interrogations—*POETICAL WRITINGS —Contempt for the world—The Bark—The Lord's Prayer or confession of sins—The new comfort—The new sermon— The Parable of the Sower—The Father Eternal—Finally, the Noble Lesson, with critical notes—The conclusions from this chapter summarized.*

WALDO commenced his work with the assistance of two scribes. Without being a man of letters, he gave birth to a literature which was not only fortunate enough to live, but to survive much that disappeared ; that of the Cathari, for instance.[563] Viewed from a distance, it strikes the eye, much as might an oasis in the desert. Gleaners have been attracted to its field even before the harvest not yet ended. Let us also enter there to bind, if it may be, our sheaf, or glean at least a few ears of corn. In order to enter, it is necessary to have the key. Now everyone knows that the key to any literature is the dialect in which it is written.

For the sake of greater clearness, let us with a good guide begin on this subject at a somewhat early period.

"After the Romans had conquered a country, they wished to force their language upon it. They were, in many cases, almost completely successful; but by the continual commerce between the conquerors and the conquered, Latin soon became corrupted. This corruption was, in different parts of the vast empire of the Cæsars, according to the influences which were at work, brought about in different ways. We may say that the popular language was soon subdivided into as many varieties as there had been, before the Conquest, populations speaking different languages. Of the dialects thus produced, some, owing to a combination of fortunate circumstances, obtained a political and literary development, which has raised them to the rank of *languages;* such are French, Spanish, Portuguese, Italian, Provençal, and Wallachian. Others, on the contrary, remained uncultured and confined within narrow limits; these fell to the level of *patois.* The different patois or dialects of France are not, as has long been supposed, degenerate offspring of the French language; they are its real brethren, humble and rustic, it is true, but legitimate offshoots from the same stock, though their development ceased at different periods of their growth. The patois of France may be subdivided into two great classes; some approximate to the French language or *langue d'oïl*, others to the Provençal or *langue d'oc.* The *langue d'oïl* prevails in Dauphiny, as far as the right bank of the Isère, between the Rhone and the mouth of the Bourne, there it crosses the river to take in a portion of Royannais, Vercors, the valley of Gresse, that of Drac, as far as the Trièves, and finally, the lower portion of the valley of Romanche. From the Grave, the boundary line seems to follow high crests of mountains, almost deserted, in the direction of Mount Thabor, and onwards to Mont Cenis. Following from north to south, between Mount Thabor and Mount Viso, the principal chain of the Alps, which forms the dividing line of the waters, there is found on the eastern slope the valleys of Bardonnèche, Oulx, and Pragelas, which now belong to Italy. Descending toward the south there are found the valleys of St. Martin, Angrogna, and Luserna, generally known by the name of the Waldensian valleys. Still further south, upon the side of Mount Viso, the valley of the Po begins, and debouches in the plains of Saluces. At the southern extremity of the Marquisate of Saluces lies the valley of the Vraite. On the western slope are the valleys of Monetier, Nevache, Bryançon, Queyras, Vallouise, and Argentière. These last two extend as far as the slopes of Mount Pelvoux. The region we have just indicated, forms, in the very centre of the Alps, a distinct country, with customs and languages peculiar to itself. This latter, which is a dialect of the *langue d'oc*, has almost become a language, thanks to the writings of the Waldenses, but being constantly encroached upon by its two powerful neighbours—Italian and French—it has shown a tendency to disappear. Reduced to the condition of a mere colloquial patois, it is losing its traditions, its rules, its unity, and is becoming subdivided into a certain number of local varieties, in which the ancient terms are gradually making way for the words of the languages taught in the schools, these being more or less disfigured by the effects of local pronunciation." [564]

Thus far philologists being thoroughly agreed, we may enter upon the special subject under consideration.

If the dialect of Queyras appears to have withstood foreign influences better than the others, that of the Waldenses has not been totally absorbed. Having been more than its neighbours employed in writings, we can understand how that circumstance would for centuries contribute to the preservation of the Vaudois dialect, and we might be amazed that to this day its character has not been more perfectly described, if we did not know that it had not been sufficiently used in writing to become thoroughly established as a language. This is no doubt the reason why its origin and formation are still discussed, without any definite or unanimous conclusion being arrived at. Let us first repeat the contradictory opinions brought out by the discussion. Perrin hardly touches the point. He simply says that the writings of the Waldenses have been recorded ,in a language " partly Provençal and partly Piedmontese." Gilles, Léger, and their successors, do not question his opinion, which is probably based upon tradition. If this be so, from the very first, criticism has attempted to correct it. It is well known that the researches of the critics were inaugurated by their leader, Raynouard, and that he expressed himself most unmistakably on this subject. " The Waldensian dialect is identical with the Romance language," he says; and goes on to state that " the slight modifications, noticeable when it is compared with the language of the Troubadours, are explainable in such away as to render additional proofs of this identity."[565]

Those are the two principal opinions, which to this day have striven for the mastery. We may profitably examine authorities before arriving at any conclusion as to which view should have the preference.

Diez writes : " The original birth-place of the Waldensian dialect must be the Lyonnais, where Peter Waldo lived. The dialect became properly Waldensian, only by the emigration into Piedmont of Waldo's followers, the dialect of that country having an influence upon the language, which was originally Provençal." [566] As to the relation between the Provençal and the Lyonnais, W. Foerster, a worthy successor of Diez, in a letter addressed to the writer, has shown that in certain particulars, the Lyonnais escapes from the influence of the Provençal, and that it deviates from the Waldensian dialect and approaches the French.[567] Therefore, there is no reason for deriving the Waldensian dialect from that of Lyons.[568] There may be nothing to prevent the idea that the primitive Waldenses carried the Lyonnais dialect with them into the Valleys ; but before admitting that it was implanted, there some traces of it should be pointed out. Thus far, no one has succeeded in doing this. Furthermore, the influence of the Piedmontese dialect must not be exaggerated. Diez lays too much stress upon it. If the old Waldensian seems to him already different from the Provençal in some of its phonic characters, the modern Waldensian is still further removed, " approaching the Italian " to such a degree that " its derivation from the ancient language is subject to great doubts."[569] Grüzmacher was inclined to favour this opinion,[570] as well as Herzog and Dieckhoff.[571] Montet adopts it resolutely, almost word for word ;[572] he even goes further. According to him, " the Piedmontese dialect eventually took the place of the Waldensian " as early as the times of the Reformation. As a proof, he states that " the acts of the

Synod of Angrogna of 1532 are written in a language greatly resembling the Italian "[573] But the language in which these acts are recorded not only *resembles* Italian, it *is* Italian, as it was then spoken. It would be a rash conclusion to determine the character of the local dialect from the more or less frequent use of that language in official documents, and we should be obliged to draw an altogether different one from the use of the French language, when it in turn was introduced. Montet is on this point quite moderate when compared with Muston, who dates the first influence of Italian a few centuries back, in order that the birth of the Waldensian dialect may be attributed to it. He gives himself up so entirely to this opinion, that, in the face of the most reliable results obtained by the study of the Neo-Latin languages, he has quite the appearance of wishing to uproot Waldensian dialect from its natural soil for the purpose of relegating it, we know not whither ; for he does not succeed in classifying it as he claims, " with the family of dialects of Italian formation."[574] Perhaps he hopes, by this new device, to restore faith in Waldensian apostolic antiquity.[575] If so, his argument is founded on a wrong basis.[576] On the one hand, he tries to prove that which needs no proof, namely, that the Waldensian language cannot be numbered amongst " the French family ;"[578] while on the other, he invokes the support of the masters of comparative philology to refute the results obtained from the history of the Neo-Latin idioms.[579] Indeed, if there be a point now thoroughly established, it is that the origin and character of the Waldensian dialect are Provençal. The facts are indeed so striking—at least for those who make the matter a subject of special and thorough study— that it is useless to contest them. Professor W. Foerster writes : " The Waldensian dialect prior to the Reformation was purely Provencal in its idiom. With regard to the modern Waldensian dialect it also is pure Provençal ; but we must be on our guard against comparing it with the old Provençal. We shall be convinced of this if we compare it with the modern patois of Provence on the Italian side of the Rhone. I must, however, after my recent researches, confess that the traces to be found in it of the influence of the Piedmontese, are more insignificant than I had expected to find, though La Tour is, of course, not the place in which it would be easiest to find these influences. Wherever the Piedmontese of the plain had not penetrated, the Provençal dialect has as to its construction remained intact. It is true that there exist a certain number of words common to the Waldenses and Piedmontese and unknown on the other slope of the Cottian Alps ; but that number is exceedingly small." As for the words which we owe to the slow but irresistible influence of the French language, it is very well known that they do not suffice to alter the fundamental constitution of Waldensian dialect.

Thus the progress of linguistic science brings us back to the principle established by Raynouard, according to whom the Waldensian dialect is Provençal, both in origin and character, though contrary opinions are still by some maintained, less, however, with reference to the more or less ancient written speech than to the colloquial dialect, which has a tendency to deviate from it.[580] While the French continues its deleterious reducing action, the influence of the Piedmontese patois and of the Italian language have grown stronger, especially since the political events, which unified Italy and gave the Waldenses public life. Waldensian dialect, Provençal as to its origin, is being transformed and resolved into its constituents, not only in the Valley of Luserna, but also in that of Pérouse, more and more may we, therefore, expect it to assimilate the patois of Piedmont. Some think that a process of degradation may go on, which will ultimately cause it to be classed with secondary or tertiary groups of dialects still unspecified. A " secondary group of dialects, having a Latin basis, and holding an intermediate place between the tongues of *oc* and of *si* on the one side, and the tongue of oïl on the other," is vaguely spoken of, upon the authority of Professor P. Meyer, who seems at one time to maintain that the language of the Waldensian Valleys resembles the Provençal most ; at another, that it has most affinity with the Italian, while at yet another time he impartially declares that it is a " romance language, like Italian and Provençal, but equally distant from both."[582] Facts show that if the influence of Piedmontese and French be undeniable, the Provençal basis is still there, evident and visible.

When we go back to the early transformations of the dialect, or seek to separate it from the mother branch, there is difficulty in understanding how the genesis and formation of Waldensian literature may be explained. Muston, the poet, in his mind's eye, saw literature springing up upon the Italian side of the Alps, even before Waldo's time ;[583] but such an idea need only be mentioned to be dismissed. Herzog himself was not far from going astray, when he thought that the Waldensian writings, already partly compiled upon a Latin basis, had donned a Provençal form in their second edition, and had afterwards undergone a new revision in order to become Vaudois.[584] A literature so edited would thus be the one presented by the existing manuscripts. There is no need for such an hypothesis as that of Herzog. The ancient writings did not need to be re-translated into Provençal; they *were* Provençal, and their Waldensian character is revealed by very slight modifications, of which Montet, as quoted by Grüzmacher, has given us an interesting specimen.[585]

The origin and place of the Waldensian dialect having been indicated, the writings now come up for examination.

These writings, as MSS. of the thirteenth, fourteenth, fifteenth, and sixteenth centuries, are to be found in some ten libraries, namely, those of Cambridge, Dublin, Paris, Grenoble, Carpentras, Geneva, Zurich, Munich, Lyons, and the village of Tepl in Bohemia.[586] Unfortunately, the history of these MSS. for the most part escapes research, and we must be content to glean a few items of information about the collections of Cambridge and Dublin. Archbishop Usher was the first to conceive the idea of making these collections. As early as 1611, he was in search of documents relating to Waldensian history, and in 1634, he obtained from a French lawyer a series of very rare Waldensian writings, for which he paid about 550 francs. The series passed in its entirety to the library of Trinity College, Dublin. When in 1655, by order of Cromwell, Samuel Morland betook himself to the Duke of Savoy to plead the cause of the persecuted Waldenses, he was exhorted by the old Archbishop, then almost on his death-bed, to profit by this opportunity for procuring memoirs, and other authentic writings which might serve to throw some new new light on Waldensian tenets. The British envoy took the matter up heartily, and, on his return, placed a valuable collection of ancient manuscripts in the library of Cambridge University. During the eighteenth century, an Italian assistant at the library catalogued the collection among the Spanish writings, so that until 1862, their existence was unknown. We can only surmise whence the manuscripts which are kept in the library of Geneva came. In 1662, Léger deposited there a volume which cannot be identified from the description he gives of it.

Upon the cover of one of the manuscripts there is found an endorsement, which states that it belongs to the churches of the Valleys of Piedmont, "who pray the Genevese to keep it for them."

As will be readily seen, these details are far from furnishing us with the necessary elements for an historical description of the sources of Waldensian literature. It might be thought that a chronological catalogue of these writings would be of service, but as yet no arrangement of them has been made, and what is to be desired is the work of elimination and expurgation, rather than any addition to the compilations already in existence.[587] Meanwhile, such a general classification as will serve the purpose of the narrative, must for the present be made to suffice.

The two scribes who worked with Waldo—one in the capacity of a translator and compiler, the other as a copyist—seem to have been the prototypes of a long succession of translators or compilers and copyists. If Waldensian literature does not shine by its originality, it must be remembered that the ancient Waldenses were not ambitious for literary fame. Those who reflect, will agree that they had not leisure for writing, their whole lives being spent in action.

Below is given a list of the versions of the Bible due to that zeal in them for the Word of God; which absorbed, as it were, nearly all the literary faculty they may have possessed. Afterwards some mention will be made of their profane writings in prose and poetry.

## I.—THE EARLY VERSIONS.

It is admitted, without contention, that attempts at the translation of the Scriptures into the vulgar tongue had been made before the appearance of Waldo, and that they served to sustain, in some measure, the faith of believers, and to feed dissent. Whether the Cathari were the authors, or even the users, of some of the translations is not certain.[588]

"The French Bible of the Middle Ages dates its origin back to the first years of the XII. century at least."[589] Lambert le Bègue, a contemporary of Waldo, busied himself with the translation of the Scriptures. Nevertheless, it may be said with truth that the study of the Bible, which marks the commencement of

Waldensian history, also imbues its primitive literature in an eminent degree.[590] This is an incontestible fact, but it has been exaggerated—so much so, that every time a new feature comes to light in connection with the Scriptural movement of the Middle Ages, more than one writer hastens to recognize its Waldensian origin.[591] Is a discovery of translations prior to Waldo made, straightway without pausing they dash at a conclusion. They argue that, as they find in the writing under investigation, literal quotations from the Scriptures which are also found in this or the other ancient poem of the Waldenses, the poem must necessarily date from Waldo's time, or perhaps to a time anterior, and thus a conclusion is rapidly and illogically arrived at. If such reasoners were satisfied with agreeing that Waldo had predecessors, their logic would not be so much at fault; but with this they do not rest content—they claim that the versions anterior to Waldo are necessarily Waldensian, without considering that what they advance as proofs are only very bad speculations, and they cite quotations which are nowhere to be found. "I formally deny," says Reuss, "that in any of those poems there is a single literal quotation from the Bible; if there were any they might be taken directly from the Latin."[592] Moreover, there is no Waldensian poem which dates back so far as the time of Waldo.

### (A) Waldo's Translation.

The circumstances of the coming into existence of Waldo's translation will be remembered.[593] Waldo desired to understand the Gospels, and being a man of little education, he procured the assistance of two priests, residents of Lyons, like himself. One was a grammarian called Stephen, from the city of Anse, above Lyons, on the Saône, where at a later period he held an office in the cathedral. The other, Bernard Ydros, was a scribe by profession. The merchant divided the work between them in the following manner:—One was to dictate the translation in the vulgar tongue, the other was to write it. "In this manner they wrote several books of the Bible, together with numerous *excerpta* from the Saints, grouped under titles; these they called sentences."[594] According to this testimony, which is entitled to more credit than any other [595] Waldo's share in this work was large though modest. He is really entitled to the whole merit, though to give him this it is not necessary to surround him with a literary aureola or make him out a critic. Gilly, with misplaced zeal, goes so far as to see in Lyons, a committee of revision analogous to those that have sprung from the modern school.[596] However powerful our imagination may be, we cannot picture to ourselves Waldo shut up in his study, like a cathedral Canon, carefully and painfully collating the manuscripts of Vercelli, Brescia, and Verona, to disentangle from them the reading to be adopted in the subsequent versions, in France as well as in Italy, and even in Spain.[597] Amusing though it be, under this fiction lies concealed, nevertheless, a serious idea, of which we shall speak further on. In the domain of fact we shall find something which concerns the early Waldensian version.

From 1173 or 1177, the date of Waldo's conversion, to 1179, the date of the third Lateran Council, to which from Lyons went the Waldensian deputation, the interval is too short to expect that in it there originated any new translation, other than that of which we have been speaking. The Waldensian translation, seen at Rome, and presented to Alexander III., was therefore Waldo's, augmented perhaps, and already revised. Now, what follows is the testimony of an onlooker; it has already been cited, and need now merely be recalled. "We saw at the Council," he writes, "some Waldenses, who presented our Lord the Pope with a book, written in the Gallic tongue, and containing the text and the gloss of the Psalter, and a great number of the books of the two Testaments."[598] That is what Map, according to Stephen of Bourbon, tells us. Both of them might well have been more explicit—we should like to know more of the nature of that translation, its extent and its language. Two elements in it must be kept separate—the translation and the annotations; Reuss attempted to define them, but did not succeed. If it were proven that Map examined the books to which he alludes, and that he was sufficiently well acquainted with the dialect in which they were written, Reuss thinks that "we should necessarily be obliged to admit that the work of the Lyonnese was an annotated Bible, and as that kind of edition or copy was very common, that would create no difficulty."[599] On the other hand, is it not probable that if Map had been commissioned to carry on a discussion with the Waldensian deputies, he must have been able to go into their affairs with some knowledge of the matter ? If we admit that, we are therefore brought to believe that the first Waldensian version comprised a certain number of more or less isolated books, accompanied by notes, if not commentaries, all collected into one volume.[600] It was at most a collection, as Tron says, "somewhat complete." As for the language employed, that is sufficiently indicated by the local circumstances attending its publication. It was the language then spoken at Lyons. But what was that? This question, so natural thirty-five years ago, is now about to find a definite solution. The ancient Lyonnese dialect would seem to be "one of the best known" among those which abounded in France. It is classified with the Franco-Provençal group.[601] If this be so, Reuss may legitimately repeat, that it is "impossible to admit that the dialect used by the three citizens of Lyons in their work was the same as we find in the Waldensian documents."[602] There is no longer any danger of confounding it with that of Provence, which served for other translations. What are we to conclude, if not that the original Waldensian translation has disappeared ? Only, that this disappearance may, after all, be more apparent than real. It is thought to be lost, and rightly so ; but it might be buried where it is not sought for, namely, in one or several of the subsequent versions, commencing with that of Metz, to which we are now about to turn our attention.

(B) *The Translation of the Waldenses of Metz.*

Here, again, let us briefly recall some circumstances which have already been adverted to.[603] This time we have a Pope for witness ; but his testimony is not immediate. The reader will remember, that in his answer to Bishop Bertram, Innocent III. wrote : " You intimated to me by letter, that in the diocese of Metz, as well as in the city itself, a multitude of laymen and women, carried away by I trow not what desire to know the Holy Scriptures, had the Gospels, the Epistles of St. Paul, the Psalter, the Moralities on Job, and several other books translated for them into French." [604] On this subject he asks for certain explanations which have been lost to us.[605]

The testimony of Innocent III. does not take us very far; still he learned what he here states, from a man at Metz, best qualified to supply information ; he adopts the report unquestioningly, as in fact his investigation is founded thereon. Indeed, he requires nothing further than to discover the author of the translation, and to verify in what spirit it was written.[606] We can form a shrewd guess from a hint that follows. Possibly the author was one Crespin, a priest, if not a friend of the Bishop, for the latter particularly complains of the clergy.[607] Be that as it may, the translation was made at the express invitation of the Waldenses,[608] who in this imitated the example of their leader. It could only have been written from the Latin text, in the dialect of the country.[609] When the clergy came on the scene to destroy it, some copies that fell into their hands were consigned to the flames.[610]

This seems to us to be clearly shown by the testimony we have just adduced, wherefore we must, to our regret, decline to follow Berger in his somewhat speculative deductions. " Did it occur to anyone," he writes in connection with this, " to consider that the question may here refer to something altogether different from a translation of the four Gospels and the fourteen epistles of St. Paul, which are supposed to have disappeared without leaving any trace ? Suppose we were to light upon a manuscript of *The Gospels and Epistles for Sundays and Feast Days*, with an extensive commentary; suppose this manuscript were by its language referable to Lorraine, by its origin to Metz, and that its date carried us back almost precisely to the time of Innocent III., could one refuse to recognize in it a stray relic of Waldensian literature, and even a witness of the persecutions of 1139 ? What if the very size and the whole condition of the manuscript seem to indicate one of those little unpretending, inexpensive books made to be kept concealed, such as the books favoured by the middle classes at Metz and the Poor of Lyons must have been ? It is a small volume, written in long lines, the text in red, the gloss in black. The character of the handwriting belongs to a period, not later than the beginning of the XIII. century. The last sheet contains Indulgences granted to the Minorite Brethren, written a hundred years later. As Abbé Lebeuf remarked, the volume contains the Gospels appointed for the last fortnight in Lent, with some Epistles for the same season, and the gloss attributed to Haimon."

Berger then goes on to quote the first lines of this gloss, adding these reflections: "There never was seen a more pious work, more sober in sentiment, less tainted with the jargon and subtleties of the Schools—in a word, more suited to the edification of those simple and pious folk called the Waldenses. Nor would its title in those days imply the slightest reflection upon their religion, while in point of orthodoxy, the commentary is irreproachable, and this, too, is quite the character which marks not a Vaudois book, for the Waldenses were not at that time bringing out books, but a pious work, such as they would have got translated and must have cherished. Among the hundreds of manuscripts of the French Bible which have been preserved, almost all more or less annotated and with commentaries; this assuredly is the only one in which both commentary and text might find acceptance with Christians even at the present day, whatever their form of worship."[611]

Curious and interesting as are such reflections, they do not suffice to convince us. We shall offer no objection on linguistic grounds, although the question of language, discussed by the Secretary to the Protestant Theological Faculty of Paris, is from what we can learn still far from being solved. We will assume that "this New Testament in the Lorraine dialect, presents all the features of the orthography used at Metz in the most ancient records;" nor shall we stop to "inquire whether this manuscript, in the same hand throughout, does not present inequalities of idiom, warranting the conclusion that there is a difference between the dialect in which it was written, and that in which it was copied." Even if that be granted, would that solve the question as a whole? With difficulty, for in the first place, whereas it was a question of a translation, it is now only that of Lessons, with comment and gloss;[612] secondly—and this point seems important—the Vaudois' version contained the Psalms, but the book referred to by Berger does not. He is surprised that the Metz translation should have disappeared "without leaving any trace;" but is he not content to believe that perhaps the same thing happened to that of Lyons—a hundred times more important from the greatness of its prestige and the precious recollections which surround it? If the Metz translation did disappear, it was probably because it was Waldensian; while Haimon's paraphrased version survives, doubtless because nothing about it rendered it suspicious ;

neither its orthodoxy, which is irreproachable, nor the name of its author, who was no less a personage than the Bishop of Halberstadt.[613] Could Bertram have been ignorant of the fact that this was the translation of a pious Catholic manual, written by a brother Churchman? If he knew, why keep silent about it in his first letter to the Pontiff, and above all, why be scandalized? If he did not know, must we assume that the inquiry directed by Innocent III., and carried out by the clergy was insufficient to open his eyes? But then, why should the clergy burn the translation? We do not refuse to recognise the relation, if any there be, between the above-mentioned Book of the Gospels and the Biblical movement of Metz; but why should this exclude a less fragmentary translation? When Berger tells us that "the Psalters, with and without annotations, were numerous at the end of the XII. century," and reminds us "that the period about 1170, was marked by one of the most remarkable Biblical movements in all the region which extends from Lyons to the country of the Walloons," we have no option but to conclude, without him it is true, that there must have been sufficient in the world at that time, both for the Waldensian version and the translation of the manual of the Halberstadt Bishop.[614]

This is what we had to say on the subject of our early Biblical translations.

Thus far the result of our researches has only been to notice translations that have disappeared. But others survived the persecution. First, there are one or two ancient ones, more or less contested; then comes a comparatively modern version. Let us speak of them with their manuscripts, according to their chronological order.

## II.—The Ancient Versions.

Each is represented by one manuscript.

### (A) *The Manuscript of Lyons.*[615]

There are several features which call the attention of the critic to the manuscript of Lyons. It is somewhat unique, as compared with those that will follow it in this summary. It differs from them indeed, and in more than one respect—first, outwardly; then, by the order in which the books are placed. First come the Gospels, the Acts, then the Apocalypse and the General Epistles; finally, the Epistles of Paul; but with this two-fold peculiarity, namely, that the Epistles to the Thessalonians precede that to the Colossians, and that the latter is followed by the Epistle to the Laodiceans, known during the middle ages, but since forgotten. Then, if we note that it is not divided into chapters as at present, we have proof that the manuscript of Lyons dates back to a remote period, inasmuch as this division was introduced in the year 1260, and was not received until much later.[616] The text presents but two omissions.[617]. To this in itself very significant feature, are added others, which show it to be necessarily a manuscript of the XIII. century. It betrays, moreover, a hand that is ill-acquainted with Latin. Is it the hand of a Waldensian? Fleck, of Giessen, who was the first to examine the manuscript of Lyons, attributed the translation of it to the Waldenses; he hesitated a little, however, doubting whether it might not come equally well from the sect of the Albigenses. He conferred with Fauriel, who went no further than to establish that its language differs from the Roman spoken in the valley of the Rhone. Gilly as well as Muston number it among the Waldensian manuscripts, without taking into account the considerable difference there is between it and the dialect of the Alps. According to Reuss, the contrast is striking. Comparing, from a linguistic point of view, the Lyons translation with the version of the manuscripts of Zurich and Dublin, he writes: "Not only does the linguistic material differ, each making use of a great number of words unknown to the other, but the grammar also is subject to other rules, other forms, other terminations. Of course, in comparing the two dialects with Northern French, and that of to-day, these shades of difference seem to disappear. On both sides is found a form of language which may be called Provençal, if this term be taken in a very wide sense; but only the most superficial carelessness, and a total absence of philological instinct, can avoid noticing the differences. The dialect of the manuscripts of Zurich and Dublin, which we are told is really of the Valleys of Piedmont, is akin to the Italian; it is most certainly an Alpine dialect, and we readily admit that it belongs to the eastern slope of the range. The dialect of the Lyons manuscript has nothing in common with the forms peculiar to the Italian; it is akin to

Spanish. It belongs to the family of those dialects that were comprised in the Limosine language, one which was formerly proper to the countries that extend from Auvergne to Murcia, and whose principal seat was Catalogne and Languedoc."[618] Thereupon Reuss states, " with perfect assurance," that the translation we are speaking of is the Cathari in origin and character. His opinion is the generally received one, and more especially so since the discovery made by one of his colleagues. This, in a few words, is the question.

The text of the Lyons translation is followed by a few leaves, containing, as some have thought, a small ritual belonging to the sect of the Cathari, or Albigenses. Cunitz is the author of that discovery, and he hastened to publish the said ritual with some very useful notes.[619] From that moment the question was settled, for Reuss first of all, and then for Herzog, Berger, and other writers, with the exception of Pœrster, who has not yet hauled down his colours, and who deserves attention. In 1872, this learned philologist devoted his holidays to the transcription of the entire Gospel of St. John, which he printed six years later.[620] He did not lose sight of this work, which he must have desired to complete. His opinion is therefore also based upon experience, as well as that which, as we saw was so positively expressed. Here it is: "The dialect of the Lyonnese New Testament is pure Provençal, as spoken on the right bank of the Rhone, probably in the departments of the Aude or the Tarn. I believe that version to be Waldensian ; only the dialect in which it is written is not the same as it was known in the valleys. It is only quite in its infancy, and the homogeneous relations between the two, does not imply an identity, which is lacking. I repeat, in my opinion, the Lyonnese manuscript belongs to the Waldenses. It is well known that they were numerous, especially in the department of Tarn." This is what the Professor at Bonn writes : " Here again we would not desire anything better than to be able to adopt his· view, but there is one little difficulty we cannot get over. Admitting, what does not seem to be absolutely incontestible, that the Lyonnese manuscript was written in the district indicated by Fœrster, what positive reason have we for believing that it was the work of the Waldenses ? They were numerous there, he observes, but were not the Albigenses there before them ? It seems sufficient to us to recall the fact that, among the localities comprised in this department, is that of Albi, whence the Cathari derived the name which they bear in the South of France. However, we desired to place on record here the statement of the learned philologist, and we shall follow it up with an avowal made by Reuss himself. "I can affirm in the most formal and positive manner," writes the latter, "that the version of the Cathari, such as I know it through the manuscript of Lyons, shows not the slightest trace of the dogmas peculiar to that sect."[621] After this, what can we say, but that the ritual alone may decide the question, to some extent at least? Fœrster, who has lately examined it again, thinks that it is not as certainly belonging to the Cathari, as is pretended, and he inclines to the belief that it is Waldensian.[622] This is not our opinion. We believe the ritual presents unequivocal traces of Catharism. The mention of the doxology in the Lord's Prayer, which is foreign to the Vulgate and Romish worship; the quotation of the Prologue to the Gospel of John, which was ordinarily used in the Albigenses' worship; the act of confession and the expression referring to the sins of the flesh, especially the ceremony of the *consolamentum* or spiritual baptism, are enough to give us grounds for an opinion as to the origin of the ritual,[623] even though we do recognize that it does not reveal that dualism which distinguishes, even in its moderate creeds, the sect of the Cathari; but for this, there is a very simple reason after all, namely, that to proclaim this dualism in acts of worship was contrary to usage.[624] With these reservations, it seems to us that too absolute an importance has been given here to the fact of the ritual being appended. It has been held, indeed, that the biblical passages quoted, agree in a striking manner with the corresponding text of the translation opposite; but care has been taken to add also, that there is more than one variation, hence some exceptions. This ritual does not prove that the version it accompanies is of Catharin origin, but only that the Albigenses adopted it. If the fact of a ritual being appended were sufficient to settle, once for all, a question of this kind, this argument in itself would settle the question relating to the version of Tepl, which is at present so much the subject of controversy.

## (B) *The Paris Manuscript.*

This manuscript presents to us the books of the New Testament, with several omissions.[626] The order of these books is not that of the Vulgate, nor that of our ordinary Bibles. The Acts follow the Gospels it is true, but the General Epistle precede those of Paul, as in the Greek manuscripts, as well as in diverse documents of the Middle Ages. The text is not here divided into chapters, as it is now; it reminds one of the lectionaries of the ancient Church. The portions taken for the Gospels and Epistles for Sundays and Feast-days are marked, either by means of special titles, or by an intervening space and a difference in the writing. Thus far the age of the manuscript has not been ascertained; but several indications—notably those having a bearing upon the language—serve to show that it is very ancient. The preface fixes the date of it within the first half of the XIV. century, and Berger confirms this point. The dialect in which it is written was the Provençal; hence it is not demonstrated that the editing was the work of the Waldenses; nay, more, there is nothing to prove that it was done by their desire. Still, this or that feature seems to betray a significant usage; thus, for instance, the index, which marginally notes those passages which were the ordinary subject of Waldensian preaching. According to Berger, that indication betrays the hand of a Waldensian collater.[627*] More than one passage should be read, however, before arriving at conviction. Here are a couple of examples :—

Non vulhas temer, petita companha, quar plac a vostre payre dar a vos lo regne. Car ieu habitaray en els e seray lur dieus et il seran mon pobol. Car laveniment del senhor sappropria. Car ancar un petit tant o cant cel que es avenir venra e non tarzara.[627*]

The following passage betrays both grotesque and menacing features :—

O vas ricz fatz ara ploras u dolas. Las vostras riquezas son fachas poyridas e las vostras vestimentas son maniadas darnas.[628]

We again affirm that it would be arbitrary, from such examples, arrive at a final conclusion with respect to the origin of the version in question. We admit, on the other hand, that it is much less controverted than that of Lyons; indeed, one can hardly say that any doubt is thrown upon it.  Reuss, who does not easily take things for granted, recognized the authenticity of it, although he had not the opportunity of examining the manuscript of Paris as thoroughly as he did that of Lyons.  The only reservation he made was the expression of a doubt whether the translation of which we are speaking, although Waldensian, ought to be grouped with those we are about to mention.[630]

We shall now deal with a translation of which there are several copies, all, with the exception of some slightly different readings, agreeing.

### III.—THE MODERN TRANSLATION.

This is represented by four manuscripts.  We will say a word about each of them.

#### (A)  *The Cambridge Manuscript.*[631]

This was thought to be lost.  It was not even mislaid, but simply ignored ; which fact afforded the Librarian of Cambridge University the satisfaction of bringing it to light, about a quarter of a century ago.  Its place of origin interests us directly, for Sir Samuel Morland, who deposited it where it now is, received it from the hand of Léger.[632]  It comprises, as a whole, the New Testament, with the addition of a few fragments of the Old Testament and of the Apocrypha.  Its omissions make it more defective than its predecessors.[633]  The order is as follows :  The four Gospels, the Epistles of Paul, Chapter vi. of Proverbs, and Chapters v. and vi. of the Book of Wisdom, Acts, the General Epistles, the last few of which, as well as the Apocalypse, are wanting.  The present division into chapters appears here for the first time ; it is marked in red, with Roman figures, and with ornamental initials.  According to Bradshaw, the writing belongs to the end of the XIV. century, and Montet confirmed his opinion.  Were other indications wanting, the dialect leaves no doubt as to the origin of this translation.

#### (B)  *The Grenoble Manuscript.*[634]

Muston writes : " I have reason to believe that this Bible is the one which the Waldensian Synod purchased of an inhabitant of Pragela, for the purpose of sending it to Perrin, to whom it was conveyed by the son of Vignaux. Perrin exchanged it for historical documents, furnished by a counsellor of the Grenoble Parliament, named Vulçon. This man bequeathed his library to the parliament, or the bishopric, and after their suppression, most of the books passed to the city library." [635] The manuscript of Grenoble, however, does not contain the entire Bible, but only the New Testament—complete this time ; together with Ecclesiastes, twelve chapters of Proverbs, ten chapters of the Book of Wisdom, and fifteen chapters of the Book of Jesus, son of Sirach. [636] This is the order of the books : the four Gospels, the Epistles of Paul and General Epistles, Acts, and Apocalypse. Then come the *excerpta* of the Old Testament we have just mentioned, as well as the Apocrypha, and a few exegetic or homiletic selections, on the Beatitudes and the Lord's Prayer, with a table of Lessons for Sundays and Feast-days. [637] The division into chapters is that of the Vulgate. [638] The books have each a prolegomena, borrowed from St. Jerome. The writing is of the XVI. century, according to Herzog; [639] at any rate sufficiently close to the date of the manuscripts that still remain for us to mention.

## (c) *The Dublin Manuscript.* [640]

This is so legible, that one is tempted to believe it to be the one referred to by Perrin, when he writes : " We hold in our hands a New Testament, on parchment, in the Waldensian dialect, very well written, although in very ancient characters." [641] This is the more probable, as among the Waldensian manuscripts preserved in Dublin there is a certain document annotated by his hand. Herzog, having transcribed it, deposited the copy in the Royal Library of Berlin, [642] in the hope that the Prussian Government, which had favoured him in his work, might direct it to be printed. This, however, did not take place. There we have the New Testament entire ; also, Proverbs, Ecclesiastes, Canticles, the Book of Wisdom, and the first twenty-three chapters of the Book of Jesus, son of Sirach. Nothing is omitted in this version. In examining this manuscript, we are led to believe that it is the copy of one more ancient, [642] which Gilly and Muston erroneously thought to be that of Grenoble. [644] The former has abandoned that opinion, and claims only a " certain affinity." [645] The books come

in the following order :—The four Gospels, the Epistles of Paul,
Acts, the General Epistles, and the Apocalypse ; then, as a sort
of appendix, come the five Books of Wisdom, of the Old Testament, following the Vulgate, as we have mentioned them. Almost
every book is preceded by a prologue from St. Jerome. The
division of the text corresponds with that of the present chapters,
with very slight exceptions, and there is no sub-division. In the
handwriting of the copyist, at the end of Apocalypse, the words,
"Deo gratias, 1522," are added. This date manifestly indicates
that of the manuscript, and the point is not disputed. Another
hand has noted on the margin a considerable number of parallel
passages.

(D)  *The Zurich Manuscript.*[646]

According to a note found at the head of this manuscript, we
learn that it was presented to the Academy of the town in 1692,
by a Waldensian pastor named Guillaume Malanot.[647]  A second,
more recent note, also states in Latin that the New Testament
therein contained was translated and written "in the ancient
Waldensian-Piedmontese dialect, by a certain Barbet, or minister
of that church."[648]  Once more, therefore, we are dealing with a
copy of the New Testament that came from Waldensian valleys ;
indeed, we find here all the New Testament, with a very few
omissions.[649] The books follow in the order adopted at present,
namely : the four Gospels, Acts, Epistles of Paul, the General
Epistles, and Apocalypse. Excepting slight variations of reading, which have been marked,[650] the text again presents the
ordinary division into chapters, as well as the sub-division of
chapters into four or seven sections, or portions, indicated by
the first letters of the alphabet. Finally, we read on the margin, references to a large number of parallel passages, of which
several are from the Old Testament and Apocryphal books.[651]
These references are written by the copyist. The age of the
manuscript is fixed. The subdivision alone proves that it cannot
date further back than the year 1490, nor further forward than
1550.[652] But we find a still more significant feature. It has been
proved for some time past, that this version, especially subsequently
to the Epistle to the Romans, took into account the Greek text published by Erasmus in 1516.[653] This fact does not constitute a

separate version. The manuscript of Zurich is a copy of an older version, somewhat corrected, and that is all.

After these rudimentary remarks upon the manuscripts that have preserved for the Waldenses the existing versions, it may not be out of place to extract a few parallel passages from them, in order to present a small comparative specimen. It is for this purpose that we reproduce here the prologue to the Gospel of John, and *excerpta* from the Sermon on the Mount, among others the Lord's prayer, and finally, the parable of the Prodigal Son.[654]

LE PR

### MS. de LYON.

In principio erat verbum, et verbum erat apud Deum e Deus era la paraula. Aisso era el comenzament ab Deu. Totas causas so faitas per lui, e senes lui es fait nient. Zo qu'es fait en lui era vida e la vida era lutz dels homes. E la lutz lutz en tenebras, e las tenebras no la presero.

### MS. de PARIS.

Lo filh era al comensament, el filh era am Dieu el, filh era Dieus. Aquest era al comensament am Dieu. Totas cauzas foron fachas per el, e nenguna causa non fon fach senz el. So que fon fach era en lui vida, e la vida era lus dels homes. E la lus lus en tenebras, e tenebras non compreenseron lui.

### MS. de CAMBRIDG

Lo filh era al comme ment, e lo filh era en Dio e Dio era lo filh. era al comenczament en Dio. Totas cosas son tas per luy, e alcuna non es faicta sencza luy que fo faict en lui era e la vita era lucz de li E la lucz luczit en las bras, e las tenebras compreseron ley.

FR

*DU SERMON S*

### MS. de LYON.

Bonaurat so li paubre per esperit, quar de lor es lo regnes del cel.

Totz hom qui au la mia paraula aquesta et la fa, es semblantz a l'home savi qui endefiquet sa maiso sobre peira. E deissendet la pluia, e vengro li fium, e bufero li vent, et espeissero la maiso, e no cazet, quar fermada era sobre ferma peira. E totz hom qui au la mia paraula e no la fa, es semblantz a l'home fol qui endefiquet la sua maisso sobre arena. E deissendet la pluia, et vengro li fium, et espeissero, e la meissos cazet, e fo grans lo cazementz.

### MS. de CAMBRIDGE.

. . . . . . .

. . . . . .

Tot aquel loqual au aquestas mia rollas e fay lor sere semblant al baro loqual hedifique la soa maison sob peira. E la ploya deiscende e li fium gron e li vent bufferon e embriver aquella meison e non cagic. Car era sobre la ferma peira. E tot aquel q aquestas mias parollas e non fai lor semblant al baron fol loqual hedifique maison sobre larena e la ploya deisen fium vengron e li vent bufferon e embri en aquella maison e cagic. E lo tra ment de ley fo grant.

### MS. de LYON.

Le nostre paire qui es els cels sanctificatz sia lo teus noms, avenga lo teus regnes e sia faita la lua volontaz sico el cel et e la terra. E Bona a nosoi lo nostre pa qui es sobre tota causa. E perdona a nos les nostres deunts aissico nos perdonam als nostres deutors e no nos amenes en temtation. Mais deliura nos de mal.

### MS. de CARPENTRAS.

O tu lo nostre payre lo cal sies en lo tio nom sia santifica. Lo tio regne v La toa volonta sia fayta enayma ilh es al cel sia fayta en la terra. Donas n coy lo nostre pan cotidian e perdona li nostre peca enayma nos perdonen a que an peca de nos. El nod nos me temptacion mas deyliora nos de mal.

# )GUE

| S. de GRENOBLE. | MS. de DUBLIN. | MS. de ZURICH. |
|---|---|---|
| filh era al comenza-e lo filh era enapres Dio era lo filh. Aizo l comenzament enapres Totas cosas son faitas ui, e alcuna cosa non ta senza lui. Zo che t en lui era vita, e la ra luz de li ome. E la içic en las tenebras, e enebras non compre-ley. | Lo filh era al comencza-ment, e lo filh era enapres Dio e Dio era lo filh. Aiczo era al comenczament ena-pres Dio. Totas cosas son faitas per luy, e alcuna cosa non es faita sencza luy. Co que fo fait en luy era vita, e la vita era lucz de li home. E la lucz lucit en las tene-bras, e las tenebras non cum-preseron ley. | Lo filh era al comencza-ment, e lo fllh era enapres Dio, e Dio era lo filh. Aic-zo era al comenczament ena-pres Dio. Totas cosas son faitas per luy, e alcuna cosa non es fayta sencza luy. Czo que fo fait en luy era vita, e la vita era lucz de li home. E la lucz luczit en las tenebras, e las tenebras, non compreseron ley. |

## NTS

### *MONTAGNE.*

| MS. de DUBLIN. | MS. de ZURICH. |
|---|---|
| aure per sperit son beneyra, car lo ne de li cel es de lor messeyme. | Li paure per sperit son beneura, car lo regne de li cel es de lor. |
| t aquel que au aquestas mias parollas lor sere semblant al baron savi loqual que la soa meyson sobre la peyra. E za deysende e li fium vengron e li vent on e embriveron en aquella maison e agic. Car era funda sobre la ferma . E tot aquel que au aquestas parol-non fay lor sere semblant al baron fol l ediffique la soa maysen sobre larena. ıloya deysende e li fium vengren e li ȷufferon e embriveron en aquella may-cagic e lo trabucament de ley fo . | Tot aquel lo qual au aquestas mias pa-rollas e fay lor sere semblant al baron savi loqual a edifica la soa meyson sobre la peyra. E la ploya desende e li fium vengron e li vent bufferon e embriveron en aquella may-son e non cagic. Car ilh era fonda sobre la ferma peyra. E tot aquel que au aques-tas mias parollas e non fay lor sere sem-blant al baron fol loqual eydifique la soa mayson sobre larena. La ploya deysende e li fium vengron e li vent bufferon e em-briveron en aquella mayson e cagic e lo tra-bucament de ley fo grant. |

| MS. de DUBLIN. | MS. de ZURICH. |
|---|---|
| u lo nostre payre, lo qual sies en li cel, ▸ nom sia sanctifica. Lo teo regne . La toa volunta enayma ilh es fayta sia fayta en la terra. Dona a nos y lo nostre pan quottidian, e pardona li nostre debit enayma nos pardonen ostre debitor. E non nos menar en ion, mas lesliora nos de mal. Amen. | O tu lo nostre payre loqual sies en li cel lo teo nom sia santifica, lo teo regne vegna, la toa volunta sia fayta enayma ilh es fayta al cel sia fayta en terra. Donna nos encoy lo nostre pan cottidian. E nos perdonna li nostre pecca enayma nos perdonen a aquilh que an pecca de nos. E non nos menar en temptacion. Mos deyliora nos de mal. |

# LA PARABOLE

## MS. de LYON.

Us hom ac dos fils e dix lo plus ioves daquels al paire, paire dona a mi ma part de laver que mi pertanh. E departic ad els laver, e no seguentre moutz dias aiustec totas sas causas lo fils pus ioves. E anec sen en autra terra en regio londana, e aqui espendec tot so aver ab las meretretz (1) vivent luxciosament. E seguentre que fo aio tot cosumat, faita es grans fams en aquela regio. Et el comenzec fraitura az aver. E anec et aiustec se ab u ciutada daquela regio, e trames lo sa vjla que gardes los porx. E cobezeiava omplir so ventre dels esparx de que maniavan li porc, e negu hom no li dava. Mais essi tornatz dix cant servent e la maiso de mo paire avondo de pas, mais eu aici perisc de fam. Levarei e anarei al meu paire, e direili : Paire pequei el cel e denant tu e ia no so dignes esser appellatz tos fils fai me sico i de tos sirventz. E levant venc a so paire. E cum encara fo lunh vi lo lo paire de lui, e pres lui misericordia, e corentz gite se sobrel col de lui e baisec lo, e dix a lui lo fils : Paire pequei el cel e denant tu; ia no so dignes esser apelatz tos fils. E dix lo paire a sos sirventz : Viasament aportatz u vestiment prim e vestetz lo, et datz li anel e sa ma, e causamenta els pes, et aduzetz i vedel gras et aucisetz lo, e maniarem largament. Qui aquest meus fils era mortz e resuscitec, peric es atrobatz. E comenzero a largueiar. Et era lo fils de lui maier el camp. E cum venc et apropiec de la maiso auzic las simphonias els corns (2) e apelec us dels sirventz e demandec a lui que era aiso, et el dix a lui ; Tos fraires venc e aucis lo teus paire i vedel gras que salv lo recep. Et saub li mal, e no la vols intrar. Peraico lo pairo de lui issitz comenzec lo apregar. Mais el respondentz dix al paire. Vec te que tot an eu servisc a tu et anc lo teu mandament no traspasei, et anc nom donest i cabrit que ab los meus amix manies. Mais al seguentre lo teu fil aquest que despendec tot so aver ab las meretritz venc et aucizest a lui u vedel gras. Et el dix a lui ; Fils tota ora est ab mi e totas las mias causas so tuas. Mais largueiar et alegrar nos covenia, que tos fraire aquest mortz era e resuscitec, peric es atrobatz.

## MS. de PARIS.

Uns ome at dos filhs, e dis al pair plus iove des filhs : payre dona a mi la della sustancia que me aperte. E dep lur la sustancia. Et apres non gaire lo filh plus iove aiostadas totas sas c annet en pellegrinage en lunhana ter aqui vivent luxurie sament destrui sa tancia. E pueisque ac degastadas tot cauzas fon fac grans fams en aquella Et el meteis comenses a besonhar et tet se amb u daycella terra e trames sa vila que pogues payser los porc desirava implir son ventre de las casta que maniavan li porc e nenguns no donava. E retornat en si dis : O q logadiers an habundancia de pan en la zon de mon paire e ieu perisc aysi de Levaray me et annaray e mon paire e l : Payre peccat ay contra lo cel e d tu, e non sui dignes que sia appellat filh. Si tis plas fay me aysi con u d loguadiers. E levet se e venc a son p E can fon davant son paire el paire l fo mogut de misericordia. E corret v et abrasset lo. E dis li lo filh : Paire ay peccat contra lo cel e davant tu non sui dignes esser appellatz ton fill l paire dis a sos sers : Aportatz tost la p estola e vistes lui e das li lanel en la causamenta es pes de lui, et aduzes lo gras et aucizes lo e maniem e sade nos, quar aquestz mos filhs era mortz vioudes, era perit e es trobatz. E co ceron a maniar. E l plus ancians fill lui eran el camp. E vengron de fo can foron prop de lostal auziron estru e van demandar a un lur sers que es a l sers va dir : Tos fraires es vengutz payres fes aucir lo vedel gres e fa festa. Et aquel fon endignat e non intrar. Adonc lo paire issi e comen a pregar, et el dis a son paire : Yeu a vit a vos per tant de temps et anc no passiey ton comandament, ni anc n doniesti mosel que manies am mes Et aquest ton filh que es vengut a d sa sustancia en mala vida e per el as lo vedel gras. E l paire va li dir : E iest am mi tota ora e totas mas cauza tieu as e covenia far festa, quar aque fraires era mort e revioudet, era perit trobatz.

---

i. *Ab las mtretretz* is foreign to the text, and is taken from v. 30.

ii. The Latin text has *chorum*. The translator has doubtless read *cornua*.

# :NFANT PRODIGUE.

## MS. de GRENOBLE.

home ac duj filh, e lo plus jove dis al
: O paire, dona a mi la partis de la sub-
a que se coven a mi.    E departia a los
·stancia.    E enapres non moti dia, lo
·lus jove, ajostas totas cosas, ane en
·rinage en lognana region, e degaste
.a soa substancia, vivent luxuriosament.
·s quel ac consuma totas cosas, grant
'o fait en aquella region.    E el com-
·e have besogna, e ane e se ajoste a un
·lin da quella region.    E trames le en
·vila qu'el paisses li porc.    E cubitava
·r lo seo ventre de las silicas que man-
·li porc, e alcun ne donava a le.    Me
·ia en si dis : Quanti mercenar habun-
·de pan en la meison del meo paire,
·?) yo perisso aici de fam.    Yo me
·y e anarey al mio paire e direy a le :
·re, yo pechey al cel e devant tu e ia
·ɔy degne esse appela lo teo filh, fay mi
·ɔa un de li teo mercanar.    E levant
·al seo paire.    Mos come el fos encara
·ɪg, lo seo paire vec lui e fo mogu de
·icordia, e corrent, cagic sobre lo col
·e bayse le.    E lo filh dis a le : O paire,
·chey al cel e devant tu yo ne soy
·· esse apela lo teo filh.    Mes lo paire
·seo serf : fo (?) raporta viaçament la
·era vestimenta e vestic le, e done anel
·man de le e cauçamentas en li pe, e
·vedel gras e l'occien, e manjen a ale-
·. car aquest meo filh era mort e es
·ola, e era perdu e es atroba.    E com-
·ɪron alegrar.    Mes lo filh de le
·velh era el camp e cum el vengues e
·ɔpies a la meison, auvie la calamella e
·npania, e appele un de li serf e de-
·e qual fossan aquestas cosas.    E el dis
·Lo teo fraire venc e lo teo paire oceis
·gras, car el receop lui salf.    Mes el
·legna e non volia intrar.    Me lo paire
·issi, commence pregar li ; mes el re-
·nt dis al seo paire : Vete yo servo a
·r tanti an e unque non tranpassey lo
·ɯmandament, e unque non dones a
·ɔri que yo manjes cum li meo amic.
·ɔoisque aquest teo filh lo qual devore
·substaucia cum los meretrices es vengu
·ies a le vedel gras.    Mes el dis a lui :
·tu sies tota vi cum mi, e totas las
·osas son toas, mes la conventava man-
·ɪlegrar, car aquest teo fraire era mort
·viscola, e era perdu e es atroba.

## MS. de ZURICH.

Un home havia duy filh, e lo plus jove dis
al seu payre : O payre donna a mi la partia de
la substancia que se coven a mi.  E el departic
a lor la substancia.  E enapres non moti nia lo
plus jove filh aiosta totas cosas, anne[en pele-
grinaie en lognani region e degaste aqui la
soa substancia vivent luxuriosament.  E pois
quel hac consuma totas cosas grant fam fo fait
en aquella region.  E el comence a haver be-
song e anne e aioste se a un cittadin da-
quella region.  E el trames luy en la soa
vila quel paisses li porc.  E desirava de
umplir lo seo ventre de las silicas que
maniavan li porc, e alcun non en donava
a luy.  Mas el retorna a si dis.  O
quanti mercenar habundia de pan en la
maison del meo payre, mas yo periso aici
de fam.  Yo me levarey e anarcey al meo
payre e direy a luy : O payre yo pequei al
ciel e devant tu e ia non son degne esser
apella lo teo filh, fay a mi enayma a un de
li teo mercanar.  E levant venc al seo
payre.  E cum el fossa encara de long lo
seo payre vec luy e fo mogu de misericordia
e corrent cagic sobre lo col de luy e bayse
luy.  E lo filh dis a luy : O payre yo
pequey al cel e devant tu jo non soy degne
esser apella lo teo filh.  Mas lo payre dis a
li seo serf : Aporta viaczament la prumiera
vestimenta e veste luy e donna anel en la
man de luy e cauczamenta en li pe de luy.
E amena vedl gras e aucie luy e manien
e nos alegren ; car aquest meo filh era agu
mort e revisque e era peri e es atroba.  E
comenceron a maniar.  Mas lo filh plus
velh era al camp e cum el vengues e se
apropies a la mayson, auvic la sinfonia e la
cumpagnia, e el apelle un de li servitor e
demande qual cosa fos aiczo.  E aquest dis
a luy.  Lo teo fayre venc e lo teo payre
aucis vedl gras e receop luy salf.  Mais lo
frayre fo endegna et non volia intrar.
Donca lo payre issic e comence a pregar
luy.  Mas el respondent dis al seo payre :
Vete yo servo a tu per tanti an e unca non
trapassey lo teo comandament, e unca non
donies a mi un cabri que manjes cum li meo
amic.  Mas pois que aquest teo filh venc
loqual degaste tota la sua substancia cum
las meretricz, tu aucies a luy vedel gras.
Mas el dis a luy : O filh tu sies tota via cum
mi et totas la mias cosas son toas.  M s la
coventava anos maniar e alegrar.  Car
aquest teo frayre era agu mort e rev que,
era perdu e es atroba.

Of course the reader will understand that these specimens are not intended to serve for a comparative study, from an exegetic point of view; but only to show the difference of the dialects. An exegetic study would require a more extended table, containing, at least, numerous fragments from the Book of the Acts of the Apostles, in which, more than elsewhere, are evident the variety of sources, or readings, followed by the translator. Still, it is quite clear from these specimens that the six manuscripts we have referred to represent but three principal versions, rendered into as many distinct sub-dialects. The third version has given rise to a series of revisions differing only in slight peculiarities. It is true that the Zurich manuscript possesses peculiarities which make of it almost a revised edition; but it is only in the second part of the New Testament that we find these peculiarities. The above are by no means all the manuscripts that have been identified with the history of the Waldensian Bible; but such as are mentioned, besides these, could not be inserted in the above table. A manuscript belonging to Aix has been mentioned, but it is not known,[655] and as for the others, they are not Waldensian.[656] Who can tell us, however, whether such a revised edition may not have met the fate of the primitive versions? Who can enumerate all the manuscripts that have been lost? If we think of the manner in which the translation of the Scriptures was so frequently treated, as mentioned in the records of the Inquisition, the decrees of the Councils and the chronicles that reflect the Waldenses' religious life; if we consider that the same persecution which has annihilated the Albigenses' literature, endeavoured to deal with the Waldensian in the same way and was bent on destroying it in a like manner, so that it would probably have disappeared in its turn, but for the refuge it found in the valleys, or in the hands of benefactors, it will be easy to see that one or more revised editions of the translation of the Scriptures may easily have perished, together with the manuscript copy. Even such refuge as it had was none too well sheltered from surprisals of the " enemy " and certain " false brethren," notwithstanding that the Barbes were diligent " in transcribing the books of the Holy Scripture, as much as they could, for the use of their disciples."[657] It is well-known that almost all the manuscripts which survived the destruction that threatened them, came from the Waldensian Valleys.[658] Several almost went astray, even though kept under lock and key in libraries ; although such institutions are certainly more desirous of "preserving" them, as the register of the Geneva library has it, than of permitting their "glorious re-entrance." In a word, the Waldenses' manuscripts shared to the full the "miraculous" preservation accorded to their faith. It is therefore natural to believe that at least a hundred copies of the versions have disappeared into oblivion, where our researches and regrets may easily follow them, though they will not bring them back. The best thing for us to do is to devote our attention to these precious relics of the Waldensian Bible, in order to ascertain their inter-relation, to know if we can establish that original unity, which Gilly hoped to discover, when he endeavoured to reconnect these versions with Waldo's—the fountain head.[652]

The six manuscripts we have recorded above differ, in the first place, with regard to age. If that of Lyons belongs to the XIII. century, and that of Paris to the XIV., the other four bring us down to the eve of the Reformation. They are to be distinguished, as we have seen, by their language, but they are not radically different. It is the same language, nay, even the same dialect ; but, while the former still reflects the period of the Troubadours, the latter indicates decadence and need for a helping hand. There is nothing, however, in that which would militate against the idea of their springing from a common origin. As to the theological point of view, there is no trace of that dualism which was in a high degree characteristic of the theology of the Albigenses, nor indeed of any heresy whatsoever.[660] If this feature be somewhat embarrassing for those who persist in tracing the hand of the Cathari in the oldest translation, it weighs in favour of the hypothetis that would attribute it to the Waldenses. The latter are at least free from the influence of any particular dogma. Their ideal is, the Bible made known to the people with the most scrupulous faithfulness ; that is their ambition—that is what they care for. This was noticed by an Inquisitor. He states that seeing that the Gospel was not in the letter known, they presumed to translate it into practice,[661] from which we may be permitted to infer that they did not aim at translating it differently upon parchment. Now the translation presented by Waldensian versions is so literal, that the best judges are struck by it. " The translator has translated his text word for word," says S. Berger, in connection with this

relation.[662]  If, in addition to this, we consider that five out of six
of the existing translations passed through the hands of the
Waldenses, and that several noticeable expressions are familiar to
them and are found in their treatises,[663] must we content ourselves
with coming to the conclusion that usage does not prove an origin,
and that similarity of expression only indicates the influence of
the assiduous reading of the Sacred Books ?  That would seem to
be straining a point.  If the Waldenses did not write the
version which passed through their hands, can it be the production of a Catholic pen ?  We must admit that certain analogies
would render that supposition admissible ;  only, in such case,
how can we explain the fact that the version so dear to the
Waldenses and so odious to the Church—which could not find
decrees sufficient to condemn it— should be of orthodox origin ?
The first prohibition issued to laymen, forbidding them to keep in
their homes  the books of the Old and New Testament, was
obtained specially through the efforts of the Councils of Toulouse,
Tarascon, and Béziers.  The decree is conceived in terms, which
betray both great irritation, and a settled purpose  to resist some
radical tendency, which was the distinguishing trait of heretics in
general  and the Waldenses in particular.[664]  Where then shall we
look for the authors of the forbidden version, if not in the ranks of
the Waldenses ?   If that  version be not too old, it may well be
directly connected with Waldo's.  If it be more ancient, then we
should not be very well able to see, either the opening for Waldo's
work  or the importance he attached to it—an importance which his
persecutors also have  recognised after  their own  fashion.   Still,
in order to arrive at a  solution, we  lack several  positive  data,
especially with  respect to the text  that served as a  basis for the
work.  Haupt was inclined for a moment to believe that it might
have been the Latin version, anterior to St. Jerome, but he does
not insist upon this supposition, and Berger absolutely rejects it.
" For the present," writes the latter, " we may state with all
appearance of probability, that the Latin text from which the
Provençal Bible was translated, was scarcely used in the South of
France, after the middle of St. Louis' reign ; and that this text
differed very little from the  ordinary version, except in the  Book
of the Acts of the Apostles."
    With regard to this book, it is impossible to believe, as Haupt
seems to, that the Waldenses knowingly preferred the lessons of

the Itala, in which we are told they loved to find quotations from the Fathers. On the contrary, it is certain that whoever may have rendered the Bible into Provençal, simply translated a certain text, mixed with fragments of the ancient Latin version, which we find in a more or less complete form in several manuscripts, the first of which is the famous Codex Toletanus. This text was probably very widely spread upon both slopes of the Pyrenees, ever since the time of the Visigoths."[665] If this be so, the text we are looking for would bring us back into Languedoc, toward the beginning of the XII. century; from which we should gather that the translator lived about that time, and nearer to the Pyrenees than to Lyons. In this way, the origin of the version of the Lyons manuscript would be in a fair way of being explained ; but the link, which connects it with that of Waldo, becomes more than ever indistinct, and it may be wondered whether any such connection ever existed. Was the text spoken of well understood ? "Fairly," says Berger. Therefore, the foundation we are seeking is not even absolutely identified. If this foundation, be it what it may, were to date yet a little further back, and if we should discover that it had been within Waldo's reach, we should not be far from admitting that Waldensian manuscripts, beginning with that of Lyons,[666] refer to more or less distinct revised editions of the early version, or to certain phases of that slow evolution, which constitutes the history of the Waldensian Bible. Meanwhile, with the knowledge we have, the paternity of these versions cannot, as Gilly thought, be attributed to Waldo. The last word, spoken by contemporaneous criticism upon this question, confirms the answer that was made to Gilly more than thirty years ago, namely, that as nothing indicates a tangible connection between the most ancient Provençal version and Waldo's, the origin of the Waldensian Bible, notwithstanding all conjecture, is still shrouded in utter darkness.[667]

Before closing this notice concerning the translations of Scripture there must here be mentioned a version, written in a foreign tongue, in the native atmosphere of the Waldensian reaction.

## IV.—A VERSION IN A FOREIGN TONGUE.

This is the one at present being discussed with reference to the recent discovery of a manuscript of Tepl.[668] The discovery has re-kindled the latent fires of an old controversy. While popular tradition hailed Luther as the first translator of the Bible into German, the reader knows that the Catholic party did not acquiesce in the assumption, and that it had good reasons for contesting his right to this honour; for that matter, the reformer himself laid no claim to it. He could not even have thought of so doing, knowing that the German Bible had been printed in at least 17 editions before his time.[669] It has been proved, indeed, that he actually made use of the German version.[670] This, however does not alter the fact that his translation, which was both classical and popular, did really inaugurate a new literary epoch. Now we are very much interested in knowing to whom belongs the credit of the first translation. Catholics and Protestants vie with each other in putting forth their claims. The latter are very much inclined to see in this translation some of the fruits of the opposition which preceded the Reformation. When the manuscript of Tepl appeared, the attention of the learned was aroused by the fact that the text it presents corresponds word for word with that of the first three editions of the ancient German Bible.[671] Then Louis Keller, an original writer, with the decided opinions of a layman and versed in the history of the sects of the middle-ages, declared the Tepl manuscript to be Waldensian.[672] Another writer, Hermann Haupt, who belongs to the old Catholic party, supported his opinion vigorously.[673] His work soon became the subject of a virulent rejoinder from the Catholic pen of Franz Jostes.[674] The discussion was resumed once more on both sides;[675] more than one theologian taking part in it, the strident echoes of the strife reaching even to France, England, and far America.[676]

That is enough to excite in some degree everybody's interest in this Tepl manuscript, which seems to conceal a mystery, if not to prepare a surprise for us. It contains the New Testament entire, with the addition of the Epistle to the Laodiceans. If this latter reminds us of the manuscript of Lyons, the order of the books carries us back to that of Grenoble. Indeed, we find first the Gospels, then Paul's Epistles, and the General Epistles; finally, the Acts and the Apocalypse. The Epistle to the Laodiceans is interpolated between the Second Epistle to the Thessalonians and the first to Timothy. This manuscript commences and ends with fragments, recalling the ritual of Lyons, but this time it is not reminiscent of the Cathari. There is first a word from St. Victor upon the confession of the sick, followed by a record of the lessons for Sundays and Feast-days, and three passages from St. Chrysostom's Homilies, intermixed with words from St. Augustine, upon the usefulness of reading sacred books and the priesthood of laymen. Those passages are in Latin. So much for the beginning. At the end there is a succinct exposition of the seven Articles of Faith and the seven Sacraments. If we add that the volume is of a very small pocket-size, annotated on the margin and worn, it will be easy to imagine that we have here a religious manual, both convenient and practical. As to its age, from several indications it belongs to the XIV. century.

Now let us come to a point which is particularly interesting. This manual, beyond a doubt, points to a dissident origin. This is the opinion of those who, like Biltz, for instance, examined it without ecclesiastic prejudice. " I have more than one reason for believing it to be a certain fact," says this learned philologist, " that the first German translation originated outside the orthodox centre, and in the midst of dissidence."[677] Keller noted emphatically certain distinctly characteristic differences between the text of this first translation, which was followed by Luther, and that of the version adopted by the Romish Church ; the result is a striking contrast in the dogmatic colouring.[678] But the dissident origin once admitted, we are not necessarily entitled to conjecture that the version is Waldensian.[679] We are brought to this point only by special indications, which must at least be touched upon.

The version of Tepl, Haupt observes, strikingly reminds us of that of Dublin; it presents a certain number of expressions peculiar to the Waldenses, such as " Son of the Virgin " and " torment," instead of " Son of Man," and " Gehenna."[680] The same divergences from the Vulgate are found in the latter, and the list of Lessons, corresponds with that which accompanies the New Testament of Grenoble ; and the Seven Articles of Faith mentioned at the end, are precisely those which the Waldensian missionaries professed at the commencement of their ministry.[681] Jostes, on the other hand, generalizes the use of these expressions— Lessons and Articles of Faith—for the purpose of showing that there was nothing characteristic or definitely marked about them. Berger intervened to point out an unexpected solution. In his opinion, the early German translation, with which the New

Testament of Tepl corresponds, shows unequivocal traces of inter-
polations taken from the ancient version, anterior to Jerome, the
author of the Vulgate, as well as expressions borrowed from some
Provençal translation.    Might it not have been "translated
partly under the auspices of the Waldenses, from an original,
written in one of the Provençal dialects ? " That is his hypothesis.
Jostes thinks it somewhat far-fetched, but Berger, comparing the
texts, came upon fresh indications, and was confirmed in his
opinions, so that it begins to be tentatively accepted, although it
is not yet quite decidedly adopted.    If it can be proved that the
German version is based upon the Provençal, it is but one step
further to conclude that it was the work of the Waldenses ; for
let us not forget that the catechetical fragments, which are found
along with it in the Tepl manuscript, indicate of themselves that
it might have been used in their worship.    If this be the case,
the Romish Church had more reason than is at first apparent for
reproaching Luther with having followed in the footprints of the
Waldenses ;[682] but caution should be used in anticipating a
solution, which may probably elude the grasp of investigators, and
which, after all, may well surprise us.

After the translations of the Scripture, we must consider the
other writings, both in prose and verse, which are attributed to
the Waldenses.    It is surprising, at the first glance, that they
should be so numerous, when hardly any trace of them is discover-
able in the records of the Inquisition ; and we cannot help thinking
that this field, which—thanks to the conscientious researches of
more than one writer, and especially as contained in the beautiful
book of Montet, to which we shall often have to refer—is no
longer unexplored, may still contain more than one surprise in
reserve for us.  Often, while reading certain pages, a doubt suddenly
arises in the mind, and forces the question : Is this really the
Waldensian style ?  Further reading dispels the doubt, whilst as
we go on it arises again.    But we do not intend to lose our way
in the labyrinthine regions of hypothesis.  We propose here to
deal with facts, more or less authenticated.  Between the blind
prejudice of those who accept as Waldensian all that comes pour-
ing out of the cornucopia of tradition, without even seeking to
tabulate them methodically, and the denials of a boldly sceptical
criticism, there is a vast field, which is all that we desire for our
task, consisting as it does in taking account of the condition in

which we find the question, without pretending to solve it completely. Furthermore, we reserve general remarks for the end of the chapter.

" We have been called upon to pass through innumerable persecutions, which have often threatened to destroy all our writings ; so that it was with difficulty that we were able to save the Holy Scripture."[683] These touching words of the brethren of Lombardy are susceptible of a general application. They tell us plainly enough that the list of the writings which have disappeared would not be insignificant if it were possible to make one. We must, however, be content with some brief remarks.

The gloss which accompanied Waldo's version disappeared with it we believe, being replaced doubtless, by one of those more or less discursive expositions which we afterwards find coming to light. An Inquisitor, subsequent to the year 1250, mentions that the Poor of Lyons knew how to take advantage of isolated texts which they borrowed from the Fathers, from Saints Augustine, Jerome, Ambrose, Chrysostom, and Isidorus ; they translated them he says, and impressed them upon their hearers.[684] To do that, it would have been necessary to have a collection at hand. Was this the original collection more or less revised and augmented, or was it a new treatise, after the style of those which have come down to us ? We are unable to say. At Friburg, a woman was questioned concerning a book containing the explanation, if not the simple translation, of the Gospel and the Epistles of Paul.[685] Naturally it is impossible to say whether any connection whatever existed between this book, the work of Waldo, and that of the disciples at Metz ; or whether there is nothing to connect these first essays with any one of the then existing compilations which we are about to mention. A writing in verse, mentioned under the title of the *Thirty Degrees of St. Augustine*, and containing a description of the gamut of Christian virtues,[686] has given much trouble to the critics. Herzog believed that he had found the translation of it in the treatise on the Virtues, which we shall speak of hereafter ;[637] but Montet, after careful examination, declares that he is not inclined to admit this hypothesis. There is another writing that has disappeared, and it seems that it is not the last. Much discussion in connection with analogous *excerpta* to be found in the manuscript of Tepl has taken place lately, concerning a little Waldensian Catechism, containing the *Seven Articles of Faith in the Divinity, and the Seven Articles in the Humanity* (of our Lord), as also the *Ten Commandments* and the *Seven Works of Mercy ;*[688] but as a matter of fact no claim that the entire work has been found[689] has yet been set up.   Finally, what shall we say of the treatises like the *Book of the Just*, barely mentioned in an epistolary fragment of the XIV. century,[690] and of other books, to which the Inquisitors allude, without even naming them, as was the case at Friburg and Strasburg, and undoubtedly in other localities ?[691]   Let us leave all that and devote our attention to existing literature.   Our review will begin with the prose writings.

Perrin, Léger, Monastier and others incorrectly assign an ancient date to diverse writings not here classified.   The reader knows we are dealing with a confession of faith, a catechism, and a few polemic treatises relating to Purgatory and Antichrist, and, the worship of Saints.   These writings, according to Gilly's own words, "were of a much later period."[692]   Discussion of the legend even for the purpose of refuting it is unprofitable, and therefore to be avoided.

We may inquire whether none of the early Waldenses has settled the question of the historical tradition concerning Waldo and his first disciples.   Gilles, it is true, observes that " our fathers were always more careful to do what was right in all things, than to note down and preserve the memory of their actions."[693]   Still, this does not prevent our believing that their minds at times must have been, were it only for polemical purposes, exercised with the problems of their origin.   Thus, the *Book of the Just* which has disappeared, touched, at least in one passage, upon the origin of the Waldenses.   In our opinion, this reference is contained in the historical fragment quoted in the chapter in this book that discusses the origin of the Waldenses.

Where the original text is we cannot say.   Our early historical literature is therefore reduced to so small a compass, that we can understand how Gilles had no knowledge of it.   It would be of great importance that we should possess at least, the most important letters ; but we believe that the very persons for whom they were intended must, for a very obvious reason, have decided upon destroying them.   Whatever the reason, there remain to us only some three or four of their circular epistles.   The most ancient has already been mentioned ; it is that of the heads of the community of the Poor of Lombardy, written after the conference of Bergamo to their brethren of Germany. It was not the only one of its kind, and we are glad to be able to insert here in full, a letter of the year 1368, recently transcribed from the manuscript of St. Florian, in Austria. It was written by the Lombard Brethren, named John, Gerard, Simon, and Peter, and was addressed to their co-religionists who were grieved by the falling away of some regenades.[694] The document runs as follows :—

"We received your letter with the respect that is due to it. It informs us of several matters which greatly afflict us. But we belong to a good school, and we must profit by the example of our forefathers, remembering that the crown of glory is the reward of a patience which surmounts all trials. Does not the word of God say that it is 'in patience we should possess our souls?'[695] For otherwise, after having been uplifted in the time of prosperity, we should soon be cast down. Let us remember what the Psalmist says, 'Thou, O God, hast proved us: thou hast tried us as silver is tried. Thou broughtest us into the net; thou laidst affliction upon our loins.'[696] We sympathize with you, brethren, in your adversity, as we did in better days, according to the words of the Apostle, 'If one member suffer, all the members suffer with it.[697] Therefore we exhort you to render thanks in the evil days, to Him who is powerful to turn your sorrow into joy.'

"You have informed us to what perfidy you are exposed, from those who are our common enemies, as regards the faith, but it will be no hindrance to us if we listen to the voice of the Psalmist, 'Happy shall he be that taketh and dasheth thy little ones against the stones.'[698] We must break our little passions upon Christ our Rock, looking to the example He has given us, and to His precepts.'[699] It must needs be," he says, 'that offences come.'[700] We read in the book of Job that when the sons of God appeared before the Almighty, Satan also came among them. These people do the same. They would by their wavering hinder your steadfastness, and introduce by wicked means their errors into your midst. 'Lo, the wicked travaileth with iniquity, and hath conceived mischief and brought forth falsehood. He made a pit and digged it, and is fallen into the ditch which he made. His mischief shall return upon his own head, and his violent dealing shall come down upon his own pate. I will praise the Lord according to his righteousness, and sing praise to the name of the Lord most high.'[701] Now, as you have sought our aid in this matter, according to the saying of Solomon, who says that ' the brother succoured by his brother is a strong city,'[702] we feel that it is a question here of protecting our own members, and of our striving to bear with you the burden which, after all, weighs upon our own shoulders, as the Apostle teaches us.[703] In the first place, we pray to God that He may hear your groaning, and answer you in the day of distress, as it is written in His word,[704] where He still says to us, ' Call upon me in the day of trouble ; I will deliver thee, and thou shalt glorify me. Give us help from trouble, for vain is the help of man. Through God we shall do valiantly ; for it is He that shall tread down our enemies.'[705] Then, as we cannot and will not answer all the objections of the wicked, we pray with all our heart that the Author of all things may be praised out of your mouth, as by the mouth of children. Say unto Him, ' Lord, open thou my lips, and my mouth shall show forth Thy praise.'[706] Let it suffice for us to answer some of the accusations that are brought against us.

" It appears, that they are endeavouring to prove, by many arguments, that our life is of no merit, as respects salvation, and that for three principal reasons : (1) Because we lack knowledge ; (2) Because we lack authority, which is false, as we shall soon show ; (3) Because, according to our adversaries, our life is neither good nor honest ; hence, neither holy nor meritorious. Let us examine these charges, point by point.

" They reproach our brethren then, for being ignorant and without culture. We admit it, at least to a certain extent. We acknowledge with the Apostle that we do not excel in learned discourses and subtle reasoning ; but after all there remains to us some spiritual knowledge.[707] A peasant taught by the grace of God, needs in nothing to envy a prince, who has learned all that worldly science can teach. Bernard said that, in this respect, the simple will be happier on the last day than lawyers. But read rather what St. Paul writes to the Corinthians : ' I will destroy the wisdom of the wise, and will bring to nothing the understanding of the prudent. Where is the wise ? Where is the scribe ? Where is the disputer of this world ? Hath not God made foolish the wisdom of this world ? Because the foolishness of God is wiser than men, and the weakness of God is stronger

than men.  For ye see your calling, brethren, how that not many
wise men after the flesh, not many mighty, not many noble, are
called.  But God hath chosen the foolish things of the world to
confound the wise ; and God hath chosen the weak things of the
world to confound the things which are mighty ; and base things
of the world, and things which are despised, hath God chosen,
yea, and things which are not, to bring to nought things that are ;
that no flesh should glory in his presence.  But of him are ye in
Christ Jesus, who of God is made unto us wisdom, and righteousness, and sanctification, and redemption ; that, according as it is
written, He that glorieth, let him glory in the Lord.'[708]  You see
therefore, dearest brethren that according to the teaching of the
Apostle, Christian faith is not to be confounded with the wisdom
of this or the other preacher.  It has seemed fitting that this faith
be preached by people, who could not be vain of their power, of
their wisdom, or of their birth.  This was the case with the
Apostles, who were the first preachers ; for, as Gregory says, God
hath chosen for the message of preaching, not rhetoricians and
philosophers, but simple fishermen, absolutely devoid of all
scientific culture.[709]  You can therefore understand how Jesus
exclaimed : 'I thank Thee, O Father, Lord of heaven and earth,
because Thou hast hid these things from the wise and prudent,
and hast revealed them unto babes.'[710]  Why so ?  Because, as
St. Paul adds, 'Knowledge puffeth up, but charity edifieth ; and
if any man think that he knoweth anything, he knoweth nothing
yet as he ought to know.  But if any man love God, the same is
known of him.'[711]  From this we learn that perfect knowledge
must fulfil the seven following conditions :—

" 1.—It must be humble, and not puffed up : *humilis sine
inflacione.*  Knowledge that is humble says, with the Psalmist,
' Lord, my heart is not haughty, nor mine eyes lofty, neither do I
exercise myself in great matters, or in things too high for me.[712]
On the contrary, knowledge that is puffed up reminds us of one of
the plagues of Egypt ; the dust that produced a boil, breaking
forth with blains upon man and beast.[713]  Such is worldly knowledge.  But that of Jesus Christ is different.  It says, ' Learn
of me, for I am meek and lowly in heart.'[714]

" 2.—It must be sober, unpresumptuous : *sobria sine pre-
sumptione.*  Indeed, 'let no one presume to be wiser than
necessary,' says the Apostle.[715]

" 3.—It must be veritable and without guile : *vere sine deceptione*. Then it will not come to pass that men learn, without being able to come to a knowledge of truth.[716]

" 4.—It must be useful for the edification of others : *utilis cum proximorum edificacione*. Such is the object of these words : ' Let no corrupt communication proceed out of your mouth, but that which is good to the use of edifying, that it may minister grace unto the hearers.'[717]

" 5.—It should be salutary, being accompanied by the love of God and of our neighbour : *salutifera cum dei et proximi dileccione*. For which reason it is written : " Though I under-stand all mysteries and all knowledge, and have not charity, I am nothing.'[718]

" 6.—It should be liberal, and be communicated gratuitously : *liberalis cum gratuita communicacione*. We must be able to say : ' Freely I have received, freely I give ; nor do I hide wisdom's riches.'[719]

" 7.—It must be active, prompt, and efficacious : *efficax cum prompta operacione*. Because, says the Scripture, ' To him that knoweth to do good, and doeth it not, to him it is sin.'[720]

" Finally, let us recall a few maxims of Bernard on this sub-ject. Our knowledge must fulfil a threefold condition : as regards the order, the mode, and the object. First, as regards the order ; for to know what we do, and not the order in which it ought to be done, is not to know perfectly. Secondly, as regards the mode ; because it must be accompanied by charity, which consti-tutes the mode and form of knowledge and of all virtue ; so that without it knowledge would be vain. Finally, it is important that our knowledge have an object : for it is not for vain glory, but for the glory of God that we ought to have knowledge. There are those who have knowledge to make themselves known. Such knowledge is but shameful vanity. Others have knowledge, but only for the sake of knowing. Their knowledge is but shameful curiosity. Others aim at selling their knowledge. This is nothing but shameful cupidity. But there are also those who apply their knowledge to the edification of themselves and others. That is the knowledge of prudence and charity.

" Thus, dearest brethren, be not in doubt as to knowledge. It is not a question of being without it, or of abounding in it, after the manner of the men of this world ; but to possess in abundance the truth which edifies. Let ue hope that the Lord by His grace will exalt us out of our abasement, for it is written : ' Whosoever humbleth himself shall be exalted.'[721]

"Let us come to the second head of accusation. Our adversaries say that we lack authority. To hear them, one would think that our order is not established on the true foundation; that we do not hold it from the Apostles, since we do not adminster all the sacraments. They allege the well-known passage : ' I will give unto thee the keys of the kingdom of heaven ;'[722] and then, the directions of the Apostle Paul to Titus, for the establishment of presbyters in the island of Crete ;[723] then again, the Levitical sacerdotal tradition ; concluding finally, that no one can give what he has not received. We concede all that. Does it follow that our authority is thereby diminished ? On the contrary, it will only be the greater. Let us grant them the origin and descent of which they speak, and ask them : Were those Bishops which were ordained by the other Apostles, who received plenary authority from Peter, ordained as though by him ? If they answer no, we reply with these words : ' Having called His twelve disciples, He gave them power ;' and further : ' Whatsoever ye shall bind on earth shall be bound in heaven, and whatsoever ye shall loose on earth shall be loosed in heaven.'[724] If they answer yes, then it is clear that all their successors had the same power, according to the words of the Psalm : ' Their line is gone out through all the earth, and their words to the end of the world.'[725] This is the explanation of those words of our Lord : ' Neither pray I for thee alone, but for all them which shall believe on me through their word. And the glory which Thou gavest Me I have given them.'[726] Now, our order is derived thence, namely, from the Apostles. On this point it is a fact worthy of notice, that in the time of Constantine, Pope Sylvester having received the treasure, his associates protested, saying : ' We have received of the Lord the precept that we shall possess no earthly goods. He said : " Provide neither gold, nor silver, nor brass in your purses, nor scrip for your journey, neither two coats, neither shoes, nor yet staves ; for the workman is worthy of his hire." And again : " If thou wouldst be perfect, go and sell that thou hast and give to the poor, and thou shalt have treasure in heaven : and come and follow Me." And so it was done : " Peter said unto Him : Behold, we have forsaken all and followed Thee." '[727] But Sylvester replied : ' If

you do not remain with me, I will send you into exile.'[728] On
hearing these words they rejoiced, saying : ' We give thanks to
God, because if the earth is denied us for having observed His
precepts, He offers us Heaven. Did He not say : "Everyone
that hath forsaken houses, or brethren, or sisters, or father, or
mother, or wife, or children, or lands, for my name's sake, shall
receive an hundredfold, and shall inherit everlasting life ?" '[729]
The following night, whilst they were still disputing with Sylvester,
a voice from heaven was heard, saying : ' To-day poison hath been
poured into the Church of God.' Having heard this voice, the Poor
of Christ went forth with more courage, and they were driven out of
the synagogue. Thus were fulfilled the words which are written :
' They shall put you out of the synagogue ; yea, the time cometh,
that whosoever killeth you will think that he doeth God service.'[730]
They were thereupon dispersed over all the earth. As they went
away, they said to Sylvester and his successors : ' We leave
the earth to you, but we shall seek after heaven.'[731] It was
Sylvester who had bidden them depart. They endeavoured to
lead a life of poverty, and their number multiplied for a long time.
At last, owing to the envy of false Christians which raged
against them, they were driven to the ends of the earth. Their
enemies said : ' Let us break their bonds.'[732] This does not, however, prevent our adversaries from pretending that Christians have
only been persecuted by Pagans. They read the Scriptures badly ;
for in them we find that the prophets were not put to death by
Pagans, but by Jews. John the Baptist was beheaded by Herod.
Jesus Christ came unto His own, and His own received Him not,
but delivered Him unto death. James, the brother of our Lord,
was also killed by them, and many other disciples suffered persecution of them. All of which is written for our instruction,[733] and
to serve us for an ensample.[734] That which happened to Paul
proves this sufficiently.[735] It is, therefore, evident that the elect
are exposed to persecution on all sides, as much from Pagans and
Jews as from false Christians and all the world, according to the
words of our Lord, who said : ' Ye shall be hated of all nations
for my name's sake.'[736] When He says ' all,' nothing is excluded.
It is, therefore, certain that the saints will be persecuted by their
brethren to the end of the world. Nevertheless, they cannot be
entirely destroyed.[737] The power of the wicked has limits ; it
could not prevail against the faith. We shall say, in our turn :

They imagined a mischievous device, which they are not able to perform.'[738]  The more the disciples of Christ are persecuted, the more their zeal is kindled and their number multiplied.  It is with them as with the tree of which Job speaks : ' For there is hope of a tree, if it be cut down, that it will sprout again, and that the tender branch thereof will not cease.   Though the root thereof wax old in the earth, and the stock thereof die in the ground ; yet through the scent of water it will bud, and bring forth buds like a plant.'[739]  Now, as regards the branches, you must know this, that formerly, when the servants of Christ seemed to have disappeared because of persecution, a man was raised up. He was named Peter of Val, and had a companion, John Lyonnais, so called after the city of Lyons.[740]  Our adversaries see in him a fool, because he was driven out of the synagogue.   He came up like a shoot from a tree watered by the grace of the Holy Spirit ; little by little he prospered.   From what is said, he was not the founder, but the reformer of our order.[741]  If he were driven out of the synagogue, it was only through the judgment of men, not of God.   That happened to others.[742]  So that he was able to say with the Apostle : ' With me it is a very small thing that I should be judged of you, or of man's judgment ; yea, I judge not mine own self, for I know nothing by myself ; yet am not I hereby justified—that is to say, I do not think myself just for all that— " but He that judgeth me is the Lord." '[743]  Such are the Waldenses, whom, doubtless, you have heard spoken of.   They were called by that name, as also by that of the Poor of Lyons, because they had long dwelt in that city.   It is said that what brought Peter to embrace poverty—which was professed before his day, and is still professed, as we believe, according to the Book of the Elect—was that word of the Gospel which he had read or heard, beginning : ' If thou wouldst be perfect, go.'[744]  He roused himself like a lion awakened from his sleep,[745] did his work, journeyed to Rome, and incurred the censure of the wicked.[746] Nevertheless he persevered, and his apostolic example brought many to embrace the rule of poverty, for he remembered that saying of our Lord : ' If two of you shall agree as touching anything that they shall ask, it shall be done for them of my Father which is in heaven.   For where two or three are gathered together in my name, there am I in the midst of them.'[747]  Of his conduct some have said that it was influenced by pride.   That is a very

rash judgment; being a transgression of the precept given by our
Lord: 'Judge not,' and of the exhortation of the Apostle:
'Judge nothing before the time, until the Lord come, who both
will bring to light the hidden things of darkness and will make
manifest the councils of the hearts, and then shall every man have
praise of God.'[748]  Does not Augustine himself say : ' He who pronounces a rash judgment upon the secret thoughts of the heart,
commits a sin ; especially when it is a question of a person known
only by their good works ?'  Knowing therefore, by experience,
that the work of this man was good, we are astonished at the
audacity of those who judge as they do.  If that work were not of
God, it would have perished already, so many persecutions did it
have to endure.[749]  It may be said that the work of Mahomet also
stands, and that it is the work of men, and not of God.  That is
true ; still, it does not prove the stability of his tenets.  Let us
say, rather, that God in His patience ' gave him over to a repro-
bate mind,'[750] and that He has tolerated him also to prove His
own, as it is written : ' There must be also heresies among
you, that they which are approved may be made manifest among
you.'[751]  Augustine, too, explains that this is necessary for the
exercising of wisdom : Peter and all the faithful were obliged to
act thus, by virtue of the Lord's precept : ' Flee out of the midst
of Babylon, deliver every man his soul, and be not cut off in her
iniquity.'[752]

"It is further objected that what we assert here is not proven,
for they read in the Book of the Just this expression of the
historian : 'from what I heard,'[753] and they found upon this a
reason for scepticism.  The writer does not, however, mean by
this expression that he doubts what he narrates ; he avoids using
rash language,[754] that is all.  The reason why we cannot prove
our statement is two-fold.  The first consists in the absence of
witnesses ; no one has seen or heard the real beginning of the
matter, because it took place very long ago.  The second reason
is still more important.  It is this : we have had to pass through
innumerable persecutions, by which our writings have often been
threatened with entire destruction, so that only with difficulty
have we been able to save the Holy Scriptures.[755]  We may,
therefore, say with the Apostle, that ' we have received of the
Lord what we have taught.'[756]  And even if the aforesaid Peter
of Val had not received ordination like others, which, God forbid

—for we claim that he received the sacred ordination as Presbyter, with John his companion and colleague of the same order, and we do not doubt that he was confirmed in it by the Cardinal, who was favourable to him—might he not, with his brethren, have received the laying on of hands from the priests who joined that order in such large numbers ?[757] Some among us still remember brother John of Burgundy, and two minor brethren, who abandoned their order to join that of the Waldenses; also Bishop Bestardi, who, because he had been favourable to us, was called to Rome and returned no more; and that other priest who was led to the stake.

"Let our authority, therefore, be no longer disputed. We received it both from the Lord and from our superiors. Moreover, we know with the Apostle that ' all things work together for good to them that love God.'[758] It is possible that this is not the case with our adversaries, and what happens may work to their detriment; for he who loves not, dwells in death.

"Let us pass to the third head of accusation, which bears upon our conduct. They condemn it for more than one reason. First, we are mercenaries in their estimation. That is what one might with reason say of those who abandon the sheep to the wolves because they ' do not care for the sheep.'[759] Then they say that we do not administer the ecclesiastic sacraments as others do. Thereupon we answer with the Apostle, ' for Christ sent me not to baptize, but to preach the Gospel; not with wisdom of words, lest the cross of Christ should be made of none effect.'[760] Moreover, we would recall what he says further on, ' Do ye not know that they which minister about holy things live of the things of the temple ? and they which wait at the altar are partakers of the altar ? Even so hath the Lord ordained that they which preach the Gospel should live of the Gospel.'[761] It appears from the above that all cannot bear the same charge. Now, because we do not administer these sacraments *in articulo mortis*, they give out that some among us die without communion. That is false, for the Lord said, ' Whoso eateth my flesh and drinketh my blood, hath eternal life ; ' and further, ' He that eateth me, even he shall live by me.'[762] Thereupon Augustine said, ' Believe, and thou hast eaten.'[763] True believers are, therefore, not deprived of the benefit of this sacrament. Alas! there are but too many who communicate, and die, nevertheless, without communion, as there

are those who die with the communion, although without communicating; union with Christ and Holy Church is communion
already."[764]

"Greet all your friends in common. The peace of our Lord
Jesus Christ and the communion of the Holy Ghost be with you
all. Amen."

Thus ends the letter of the brethren of Lombardy. We have
omitted merely such portions as have no particular interest. It
was not left unanswered. We shall quote from a letter of the
renegade Siegfried, these words only : "Indicate the places to us,
name the persons who exercise the ministry of the sacraments.
You cannot possibly do it. You hear confessions and that is all.
For the rest you send people to the Church. The Church, on the
contrary, administers the sacraments and many other benefits to
the people, while you retain only the confession which is but a
semi-sacrament. You boast, it is true, of your good works, of
your vigils, fasts, prayers, supplications, and thanksgivings."[765]
Another reply bears the signature of a renegade named John.[766]
It repels the accusation against those who abandon Christ's sheep
to ravening wolves, and contains a few observations on the origin
of the Waldenses. "Your order, from what I have learned, says
that as the light of faith has never been wanting from Abraham
to Christ, so, too, it cannot have been wanting from Christ down
to the present day. We read there also, that in the beginning
your community had increased to such an extent, that your faithful people, in Synod assembled, numbered sometimes as many as
seven hundred or one thousand. From the incarnation of our
Lord to the period of the Emperor Constantine, are 314 years.
It was then that Sylvester was head and ruler of the Church. From
the time of Constantine and Sylvester to the founder of your sect
there be 800 years ; now add 200 years which have elapsed since
the foundation. It is said that during those 200 years your order
has manifestly lived. Barely 50 more years bring us down to the
present day, that is to say, the year of grace 1368; during that
time you have ceased to preach publicly."[767]

Finally, let us mention one or two letters of the Waldenses of
France, or of the valleys. That of Barbe Tertian to the faithful
of Prajela is well known. There is a letter which deserves to be
mentioned, namely, the *Letter to the Friends*. According to the
Cambridge and Genevan manuscripts it dates back at least to the

beginning of the XV. century. It is true that Montet classifies it among the "spurious works;" but he does not say why. The original does not in any way shew that it is a work to be suspected : far from it.[768] We have here a pastoral Epistle intended for the edification of "all the faithful Friends and Servants of Jesus Christ," who are invited to remember the mercies God grants unto His people, in order by means of them to promote their sanctification. As we read it, we seem to hear the first call to the Waldenses to bring them back to the God of their fathers. We find in it at any rate, indications, of a relapsing which has to be resisted. The authoritative accent is evident. We read in it : God who has called us, blesses us all, and in divers manners ; but the devil makes the greater efforts to undo and corrupt His work in us. Be watchful, therefore, that ye may not fall into the toils of pride and covetousness. Time is short and fleeting ; therefore, let everyone make use of transitory things, whilst keeping sight of eternal salvation. Husbands, live with your wives, in such a manner that they may not turn your heart away from the fear of God. Fathers, love your children and shew your love by bringing them up under constant discipline, that they may become His children. Let nothing be a stumbling block unto you, lest the care of earthly things cause you to lose sight of the kingdom of heaven. Refrain from all evil, in thought, word, or deed. It is through evil deeds that fools perish. Everything that is evil turns us away from charity, which places us under an obligation to our brethren. Moreover, do not forget to add to the love of God love toward your neighbour, whom you ought to love as yourself. Scripture teaches us that he who does not love his brother shall perish, but that love is the fulfilling of the law. Consequently, avoid all malice and quarrelling, seek after peace with all men, returning good for evil, and blessing those who curse you, that you may inherit everlasting joy."

There ends the letter.[769] Besides these historical and epistolary fragments, there are some of a different character, both dogmatic and liturgical. Charles Schmidt has reproduced some from a Latin manuscript in the library of Strasburg.[770] He recognizes in it the statutes of the Ancient Waldenses, apparently the very one above-mentioned, which the ministers learned by heart.[771] Here we find, besides the creed in seven articles, some rubrics relating to the administration of sacraments, especially to

those of Confession and Ordination. The critics now add the
fragments preserved in the manuscript of Tepl. Moreover, we
must not forget the discourse upon the *Word of God*, in the
volume containing the historical fragments concerning the origin
of the Waldenses, which is in the library at Cambridge. This
discourse treats of the very intricate subject of ordination, or
transmission of the office of the ministry of the word.[772] It
divides it into four kinds ; that which comes from God alone ; that
which comes from God and man ; that which comes only from
man ; and finally, that which is claimed by false preachers. The
application may be inferred,the introductory words already hint at it.
" There are people who wish to bind the word of God, by following
their own will ! "[773] Here it is clearly expressed : " Priests and
curates cause the people to perish for lack of hearing the word of
God." Not only at present will they neither hear nor receive the
word of God ; but that it may not be made known, they issue
orders and frame laws according to their own will, preventing the
free proclamation of it. It shall be more tolerable for the land of
Sodom in the day of judgment than for such. The Gospel of
Christ must be freely preached, for it is manifest that it comes
from God. In ancient times all could preach ; for this, Eldad
and Medad, upon whom the Spirit of the Lord rested, preached
freely without the intervention of Moses being necessary. For
the same reason, the humble of Christ, upon whom the Spirit of
the Lord rested, were enabled to preach the word of God to the
people freely, and without any intervention of Pope or Bishop
being required. Would to God that the Prelates possessed the
Spirit of Moses ; they would not hinder those who sing to Thee,
O Lord! neither would they close their mouths." This is
language which reminds us strongly of that used by the Waldenses
at the dispute of Narbonne. It is characteristic and would, if
some of the quotations, used in the text, did not indicate a later
date, lead us back to the origin of the dissent. Indeed, in
addition to the Fathers, St. Bernard, Pope Innocent III., even
Nicholas of Lyra, and John of Andrea, are all quoted. These
last lived toward the middle of the XIV. century. From this, to
the date preferred by Montet, the distance is too great ; we cannot
cover it without hesitation. If the manuscript belongs to the
middle of the XV. century, it does not prove that the date we are
seeking should be fixed at the same period. We must admit

that, as a rule, the date of a manuscript is later than that of the original; and, unless we have absolute proof, we cannot assume any manuscript to be the original copy. The fact that our discourse is found side by side with the historical fragment in the same manuscript, and that it has one point in common with it, in its allusion to the legend of Constantine,[774] is of a nature to make us assign nearly the same date to both. Then, why not prefer the date which is assigned to the fragment; namely, the end of the XV. century? Moreover, there is no doubting the fact that the date of which we speak cannot be later than 1440; for it was at that time that Laurent Valla refuted the legend of Constantine's donation; and it is well-known that his refutation caused no little stir.

The above constitutes the chief of the original matter gleaned from our ancient prose. Let us now pass to the translations and compilations.

We were discussing, a few pages back, the fate of the *gloss* which accompanied the first Waldensian version of the Scriptures, and there seemed to be reasons for thinking that it had disappeared. There is more than one way in which such a document may disappear. It is just possible that it may still be lying concealed in some unsearched collection. Whatever its fate the sentences of the Fathers, grouped around the Waldensian Bible, seem to have accumulated and multiplied like limpets on a rock, as is shewn by the treatises, entitled the *Doctor* and the *Orchard of Consolation*. These two writings cause to dance before our eyes, as it were, hundreds of quotations, the origin of which precisely corresponds to the description before noticed in the words of the Inquisitor, David of Augsburg. They are borrowed, as a matter of fact, from Saints Augustine, Jerome, Ambrose, Gregory the Great, and Isidore of Seville, as well as from more recent writers.[775] After these two treatises, we have an acephalous work, which deals in a monotonous style with virtues and vices, its title being a mere agglomeration of headings of the *excerpta* which it contains, thus :—The *Ten Commandments, The Seven Deadly Sins, The Seven Gifts of the Holy Spirit, The Tavern, The Ball, The Sins of the Tongue, The Godly Virtues, The Cardinal Virtues, The Gifts of Nature and of Grace,* and *The Six Most Honourable Things in the World.* These different pieces, except the two upon the Tavern and the Ball, are also

present in a treatise, entitled *La Somme le Roy*, which a preaching monk, by name Laurent, composed in 1279 at the order of
Philip III., King of France.   There must be noticed next the
treatise upon the *Imposition of Penitence*, which was found to
be a manual of confession, and the *Treizaines*, a table of Lessons
for the ecclesiastic year.   This table is divided into four sections,
each comprising thirteen Sundays, and it is from this number that
it gets its title.   We will mention in passing that, if it correspond to the missals of the period, it possesses hardly any similarity
to that which accompanies the Biblical versions of Grenoble and
Tepl.   Finally, we may put on one side, without any hesitation,
all that mass of allegorical and fanciful interpretations which has
been too long known in the Church—first under the name of
*Physiologue*, then under that of *Animanczas*—for it was demonstrated many years ago that it had a semi-pagan, that is to say,
Gnostic organ.[776]   By reducing these writings to their just value,
which is very small, the critics rendered a real service, and did
themselves much credit.   There still remains, however, plenty for
them to do.   They would confer a favour if they could find a clue
to that ravelled skein called *Glosa Pater*.   A first examination
revealed in that paraphrase of the Lord's Prayer some surprising
variations.   Five copies have come down to us, not all belonging
to the same epoch.   From these different copies we can collate
at least two very distinct readings and a whole series of divergences.   According to the most ancient reading, which, through
its two manuscripts is said to date back to the XV. century, tran-
substantion—a term then crudely defined—is stated to be a true
doctrine; according to the more recent reading, which had been
subject to the influence of the Reformation, it is a false doctrine.
Progress and remodelling are equally apparent here; but we must
be permitted to question whether this early reading, which is
Roman Catholic in its tendencies, be Waldensian at all.   Montet
has some doubts upon this point.   After having classified this
among the " spurious writings," he suspends his judgment, and
wonders whether, after all, it does not belong to the category of
mere translations.[777]   After all, what is this book of *Virtues*
which the critics make so much of even to the extent of finding
therein superstitions, which they attribute to the Waldenses ?
It is true that it contains many quotations from the sacred Scriptures, intermixed with sayings of the Fathers; but is it not

Roman Catholic throughout ? Where does it betray a Waldensian tendency ? Montet, who made this the subject of patient research, has been compelled to admit, nay, he has even proved, that there is to be found in it "not the slightest trace of antagonism to the Romish Church or her dogmas."[778] We give up any idea of analysing it, and we also pass by *The Pains and the Joys of Paradise*, minutely dealt with in *Future Things*. We shall not enumerate the unmeaning homilies, crammed with monkish allegories, which are found here and there in the collections of these ancient manuscripts. We recognise at once, on reading these different productions, that criticism has by no means completed its work of elimination. Among the prose of the first period there is a book which the critics particularly appreciate, and are far from desiring to displace from the catalogue of Waldensian literature. It is the *Cantique*, which was closely examined by Herzog.[779] Montet informs us that he, too, went over the work, and he adopts Herzog's conclusions, that is to say, he classifies this book among the Waldensian writings, " imitated from Catholic works."[780] Is this correct ? It is difficult to think so, and for the following reason :—

The Cantique is a commentary upon the " Song of Solomon." Let us draw a distinction between the translation and the commentary, properly so called. The translation closely follows the ordinary Vulgate, whose very alterations it imitates. Its divisions do not correspond with the chapters. Nothing, therefore, would prevent this book from dating quite far back in the XIII. century, were it not that some expressions are found, which are said to be borrowed from Thomas Aquinas. As to the commentary, it flows on in the full stream of Roman Catholic—nay, monkish—tradition, with its quadruple method of interpretation ; very slightly historical, but on the other hand, tropological, anagogical, and all allegorical.[781] Moreover, its origin may be easily guessed from the analogies already pointed out, which it presents to the writings of Apponius, Angelomus, Bruno of Asti, and the Abbot of Clairvaux. If, moreover, we find evident traces of a Latin original,[782] we shall be inclined to imagine that we have before us one of those numerous paraphrases on the aforesaid Book of Scripture, for which we are indebted to the Middle Ages. Herzog grants this at first ; he even goes so far as to say that it could not have been written within the boundaries of the Cottian Alps, and that

it was only amended there, for the purpose of facilitating the
reading of it.   But he draws a totally unexpected conclusion from
these premises.   He would have it, that the condition of the
Waldenses was more clearly reflected in the Cantique than in any
other writing.[783]   Montet shares his opinion ; he even affirms that
this commentary evidently indicates " a long-continued development of the sect."   We do not think that to be really the
case.

In the Cantique we meet more than once with references and
quotations from the Scriptures ; but there is nothing unusual in
that.   So much is admitted by Herzog, therefore, there is no
reason for us to stop to examine that point.   We also find censures
of unworthy Priests, bad Catholics, heretics, schismatics—in
short, against " the Church of the wicked."   The times are
sad ; the faithful are persecuted, put to death, and given as
a prey to the wolves and leopards.   Are not these the plaints of
the distressed Waldensian family ?   Not necessarily so, perhaps ; they are only the stereotyped tones of the old clerical
lamentation used by Apponius, Angelomus, and so many others
before this period.   Let us take up at random one of St. Bernard's
sermons ; there we shall read the exhortation " to hate the
Church of the malicious," according to the words of the prophet :
" Ju hái l'église des malicious, et ensemble les fellons ne serai
mies."[785]   Then let us take the Gallo-Italic sermons preached about
that time in Piedmont, probably by a cleric to clerics, and therein
we find analogous expressions.   Mention is made of persecutions,
of martyrdoms, of lions and leopards, only there it is a question
of the persecution of Jews by the Emperors.   The latter are
the lions.   As for the leopards, they are the heretics, spotted with
perverse doctrines, which devour the Church ; like Arius, Sibellius
and the Simonides, the race of whom is not yet extinct.[786]   The
writings of the monks during the XIII. and XIV. centuries bristle
with analogous expressions, even more strikingly similar ; for the
divers protests made during the Middle Ages, are no more Waldensian by reason of their virulence, than those of the Canons of
the Renaissance are Calvinist or Lutheran.   But there are other
indications which seem to be more to the point. They are—first :
certain passing but repeated allusions to the " Poor of Christ," to
the " people," the " Church of the Poor," the " perfect," and the
" saints," as opposed to " the wicked."   Who could they have

been, if not Waldenses, asks the critic ? We answer that these last appellations were in common use amongst Catholics,[787] and the word " perfect " is susceptible of a variety of applications, especially when it is employed in a general sense, as is here the case. Finally, what can be more vague than the appellation " Poor," at a time when poverty was the ideal of so many people— the monks themselves included ? " Poor of Christ " existed even before Waldo, as a proof of which we have the nunnery into which he placed his daughters. The Beghins also bore that name. There exists an ancient " Bible of the Poor," which has no connection with the Waldenses ; and the reader will not have forgotten the order of the " Catholic Poor," revived, as it were, by that of St. Francis, entirely composed of brave knights of the goddess Poverty, for whom many endured the scorn of the world, and the anger and persecution of the Prelates. Moreover, if there be some feature here which corresponds with the style of the Waldenses, it will serve to make us understand the object of the translation, unless we are to recognize in it, after all, merely the traces of an amended copy.[788] Let us not exaggerate the importance of this, the more so, as besides similarities, there are also discrepancies to be found. Thus, what has this manifold interpretation, which destroys the real sense of the text, in common with Waldo's school ? We shall clear up this point further on ;[789] but, meanwhile, let us quote some examples. The commentator of the Cantique tells us that all numbers up to 10 are perfect, as well as those from 100 to 1,000 ; that by queens, we must understand the souls of the saints ; by concubines, the heretics and false preachers. Elsewhere, he analyzes the walnut, dividing it into the " scorcza," or outer shell, the " grolha," or shell, and the " garilh," or kernel, in order to unfold to us that the first signifies tribulations; the second, patience ; and the third, the soul devoted to good works. The preachers are represented in a thousand different ways, as, for instance, by the pomegranate or the navel.[790] Is that the style of Waldo's disciples ? We doubt it. Furthermore, it is to be observed, that not only is the doctrine of the treatise Catholic, but it is that and nothing else. Quotations from the Scriptures recur frequently ; but so they do in more than one other Catholic treatise of the same kind ; but why, instead of adhering so closely to the Vulgate, did not the editor follow the translation in common use, and more especially as he was address-

ing his brethren ? He is positively addressing an entire community, even women, recommending the exercise of discipline and
chastity, and finally, he commends himself to them lest the
"preyres al poble de Dio" despise his teaching because of his
youth: "per la mia joventu." Herzog here observes that a
Catholic would not have dared to express himself so freely, and
that it is not probable that he would have spoken Latin to women.
But does this language become more natural in the mouths of the
Waldenses ? Let others judge of that ; to us it would seem that
the first editor was an ascete affiliated to the Beghins, if not to a
regular order. If this be so, then all is clear : the Latin, the
allegory, the dogmas, the style. If, after that, the editor chooses
to designate himself a "knight" carried away by the "gloriosa
lautissima pauretà,"[701] we shall not be tempted to seek for his
comrades among the shepherds of the Waldensian Alps.

For all these reasons we must claim permission to conclude
that the treatise of the Cantique, probably carries us back, for its
origin, to a source outside of the Waldensian dissidence.

The other prose-writings, which remain for us to mention,
escaped Roman Catholic influences. On the other hand, they
bear the mark of the Hussite reaction ; but let us hasten to add
that the latter seems to us to have been exaggerated on certain
points.

The first which presents itself is a letter, the *Epistle to King
Ladislas*, a boldly sarcastic apology, already quoted.[792]

The second is, the treatise upon the *Cause of the breach with
the Romish Church*. The Hussite influence here is conceded.[793]
It contains an exposition of doctrine, morals, worship, and
discipline, from an altogether dissident point of view, both
Waldensian and Hussite ; finally, a general refutation of
Catholicism. The reasons for the breach with the Romish
Church, are therefore given in detail. The chief reasons assigned
are of a purely moral character, and may be reduced to this one,
viz., the vices of the clergy and their indifference to the salvation
of souls. These vices are lashed without mercy. Dogma also
counts for something amongst the causes of the rupture, but does
not really constitute "la causa," as was the case, in the days of
the Reformation. The points of contact with Rome are still
distinctly marked, and it is curious to notice, even when rupture
is spoken of, the existence of a remnant of admiration for the

Church about to be quitted. As to the basis of this compilation it is well-known; it consists of a less widely spread Hussite writing of the year 1496, relating to the "causes of the rupture."[794] From several indications, it would appear that it came to light in the interval which separates the erection of the pile upon which Savonarola was burned in Florence, and the bull of Leo X. at Wittemberg.

Now we come to a series of treatises, the sources of which will appear more and more evident. As to these sources, we must remind our readers more especially of the Taborite Confession of Faith in 1431. The treatises are known for the most part under the title of *Treasure and Light of Faith*.[795] We shall proceed to enumerate them.

First, we have the treatise of the *Ten Commandments*. We find here a compilation possessing a two-fold origin, Catholic and Hussite. By the former it dates very far back; the latter contributed to render its arguments clear and vigorous, especially with regard to the worship of the Virgin and Saints, which, by-the-way, the Waldenses no longer admitted.

Secondly, we have the treatise of the *Seven Sacraments*. It is almost copied from the Taborite confession, though it presents certain divergences. If the number seven is still the rule, the exception has manifestly a tendency to come in. The second sacrament of the "Chrisma," is looked upon as devoid of scriptural basis; others are modified as regards their interpretation, particularly those of Penitence, Ordination, and Extreme Unction.

Thirdly, the treatise of the *Dreamed Purgatory*[796] The title itself is sufficient. The dream of purgatory constitutes the fact of the Latin or Romish Church. Among the names quoted is that of master John Huss, "of blessed memory." This treatise, however, is hardly anything other than a translation of the two fragments of the Taborite confession.[797]

Fourthly, the *Invocation of Saints*. This treatise consists of a formal refutation of the worship of saints, upon the basis of the said confession. According to the compiler, that worship is a veritable act of idolatry, by which man turns his back upon God to worship the creature. Quotations from the Scriptures and the Fathers abound; even Wycliffe, "lo doctor evangelic," finds a place here.[798]

Fifthly, we have the treatise on the *Power given to the Vicars of Christ*, a translation of a fragment of the *Treatise on the Church*, by John Huss. Although literal, this translation seems to deviate slightly from the train of thought of the author, at least upon the question of faith. While Huss speaks of receiving Christ through faith, the translator would receive Him through the *fides formata*, according to the formula of Thomas Aquinas. This point has been especially pointed out.

Sixthly, we come to the treatise on *Antichrist*. This exists only in quotations, fortunately, very extensively furnished by Perrin and Léger. Dieckhoff had suspected its Hussite origin, but to Goll belongs the credit of having demonstrated the fact.[799] Ineed, it dates back to Lucas of Prague. The Waldensian compiler did not adhere strictly to the original arrangement of the matter, but the divergences appear to be very insignificant. According to his definition, Antichrist is not a person, but merely a vague personification of the hypocritical rebellion against the Church of God and its legitimate ordinances. Its acts are described, as well as the consequences thereof, and the appearances by which they are concealed. Montet concludes that originally this treatise must have been one with that which turns upon the causes of the breach with the Romish Church, because the latter is partly found again in the fragments of the treatise on Antichrist, preserved by Perrin and Léger.

Finally, let us record the treatise of the *Minor Interrogations*. It is a Catechism, the origin of which has greatly puzzled investigators, at the head of whom are Professors Zezschwitz and Goll. At first this was considered to be simply a revision of the Catechism of the year 1524, belonging to the Brethren of Bohemia. Dieckhoff and Herzog were of opinion that the two Catechisms should be attributed to a common source, Bohemian, but lost. According to Zezschwitz, the Waldensian Catechism is older than that of the Brethren of Bohemia, which would not at all prevent their having a common source ; only it would have to be sought for farther back, in the literature of that country. Since then Goll has discovered a manuscript in the Tzech language, in which he thought he recognized the original text of the Bohemian Catechism. There the question rests.[800]

This concludes our review of the prose writings of the first period. To be absolutely complete, we ought still to mention one or other production, which, under the mass of compilations, may have escaped us. We ought to notice the rescript of more than one writing already mentioned—of *Penitence* or *Glosa Pater* for instance ; or, again, some letters and memoirs which appeared on the eve of the introduction of a Reformation in the valleys of the Cottian Alps. A summary review has limits, however, beyond which it is impossible to pass. Moreover, the direct connection of such letters and memoirs with the subsequent period will compel us to deal with them later on. Let us now, therefore, pass to the last division of our chapter, which we shall devote to the poetic writings.

After having threaded our way through the somewhat dark tangle of the prose literature, encumbered with quotations, and bristling with unsolved and insoluble problems, we do not regretfully look back upon its charms ; they are too few and mixed. We rejoice rather at the prospect of coming out into the bright light of day, or to gaze upon the stars that shine in the sky of poesy. Our metaphor, somewhat bold perhaps, will serve to introduce in a measure the subject which is now about to engross our attention.

The sky of Waldensian poetry is far from being as thickly covered as is the forest of prose. No stars of the first magnitude appear, though some luminaries are visible even to the naked eye; of course, more than one has disappeared. Had they shone with a brighter lustre, would they not have been noticed ? We have already mentioned a piece of rhymed prose, called *Rithmes de St. Augustin*, a modest little comet, which has passed into oblivion,[801] and we can hardly hope that any new discovery will be made. The last, which we owe to Muston, was made in 1849, and relates to an already known writing ; but one whose somewhat halting measure and rhythm, had not been made out. All that has come down to us forms a graceful little group. The *Noble Lesson* is the principal poem ; then come seven less brilliant pieces of verse: *The Scorn of the World*, *The Bark*, *The New Comfort*, *The New Sermon*, *The Lord's Prayer*, *The Parable of the Sower*, and *The Father Eternal*. Have we here works that are united only in appearance, as the stars of some constellation ; or, do they really form a group—like that of a planet for instance, with its little train of satellites ? Montet observes that they present " something like an appearance of relationship," yet he does not venture to infer from this a common origin. According to Muston they were seen to rise in the east and follow a westward course ; but others are of a contrary opinion, and hold that the Waldensian group, even though not a planetary one, naturally follows the reverse course ; that is to say that the majority of the poems have the same source as the Waldensian versions of the Scriptures and most of the other prose writings, and came from France with the refugees who escaped the persecutions. We shall look into that question at the proper time and place. We have now to deal with these eight poems, one by one, reserving to the last a few critical notes upon *The Noble Lesson.*[802]

## I.—THE SCORN OF THE WORLD.[803]

This poem treats of the vanities of life and its fictitious treasures down to the 95th verse, which says :

L'onor del mont yo te volk racontar.

Here we expect a new departure ; but twenty lines further on the poem is suddenly interrupted. It would seem, therefore, to be incomplete. More than one author has remarked, towards the end of it, certain allusions which seem to be inspired neither by the spectacle nor the experience of the hard life endured in the valleys of the Alps. Those towers, palaces, great banquets, beautiful vineyards, and spacious gardens, carry the mind back to the luxurious life of the plain and the opulent Lords of Provence, rather than to the humble domains of the castle of Luserna and the shepherds of the valleys. Among those descriptions one is particularly admired ; it is that of death which we give here :—

Tot czo qu'es crea de carn la mort destruy e auci ;
Ilh apremis li grant é li petit asi ;
Ilh ten de li noble la poysencza,
E non ha d'alcun neuna marczeneiancza.
A li duc e a li princi ilh es mot cuminal ;
A jove asi a velh ilh non vol pardonar.
Par alcun enging non po scampar lo fort
Qu'el non sia atrissa sot lo pe de la mort.

## II.—The Bark.[804]

This poem begins by describing

De la humana condicion la vilecza.

Man, formed of the basest of the four elements, lives in a world full of misery, iniquity, and vanity of all kinds. At last he will be the food of worms. It would have been better for him had he never been born. Death menaces him. He knows not when it will come. If he be not prepared, he will be taken unawares, and the result will be ruin and perdition; therefore let us awake and lead a wise life. Life here below may be compared to a bark making for a port—the Kingdom of God. We are the passengers. All depends on the manner in which the bark is laden; for, once arrived, the cargo cannot be changed. Happy is the careful man who shall be found to have laden it with gold and precious stones, rather than with wood, hay, and stubble; but the plight of the careless will be pitiable.

Lo paure marinier que la barca guidaré
A l'nitra d'aquest port trey gran cri gittaré,
Diczent : Ay, ay, ay ! del grant paur qu'el auré ;

and he will be cast into hell. What use will his amassed riches be to him then ? Therefore, O sinner ! look and recognize thy misery. Would'st thou have nothing to fear ? Then humble thyself before God. Cry to him that he may have mercy upon thee ; and, going to thy confessor, say unto him :—

Yo peccador, a Dio e a vos soy veugu
Qui vos me done bon conselh a vera penetencia.

Make confession with an open heart, concealing nothing.

E cant tu te scres confessa entieramant
De tuit li teo pecca, cum plor et pentiment.

resolve to commit no more sins, and keep the resolution.

E non te sia greo d'far bona e vera penedencza

while it is time.

Car en enfern non ha redempcion
Ni alcuna perfectivol ni bona confession,
Del cal nos garde Dio per la soa passion
E nos alberge tuit en la soa sancta maison.

Muston claims that the poem concludes with the sinner acknowledging his faults, and accepting as his only pilot, Jesus Christ, and as his only treasure His merits.[805] If this were so, we should have before us a Protestant poem, whereas, it is hardly Waldensian. Certain rather trivial expressions betray the jargon of the monks ;[806] whilst some words seem to indicate a relatively modern period.[807] At any rate it is very doubtful whether this poetry was written in the valleys of Piedmont, unless we admit that there, as elsewhere, there was occasion for saying :—

> Li autre meton lor temps en servir ben lo cors,
> De beore e de manjar e pilhar grant deport;
> En cantar e ballar meton poc de mesura,
> E la noyt e lo jorn segont lor grant luxura,
> Durmir e repausar sencz neuna mesura ;
> En ornar ben lo cors, aquil es lor grant cura.

### 3.—THE LORD'S PRAYER.[808]

This production somewhat disguised by the prose accompanying it, was first noticed by Muston.[809] Perrin and Léger translated it, without noticing that it was poetry, under the title of *Confession of Sins of the Ancient Waldenses*. It is indeed a confession of sins. It begins thus :—

> O Dio de li rey e Segnor de li segnor, yo me confesso a Tu,
> Car yo soy a quel peccador que t'hay mot offendu.

We soon discover here the idea derived from reading the Psalms, and an example of that confession to God recommended in the Bark. It is very different to analyse this piece; it abounds so much in parallelisms and repetitions. Nevertheless, we will try.

O Lord, I implore Thy forgiveness, for I have greatly sinned. I have no excuse to offer, for I have done evil, not through ignorance, but through wickedness and ingratitude, and have forsaken Thy commandments, to give myself up blindly to covetousness. Not only have I sinned against Thee directly, but I am also guilty toward my neighbour. Now, I confess that my repentance is valueless. What is it, as compared with my iniquity? Nevertheless, Lord, Thou seest; I cast myself at Thy feet, with tears and groans.

Segnor Dio, tu sabes tot czo que yo hay confessa;
Encara hi a moti mal que yo non hay reconta.
Mas tu sabes li mal pensier e li mal parlament
E las perversas obras que yo fax a temp present.
Segnor, perdona me, e dona me alongament
Que yo poisa far penitencia en la vita present;
E dona me tal gracia al temp que es a venir
Que ayre tant lo mal que yo non lo facza plus.
E ame tant las vertucz e las garde al meo cor;
Que yo ame tu sobra tot, e te teme tant fort
Que yo haya fayt lo teo placzer al jorn de la mia mort.
E dona me tal flancza al jorn de jujament
Que yo non tema demoni, ni autre pavantament,
Ma iste a la toa dreita sencza defalhiment
Segnor, tot ayczo sia fayt per lo teo placziment.
            Deo gracias! Amen.

Muston does not admire these verses unreservedly; but their
very defects seem to him to be a sign of " great antiquity."[810]
Now and then a verse would lead us to suppose the author had
read the *Noble Lesson*. At any rate, this piece unmistakably
bears the seal of the Waldensian dissidence.


## IV.—The New Comfort.[811]

The subject is indicated at the very commencement :—

> Aquest novel confort de vertuos lavor
> Mando, vos scrivent en carità e en amor;
> Prego vos carament per l'amor del Segnor,
> Al andona lo segle, serve a Dio cum temor.

First comes a somewhat monotonous description of the
wretchedness of life; after that, some striking passages; for
instance these three quatrains upon faith and works :—

> San Jaco mostra e aferma clarament
> Que l'ome non se salva per la fe solament;
> Se el non es cum las obras mescla fidelment :
> La fe sola es vana e morta verament.

E sant Paul conferma aquest tal parlar,
Que l'auvidor de la ley non se poiré salvar ;
Si el non vol cum la fe las obras acabar,
La corona d'gloria non es degne de portar.

Car enayma en l'ome son dui compliment,
L'esperit e lo cors en la vita present ;
Enayma la fe e las obras son un ligament
Per local l'ome se salva, e non ja d'autrament.

Further, the poet resumes the law of Jesus Christ, and
exhorts the reader to yield his rebel heart to Him :—

Emperczo al seo cor se conven batalhar
E a li seo desirier fortment contrastar,
Cum la sancta scriptura lo cor amonestar,
D'esperita cadena fermament lo ligar.

Let him therefore serve the Lord in a spirit of fear and
fidelity, patiently enduring tribulations, even persecutions and
martyrdom ; let suffering complete the purification of his soul and
its preparation for heaven. Moreover, the eye of Christ, the
Good Shepherd, is upon them who follow Him, to keep them.
Has he not sealed them as His own ? They are "His little
flock," His sheep and His lambs. Therefore, He calls them by
their names, leads them to His pastures and to the very fountain
of life. It has been so from the beginning, and He is faithful to
the end. Those who follow Him shall be partakers of His
victory, coronation, and triumph. The poem concludes with the
following lines :—

O car amic ! leva vos del dormir,
Car vos non sabe l'ora que Xrist deo venir :
Velha tota via de cor en Dio servir,
Per istar a la gloria, lacal non deo fenir.
Ara vene al dia clar e non sia negligent,
Tabussà a la porta, faczè vertuosament.
E lo sant sperit vos hubrirè dvoczament
E amenaré vos a la gloria del cel verayament.
Vene, e non atendè a la noyt tenebrosa,
Lacal es mot scura, orribla, espavantosa ;
Aquel que ven de noyt, ja l'espos ni l'esposa
Non hubrire a lui la porta preciosa.

Raynouard, struck with the relative perfection of the rhythm, was the first to state that this piece could not be very ancient. Moreover, does not its language prove this sufficiently ? If we admit a date that brings us near the Reformation, we shall be more easily able to account for what is said in it concerning persecution, and the allusion to the "wicked Antichrists."

## V.—THE NEW SERMON.[812]

In this we have depicted the contrast between the being who wallows in his sin, and the sacred nobility of the penitent. First, we have a description of those who live for earth, then of those who live for heaven. The poet begins by saying that men have gone astray ; there are but few who care to do right, to be numbered with the elect. They would like to enter Paradise without taking any trouble to gain it. Now, who does not know that the work of our salvation demands our whole energy ? Here again, to will is to be able, if we be guided by knowledge. Wisdom advises everyone to serve God ; but many a one, who has grasped this fact, goes to perdition just the same. Such is the fate of many who allowed themselves to be seduced by covetousness. In this respect princes, peasants, merchants, usurers, artisans, and clergy, all join the same path. The latter have the greater blame, for :

> Aquesti han promes, per propria voluntià,
> De segre Yeshu Xrist per via de povertà,
> E ensegnar a li autre la via d'vita e d'salvacion ;
> Ma car fan plus lo contrari ilh son fait pejor d'tuit.
> Entende saviment que yo non dic d'li bon,
> Que son serf del segnor, ma dic d'li fellon.

Do any of them enjoy the money they heap up ? No, indeed ; they live too much in dread of losing it ; meanwhile, death steps in, and then they are compelled to part with their treasure ; therefore let us avoid coveting the goods of this world. On the other hand, excessive poverty has its snares ; we must not be entangled in them. Let us earn our living honestly, giving away any surplus, and we shall lay up for ourselves treasure in heaven. Yet, while some heap up treasures, others follow the lusts of the flesh, and give themselves up to idleness, gluttony, and luxury. They will find at last that they have served a false god. Death will precipitate them into hell, where every sin will receive its appropriate punishment. If, during life, you wore sumptuous apparel, you shall be naked and cold. If you slept too much your couch will be invaded by insects. If you enjoyed good cheer, you will be consumed by hunger and thirst. The impure, freezing with cold, will be lashed by the storm.[313] Ribald laughter will be followed by unceasing tears; foolish songs will be changed into curses, and he who shone by his comeliness, will be black as coal. Let us learn, therefore to give our body nothing but clothing and food, and to hold it in check. But here is yet another band of sinners; pride is their banner. This one because he was placed in a position of authority, has no feeling but that of scorn; another can only breathe forth vengeance. another prides himself on his own sense, or else he swears and prejudices himself, and threatens and curses. Their end is in the burning lake of fire and brimstone.

Such is the triple cohort of those who serve the world, the flesh, and the devil. But there are also those who serve the Lord. These may be classified into three categories.

> La primiera paria es de li contemplant
> Lical son dit perfeit en seguent paureta,
> Vivent concordialment en pacz e en carità;
> Per paya auren lo regne que Dio lor ha dona.
> Ma l'autra compagnia que ven al segont gra
> Es la nobla guarnacion, clara per castità,
> Amant Dio e le proyme, lavorant justament,
> Retenent per lo vivre, donant lo remanent.
> Aquesti auren terra nova per la dreita hereta,
> La call Xrist ha promise a li sio benaura.
> Ma la tercza paria es de li noceia
> Gardant lo matrimoni fidelment e en bontà,
> Departent se de mal, faczent vertuos lavor,
> E ensegnant a li lor filh la temor del Segnor.

Taken altogether, these are the elect, the redeemed of Christ. Humility is their banner. They are a "small company," but their valour is not measured by their number.

Aquilh son poc per numbre, que portan aquella ensegna ;
Ma ilh son mot per valor, car en compagnia degna,
Czo es Jeshu Xrist, filh de sancta Maria,
Que li conforta mot e lor mostra la via
Novella, e vivent, e de salvacion.

From this language, it is evident that this poem is not ancient.
It dates, perhaps, from the XVI. century. The allusions found
in it relating to the pleasures of an opulent, luxurious, and
frivolous state of society, recall much more forcibly the civilization
of large cities, than the rustic and arduous life of the Alps.

## VI.—THE PARABLE OF THE SOWER.[814]

This is a paraphrase on the parable of Our Lord. An analysis
would therefore be superfluous. The exposition proceeds without
protection. It is sober, simple, and touching. It afforded a
favourable opportunity for polemical allusions ; but the author
avoids them, as will be seen from the following verses :—

Aquisti fals oysel son li maligne sperit,
L'escriptura o demonstra, e en l'evangeli es script :
E volon devorar lo tropellet petit
Del cal es bon pastor lo segnor Yeshu Xrist.

Aquesta mala herba, semencza de tristicia,
Czo son li filh feilon, plen de tota malicia,
De persegre li just ham mota cubiticia,
Volent lor deviar la divina justicia.

Tribulacions lor donan e li trabalhan fort,
Faczen a lor motas angustias e torment entro a la mort ;
Mas li just son ferm ; en Xrist han lor confort ;
Al regne de paradis istaren cum deport.

Emperczo temon Dio, gardant se de mal far ;
La ley del Segnor s'efforczan de gardar
E totas adversitas en paciencia portar,
Entro que sia vengu lo temp del meisonar.

The applications, which have reference to the good seed, are
particularly interesting to us. Let us note the principal ones.

D'aquesta tal semencza son li bon auvidor,
Que scoutan volentier la vocx de Salvador ;
Ben lor par docza, bona, complia d'resplendor ;
De bon cor la recebon, cum spiritual amor.

La parolla divina se planta en lor cor,
E ferma la soa reicz dedincz e de for,
Que per neuna adversita non es arracha ni mor.
Fin son, a tota prova, coma lo metalh de l'or.

Ben venczon lo demoni e la soa temptacion,
E la soa grant batalha, e la soa decepcion.
La parolla de Xrist tenon cum devocion
Cum tota bonas obras, complias de perfeccion.

Non lor po noyre vent ni autra mala tempesta,
Ni la perseguecion, ni autra caus molesta,
Non volon laisar Xrist qu'es lor veraya testa,
Mas amon lui e lo temon, e lo servon cum festa.

Non temon lor torbilh de la cura mondana,
De la mala cubicitia, ni de la gloria vana,
Ni desirier carnal ni temptacion humana ;
Car servison a Dio cum la fe cristiana.

Lor mayson hedifican per durar longament,
Cavant en aut fan ferm fundament
En la cantonal peira de Xrist omnipotent.
Non la po more fluz, ni u dilivi ni vent.

Paures son per sperit de la cura temporal ;
Non segnon avaricia, la reycz de tuit mal :
Mas queron las riqueczas e lo don celestial,
La corona de gloria, lo regne perpetual.

Per czo meton lor cor en servir Yeshu Xrist
Per aquistar riqueczas al regne sobre dit,
Al cal non pon intrar li avar e li cubit ;
L'escriptura o demostra, e en sant Paul es script.

Si alcona vota ploran en la vita present,
Suffrent las angustias e moti apremiment,
Ilh serén benaura al dia del jujament ;
Istaren a la dreyta de Xrist alegrament.

Mot son pacific, human e ben suffrent ;
Non se volon deffendre, non son mal repondent,
Mas porton en paciencia greo cosas entre la gent ;
Emperczo son apella filh de Dio tot poysant.

Tribulacions suffron, e perseguecion grant ;
Son tormenta e aucis e en grant carcer istant ;
Per czo son plen de temor e de grant spavant,
Sovent d'un luoc en autre fuon trafugant.

E cant perdon la roba de que devon campar,
Conven qu'ilh se fatigon en fort lavorar,
Car non van mendigant, ni almona demandar :
Del lavor de lor mans se volon ajudar.

Per czo son benaura, enayma es script,
E volon ben complir czo que lo Segnor ha dit,
Que non faczan venjancza de grant ni de petit ;
Non rendan mal per mal ni maldit per maldit.

After what we have just read, we shall have no difficulty in
admitting that the origin of this poem must be looked for not far
from the refuge of the Cottian Alps, perhaps even before the time
of the last great persecutions.

## VII.—THE FATHER ETERNAL.[815]

We have here a poem *sui generis* in the Waldensian group.
First, it differs from the others in the train of thought ; though
that is dogmatic, or even scholastic ; secondly, in the style ; the
artifice which, at the expense of simplicity, dominates it, of itself
proves that this piece has no relation to the origin of Waldensian
dissidence, but constitutes an exceptional production, if not a
foreign one, in which we vainly seek for that grace accompanied
by picturesqueness of figure and that natural style which we admire
in the other poems. A short quotation, however, will say more
than many words. Here are the first three, and the last
stanza :—

O Dio, payre eternal poisant conforta me !
Enayma lo tio filh l'armé gouverna me :
Enayma degainant, retornant a tu, recep me !

I

Ameistra me, Dio filh sapiencia
D'entendament e d'auta sciencia,
En parolla e en veraya speriencia.

Dio sperit, bonta, vita de tota gent,
Dona me la toa gracia en la vita present;
E a la fin tu me garda de tot amar torment.

Dio autic, novel, per ta bonta un en tres,
Hosta de mi lo ment que destruy en mi czo qu'es,
Lausor sia a tua, ben compliament de tot cant es.

Ought we, with Herzog, to admit that this poem is full of allusions to Catharism, and think, as Montet does, that the author had left the sect of the Albigenses to embrace the principles of Waldo, and that in this poem " he poses as the adversary" of the doctrines of the Cathari? We are not convinced of this; the passages quoted to support this hypothesis seem to us insignificant, and to perceive all that in it appears to us to require a great deal of the wish that is father to the thought. We have also been unable to perceive that the Albigenses were pointed at in the peaceful Parable of the Sower, and if there is " an intentional enunciation of the Anti-Catharin truths," we confess that it has escaped our attention; in other words, we are not prepared to believe anything of the kind. It is pretended that this allusion to Catharism is found again in the principal Waldensian poem, which we shall now examine.

## VIII.—THE NOBLE LESSON.[816]

The poetry of the Waldenses naturally savours of their school. The title of Sermon or Lesson corresponds very well with the character of its most remarkable pieces. Still, lessons differ in kind. This one excels in its contents, so that it is especially entitled to our attention.

The object of the Noble Lesson is indicated in the first lines:

O frayres, entende una nobla leyczon:
Sovent deven velhar e istar en oracion,
Car nos veyen aquest mont esser pres del chavon;
Mot curios deorian esser de bonas obras far,
Car nos veyen aquest mont de la fin appropriar.

As to the matter of the poem itself, here is an epitome of it :

Breoment es reconta en aquesta leyczon
De las treys que Dio done al mont.
La prumiera ley demostra a qui ha sen e raczon,
Co es a conoiser Dio e honorar lo seo Creator.
. . . . . . . . . . . . . . .
Ma la seconda ley, que Dio done a Moysent.
Nos ensegna a temer Dio e server luy fortment,
Car el condampna e punis tot home que l'offent.
Ma la tercza ley, lacal es ara al temp present,
Nos ensegna amar Dio de bon cor e servir purament.
. . . . . . . . . . . . . .
Autra ley d'ayci enant non deven plus aver,
Si non en segre Yeshu Xrist, e far lo seo bon plaçer.

Such a *resumé* as we can give here cannot be satisfactory.[817] The verses we have just quoted indicate one of the salient features of the poem, or, we might say, the skeleton of it ; and it is evident that, looked at from this point of view, the Noble Lesson presents the three successive divisions marked by Muston : the first ending at the 138th verse ; the second at the 207th ; the third at the 348th ; then follows the final application or conclusion. We shall not endeavour here to substitute any other division. Only, this skeleton being admitted, we must try to clothe it with what is necessary to constitute a body. What we have to say further will serve that purpose.

The end of the world is near ; it is foretold by signs. The hour of judgment is about to sound for all. Then

Li bon iren en gloria e li mal al torment.

To be convinced of this, one has but to consult the Scriptures. There we shall also find that the good are in the minority. If we desire to belong to that number, let us learn to invoke the aid of the Holy Trinity, love our neighbour, and turn a hopeful eye upon the blessings to come. Our salvation depends upon that. But the wicked find no pleasure therein. Carried away by love of the world, they forsake the promises and God's laws ; they even compel others to follow them ; and evil has invaded everything. Whence does this arise ? In this way : Adam sinned first ; the seed of sin passed to his descendants, and with sin, death ; but the good are redeemed by the sufferings of Christ. Evil has only increased with the generations of mankind. First, we have corrupted in ourselves that noble law of nature which taught us to love God, to serve Him, to keep inviolate the holy marriage bond, and to love our neighbour as ourselves. Then God's threat was fulfilled, contrary to what men now say, namely, that He did not create man in order that he should perish. The deluge came and destroyed the idlers. Noah and his house were spared, and God promised to send no more deluge upon the earth; but Noah's descendants having greatly multiplied, gave themselves up to evil, and doubted of God's faithfulness. In order to guard themselves against the deluge, they built a tower or city of refuge. God rendered their foolish undertaking of none effect; He confounded their language, so that they were obliged to disperse. As they continued to transgress natural laws, five cities were destroyed by fire from heaven. All their inhabitants perished except Lot, his wife, and his guests—though afterwards his wife, because of her disobedience, perished also. After that, God called upon Abraham to leave his own country. Through him He prepared a separate people, which first lived in Egypt. Afterwards, being delivered by the hand of Moses from the yoke of oppression, it crossed the Red Sea and entered the desert, where it received the law, written upon tables of stone. At that time discipline reigned amongst the people of God. When they were finally established in the promised land, they prospered by reason of their faithfulness; and, finally, having become unfaithful, they were carried away captive into Babylon. When they repented they were restored to Jerusalem; this repentance, however, was of short duration, and soon there remained to observe the law but a small number of the pious.

> Mas hi ac alcuna gent plen de si gran falsità ;
> Co foron li Pharisio e li autre scripturà ;
> Qu'ilh gardesan la ley mot era demostra,
> Que la gent o veguessan, per esser plus honrà ;
> Mas poc val aquel honor que tost ven a chavon :
> Ilh persequian li sant e li just e li bon.
> Cum plor e cum gemament oravan lo Segnor,
> Que deisendes en terra per salvar aquest mont,
> Car tot l'uman lignage annava a perdicion.

Then God sent His angel to " a noble maiden of royal lineage," to announce to her that she would bring into the world Jesus, the Saviour. Jesus was born poor ; he escaped the persecution occasioned by the visit of the " trey baron," and selected twelve Apostles,

> E volc mudar la ley que devant avia dona.;
> El non la mude pas, qu'ilh fos habandona,
> Mas la renovelle, qu'ilh fos mehl garda.

The new law is superior to that of Moses ; the Sermon on the Mount is a testimony to that. Jesus having himself been baptized for the salvation of men, conferred upon His Apostles the power of baptizing and instructing every creature in the law of the Gospel. To this power He added that of performing miracles, and of foretelling the future. He had instructed them to follow the path of poverty, and had taught them by means of parables, which have been preserved to us in the New Testament ; hence it follows that if anyone love Christ, and desire to imitate Him, he must begin by reading the Scriptures. We find there

> Que solament per far ben Xrist fo persegu
> . . . . . . . . . . . . . . . . . .
> E cant el faczia mais de ben, plus era persegu.

Finally, Jesus was betrayed and crucified.

> Taut foron li torment amar e doloyros
> Que l'arma partic del cors per salvar li peccador.

After His resurrection, He appeared to His disciples, and promised to be with them to the end. Then He ascended up into heaven, whence the Holy Spirit descended upon the Apostles on the day of Pentecost. Since that time these latter have gone into the world preaching the Gospel, and there soon sprung up a people of believers.

> Cristians foron nomma, car ilh creyan en Xrist.

All were persecuted, not by the saints, for that has never been seen, but by people who acted mostly from ignorance. To-day, as then, there are those who persecute, and they call themselves His disciples !

Mas enapres li apostol foron alcuns doctors
Lical mostravan la via de Xrist lo nostre Salvador.
Mas encar sen troba alcun al temp present,
Lical son manifest a mot poc de la gent,
La via de Yeshu Xrist mot fort volrian mostrar,
Mas tant son persegu que a peno o pon far ;
Tant son li fals Xristian enceca per error ;
E maiorment que li autre aquilh que devon esser pastor,
Car ilh perseguon e aucion aquilh que son melhor,
E laysan en pacz ll fals e li enganador.
Mas en czo se po conoyser qu'ilh non son bon pastor,
Car non aman las feas si non per la toyson.

After that, praise was reserved for the wicked. It was he who
was exalted as " prudom e leal home." But let such as act in
that manner beware ; they will be confounded at last. It will
avail them nothing to call in the confessor in their last moments.
However, we shall see by an example how they are accustomed to
act :

Cant lo mal lo costreng tant que a pena po parlar
El demanda lo prever e se vol confessar ;
Mas segont l'escriptura, el ha trop tarcza, lacal di :
" San e vio te confessa e non atendre la fin ! "
Lo prever li demanda si el ha neun pecca ;
Duy mot o trey respont e tost ha despacha.
Ben li di lo prever qu'el non po esser asout,
Si el non rent tot l'autruy e smenda li seo tort.
Mas cant el au ayczo, el ha grant pensament,
E pensa entre si que, si el rent entierament,
Que remanrè a li seo enfant, e que dirè la gent ;
E comanda a li seo enfant que smendon li seo tort,
E fay pat cum lo prever qu'el poysa esser asout :
Si el n'a cent lioras de l'autruy o encara 2 cent,
Lo prever lo quitta per cent sout o encara per mencz
E li fay amonestancza e li promet perdon,
Qu'el faça dire mesa per si e per li sio payron
E lor empromet perdon sia a just, o sia a fellon. [818]
Adonca li pausa la man sobre la testa ;
Cant el li dona mais, li fay plus grant festa,

E li fay entendament que el es mot ben asout :
Mas mal son smenda aquilh de qui el ha li tort.
Mas el serè enganna en aital asolvament;
E aquel que lio o fay encreyre hi pecca mortalment.
Ma yo ruso dire, car se troba en ver,
Que tuit li papa que foron de Silvestre entro en aquest,
E tuit li cardenal e li evesque e li abba,
Tuit aquisiti ensemp non han tanta potesta
Que ilh poissan perdonar un sol pecca mortal :
Solament Dio perdona, que autra non ho po far.

The pastors and the faithful who are worthy of the name do not act so. Their confession is sincere and thorough; for if any-one desire to follow Christ he must practice these three virtues : spiritual poverty, chastity, and humility.

Such is the permanent law—the way open to us. Let us walk in it, and remember we are told to watch.

E esser mot avisa del temp de l'antechrist,
Que nos non crean ni a son fait ni a son dit,
Car segont l'escriptura, son ara fait moti antechrist,
Car antechrist sont tuit aquilh que contrastan a Xrist.

Once more, the end is near at hand ; the judgment will soon come, when heaven and earth shall be shaken. God grant that on that day our place be found on the right hand of the just Judge for ever and ever.

Such is a summary of the Noble Lesson.[819] We shall not here consider the special doctrine that characterizes it ; but we already feel, and shall moreover demonstrate further on, that it coincides in every respect with the doctrine of the Waldenses. We would prefer to examine the question of the date of the poem, which is still such a subject of dispute.

According to an interpretation, which has become traditional, the Noble Lesson dates back to a period before Waldo. According to modern criticism it goes back only to the eve of the Reformation. We shall show that this tradition is tainted with prejudice, and that the critics in this matter have proceeded with a certain degree of haste, which has not accelerated a definite solution.

The great point in the dispute that has taken place with regard to the date of the poem is furnished by two lines, which

are read in two different ways. The reading first followed was
this :—

> Ben ha mil e cent ancz compli entiérament
> Que fo scripta l'ora car sen al derier temp.

The other reading, generally followed now-a-days, is as
follows :—

> Ben ha mil e 4 cent an compli entierament
> Que fo scripta l'ora car sen al derier temp.

Of these two readings which is the correct one ? That,
really, is what the whole question is about. Let us enter
into some details, and examine first the one that bears the most
ancient date. Raynouard translated it literally. He says :

> Bien a mille et cent ans accomplis entiérement
> Que fut écrite l'heure que nous sommes au dernier temps.[82]

But did he interpret it aright ? "The poem of the *Nobla
Leiczon*, he writes, bears the date of 1100." Raynouard did not
well consider that statement ; undoubtedly because he thought
only of appropriating the popular and traditional interpretation of
Morland, Léger, and their repeaters ; moreover, he was interested
in making it fit in with his theory of the primitive Romance language. Reuss, accustomed to more strictly accurate language,
opens his eyes in astonishment, and exclaims : "Can it be
believed ? almost all the authors who have written upon these
verses, and the poem from which they are taken, claim that they
contain directly and explicitly the poet's indication of the epoch—
the year 1100 of our era.[81] This would mean that, at the
moment of our Lord's birth, someone predicted the end of the
world at a given time, and that his writing was accepted as
authoritative at the end of the XI. century ! Is that common
sense ? Where are the inspired books, or those passing as such,
which are contemporary with the year one ? How could those
writers, one after the other, repeat a statement contrary to the
best established facts recorded in sacred history, which even
our children know by heart ? Evidently the date, from which to
compute the 1100 years of the poet, must be the epoch of a
writing, containing a similar prediction ; which writing, in its
time, preoccupied the minds and awakened the anxious attention

of the party to which it belonged."[822] Now, what is that writing?
According to Reuss, " it can be none other than the Apocalypse,"
and he does not even think it necessary to prove his statement.
Herzog is not of that opinion; he believes that the writing
designated by the poet must be the first Epistle of the Apostle
John, which the Waldenses all knew quite as well as the Apocalypse.[823] Be this as it may, as, according to tradition, those two
writings date from the end of the first century, whether it be one
or the other, the questions remain unchanged. We must,
therefore, count the 1100 years from the year 100 or thereabout.
If we take the indication given by the poet, in its literal sense,
we come down to a period later than the year 1200; for it is only
fair to recognize that this indication— somewhat approximative
and general as it is—refers less to the year than to the century;
it means that the XII. century was ended and past sometime
before.[824] Our conclusion is, that if the reading of the verse
quoted be correct, its literal interpretation fixes the date of the
poem at the beginning of the XIII. century; that is to say, from
the year 1200 to 1240. Muston has not yet given his adherence
to this view; still even he no longer dates the Noble
Lesson back to the year 1100; the name of Vaudès
found in it no longer seems to him a proof that the Waldenses
existed before Waldo; and he is ready to " bring that composition
down to a period posterior to that of Waldo." We make a note
of this concession. But why stop short of the term indicated in
the poem? That is what the historian does when he states that
the Noble Lesson " belongs to the second half and probably the
end of the XII. century," whilst at the same time adding " it might
without anachronism be brought down still nearer to our time."[825]
It must, in our opinion, be so brought down—arithmetic and logic
demand it; and that is undoubtedly the reason why, in a recent
study of the Noble Lesson made by a Waldensian pastor, the
following conclusion, as here quoted, is arrived at:—" We are
led to fix the dates of the composition of the poem at the end of
the XII. century, or the beginning of the XIII., say between 1190
and 1240."[826] On this point we are nearly in complete agreement
with the writer.

It remains to verify the date. From an historical point of
view nothing can be easier. Everybody knows that at the beginning of the XIII. century the end of the world was expected:

many predicted a universal upheaval ; in short, it was an hour of general expectation.[827] Without being won over by the Apocalyptic ideas of Joachin de Flore and his school, the Waldenses yielded in part to the spirit of the age ; they, too, distinguished the great epochs of the human race, but after their own fashion ; that is to say, according to the Scriptural reading. This, however, is the fact which may most clearly indicate the date of the document we are considering : the Noble Lesson corresponds fully and distinctly to the testimony of the Inquisitors, respecting principles of doctrine and morals of the Waldenses during the Middle Ages. This point will be made clear further on ; only we must acknowledge that the considerations ordinarily brought forward on this subject, our own included, do not apply exclusively to the XIII. century ; they do not prove that the composition of the Noble Lesson was, in the following century, out of the question—far from it. That which makes us insist upon the XIII. century, is solely and entirely the indication of the poet. Had he written :

Ben ha mil e 2 cent an compli entierament,

we should feel quite easy in our minds ; the entire poem would still be accounted for by reasons of a general kind, such as justify the accepted date.

But is that date authentic ? That is the kernel of the question. The critic, Dieckhoff of Goettingen, doubted it before he could adduce any apparent reason for his doubts. This learned man, gifted with great perspicuity, but with too fertile an imagination, bethought himself one day that the Noble Lesson did not emanate directly from the Waldensian reaction, and might have issued from that of the Taborites of the XV. century. In that case, what became of the verses that indicate the date ? Dieckhoff explains away their significance, by stating that the verses had been interpolated. The idea that the poem should have originated in Bohemia is almost ridiculous. That notion had no interest for philologists, nor did it long attract the attention of readers ; Herzog mentions it, only in a few words to refute it.[828] That point had been reached when the librarian of Cambridge University laid his hands upon the manuscripts —deposited by Sir Samuel Morland—thought to have been lost, perhaps stolen, by the Waldenses or their friends.[829] On that day fortune favoured Bradshaw. He was looking over

the old manuscripts, when his eye was attracted by a copy of the
Noble Lesson. Whilst reading the verses, which we are now
discussing, he came upon a variation :—

> Ben ha mil e* cent an compli entierament
> Que fo scripta l'ora car sen al derier temp.

The point, marked with an asterisk, showed an erasure.
By the aid of a magnifying glass, the librarian eventually made out
—so he said—a 4, barely recognizable, owing to the action of an
eraser. " Habemus confitentem reum," cried he, with great
satisfaction.[830] A meeting was called, and Bradshaw proved himself equal to the occasion. After having mentioned with pride
the discovery of the manuscripts—slurring over the fact of their
long oblivion, the result of ignorance—he showed all the
resurrected volumes, and at last came to the subject of the erasure.
He pointed it out and indicated the figure, which had been
operated upon by the blade of the forger, proceeding by comparing
it with the other " 4s " which are to be found, in more than one
article forming part of the same volume, to establish its identity
with them. The similarity was evident, and constituted a
primary indication. But the proof was to come. In the following
volume of the series, discovered by him, was a very short fragment,
till then unexamined, containing the first verses only of the Noble
Lesson, written like prose, in uninterrupted lines. Then the
mystery was solved ; for here the four hundred was evident, in
Roman figures :—

> Ben ha mil e cccc anz compli entierament
> Que fo scripta l'ora ara sen al derier temps.

That is the second reading. It is more authentic than the
first ? Criticism this time scarcely admits of any discussion ;
one would think that, weary of doubting, it had become credulous.
The manuscripts produced are four in number. Their age seems
to be fixed. Two are at Cambridge, and date, one from the
beginning and the other from the middle of the XV. century.
These bear the modern date. The others are in Geneva and
Dublin ; the former belonging to the end of the XV. century, the
latter only to the XVI. These bear the ancient date. Now,
according to Bradshaw, Todd, Herzog, and Montet, there is

nothing more to be said on the matter; a decision has to be
arrived at. Only lately Montet wrote : " The question of the time
of the Noble Lesson, the only poem whose date can be approximately fixed, is decided by the respective age of the different
codices which contain it."[831] However, if the truth must be told,
for us the question is not solved. Can we be sure that no manuscript of the Noble Lesson existed prior to that of Cambridge and
the accompanying fragment ? If such a manuscript did exist, did
it bear the ancient or the modern date ? In other words, what
guarantee have we that the reading of the Cambridge manuscript
is the only authentic one, when, in order to believe that, we must
give up the idea of taking it literally ? The attempt to count the
centuries from the year 100 is now given up ; for that would bring
us to the century of the Reformation. Montet seems at first to
wish to make an exception in this case, but he rapidly becomes
confused. He may be judged by his own words. He says : " In
the more ancient manuscripts, the manuscripts B and C of Cambridge—one of the first half, the other of the middle of the XV.
century—the Waldensian author states that he writes in  the XV.
century.

Il y a bien mille et quatre cents ans accomplis entièrement
Depuis que fut ècrite l'heure que nous sommes au dernier temps.

" The author taking as a point of departure for his chronology,
the time in which the First Epistle of St. John was written,
namely, about the end of the first century of our era, the fourteen
hundred years of which he speaks, bring us down well into the
fifteenth."[832] We beg to correct this ; one century, plus fourteen
centuries fully elapsed, bring us to the beginning of the XVI.
century. Let us not forget that, according to Reuss, it is a
question of " common sense." If any one possessed that kind of
sense, it was surely the poet, who thought of what he was saying;
but with the copyist it is a different matter. Little zealous for
the integrity of the text, uneducated, or, it may be,
moderately mindful of the rules of prosody, he may have
been ; hence the mistake. It is not necessary to imagine,
with Muston, that the four manuscripts may have been written
from the same dictation, in order to agree with him, that
it is possible the copyist on arriving at the words, " Ben
ha mil e cent an," may have said to himself, " This will not do,

we are in the fifteenth century"; we must therefore write, "Ben ha mil e 4 cent an."[833] A copyist might commit such an error; common sense is not as necessary to such an one, as to the inditer—and, shall we say? to his critics.

This is, as far as we are concerned, the main obstacle; for all the other allegations with regard to this less ancient date have no real value. For instance, what have we to do here with arguments derived from the mention of persecutions, or allusions to the coming of Antichrist? Persecutions belong to all ages, and the idea of Antichrist was as widely spread, if not more so, during the XV. century as at any former period. One may be surprised that the poem should speak of Saracens; still, although the expression was an old one, does that prove it to have been obsolete? Again, the mention of Bishop Sylvester has seemed to betray a recent date, because it is said the legend concerning him was not known among the Waldenses in their early days. What does that signify? Traces of this legend are not to be found in all the revised editions of the poem. The Dublin manuscript is free from it, Sylvester not being named therein. Herzog verifies the fact only to observe that "his name may have been introduced in a subsequent revision!"[834] Here is another *imbroglio*. According to the unanimous opinion of all the students of ancient writings, the Dublin manuscript is the most modern, and Sylvester is mentioned in the *codices* of Cambridge and Geneva. These manuscripts, therefore, present variations that are not insignificant; they indicate more than one revision. What is there to tell us whether the Geneva or Dublin revision may not be anterior to that of Cambridge? The age of the manuscripts by no means decides the question; their independence is possible, notwithstanding their age, which, after all, does not appear to be fixed with great precision. The most recent manuscript may give a more ancient version; so that the reading of those of Geneva and Dublin, with reference to the date of the poem, is not necessarily explained by a pious fraud; whilst the erasure at Cambridge, attributed to the hand of a forger, was, perhaps, the act of an awkward but scrupulous corrector. Who knows, even, whether we do not owe the erasure to the hand of the copyist himself? In my case the explanation is not clear, and the question of the date of the poem is so far from being solved, that we despair of its ever being so on purely historic ground. Let us, therefore, consign the solution to the hands of philologists ; at the same time, however, warning them that, as has been too often the case, if they take upon themselves to decide the question lightly, their verdict will have no other effect than to confirm others in their previous opinions. We hope for a more satisfactory result, which must necessarily be facilitated by the recent progress made in Neo-Latin philology.[835] We heartily wish them God-speed, the more so as the date of the Noble Lesson, once established, will serve as a basis from which to determine that of the other poetical writings.

We have now arrived at the end of our chapter, which may be here recapitulated in a few words. Let us confess, without hesitation, that the impression it leaves is not a very clear one, this being partly explainable by reason of the imperfection of our analysis ; but, besides this, we would also ask the reader to take cognisance of a much more serious and deeper-lying cause, which belongs to the very nature of Waldensian literature, such as we of the present day imagine it to have been. Indeed, the two principal elements of which it is composed diverge too much in thought ; they are not homogeneous. The poetry, as a rule, bears the Waldensian imprint ; but the prose bears it only in exceptional cases. The former is authentic in matter and in form ; generally, one needs but to read to be convinced. Everything, except some very slight peculiarities, recalls what we learn from the judges of heresy, concerning the dogmatic and moral character of the Waldensian reaction. The prose, on the contrary, is derived from concealed foreign sources ; so much is this the case, that, to become doubtful regarding its authenticity, it is here also only necessary to read it. How many pages are Waldensian only in form, or in translation ? It may be that the name Waldensian is all that many have. We need not then be surprised, if critics have found in these writings material for showing the early Waldenses to be Catholics.[836] We shall see that the Inquisitors were more just towards them. Verily, what the Waldenses lose in being known by the prose attributed to them, they regain through the writings of the judges of heresy and the testimony of persecutors. What does this amount to, but a confession that side by side with a poetry that is truly Waldensian, we have a prose that is very little so ? This doubt crossed our minds at the commencement of this research. It continued whilst we proceeded ; and now that we have reached the end, we confess that it has not left us.[837] Doubt has its advantages; it will preserve us from making the contradictory statements for which critics are now-a-days notorious, and it may furnish us with the means of re-establishing the facts concerning the religious life of Waldensian dissent.

# CHAPTER THE SIXTH.

## THE RELIGIOUS LIFE.

*The materials for this picture refurnished by Waldo—The rule of religious life is Christ's law according to the Scripture— Have the Waldenses adopted the scholastic method of inter- pretation ?—Their articles of faith, mainly derived from Catholic tradition, are reformed as regards two points : eschathology and worship—Their morals, copied from the precepts of the Gospel, give evidence of the influence of Catharism, and are especially marked in the protest against falsehood, oaths and the death penalty—Divers names : the one that remains—The community and the triple vow of admission—Bishops, Presbyters, and Deacons ; the Bishop and the general administration—The Chapters—Worship : remarks upon the times, places, and elements—The Bene- dicite Prayer : the Lord's Prayer only used, the Ave Maria given up—The reading of the Holy Scriptures: reading, learning by rote, preaching—The Sacraments : their number according to Waldensian usage—Variations in the conception and observance of baptism—Ordination by the laying on of hands : rubric—Confession and Penances—The Eucharistic rite and the consecrated bread—Polemics—Ethics : praise and calumny—Different usages : costumes, disguises ; the hawker—The epoch of decadence ; religious life in the valleys of the Alps toward the end of the XV. century and at the approach of the Reformation, according to the testimony of Inquisitors, of Bishop Seyssel. and of the Barbe Morel— Concluding remarks.*

THE framework of Waldensian history is now completed. Let us then endeavour to sketch an outline of Waldensian religious life. It should be a finished picture, but that is not possible for us. We shall try to give the main features of it at

least, and our first question is : Where shall we find the initial conception of the ideal which determines the real character of the
reaction we are studying ?

There is no doubt upon that point. We must look for it in
Waldo. He was the Father, the Abraham of the Israel of the
Alps, before he became it's Moses. He possessed, in short, all
the qualities that constitute a Reformer, and he excelled in
communicating his own convictions to others ;[838] consequently he
has left a deep, indelible impression. His powerful individuality
towers above all others in the period prior to the Reformation ; he
arose in the midst of a world of serfs attached to the Papal glebe,
to follow Christ and obey His word. His entire programme is
contained in the command that re-echoed from the depth of his own
conscience : "Come, thou, and follow me." It includes all the precepts of evangelical law, from that of voluntary poverty to that of
free preaching. These two precepts of opposite extremes meet
here ; in reality they constitute but one, and that unity is the
ideal of the Waldensian reaction. The Franciscans and Dominicans understood it well ; they were even influenced by it ; but,
making it subservient to Papacy, they changed its nature. If the
Waldensian reaction presents an original type, it owes it to
Waldo. The Mendicant Orders are only an imitation or a carica-
ture of it.[839] Between the Waldensian principle, and that of the
monks, there is all the difference that separates obedience from
servile cringing. If, according to his disciples, Waldo was "like
a lion that awakes from his sleep," the monks were *canes Domini*,
but dogs that allow themselves to be muzzled. In a word, the
Waldensian idea is summed up in the apostolic word : "It is
better to obey God than man." Thus Waldo imitates the
Apostles; he is a continuation of them more than the Popes, for they
do not maintain their veritable tradition as he claims to do. Hence
the double aspect assumed by the Waldensian reaction, according
to the point of view from which it is regarded. On the one hand
it is positive, for it is, above all, an act of obedience to Christ ; on
the other, it is negative, in that it necessarily implies rebellion
against His pretended Vicar. Some think that it bears upon its
banner the vital principle of all reform worthy of that name ;
others, that it proclaims heresy, the mother of all discord.
Nothing in it, however, points to anarchy, and there is a wide
difference between the free investigation practised by Waldo, and

that which is preached in modern times. Liberty is looked upon by the early Waldenses as a condition of obedience; it emancipates the soul from the yoke of the Church, only to bring it back captive to the feet of its Divine Master.

Such is the initial conception which dominates the Waldensian evolution. Let us descend from these general considerations to the facts, which we desire to determine; and first, let us see what is the rule that governs the religious life of the Waldenses.

This rule was not new. It was but necessary to put forth a hand in order to take it from the ark of tradition, wherein lie the treasures of faith, "sacred, only, because never touched."

It was not absolutely forbidden to touch them; but it was no longer customary to do so, owing to clerical prejudice, which had almost consigned to oblivion both ancient practice and the voice of the Fathers of the Church, such as Saints Augustine and Chrysostom. From time to time that voice found a feeble echo in the words of the pastors; then the Waldenses listened. Waldo, it will be remembered, did so, and his disciples likewise. A priest one day composed a homily upon this text of the Gospel : "The sower went forth to sow the seed." If ever there were a text likely to interest the Waldenses this was it. On that occasion the preacher spoke words which were recorded in Waldensian dialect. Here are a few of them :—

"The word of God is the salvation of the souls of the poor; it is the medicine of those who faint; it is the food of those who hunger; it is the teaching of those who remain ; it is the consolation of the afflicted ; it is the rejection of vices ; it is the acquisition of virtues ; it is the confusion of devils ; it is the light of hearts; it is the path of the traveller. The word of God fills the thoughts of man with all virtues. The word of God tells thee whether thou be an unreasoning animal or a reasonable man. The word of God is the beginning of spiritual life. The word of God is the preservation, not only of the virtues and graces, but of all Christian faith."[840]

The Waldenses, however, were not satisfied with these pious sentiments alone ; they also used their reason. The Scripture was for them the very fountain head of religious knowledge. Superior to reason, tradition, and the authority of the Church, it takes its stand as the rule of faith.

L'Escriptura di, e nos creire ho deven
Ayczo deven ereire car l'Avangeli o di.[841]

They distinguish in it three successive laws : the natural law,
the law of Moses, and the perfect law of Jesus Christ. This
latter alone is permanent. To meditate upon it and observe it is
all their wisdom, as it also is their life.

Se Xrist volen amar ni saber sa doctrina
Nos coventa velhar e legir l'Escriptura.[842]

It would be puerile to pretend that the early Waldenses attempted
to criticise sacred questions, at a time when nobody thought of so
doing. They knew the Scriptures according to the Vulgate ; but
after what we have just seen, it is not surprising that they should
prefer to translate the New Testament.[843] In this they were
acting logically. They only partially attempted to translate the
Old Testament, if we may judge from such portions as have come
down to us, and they did not exclude the Apocryphal books. If
their notions regarding the canon of the Scriptures betrayed at
first the influence of Catholicism, they became modified later on
by that of the Renaissance and Reformation.[844]

The rule being given, how do they interpret it ?

In Waldo's time, a knowledge of the meaning of the Scriptures
was arrived at by four roads. These had been traversed by the
Fathers, the theologians and the monks. Waldo did not much care
for these beaten paths ; he had no time to lose. Had he heard the
precept, which caused his conversion, preached in several different
ways, it is probable that he would never have quitted his farm
and mills. He brought to the study of the Scriptures that
practical common sense which had guided him in his business
transactions. Fault was found with his interpretation for being
too literal, and on that account it did not, whatever some writers
of our day may think, agree with the scholastic method.[845]
Is it even probable that Waldo selected any particular method ?
We think not. He seems to have gone on his way without any
theory or interpretation, even in the theological sense of the
term.[846] The word of Christ was clear enough ; for Waldo it was
simply a question of furnishing a literal translation. His school
remained faithful to this principle ; nowhere did it produce
theorists. Bernard Gui states, concerning the Waldenses scattered

in the South of France, that they insisted upon the observation of the precepts of the Gospel, just as they were written, and without commentary.[847] It was not different in Germany. David of Augbourg and his colleague of Passau, accused their victims of adhering too closely to the literal meaning, and of rejecting all mystic interpretation.[848] It would not seem that the allegorical method was at all palatable to the early settlers in the valleys of the Alps, for Morel, writing to Oecolampadus, actually asked whether he thought that interpretration admissible, and adapted to the instruction of the people.[849] It is true that certain Waldensian compilations of Catholic origin, like the treatise on the Virtues and the commentary on the Songs of Solomon, had admitted it; and it is upon these that Herzog and Montet base their assertions, when they impute to the early Waldenses the fourfold scholastic interpretation. Of course such a mode of argument could be made to prove anything.

We repeat, the Waldenses were not theorists, we must not go to them for forms and rubrics. Their reaction, which was essentially moral, departed at first, but very slightly, from traditional dogmas; like an Alpine brook that flows a long while under the snowfield upon which it feeds, before the latter breaks down; that departure was not the result of calculated speculation, but of a practical observance of evangelical morals. It will not be difficult to form some idea of this.

A new life, according to the perfect law of Christ, commences with repentance; that constitutes the first round of the ladder of perfection.

> La ley de Yeshu Xrist haven abandona,
> E non haven temor ni fe ni carita.
> Confessar nos coventa : non y deven tarçar.[150]

As everyone ought to repent before death comes to take him unawares, there is no time to be lost. If God waits for the sinner, if he prolong the time of his patience, it is only during our pilgrimage here below.

> Car atent lo peccador e li dona alongament
> Quel poysa far penedença en la vita present.[851]

Does not this principle lead to the denial of purgatory? At least, we must confess, it is very far from leading to an admission

of that doctrine.   Let us not forget that during the XII. century,
the doctrine of purgatory was disputed not only by the Cathari,
but even in the bosom of the Roman Church ; moreover, such vague
deductions as the above are not the only proofs we possess ; we
have within reach the most explicit testimonies.   There are but
two paths, said the Waldenses—one is the path of life,. the other
that of death.[852]  The first leads straight to paradise ; the second,
to hell.   There is no middle road.[853]  The most ancient Waldensian writings ignore purgatory ;[854] it is mentioned, it is true, in
subsequent writings, but only to be refuted.[855]  Was it rejected from
the commencement : that is to say, by Waldo and his original
followers in Lyons.   This is a doubtful point ;[856] however, the
doctrine of purgatory and the monoply of Scriptural interpretation and preaching are the first Romish doctrines decidedly
put aside.[857]   There are punishments which serve to purify
the soul, but they are those of this life.[858]  From this, to
rejecting purification through punishment in another life, was but
a single step,[859] and the conclusion must be—Purgatory does not
exist.[860]  The priests invented it solely for the purpose of justifying the masses for the dead, suffrages, indulgences and bountiful
alms.   All that scaffolding therefore crumbles from the base.[861]
Even the doctrine of the intercession of Saints becomes illusory
and the worship of them is rendered futile.[862]  The fact is that neither
the Virgin nor the Saints can do anything for the salvation of
sinners, except by their example, which renders them worthy of
veneration.   The Waldenses venerate the Saints, but with discretion.   They learn in early life that worship belongs to God alone.
We read in the Gloss on the Lord's Prayer, "We owe to God fear,
honour, and obedience in all things ; also honour is due, after
that to God, to the blessed Virgin Mary, first among all created
beings, for she is the mother of Christ ; then a like honour to
all the saints who rest in glory, together with all the heavenly host."
Then we owe obedience to our superiors.[863]  It would be more
than hazardous to deduce from this passage that the Virgin and
the Saints divided the honour of worship with God, even in the
minor degree of " dulia cultus " to use the jargon of the schools.
It contains nothing more than a somewhat vague definition of a
religious homage.   Again, is that homage quite authentic ?  The
passage is taken from too mixed a source to be reliable ; and
whereas a homily of rather suspicious origin is quoted, to show

that the Waldenses looked up to the Virgin Mary as the "Queen of Heaven,"[864] it is contradicted by the testimony of the very persons who sat in judgment upon them. Indeed, the judges tell us that the Waldenses, in Germany for instance, do not admit that the repose of the Saints can be disturbed by our prayers.[865] If they had to pray for sinners every time the latter afforded them an opportunity, their state would not be very enviable.[866] No, they are not cognisant of our miseries, neither can they prevent them.[867] They cannot see them, being absorbed in the contemplation of the Godhead.[868] To invoke them is a waste of time, nay more, a moral sin.[869] Help comes from God, the only object of our faith.[870] He has atoned for our sin on the Cross, in the person of His Son, born of the Virgin Mary, and he expects from us obedience to His holy law, and works meet for repentance. That is the price of our salvation. Man is not saved by faith alone.

> Si el non vol cum la fe las obras acabar.
> La corona de gloria non es degne de portar.

Works are the demonstration of faith, and an earnest of our election. There are but few who endeavour to put them into practice ; with most it is as though it were sufficient to desire an entry into Paradise to obtain it. That is a mistake. God has promised it to us as He has promised our daily bread—but we must earn it.

> Poc curan d'obrar per que ilh sian eleit,
> Ben volrien paradis, a cant per desirar,
> Ma czo per que el s'acquista non volrein gaire far ;
> Ma segout l'escriptura la lo conven comprar.[871]

Here we are, back again in the full blaze of Catholic tradition. We shall, whatever ultra-apologists may say, seek in vain in the creed of the early Waldenses for those tenets which characterise Protestantism. " When the Waldenses separated themselves, they held but very few dogmas opposed to ours," says Bossuet. He would have been right had he stopped there ; but when he goes on to add that they had " perhaps none at all,"[872] he goes half-way to meet modern criticism, which is on the point of going astray. We must recognize the fact that the Waldenses did not aim at reforming creeds. They bear on their banner a moral ideal ; that perfect standard which is practically summed up in the triple vow of poverty, chastity and obedience to the law of the Gospel.

> Si nos volen amar ni segre Yeshu Xrist,
> Paureta sperital de cor deven tenir,
> E amar la castita, Dio humilment servir.[873]

We may mention that just as their dogmas adhere to Catholic tradition, so, too, their moral teachings recall those of the Cathari ; at least in such precepts as escape the influence of the double principle. Here again the analogy is striking. The Waldenses, following the Cathari, rejected the doctrine of purgatory and the practices relating thereto, whilst the Cathari have quite the appearance of having borrowed the articles that condemn falsehood, the oath and the death-penalty from the Waldenses. The features they have in common do not end here ; we shall yet notice several others, relating to organisation and worship. It may be said that we have seen how the origin of the Waldensian movement was free from Catharin admixture. True ; but the first deviations from Catholic tradition, except the one referring to lay preaching, do not date back to Lyons. Nevertheless, it seems to us, that the influence of the Cathari has been exaggerated,[874] and that the following fact has not been taken sufficiently into account, namely, that the moral teachings of the Waldenses are copied, as it were, from the Sermon on the Mount and the precepts of Christ.[875] Here are the salient features :—

> Se n'i a alcun bon que volha amar Dio temer Yeshu Xrist,
> Que non volha maudire ni jurar ni mentir,
> Ni avoutrar ni aucire ni penre de l'autruy,
> Ni venjar se de li sio enemic.
> Ilh diçon quel es vaudes e degne de punir.[876]

Three of those precepts have been much emphasized. They are those to which we have just alluded, and which we shall consider separately.

## I.—The Precept Condemning Falsehood.

According to the Waldenses, every man is bound to tell the truth, as much out of regard for his neighbour as from self-respect. Lying kills the soul.[877] The judges of heresy must at first

have greatly relished this scruple, which so much facilitated their
task. It is true, that face to face with torture and the stake, some
tried to compromise. Hence the ambiguous, equivocal language,
extorted by suffering from so many poor victims who had not
courage enough to face martyrdom. This is sufficiently laid
down by the questioners, who minutely analyzed the answers
with a sagacity becoming enough in mere grammarians, but
repugnant to all our feelings at such an occasion. To follow the
analysis still makes us feel as though assisting at an operation
when the knife is cutting through the living flesh. These
sophisms are even classified and ticketed, with all the care that
might be bestowed upon a collection of shells, flowers, or
precious relics.[878]

## II.—THE PRECEPT CONDEMNING OATHS.

Every man must abstain from swearing. According to the
Waldenses the oath is in no case allowable. " Swear not at all,"
says the Gospel, " neither by Heaven, for it is God's throne, nor
by the earth, for it is His footstool ; neither shalt thou swear by
thy head, because thou canst not make one hair white or black ;
but let your communications be 'yea, yea,' 'nay, nay ': for whatsoever is more than these tendeth to evil." They assiduously inculcated this precept; so we are told by one of their judges, and
they cared not at all for commentaries.[879] Swearing is classified
by them as a mortal sin. If any man be compelled to take an
oath,[88J] he must hasten to confess his sin and do penance. That
is the rule everywhere in France,[881] as well as in Italy and Germany.[882] But exceptions are tolerated, even authorized, in order
to avoid the total ruin of the community, which was already
threatened by so many dangers. " Formerly," observes an Inquisitor, " the Waldenses had determined not to swear at all ; then they
easily fell into our hands and a great number were despatched.[883]
Now they are prudent ; they swear, but only to escape torture and
not to betray one another ;"[884] they were especially careful not to
compromise their teachers, who were particularly exposed. To
betray a teacher was to commit the sin against the Holy Ghost.[885]
" Hence we have," adds our Inquisitor, "those evasive and deceptive answers which give us so much trouble and render our task
almost desperate.[886] Rather than die, they deny, swear and per-

jure themselves, unless in cases where we are dealing with their teachers or other persons determined to confess their faith to the end."[837]

## III.—THE PRECEPT CONDEMNING THE DEATH PENALTY.

We must get an accurate conception of this precept, for it has been the cause of misunderstanding and false deductions. Let us again hear the testimony of the Judges.

" The Waldenses affirm," says Bernard Gui, " that all judgment, being forbidden by God, is a sin ; and the judge, who, under whatever circumstances, and for whatever motive, condemns a man to torture or to death, acts contrary to the Gospel, in which it is written : ' Judge not, that ye be not judged.' They also appeal to the commandment : ' Thou shalt not kill,' nor regard any commentaries thereon ;[888] and the same principle is professed in Lombardy and elsewhere.[889] It does not only refer to a particular form of the death penalty or its application to heretics, as might be imagined ; on the contrary, it condemns all manner of violent death, whether by the sword of the soldier or of justice.[890] In Germany some, perhaps under the influence of Catharin superstition,[891] seem to have extended the application of it to animals. From this, to question the salvation of professional violaters of this law, namely, Princes, Lords and officers of justice, is certainly not a long step."[892] We can now understand how the Waldenses were suspected of anarchy by people who knew them imperfectly, or were seeking for a pretext to slander them.[893]

Let us add, that the condemnation of the death penalty naturally implied the reprobation of murder, and, by implication, of all deeds of blood ; for the horror of blood was not with them a mere feint, as in the dominating Church, but a veritable and sincere feeling.[894]

Such are the characteristic features of the creed and moral teaching of the Waldenses. It is quite clear that they diverge more and more from the world and the official Church.

And do they not also form themselves into a distinct society, having a special organization ? It is now time to inquire into this. Let us begin by noticing the names the Waldenses give themselves, or permit others to give to them.

The first name they are ambitious of, that of " Poor of Christ,"
was not new, nor was that of " Brethren."[895]  Catholics sometimes
call them after the name of Waldo, their teacher; sometimes
" Poor of Lyons," or " Leonists," to mark their origin ; or again,
*Insabatés,* because of the *sabates* they were in the habit of wearing.  " They are called ' Poor of Lyons,' " Stephen of Bourbon
remarks, " because there they first began to profess poverty ; as
for them, they call themselves ' Poor in Spirit,' because the Lord
said : ' Blessed are the poor in spirit.' "[896]  If the name " Poor of
Lyons " recall to us the original root of the Waldensian reaction,
that of " Poor of Lombardy " designates the most prosperous of
its off-shoots.   In the valleys of the Alps we find only the three
names that refer to the Lyons origin and to Waldo.   The only
other one is that of " Waldenses."[897]   If the name of Waldo is
susceptible of several interpretations, as we have seen;[898] it is
different with that of Waldenses, which designates the disciples of
the reformer of Lyons in whatsoever locality they may live.  This
is proved both by the testimony of the Judges of heresy[899] and
the early Waldensian tradition,[900] again confirmed in the XVI.
century,[901] and noticed by Gilles.   " The aforesaid people, having
come from Lyons," writes the before-mentioned historian, " were
by their adversaries called ' Waldensian People ' on account of
Waldo, although the said people at first refused to accept that
title, not that they despised Waldo, but in order not to bring any
slight upon the very worthy name of Christian, nor wishing to
seem to acknowledge being sectarian and schismatical, as their
adversaries falsely accused them of being ; and of their said
refusal the proof is to be found as much in the books of the Waldenses themselves as in those of their adversaries.   In the epistle
they wrote to King Ladislas of Bohemia, they designate themselves " the little Christian flock, falsely called Waldenses ;" and
among other instances, also, in the book entitled *Vittoria Triom-
phale,* of the Cordelier monk, Samuel of Cassini, where he says in
the first chapter : " Thou sayest thou art not a Waldensian, but
a member of the Church of Christ."  " It is evident, therefore,"
Gilles concludes, " that this name was by their adversaries forced
upon them against their will."[902]   The name of Waldenses, however, is the only one that survived the first period.

Let us now consider what relates to their organization.

If the Waldensian reaction had not been in flagrant opposition to the traditions of the Church, it is possible that Waldo's co-religionists would have accepted, to the advantage of the people, the office of co-adjutors or helpers, as distinct from the clergy, as was the case with the first disciples of St. Francis of Assis. But they were condemned and driven out. Then, what were they to do? Did they decide to found independent churches by the side of the Romish Church, or resolve to pursue their missionary work at a distance, as it were, and secretly, without creating a schism? This point has not been examined closely enough by historians; nay, a schismatic movement was believed in without reason, although the Waldensian mission, in Gallic territory at least, and in the valleys of the Alps, never exceeded the limits of simple dissent. The Waldenses evangelize, hear confession and communicate; but, whilst still leaving the faithful in the Church in which they were born, these latter are benefited by their pastoral care without renouncing their membership in the Catholic Church.[903]

A distinction between the Waldenses and their faithful members is here drawn; this was only to be seen in the beginning. Afterward, it was particularly maintained in the French tradition, which was comparatively conservative, and to such an extent that, on the eve of the Reformation, this distinction had not disappeared from the valleys. The tendency to schism was one of the characteristic features of the Brethren of Lombardy; still, as we have clearly seen, it was not actually realized."[904]

We have just observed that the Waldenses liked to call themselves "Brethren." This is the more easily understood in that they observed the same rule and lived in common. Together they formed an association called the "Fraternity," or the "Community," or simply the "Society."[905] Brothers and sisters were soon designated by the name of "perfect"—a custom undoubtedly borrowed from the Cathari, because they professed the perfect law. The faithful who admired the Waldensian maxims, but were not admitted to the profession of the rule, were called "imperfect," or more usually "friends" or "believers."[906] To learn how the primitive community recruited its ranks, we must once more go back to the early period.

After Waldo had taken the vow of poverty, we saw that he gained over proselytes, who pledged themselves to imitate him.

All divested themselves of their property, led a chaste life in the ecclesiastic sense of the term, and at the call of their master, went out, two by two, from village to village, reading or preaching the Gospel. The society, thus founded in Lyons, increased after the first persecution and multiplied everywhere, especially in the South of France and in Lombardy. Before admission, the triple vow of poverty, chastity and obedience to superiors, continued to be enforced. That was the general rule. Let us now go into some details.

Bernard Gui tells us: "When a man was received into this society, called Fraternity, and had pledged himself to obey his superior and observe evangelical poverty, he was from that moment bound to observe the law of chastity, and own nothing in his own right; consequently, he was obliged to sell all his goods, hand over the proceeds to the common treasury, and live upon the alms of the faithful, which the leader took upon himself to distribute to each one according to his need."[907] These alms were of various kinds. They consisted either of money or produce, which was sold for cash;[908] to say nothing of lodging, food and clothing, which the brethren were sure to receive on their missionary visits. Further-more, the society accepted legacies.[909] It was so everywhere in a measure, only there is one difference to be noticed relating to the question of work. While the Waldenses of France renounced all material occupation, in order to give themselves up exclusively to their mission—[910] but reserving the right to take up any trade as a disguise when it was a question of avoiding the attention of the spies and hirelings of the Holy Office[911] — the Poor of Lombardy and their brethren of Germany claimed in this respect perfect liberty of action;[912] nay, more, they were proud of working and reproached the Romish clergy with their idleness.[913] We can surmise how, in their lively discus-sions, they took advantage of the words of the Apostle Paul.[914] However, they finally looked at the question from another point of view and conformed to the rule of their French brethren.[915]

The second vow was that of chastity.

Here again Waldo set the example. The reader will not have forgotten how he gave up his family life and separated from his wife. He consented, it is true, in compliance with the injunction of the Archbishop, to take his meals at her house; but this act of obedience was followed by their final separation. Could he have required his brethren to take the vow of chastity had he not observed it himself? They observed it from the very day of their entrance into the community. If the candidate had a wife he was obliged to separate from her. If a married woman were to be admitted she had to be separated from her husband whether she desired it or not.[916] Let us also add that the sanction of the community was necessary, so that no step could be taken on the caprice of the moment.[917] The Poor of Lombardy insisted that the marriage contract was indissoluble, except in the case provided for by the Gospel law, and that consequently neither husband nor wife had the right to withdraw from it, without the consent of the other party.[918] However, this in no wise restrained the Lombards from insisting, as eagerly as their French brethren, upon the observance of the vow of chastity on the part of those affiliated to the community; and that practice is found again among the Waldenses of Germany.[919] After all, the mention of women cannot always be accounted for in the same manner. In one case it is a question of women admitted into the community through the regular vow;[920] in another it might well be a question merely of some faithful person,[921] if not of some local and subordinate order, which escapes us. It is certain, at any rate, that in the beginning at least, the community gave women the right of participating in the triple vow prescribed by the rule.[922]

The third vow was that of obedience.

Waldo had made that vow to God, as others had done, for the matter of that; but, in the way that he understood it, it was not pleasing to the Pope. Waldo kept it nevertheless; and what was the consequence? He in a way supplanted the Pope in the eyes of his brethren, who recognised in him both the founder of their order and their legitimate superior. He was in the community of Lyons what Zinzendorf was during the last century in that of Herrnhut, namely, the Bishop of his brethren. He ruled them by the prestige of his powerful individuality more than by the exercise of any right conferred on him.[923] His opinion had sometimes more weight than he desired, and it is very possible that he may have felt the burden of his power as much as his subordinates. He was at the same time both Bishop and Rector-General of the community.[924] What a task and what a responsibility was his, in the midst of dispersion! Is it a matter for astonishment that he was not able to preserve unity everywhere—

in the cities of Lombardy, for instance, which were a prey to so
much discord ? His brethren assembled at Bergamo shortly after
his death ; all attributed to him a saying which is not altogether
clear to us, namely, that he did not consider it right that supreme
direction should be conferred upon any one man, either during his
own lifetime or after his death.[925] These words not only
expressed the feeling that the sole head elected by the Lombards
could not be recognised by the ultramontane Waldenses, but also
the conviction that the direction must be divided. There is
nothing to prove that Waldo ever arrogated to himself alone the
supreme power. He undoubtedly had, as colleague in the Rectorship, that Vivet, who, by his side, filled an eminent position, and
whose name is coupled with Waldo's in the recollections of the
deputies assembled at the conference of Bergamo. At any rate
we find that the two Rectors of the Waldenses of France presided
over that assembly, namely Peter of Relana and Bèranger
d'Aquaviva.[926] They were not elected for life, like the Lombard
President, but for a term—for one year only.[927] The residence of
these Presidents is not indicated ; but the Poor of Lombardy undoubtedly had their chief at Milan. Still that residence was not
absolutely fixed, inasmuch as their colleagues, Bishops, Presbyters and Deacons, upon whom devolved the different offices of the
community, led an itinerant life.

"What have we here ? Bishops ! "

" Yes ; we find here three very distinct classes of ministers ;
Bishops, Presbyters and Deacons.[928] The Bishop was elected by
the assembled Presbyters and Deacons. He had the power to
administer the Sacraments of Penance, of the Order, and of the
Eucharist, and to preach the Gospel where he thought best ;
besides, it was he who gave the Presbyters their commission to
preach and to hear confessions.[929] Finally, he could absolve from
all sin anyone who confessed to him, and although the latter
power was very rarely exercised,[930] remit fully or in part, the penalty
due for sins. The Presbyter received power to hear confessions,
but not to remit penalties or to administer the Sacrament of the
Eucharist.[931] As for the Deacon, he was by the very act of
ordination rendered subject to the vow of poverty, chastity, and
obedience. Before admission to the order of Deacons, no one is
perfect.[932] Any adherents to Waldensian practices, who have not
submitted to ordination, do not count among the members of the

community properly so-called; they are not brethren, but friends. It is from these that the brethren receive their means of subsistence.[933] The Deacons were the organs of this work of supply; it was their office to provide for the wants of the Bishop and Presbyters.[934] They had no power to hear confessions.[935]

What we have just read with respect to the Bishops is not as clear, at first sight, as that which relates to the other offices. We ask, for instance,[936] What relation was there between the office of Bishop and the Rectorship? We lack information upon this particular point. It is natural to think, however, that the rectors were chosen from among the Bishops, without such election necessarily involving any identity between the offices of Bishop and Rector; each of which had its distinct and peculiar character. But was the Bishop-Rector the sole head? It seems so, for the mention of the sole head is very explicit.[937] Did we not, however, in one case find two Rectors co-existing? That is true. Still, there is nothing to prevent us from assuming that one was the Chief Rector, and the other his co-adjutor; nay, is it not likely to have been so? Furthermore, if the chief stood alone in his capacity of Rector, he did not do so as Bishop.[938] There was more than one Bishop. Now the Bishops as such are equal. The election to the office of Bishop was therefore distinct from the election to the office of Bishop-Rector.[939] The latter presided at ordinations. If he were absent another Bishop took his place. If there were no Bishop present, the right of presiding passed to the Presbyters. It would appear from this that the difference between Bishop and Presbyter was not as great as amongst Catholics. This difference lies less in the dignity itself, than in the right of precedence. It is true that the Bishop enjoyed, in addition, the privilege of celebrating the Eucharist and pronouncing complete absolution, and that this privilege did not pass in its entirety to the Presbyters, even in cases of special delegation.

We now know who this " superior " was who received the vows of the new brothers, and of whom it is written that " all are bound to obey him as Catholics do the Pope."[940] He had supreme authority in the general direction and presided over the Chapters. He decided and disposed of all matters concerning the Presbyters and Deacons; it is he who designated them to collect at confession the alms of the faithful, and in all things he controlled their actions.

We have just alluded to the Chapters. It is time to say
something about them, in bringing our remarks respecting organization to a conclusion.

There undoubtedly were particular or district Chapters, since
mention is made of " General Chapters " ; but the chronicles are
silent concerning the former. With respect to the General Chapters, matters stand on a different footing. We learn that they
assembled, in the XIV. century at least, once or twice a year, and
ordinarily in a large city, in order more easily to avoid the eye of
the enemy. The Brothers disguised themselves as merchants in
order to succeed better, and assemblies were held without any
demonstration at the house of some co-religionist of long-stand-
ing.[941] The perfect Bishops, Presbyters, and Deacons were convened ; all were admitted to participate in the elections, perhaps
the above were joined by the faithful of the place.[942] The authority
of the Chapter was supreme ; although limited by the power of
the superior who presided in virtue of his office, and who at one
and the same time both consulted and controlled the Chapter. It
was on such occasions that the Deacons presented their accounts ;
and the general interests of the mission were decided upon,
especially the delegation of Presbyters or Deacons to the brethren
and friends of different countries.[943]

Such was the organization of the Waldenses. It was in force,
in a special manner, in France and Lombardy. In the latter
country it differed somewhat, but rather in the matter of names
and titles than in the offices themselves. The General Chapter
acted under the name of the community, used also on the other
side of the Alps, or under that of the congregation ; the simple
Bishop is called minister ; the head Bishop, as we stated, bore
the title of Prepositor. In Germany, we can very easily infer
what the meaning of this was, when we recall the influence of the
Poor of Lombardy that prevailed there. Nevertheless, as the
influence of the Poor of Lyons also counted for something, in
Bohemia particularly, it would not be surprising if uniformity was
less rigorously maintained there, than below the Alps. The union
with the Hussites and the Brethren of Bohemia afterward brought
on modifications, with which we have nothing to do. Bishop
Stephen, the martyr of Vienna, is perhaps the last Waldensian
who bore that title.

Let us now enter into the sanctuary of the religious life of the Waldenses, to examine their worship.

We might unprofitably seek to distinguish here between the worship at which Waldenses alone were present and that in which the faithful took part. We should find the same elements on both sides. Moreover, we are bound to admit that, on the first point, we have no large amount of information. We may well infer that their statutes compelled them to observe regular practices. They undoubtedly had both individual and congregational worship ; that is to say, among the members of the community, when the latter was not dispersed in a thousand directions ; but we learn very little concerning either. This is quite immaterial after all, for the principles of that private worship will be revealed to us in the outward worship to which the faithful were admitted. Only we must not here look for that regularity which distinguished the practices of the Association properly so-called. Of course there was no place consecrated for worship. In the commencement the Waldenses appeared before the people in the churches and chapels ; but persecution forced them—like the early Christians— to take refuge in the sanctuary of the family with their friends. They met in secret, in retired places ; sometimes in the caves of the earth.[944] When the wind of persecution had passed, they ventured out into the open air, in the majestic temple of nature. As to the hours of worship they were not fixed, except, perhaps, in the large cities, where adherents were numerous. In the villages the day was marked by the visit of the missionary. The opportunity was eagerly made use of, for it came only about once a year, usually toward Easter. The best thing we can do to become conversant with the forms of Waldensian worship is to follow the steps of the minister on his arrival. He shall be our guide, and, at the appropriate time and place, we shall be successively initiated into the elements of worship, especially the *Benedicite* prayer, the reading of the Scriptures, and finally, the Sacraments.

The minister, even though it be his first visit, is soon recognised by some slight conventional sign, or by some expression. He does not usually come alone, but is accompanied by his young assistant.[945] They go to a friend's house, who makes preparations for lodging them. From that moment every meal, especially the evening one, is made to partake of the character of

K

a more or less eucharistic reunion, recalling the daily communion in apostolic times. The minister pronounces the *Benedicite*. This custom is described by an Inquisitor in the following terms :—

"Before they sit down to the table they bless it saying :— *Benedicite, Kyrie eleison, Christe eleison, Kyrie eleison, Pater- noster.* Thereupon, the oldest person present says, in his own dialect: ' God, who blessed the five barley loaves and two fishes for His disciples in the wilderness, bless this table, whatever is upon it, and whatever may be brought to it.' Then, making the sign of the Cross, he blesses it saying : *In nomine Patris et Filii et Spiritus, Sancti. Amen.* In the same manner, when they rise from table, be it after dinner or supper, they return thanks in the words of the Apocalypse, pronounced by the senior present, in his own dialect: ' Praise, glory, wisdom, thanksgiving, honour, power, and might, be to our God for ever and ever.' He further adds : ' May God grant ample reward and good return to all those who do us good and bless us, and after having given us material bread, may He give us spiritual food. God be with us, and we with Him for ever ;' whereupon the rest answer ' Amen.' Either during the Benediction or at the moment of rendering thanks they often join hands and lift them up toward heaven."[946]

After the meal is over, the minister commences to exhort the persons around him, unless there be cause to mistrust some ser- vant or stranger who may happen to be present. But the preacher generally reserves himself until after supper, when the faithful, having returned from their daily work, have time to assemble, and night has come. That hour is the safest. Then all prepare themselves by meditation, and the worship, properly so-called, takes place. We shall not endeavour to indicate the ritual of it ; but at all events it closes with prayer.[947] The other elements are the reading of sacred books, preaching, and com- munion. As for singing that was out of the question, as in order not to attract the attention of the neighbours, the windows had to be closed, and sometimes even the light had to be dispensed with. Silence took the place of song, and the Waldenses preferred that to Church singing.[948] Let us examine the acts of worship a little closer, in order to discern their true character.

First, there was prayer.

The prayer of the Waldenses was the Lord's Prayer. Is it not the only one prescribed, *the* prayer par excellence? More is gained by repeating it once, than by chanting a Mass.[949] Thus, according to the proceedings of the Inquisition, the Waldenses were satisfied with that, and repeated it with a constancy that Catholics ought to have found exemplary. The following words testify to this; we borrow them again from Bernard Gui: "They say many prayers during the day, and, in like manner, they teach their followers to do the same, and join with them. This is the way they act: They kneel on the ground, bend down and lean upon a bench, or some such other piece of furniture which answers the purpose. Then all begin to pray in silence, and long enough to repeat the Lord's Prayer thirty or forty times, and sometimes more. They do this regularly every day when they are alone, with their faithful or adherents, before and after dinner and supper, in the evening before retiring, in the morning when they rise, and several other times during the day, morning or afternoon. They neither say, teach, nor practice any other prayer than that."[950] But do they not recite the *Ave Maria*? No; they are satisfied with the Lord's Prayer.[951] It has been stated, even quite recently, that it would not have been surprising "to hear Waldenses repeating the *Ave Maria*."[952] Facts do not justify that assertion. The Waldenses are as careful to leave out the *Ave* as they are to repeat the Lord's Prayer. "They think nothing of it," says Bernard Gui.[953] If they happen to recite it, it is quite an exception, and they make excuses for so doing. After all, they say—Is it a sin to recite a passage of the Gospel?[954] We must know it by heart, if only, when necessary, to foil the judges of heresy.[955] But it sometimes happens, on the other hand, that some have been brought into straits, because they neglected to practice.[956] They also suffered—and this was a more frequent occurrence—for not being able to recite the Apostles' Creed.[957] The Waldenses did not despise that Creed; as we have seen, they retained the principal articles of it, but they did not all endorse the adopted form; for, said they, Christ did not prescribe it.[958] They have a Creed drawn up in their own fashion, of which they are even proud; so says an Inquisitor.[959] It by no means follows that this Creed found a place among the elements of ordinary worship; but, even though the Lord's Prayer excluded the other prayers or practices used in the Church, did it leave no place for free or improvised prayer ?   As a rule it did not ; still if anyone ask whether this rule admitted of no exceptions our answer must be that there is not a word to indicate the fact.   Do we not read that some did not even permit themselves to adopt the Psalms as prayers ?[960]  The prayer was long or short, according to the number of times the Lord's Prayer was repeated, which absolutely depended upon the inclination of the senior minister who presided.[961]

Another element of the Waldensian worship is the reading of, and the insistence on, the Holy Scriptures.  This is characteristic, and one word will suffice to define it; it is the Lesson.[962] The part played by the Scriptures in the assemblies of Lyons and Metz has been noticed, and this will assist us in accounting for the general—sometimes extraordinary—knowledge of them, of which the least educated of the faithful were capable. If the sacred books were less wide-spread then than we generally imagine, it was not for want of zeal.   They were passed from house to house, at all hours.  Men and women, small and great—all were at work, night and day, learning them by heart in more ways than one ; no one grew weary.[963]  A disciple of seven days' standing already began to teach another.[964]  This work, like that of bees in the field, pre-supposes a hive. The hive was with them the assembly, or, better, the school; hither, for purposes of learning and teaching, the members stealthily came together.  The minister—or, as they called him, the teacher—was there, with his little book in his hand,[965] containing various portions of the Scripture, sometimes the whole of the New Testament, with chosen selections from the Old.[966]  The spirit of Waldo is here easily recognized, so faithful are his disciples to the work commenced by him.   Some who were more educated used the Latin text ; but most of them simply employed the vulgar text.[967]  A certain Inquisitor states that there were those who preached without knowing how to read. And why not ?   In such a case, he adds, they quoted from memory, and not the less faithfully for that.[968]  All aimed at inculcating the text, without commentaries ;[969] for, said they, what is not in conformity with the text of the Scripture is mere fable.[970]  Waldo had insisted upon the words of Scripture, nothing more ;  his followers did the same, and the consequence was that their hearers learnt it by heart.[971]  Men and women, old men and children, down to the humblest little one, all listened and turned over in their minds the Word of Truth.[972] According to the trite yet precious expression of one of their judges, they meditated on it during worship; then, after they got back to their firesides, each one meditated on it again with others;[973] they vied with each other in writing it upon the tablets of their memory, to meditate upon it day and night. It was their passion, but it was also their merit. However, their industrious application would have passed unnoticed if, instead of having the Word of God for its object, it had been bestowed upon the large volumes consulted by others without enduring profit. They had but one book, but it was *the* Book. From infancy everyone spelled it, line by line, learning at the same time to read, think, believe, and pray. If anyone declared he could learn nothing, it was replied: "Try to remember one word each day; at the end of the year you will know so much, and you will have made a commencement,"[974] Others distinguished themselves by their great willingness. "I have seen," relates Stephen of Bourbon, "a peasant who had been only one year in the house of a Waldensian heretic. He had so well cogitated over what he had heard, that he knew, word for word, forty of the Gospels for Sunday." He was not the only one of his kind. The same Inquisitor adds: "I have seen laymen who knew almost the entire Gospels of St. Matthew and St. Luke, especially the discourses of our Lord; so that one could hardly quote a word without their being able to continue from memory."[975] Yet another example: this time it is an Austrian peasant. "I have seen and heard," says the Inquisitor who narrates the fact, "a peasant who knew by heart the whole book of Job, word for word, and I have known others who knew the New Testament perfectly."[976] Those are the more rare cases, to judge from the manner in which they are related; still, they confirm the characteristic principle of the Waldenses. They may not be all able to recite the Creed, but they are ready to give a reasonable account of the faith that is in them.[977] This confounds the clergy, their audacity goads on the judges of heresy; the more so that such knowledge is a more or less direct protest against the learned ignorance of the high dignitaries of the Church. Indeed, it was said that it would be easier to find, among the simple Waldensian faithful, persons who could recite the text of the Scriptures, than to find a doctor capable of repeating only three chapters in succession.[978] The theologians were furious: "Very good, you recite the Gospels and Epistles ! What of that ? You have indeed great reason to be proud ! Our scholars know their grammar at twelve, and can read with ease any Latin book. Are they not a hundred times more learned than your teachers, who at sixty have no other learning than verses of the Bible stored away in their memory ?[979] If you knew your grammar better, you would read the Gospel according to the real meaning, and would not falsify it."

" Give an instance."

" Here is one : St. John says that Christ ' came to his own, and His own received Him not '—*sui eum non receperunt;* and you read, ' the swine received Him not '—confounding somewhat maliciously *sui* with *sues.*[980] You would do better to leave our Latin to us."

The reply would not fail to be given that, with all their Latin, the Catholic doctors had not succeeded in arriving at the most necessary knowledge of all, the fountain of which never ran dry during the worship of the Waldenses.

But the teacher's lesson was not confined to reading. When preaching on the Gospels or Epistles he brought forward examples and quoted maxims of the holy men of God.[981] " Thus is it written in the Gospel, or Epistle of St. Peter, or of St. Paul, or of St. James."[982] That constituted his whole argument, according to the report of an Inquisitor, who adds that " this did not prevent him from occasionally making use of the testimony of this saint, or that doctor, so long as the text of Scripture seemed to be adhered to ; otherwise he would have nothing to do with it."[982] In short, he applied the precepts of Scripture, without discussing the dogmas. His preaching ran upon virtues and vices, upon good works ; the maxim of " doing unto others as we would that they should do unto us ;"[983] above all, upon the duty of abstaining from lying, swearing, or the shedding of blood. He concluded with : " The time is short ; confess your sins and do penance."[984]

The visit being over, the missionaries resumed their journey, accompanied by some of their hearers, and on their way they still expounded the Scriptures."[985]

We may well think, however, that this visit did not conclude with the preaching of penitence. It was also the occasion for the administration of the Sacraments in use with the Waldenses.

We have now come to the Sacraments. The subject is an important one, and demands our whole attention. We must first ascertain how many Sacraments were recognized by the Waldenses, and how they modified them; more especially in practice.

" The Waldenses," Montet writes, " enter into competition with the Catholic priesthood as regards preaching; but they accept the Sacraments at their hands."[986] That was true at the very commencement of the work; but, little by little—when the first condemnation of the Waldenses was sanctioned by the Lateran Council, and persecution was let loose by means of the Inquisitors —the question of the Sacraments changed its aspect. Some were put aside, particularly by the Poor of Lombardy and of Germany. First, that of marriage, which had nothing to do with the Waldensian ordinances. It continued to exist for the faithful, and the Waldenses did not dispute with the clergy the right of administering it; only it happened that they did not appreciate it as much as celibacy, and that they curtailed the rights of it, owing to the bi-fold influence of Romish tradition and Catharin principles.[987] They also very soon disregarded the Sacraments of Confirmation and Extreme Unction, and finally rejected them, at least in some districts of Germany.[988] The other Sacraments, namely, Baptism, Ordination, Confession, and the Eucharist, were fully recognized; but the Waldenses, being forced to re-assert their right to participate therein—always owing to the intolerance which oppressed them—modified the practice of them more or less. That is the point we shall now consider; and first, as regards Baptism.

Upon this point the Waldenses neither anticipated the belief of Luther, nor of the Baptists, as has been asserted. They were originally so completely under the dominion of Catholic tradition, that a reaction was not long in taking place. Without baptism no salvation, they said unanimously; then, while still following this same tradition, added that it might be administered by any one.[989] Still, on the Italian side of the Alps, a very perceptible divergence of opinion was soon manifest. Many began to hold that children might be saved without baptism.[990] It would even seem that, for some time, this opinion prevailed in Lombardy and in some parts of Germany.[991] Whilst the Poor of Lyons continued to recognize as valid the baptism administered by the Church in Lombardy, they were liberating themselves from their superstitious practice.

Why do you not baptize ? asked the Catholics.   We have already seen the answer : " Christ did not send us to baptize ; but to proclaim the Gospel."[992]   The Brethren of Lombardy did not stop there in abandoning rites ; they went so far as to treat with levity the pretension to administer the Sacraments, of which their predecessors had been so jealous.   Otherwise how could we explain the fact of one of their perverts writing to them in a defiant tone : " What are the Sacraments you administer ?   You no longer retain more than a semi-Sacrament, that of Confession; that is all.   As for the other Sacraments, you refer people to the Church."[993]

Let us pass on to the Sacrament of Ordination.

Evidently it is here no longer a question of Ordination in the ordinary sense.   The admistration of this Sacrament is a sequel to the vow of obedience to God, which the Pope and Clergy do not accept, and which the Waldenses, from the time of their formation, had taken to their superior.   At all events, they had a rite of Ordination, properly so-called, and it is not just to imagine that, amongst the early Waldenses, " the first comer, wearing wooden shoes, could mount the pulpit steps and preach the word of God."[994]   But did they not profess equality as regards the priests ? Undoubtedly ; but we have seen that they had ordinances.   We must remember this, in order not to be deceived as to the character of their priesthood.   They condemned the exclusive sacerdotal privilege, but the distinction between the special and universal priesthood remained, notwithstanding some expressions which would seem to cast a doubt upon it.   " They say," so an Inquisitor reports, " that the Sacrament of Ordination is void, and that every good layman is a Priest, according to the example of the Apostles, who were themselves laymen.   Nay, every layman, in their opinion, even women, should preach."[995]   Still, the laity are ordained,[996] and in the following manner.   Bernard Gui describes to us, in successive order, the ordination of a Bishop, Presbyter, and Deacon.

" The election of the Bishop having taken place, after prayer in common and the private confession of sins, there follows a public and general confession ; if there be a Bishop present, it is he who performs the ceremony ; if not, one of the Presbyters who may be present prepares to pray, and, while he recites the Lord's Prayer, he lays his hand upon the head of the Bishop elect, that he may receive the Holy Spirit. After him, all the others, Presbyters as well as Deacons, impose their hands, each in his turn. Thus is accomplished the ordination of the Bishop, without further formality, without the least trace of tradition, without anointing of any kind, or sacred ornaments, but solely by prayer and the laying on of hands."[997] The ordination of a Presbyter is performed in like manner. "After prayer and the confession of sins," Gui adds, "the Bishop lays his hand upon the head of the candidate, then all the Presbyters present do the same, that he may receive the Holy Ghost." We have seen that, in case of the absence of a Bishop, the Presbyter may proceed to ordain a Bishop.[998] Much more then would he be permitted to proceed, in like case, to the ordination of a Presbyter. Finally, comes the turn of the Deacon. "When the Deacon has been elected, the Bishop alone, after the usual prayer and confession, imposes his hands upon him, repeating the Lord's Prayer, that the candidate may receive the Holy Ghost," and with that, all is over. Thus, concludes the Inquisitor, with almost naïve astonishment, the ordination is performed without any more formality than prayer and the laying on of hands. Whether it be that of Bishops, Presbyters, or Deacons, ignorant laymen, or learned persons, it is sufficient that the candidate should have been approved and elected in the manner just described.[999]

Such, according to Bernard Gui, was the practice of ordination among the Waldenses of France. This is not the only information we have on the subject. Here is more, relating to another branch of the Waldensian family.

Another Inquisitor writes: "When they wish to admit any one to their number, they first examine him during a certain time,[1000] after prolonged instruction.[1001] At the moment of ordination, they require of him a confession of all the sins he can remember from his youth up. Moreover, to be received into their ranks, one must be chaste."[1002] And here an important detail is mentioned, which apparently escaped the researches of Bernard Gui, unless—and this is not impossible—it was a subsequent addition. We read that the candidate was interrogated upon the seven articles of faith, that is to say, he was asked whether he believed :—

1. In a God, in three persons, one in nature.
2. In a God, Creator of all things, visible and invisible.

3. In the Divine promulgation of the law of Moses on Mount Sinai.

4. In the incarnation of the Son of God in the Virgin's womb.

5. In the election of the Holy Church.

6. In the Resurrection of the Body.

7. In the Judgment to come.

The other articles of the Creed are not mentioned.[1003] The candidate was further questioned upon the seven Sacraments. As to the vows required of him, they are the three we already know : obedience, poverty, chastity,[1004] in addition to the two following pledges : When he shall be in prison or in danger of death, he shall not redeem his life or that of his brethren, by a false oath or any other mortal sin ; and he shall not maintain with his kindred greater relations of intimacy than those which unite him to his brethren.[1005]

We now come to a third Sacrament assiduously practised by the Waldenses, namely, that of Penance.

This Sacrament is in such perfect harmony with the character of the Waldensian reaction, that one might almost say, if it had not existed, the Waldenses would have invented it. At first they preached penitence, but without confession. The administration of this Sacrament, on the part of the Waldenses, marked one of the first consequences of their breach with the clergy. They contented themselves with consecrating it by religiously practising it. Many believed that they had re-established it ; they said that the power of the keys, lost by the Popes, had passed to Waldo.[1006] Their notion of penance is already known by the quotations borrowed from their writings. It was taken both from the Scripture and from tradition. Their sincere and rigorous confession was addressed to God, but it was far from excluding the office of the confessor, as some have thought. This office was subject to conditions and limited, according to the spirit of the Gospel, and certain liberal notions of the time, emanating from the teaching of the Fathers. It was only re-formed. More than once the Waldenses profited by the maxims of Peter Lombard, in re-calling the fact that the right of pardoning belongs to God alone, and that the office of the confessor consists on the one hand in pronouncing or declaring forgiveness ;[1007] on the other, in directing by his evangelical councils the

soul that repents and prescribing the penance.[1008]  Between the
Romish confessional and the Waldensian conscience there was not
the needful point of unity.  Little by little the Waldenses had
drawn themselves back; their faithful disciples, who were still
seen going to the Priest it is true, but only in cases of necessity,
or to elude the vigilance of the persecutors, acted in the same
manner.[1009]  Even in such cases they seldom confessed to the
Priest any but venial sins.[1010]  They usually said : It is better to
confess to a pious layman than to an unworthy Priest.[1011]  Moreover, a layman has as much power as anyone.[1012]  One of the
reasons which urged penitents to confess to the Waldenses was
that they were sure to be well received.  Their confession was not
more frequent than that of the Church ; it took place at least once
a year,[1013] from childhood.[1014]  It was serious, complete, sure, and
efficacious.[1015]  The common people in the retired districts of
Germany went so far as to attribute to it a species of magic
virtue.  A sin remitted by the Waldenses was remitted effectually ;
the individual was as free from it as if he had just been born.[1016]
If anyone confessed to those holy men and died before the end of
the year he was sure to go straight to heaven.[1017]  The reason is
because they are not ordained like others ; they received their
authority from God ;[1018] they received it from an angel from
heaven.  Every seven years they ascend thither, to listen to the
voice of Divine wisdom, and receive the sacred seal of their
mission.[1019]

The form of Absolution varies.  Two are known, of which
one is used in France, the other in Germany.  The first is the
prerogative of the Bishop, to whom is reserved the right of complete absolution.  When he absolves, says the Inquisitor Gui, he
speaks thus : " God absolve thee from all thy sins.  I enjoin
upon thee contrition for thy sins until death, and the performance
of such a penance."[1020]  The second formula which has been preserved is less summary.  " May our Lord, who forgave Zaccheus,
Mary Magdalene and Paul, who delivered Peter from his bonds,
and Martha and other penitent women, deign to remit thy sin
The Lord bless and keep thee, the Lord make His face to shine
upon thee, and be gracious unto thee, the Lord lift up His countenance upon thee and give thee peace.  And may the peace of
God, which passeth all understanding, keep thy heart and mind
in Jesus Christ.  Blessed be thou by God the Father, and the

Son, and the Holy Spirit. Amen."[1021]    During absolution, the confessor probably laid his hand upon the head of the penitent.[1022]

Penance, always rigorous, was sometimes excessive.[1023]    It consisted of fasting and prayer.[1024]    We are already aware that by prayer we must here understand the repetition of the Lord's Prayer. It was prescribed for every day, especially for Sunday.[1025] The Ave Maria, on the contrary, never was; it was only tolerated, and the reason is already known.    As to fasting, the Waldenses in France observed it as follows : Mondays and Wednesdays, semi-fasts, not excluding the use of meats ; Fridays and part of Lent, strict fasting, not for conscience's sake—for Christ does not command fasting—but in order not to give office.[1026]    Their brethren of Lombardy seem to have followed an analogous custom, perhaps more rigid.[1027] On Fridays they fasted on bread and water, except in cases of toil, journeying, or sickness.    They also fasted on Saturday.[1028]    The confessor, although strict,[1029] had regard to the health of the penitent ; sometimes the use of a little wine or light beer was permitted.[1030]    Of course, there was no confessional ; nevertheless confession was seldom heard but in secret ; generally in the hospitable house where the minister lodged, and in which the meetings were held.[1031]

Finally, the Waldenses attached a great importance to the Sacrament of the Eucharist.

This Sacrament also underwent at their hands a beginning of reform.    Of a truth, they professed to believe in the dogma of transubstantiation, which was several centuries old ; this profession is common to the Waldenses of France and those of Lombardy.    We have seen that their differences had no reference to the dogma itself; they disagreed in their manner of explaining it. According to the Waldenses of France, transubstantiation is the result of the magical virtue inherent in the sacramental words ; or it depends upon the official character of the priest ; or again, upon the all-powerful mediation of the God-Man.    Their brethren of Lombardy emphasize this latter causation without admitting it to be sufficient.    In their opinion it matters but little whether the celebrant be consecrated or not ; he must, above all, be a good man, inasmuch as God does not answer the prayers of the wicked. Such are the diversities of opinion which entail a certain difference of practice.    The sacramental consecration was accepted even from laymen, almost the same as baptism.[1032]    The holier the celebrant was, from the point of view of the Church, the more his moral authority seemed to be questioned.[1033] Nevertheless, amid all this discussion, there was no apparent doubt of the reality of the transubstantiation. Was it always and everywhere thus ? Certainly not. A doubt soon arose, not only among a group of Waldenses of Alsace, evidently influenced by notions that were foreign to their dissidence,[1034] but also in Germany.[1035] It found a form quite ready to embody it, in the symbolic interpretation adopted by the Cathari. More than one Inquisitor tells us that, in their meetings, the Waldenses celebrated this Sacrament by reciting the consecrated words, and they administered it one to another, as at the Last Supper.[1036] The cup was then beginning to be withdrawn ; but the Waldenses retained it.[1037] Let us now go back to the manner in which this rite was celebrated among them in the beginning, that is to say, in the XIII. century.

" The Poor of Lyons," we read, " celebrated their mass once a year, namely, on Holy Thursday. At night-fall he who presides, if he have received the order of priesthood, gathers around him all the members of his family,[1038] of both sexes ; he causes a bench or a box to be set up before them, which is covered with a clean table cloth, upon which are placed a large glass of pure wine and an unleavened loaf of bread.[1039] Then he who presides says : ' Let us pray that God in His mercy may pardon our sins and transgressions, and deign to answer our prayers ; to this end we will repeat the Lord's prayer seven times, to the glory of God and the Holy Trinity.' Whereupon all kneel and say the Lord's Prayer seven times ; then they rise. Afterwards, he who consecrates makes the sign of the Cross over the bread and the cup, and, after having broken the bread, he gives a piece to each ; then he passes the cup to all. They remain standing during the whole time of the celebration ; and this closes their act of sacrifice. They firmly believe and confess that it is the body and blood of our Lord Jesus Christ.[1040] If aught of the sacrifice remains unconsumed, they keep it till Easter and finish eating it on that day. If anyone present ask permission to receive it, they give it to him. For the space of one year, they give nothing to their sick but consecrated bread and wine.[1041] Such was originally the custom of the Poor of Lyons, or Waldenses, before division came in among them."[1042]

The following deductions have been drawn from this testimony:—
The Waldenses of France did not celebrate the sacrament of the Eucharist more than once a year, on Maundy Thursday. This celebration embraced only the regular members of the primitive community. Nevertheless, other persons were permitted to attend, even to participate, if any of the consecrated elements remained. The consecration of the elements implied transubstantiation. It was performed by a Priest, and, as a rule, by the chief of the community, if in holy orders. The blessed bread and wine, which was distributed during the rest of the year, must not be confounded with the consecrated elements ; they evidently differed. Finally, this form of celebration is the one that was in use in the community at its commencement, that is to say, before the separation. It would appear that the Brethren of Lombardy did not retain it.[1043]

Such was apparently the rule ; but it had exceptions. In this case again, the Priest was dispensed with, if necessary ; that is to say, when the choice lay between a Priest suspected of mercenary motives and a good layman.[1044] Then the communion was handed from one to the other.[1045] The form therefore, we see, varied. Some, we read, celebrated their Easter communion as follows :—
One of them took an unleavened loaf, and placed it upon a little board ; beside it he placed a wooden spoon with some water. After having pronounced the benediction, he communicated and passed the elements on to the others. When the ceremony was finished, both the board and the spoon were thrown into the fire.[1046] It is true, confesses here the anonymous narrator, that this fashion is not much liked ; it is repugnant even to most of the Waldensian teachers, who desire either to communicate in the Church or to go without communion during entire years. In such case, they hide themselves so as not to be noticed.[1047] Besides, all Waldenses do not wait for Holy Thursday to communicate. The custom was general, we grant, but it did not in any case exclude frequent, even daily, communion, if opportunity should offer.[1048] Still, we are not quite free from doubt on this point. Is it not possible that the narrator confounded the Eucharistic communion, properly so-called, with that of the blessed bread ? This brings us to this last rite ; let us try to understand it.

How is this custom of the blessed bread explained ? Thus far, no satisfactory reason for its use has been assigned. It must be acknowledged that the allusions to this subject, presented by our sources of information, are few and obscure.[1049] This bread not being that of the Communion proper, does it not have some reference to the *benedicite* pronounced at meals ? That custom is known to have come, like so many others, from the Cathari. " It was the intention of those who first took part in them, that these repasts should be a renewal of the love-feasts of the early Christians, and symbolize, not the participation in the benefits of the death of Christ, but the oneness of the brotherhood existing among all the members of the sect. Where the perfect were numerous and could frequently visit their faithful members, they blessed bread for them, in sufficient quantity that they might partake of some every day. In the times of persecution, when the perfect were obliged to conceal themselves, and could not make their rounds, excepting at rare intervals, this custom must have undergone some modification ; blessed bread was at such periods eaten only on solemn occasions, especially at the feasts of Christmas and Easter ; faithful messengers carried it into the towns and villages to the believers, and the latter preserved it religiously. It was then no longer necessary to eat it in common, in order to celebrate a love-feast ; a bit of it was taken in secret, in commemoration of admission into the community of believers, and of the fidelity owed to the Goodmen and their Church.[1050] So much we know concerning the practice amongst the Cathari ; that this rite should have passed from them to the Waldenses is not at all surprising.[1051] Only, amongst the Waldenses, the blessed bread does not take the place of the Eucharist, either because they attached a different dogmatic interpretation to it, or because they still hesitated to set themselves up as a separate sect. Meanwhile, the use of the blessed bread constitutes the first deviation. From this to the reformed Eucharist is no great stride.

Such are the various modifications imported by the Waldenses into the observance of the Sacraments.

We see, by what has been said, that the religious life of the Waldenses, like their historical tree, has its various ramifications. It is, for instance, impossible to identify the original reaction which spread over Gallic soil with that which had its source in Lombardy, and from thence sprang up again under a different form in Switzerland, Alsatia, Swabia, and Austria. Moreover, those different forms became more marked during the controversy with the dominant Church.

The Poor of Lyons were dissenters and not schismatics. As a matter of fact, they did not invite the faithful to shake off the yoke of the Romish Church. They recognised the right of the clergy to administer the Sacraments, with the idea that their flocks might derive the benefit thereof.[1052] It has been claimed that the Waldenses even exhorted their hearers to frequent the Church and pay their tithes to it.[1053] That may have occasionally been the case, in order not to provoke too inconvenient reprisals, and we admit the fact; still when it becomes a question of arguing on their own account, do they not cast a doubt upon the moral authority of the Catholic priesthood[1054]—the Popes as well as the Prelates?[1055] They go even further; they betray no anxiety about being excommunicated,[1056] any more than about their decrees and statutes.[1057] They have very good reason for this; in that the Romish Church clergy have declined to accept apostolic poverty. That is the crime, the mortal sin, which renders their authority vain and their priesthood of none effect; so much so that, according to popular opinion, instead of feeding souls they would do better to go and feed swine.[1058] Here we find a decided advance made since the conference of Bergame. But this somewhat plain spoken language did not always entail corresponding results. The Waldenses consider themselves the Church within the Church; reform may be possible without schism, if not in the head, at least in the members. This remark is particularly applicable to the Waldenses of France. Those of Lombardy and other countries were less patient; their protest rose up against the Church in outspoken indignation. The Romish Church, say they, is no longer the Church of Jesus Christ, but the Church of the wicked, the beast and the whores, described in the Apocalypse.[1059] It is well to go out of her, for she is only governed by Scribes and Pharisees; whosoever obeys them shall be damned.[1060] We are the Church of Christ, and he who would be saved must follow us.[1061] The authority of the Church of Rome is null and void; the Pope has lost the right to palm himself off as successor to the Apostles, seeing that he has become the leader of the apostacy, and with him the entire hierarchy, already smitten with the interdict, totters to its fall. After that, what have we to do with tithes, royalties, prebends, donations, legacies, privileges, immunities, dispensations, indulgencies, canonizations, vigils, litanies, legends, miracles, relics, feasts, dedications, consecrations, candles, ashes, palms, fastings, Chrisms, purifications, pilgrimages, temples, water, salt, incense, mitres, chasubles, and the rest ?[1062] Everything, even to the graves, is profaned by the benediction of mercenaries. It would be better to be buried in the open fields than in the cemetery, and we should prefer it if we were free.[1063] How much money is wasted in ornaments which would be much better spent in benefitting the poor ? [1064] If we had a voice in the chapter, we would say to the Priests : Sluggards that ye are, earn your bread like other people,[1065] instead of wasting your time at Church, after having frittered it away in the seminary.[1066] All their work consists in rendering the law of God of none effect, in order to establish their traditions, after the manner of the Pharisees.[1067] The traditions, forsooth, sustain the prohibition of the seven mortal sins, whereas they should add the command-ments directed against lying, calumny, and swearing ; thus having ten precepts instead of seven.[1068] Many others are got rid of for that matter. Are not violence and persecution a continual violation of divine laws ? Conscience ought not to be forced; but should be free.[1069] Then what shall we say of murder ? Have you the power of giving life ? No. Then that of taking it does not belong to you.[1070] Death makes ravages enough, when we consider that every sin is mortal ;[1071] only a fool thinks he can rob it of its prey, by means of the mediations of Saints. As for us, we believe, as the Book of Ecclesiastes says : "In the place where the tree falleth, there it shall be." The just have no need of mediations ; they do no good to the wicked. This being the case, of what use are the masses for the dead ? The mass ! The Apostles knew nothing of the kind.[1072] All the display made there, and all the mutterings are but lies, in so far as they are not a rehearsal of the word of Christ ;[1073] but they hold to it, because it opens the money bags. What has become of the worship practised by the Apostles ? It has disappeared. Look at those images ; what idolatry is there ! They are not even ashamed of rendering homage to the infamous Cross upon which our Lord was nailed. They prostrate themselves here and there, kissing the hand of the Priest and the foot of the Pope, as if they were more worthy than the Apostle Peter, or more holy than an angel from heaven. What is their singing ? Listen to that uproar ; one would take it to be the grunting of unclean animals—an infernal noise. The temple, which should be a house of prayer,

is but a house of stone, when it is not made of straw;[1074] it would
be better to pray in one's room, or even in a stable.  Everything
is falsified, even to the parochial definitions, which form the very
basis of their ecclesiastic constitution.  It is not just so to divide
the land and the population.[1075]  As for us, we hold to the doctrine
of Christ and His Apostles, whilst we ignore the statutes of the
Church.[1076]  General rule : everything that cannot be found in the
Gospels ought to be repudiated.[1077]  To be legitimate, the
ordinances of the Church must date back at least to the day of
Our Lord's Ascension ; otherwise, they should be regarded as
non-existent.[1078]

Under these words we can trace the existence of a fire that was
ready to burst forth.  The struggle was certainly a serious one.
What impetuosity there was on the one side ; still victory
remained on the side of the fire and the stake.  After the struggle
came decadence.  The reaction drew back ; it re-entered its
original centre, that of dissidence, whilst approaching still nearer
to that of France and the valleys of the Alps, which at first
seemed too conservative.  It was, however, late in the day ; the
ranks begin to waver ; they became visibly thinner, the bravest
struggle in the shade, soon to disappear in the darkness of the
night.

We have now nearly reached the end of our review, so far as
it relates to the early religious life of the Waldenses.  Before
closing our narrative let us glance back on the field we have just
run hastily over.  There are still many more facts to be gleaned.
For instance, with reference to manners and customs.  It is true
that we have already spoken of the manners, but one point,
and a very delicate one, remains to be cleared up.

The purity of morals amongst the Waldenses has been so
generally recognized, that more than one judge of heresy testifies
to it.  We will quote, as an example, the testimony rendered by
the Inquisitor of Passau :

" They may be recognised by their manners and discourse.
These are sober and modest; they avoid pride in their dress,
which is composed of materials neither valuable nor worthless.
They have nothing to do with trade, as they have no wish to
expose themselves to the necessity of lying, swearing, or cheating.
They live by the work of their hands as journeymen.  Their very
teachers are weavers and shoemakers.[1079]  They do not accumu-

late wealth, but are content with what is needful for this life. They are chaste, the Leonists especially,[1080] and moderate at their meals. They frequent neither taverns nor ball-rooms, not being fond of that species of vanity; they refrain from anger; although always at work they find means to study or teach ; therefore they pray but little.[1081] They go to church, participate in the worship, confess, communicate and attend preaching, but for a purpose, namely to criticise the preacher.[1082] They are also known by their discourse, which is both sober and modest.[1083] They avoid speaking evil of anyone and abstain from all foolish or idle conversation, as from lying. They do not swear ; they do not even use the expressions " verily " or " certainly," or anything of the kind, for, in their estimation, such are equivalent to swearing."[1084]

That is no portrait to be lightly esteemed. It is clearly enough limned. We must now try to account for a villainous calumny, which is in strong contrast with what we have just read, as well as with all that we know regarding the morals and manners of the Waldenses.

Certain suspicions were thrown out with respect to their meetings, quite horrible enough to be simply ridiculous, if they had not been at the same time infamous. In short, more than one Catholic writer says, that at a given moment the lights were put out, and this, they add, was the signal agreed upon for misdeeds that shall be nameless.[1085] This foul calumny has been so often repeated, that it is our desire to have it looked into. For this purpose let us draw a distinction between the source of, and the occasion that gave rise to, such reports. The source is hatred and prejudice, those two eyes of the spirit of fanaticism, which has from time immemorial been the demon of a dominant state religion. The early Christians fell victims to it. " It was said that at the love-feasts which they attended, accompanied by their mothers and sisters, on a given signal the lights were put out, and adultery and incest were committed in the darkness."[1086] The slander is therefore an old one, but so much the more tenacious, and against it the apologists of that period had to defend themselves.[1087] When the reins of dominion passed into the hands of the Catholic Church, her priests repeated the old calumny, with a thousand other errors and prejudices having the same origin. From that time till now the same calumny has been uttered against the most varied sects ; but for their wickedness there can be no excuse. It is true that certain Gnostic sects of the early period may have given reason for a suspicion of immoral practices. When we see, however, that—for instance, with reference to the Cathari—this suspicion is perpetuated without the least proof being adduced in support of it, and that every movement of reform is attacked in the same way, must we not conclude that the virus of Pagan intolerance has entered into and vitiated the blood of the Catholic priesthood? The history of the Waldenses, which presents many similarities to that of the early Christians, recalls this fact to our minds in the matter under consideration. The old calumny is uttered against them in order to avenge official worship upon those who denounced the vices and scandals of its Priests.

Such was the cause, and the occasion is as follows :—

The Waldenses met in secret, protected by darkness. They lighted a lamp, and often after the reading was ended the light was extinguished, lest it might attract the attention of the neighbours. How many a time has the dim little taper been extinguished in the middle of a meeting, upon the slightest signal of alarm ! Sometimes it was not even lighted. We are not inventing ; the Inquisitors themselves tell us so. Says one of them : " The preaching being over, they kneel for prayer, and they sometimes, if there be a light, put it out, so as not to be seen or surprised by anyone from without."[1088] The timid were impressed by this ; at times even—if they were novices—frightened.[1089] Thus, there is contemporary assurance on this point as to the reasons for the practice, and, indeed, they were quite understood. It must not be supposed that the Inquisitors, because of this, withdrew the opprobrious slander. No ; it was not without its use to them.[1090] Still, they do not know how to prop it up ; witnesses are lacking, or else they contradict themselves ; more than once they are procured from amongst suspicious, unscrupulous persons, terrorized by torture,[1091] or influenced by the hope of escaping it, if not by the allurement of some reward. In any case such witnesses are not in any way entitled to credit. Indeed, an Inquisitor declares explicitly that he does not believe any such villainous stories about the Waldenses. He says: " They assemble particularly at night, during the hour of sleep, in order more freely to indulge in their iniquitous rites. It is said, that after they have extinguished the lights, they all give themselves up to fornication ; but I do not believe this can be said of this sect ; and of a truth, I have never heard any such report from the lips of trustworthy persons."[1092]  Moreover, calumny did not end there. It asserted by the mouth of gossips, that ridiculous animals made their appearance, and even the devil himself, to whom worship was rendered.  Really, an immense amount of credulity and depravity must have been required to believe such fables.  By some these old slanders, with new ones added, are still believed.[1093]

Meanwhile we call attention to the fact that the purity of Waldensian manners was attested by the testimony of those most interesting in discrediting it.  Of course they take some exceptions, for are they not theologians ?  To hear them one would think they held a brief from Satan himself.  Instead of concluding that the tree could not be evil which bore the fruit of such good manners they do just the contrary.  They say the manners of the Waldenses present a double aspect : on the one hand, there are their relations toward men ; on the other their relations toward God.  The former, the only visible one, is luminous ; the latter is in the darkness of heresy.  Here, therefore, is the reality which is falsehood ; there the outward show, which is hypocrisy.[1094]  In this way the devil gets his full share, thanks to the subtle metaphysics of the Inquisitors.  As far as we are concerned their deductions are of very little importance.  Their testimony is of value, only in as far as it bears upon outward life.  Now this testimony is such that the highest praise has, with justice, been found underlying it.[1095]  Criticism, which has searched so much, has found nothing of a nature to attentuate this.  If anyone does so, it is the Waldenses themselves, as will be further seen in their confession to the fathers of the Reformation, humility being one of the attributes of their religious life.

We shall now add a few more details about Waldensian customs.  The early Waldenses, as we have seen, were distinguished by a particular costume.  They wore a woollen tunic,[1096] a cloak and a particular kind of shoes.[1097]  They cut the upper part of these latter, so as to recall the apostolic use of sandals,[1098] and marked them with a sign resembling a shield, on account of which they were called Ensabates or Insabbatati.[1099]  They were like the Nazarenes in respect that they wore their beards and their hair long. A monk, whose halting jests have been already noticed, mocks at them in his own fashion.  He says : " They find it more convenient to cross the straps of their sandal than to crucify their members; they crown not their head but their shoes."[1100] That sign was, however, a cross in the days of the persecution. Little by little it disappeared, still not before the end of the XIII. century.[1101] Persecution obliged the Waldenses to exercise much prudence and even shrewdness; they travelled mostly by night, often carrying disguises with them in case of need, in order to circumvent spies and to be able to disappear, or to pass unperceived from one house to another.[1102] One day one of their leaders was arrested. He had enough upon him to rival Proteus, says an Inquisitor.[1103] If he had been once seen, he quickly changed his costume. At one time he would be dressed as a pilgrim, at another as a penitent; one day he was a shoemaker, another a barber, a reaper, or a bowyer.[1104] The object of the Waldenses in thus disguising themselves was not merely to escape danger; they frequently only desired to disarm prejudice and gain a more ready access as missionaries; in such cases they assumed the *rôle* of pedlars. An Inquisitor has given us such a faithful description of one of their visits, that we can almost imagine ourselves to be present. The scene is laid on the confines of Austria and Bavaria.[1105]

"They endeavour to insinuate themselves into the intimacy of noble families, and their cunning is to be admired. At first they offer some attractive merchandise to the gentlemen and ladies—some rings, for instance, or veils. After the purchase, if one ask the merchant: Have you anything else left to offer us? The latter will reply: I have stones more precious than those gems;[1106] I should be very willing to give them to you, if you will promise that I shall not be betrayed to the clergy. Being assured on this point he will add: I have one pearl so brilliant, that with it any man may learn to know God; I have another so resplendent that it kindles the love of God in the heart of whoever possesses it.[1107] And so on; of course he speaks of pearls in a figurative sense. After that he will recite some passage of Scripture, such as that of Luke: ' The angel Gabriel was sent,' etc., or some words used by our Saviour, like those beginning thus : ' Before the feast,' etc.[1108] When he begins to fix the attention of his hearer, he will add: ' The Scribes and Pharisees sit in Moses' seat,' etc., or: ' Woe unto you Scribes and Pharisees, hypocrites, for ye shut up the kingdom of heaven against men ; for ye neither go in yourselves, neither suffer ye them that are entering to go in '; or else : ' Beware of the Scribes who devour widows' houses, and for a pretence make long prayers.'[1109]   The listener will then ask : To whom are these imprecations addressed ?   He answers :   To the Priests and Monks.[1110]   Then the heretic compares the condition of the Romish Church with that which concerns his party.   Your teachers, says he, are fastidious in their dress and manners ; they like the chief places at feasts and to be called masters, Rabbi, Rabbi ! We do not look for such Rabbis.[1111]   They are incontinent ; while each one of us has his wife and lives in chastity with her.[1112] They are those rich men and misers of whom it is said : ' Woe to you that are rich, for ye have already received your consolation.' As for us, we are content if we have food and raiment.   They are those voluptuaries to whom it is said : ' Woe to you who devour widows' houses,' etc.   We, on the contrary, satisfy our own needs, in one way or another.   They fight, stir up wars, cause the poor to be killed and burned ; of them it is written : ' Whoever kills with the sword shall be killed by the sword.'   We, on the contrary, suffer persecution at their hands, for justice's sake. They eat the bread of idleness, like drones.   We, on the contrary, work with our own hands.   They wish to be the only teachers ; thus it is said of them : ' Woe unto you who have taken away the key of knowledge,' etc.[1113]   With us, the women teach like the men, and a disciple of seven days' standing teaches another. Among them it is rare that a doctor of divinity is able to repeat by heart, and word for word, three consecutive chapters of the New Testament ; while with us it is seldom you can find any man or woman unable to recite the text in the vulgar tongue. And because we have the real faith in Christ, and all of us teach a pure and holy doctrine, the Scribes and Pharisees persecute us to death, as, indeed, they did Christ himself.[1114]   Besides, those people talk and do not act ; they bind burdens that are heavy and grievous to be borne, and lay them upon men's shoulders, but they themselves will not touch them with one of their fingers.   As for us, we practice all that we teach.[1115]   They endeavour to observe human traditions rather than Divine precepts ; they observe fast-days, feast-days, and go to Church, bound as they are by the rules prescribed by men.   For us it suffices to persuade men to observe the doctrine of Christ and

His Apostles.[1116]   So, too, they load the penitent with very heavy punishments, which they do not touch with a finger.   We, on the contrary, following the example of Christ, say to the sinner : Go and sin no more, and we remit their sins by the laying on of hands.[1117]   In the hour of death we send souls to heaven ; but they send them all to hell.   After this conversation, the heretic says to his listener : Now see which is the most perfect religion— the purest faith—ours or that of the Romish Church ?  think the matter over and make your choice.[1118]   Once turned aside from the Catholic faith by such errors, our members leave us.   Anyone who credits these heretics begins to favour and defend them ; he conceals the man in his house for months together, and in this way becomes initiated in all that concerns their sect."

Here we have a truthful story, simple and charming.   There now only remains for us to discover to what class the personage, thus placed before us, belongs.   Some have thought it was a Barbe.[1119]   But let us not forget that we are neither in the valleys of the Alps, nor on the road to Calabria, and that this appears to have been a married man.   Was he a hawker ?  Some have thought and still think so.[1120]   At any rate, we have here a Waldensian, such as many were, born to evangelize, just as the Dominicans were born to hunt heretics—without consecration, perhaps without salary, without any obligation of reporting to superiors, but none the less zealous.   The zeal of such a man is capable of anything.   A river intervenes to prevent one like him from arriving promptly at the hamlet where he is expected ; winter though it be, he swims across.[1121]

It is true that with all their zeal, the missionaries generally limited their efforts to seeking for the scattered sheep, in order to lead them to the fountain of life, and to feed them with the reading of Holy Writ.   Of course they are reproached for this.   If you be right, why do you hide ? it is asked.   Come out of your retreat ; cast aside your modest, itinerant mission, and come out into the full light of day ; preach to the scandalous sinners.   But no, you prefer to go to those who are peaceful, gentle, and quiet.[1122]   The answer was easy.   How can we preach publicly, when we are pointed out as heretics, and hunted down like wild beasts ?[1123]  That is not a mere excuse, but the real truth. Under such circumstances, not only did they avoid exciting attention, but they seldom assembled, and even then in small numbers,[1124] and with a thousand precautions. Before beginning they made sure there was no suspected person present.[1125] Moreover, there were several ways whereby the faithful recognised each other, especially in the manner of shaking hands.[1126] It is evident that all had not a vocation for addressing multitudes. Many acknowledged this frankly.[1127] If opportunity offered, the Waldenses were not slow in seizing it. They were then seen disputing in the public square, preaching everywhere, even upon the roofs, and the judges of heresy were aware of it.[1128] Surely, if the Reformation did not take place before Luther came, it was not their fault.

Such was, in general, the condition of the religious life of the Waldenses during the early period.

Upon reading the foregoing, a doubt may have arisen in the mind of more than one of our Waldensian readers. We can well understand it. Having been accustomed to read romance rather than history upon the subject, certain details have seemed to him, if not new, at least somewhat odd, and at any rate inexhaustive. He feels somewhat hurt, and suspects us of concealment. The silence we have thus far maintained, regarding the particular condition of religious life in the valleys of the Alps, appears to him suspicious. Upon seeing the principles and practices of the ancient Waldenses, scattered in France, Alsace, Lombardy, Germany, and Austria, as it were unfolded before him, he has said : That sheds no light upon the faith of my ancestors, properly so-called, and there is nothing to prevent my believing that they professed in those valleys the good apostolic tradition which remained unchanged, notwithstanding the lapse of centuries. What is said concerning our ultramontane co-religionists, and even concerning those of Lombardy, is surely interesting to us ; but it could not apply to us, the more so that they did not always agree on every point. If we have seen the Waldenses of France holding fast their sentiments, upon certain secondary practices, in opposition to their brethren of Lombardy, we may be permitted to conclude that our ancestors also had something to hold fast.

Now, that is what we are anxious to know.

This objection serves our purpose, for it gives us the opportunity of returning to our narrative to complete it, and justifies beforehand certain inevitable repetitions. Indeed, it must not be forgotten that our review of the religious life of the Waldenses has not come down to the XV. century. It has thus far only marked the early and flourishing period. We still have before us the period of decadence, which precedes the Reformation. Where shall we look for what is lacking in our sketch, if not in the valleys of the Alps? This will also be a means of bringing into relief that too much ignored tradition of the more direct ancestors of the Waldenses of the Alps.

This tradition has been established by the Inquisitors; then by a Bishop of Turin; finally, by one of the Barbes. We have but to record it, according to their testimony. That of the Inquisitors relates to the time of the Crusaders, and the years immediately following, hence to the end of the XV. century.

It will be remembered that Albert Catanée subjected the Waldenses to more than one examination. There were those who sealed their faith with martyrdom, others who were weak and recanted. There can be no doubt that this great Inquisitor founded the report upon his notes of the proceedings against them. From that report we shall borrow an interesting page.

" These heretics, who do not excel either in knowledge or in mental endowments, do not cast any doubt upon the hidden mysteries of our religion, as for instance the procession of the Holy Spirit, concerning which very learned men have put forth very different opinions. Devoted to their vow of poverty, they have carried insanity and blindness to the point of denying to the Apostles, Martyrs, and others Saints, and to the Divine Majesty, the worship and homage which is their due. They think, indeed, that we ought not to build temples to God, nor sing his praises. Their scorn for the Saints is so great, that they believe their prayers to be of no benefit to mankind; and therefore say we ought neither to invoke them, nor observe festivals in their honour. Finally, they endeavour to pull down several very legitimate institutions, which serve to maintain Christians in the fulfilment of their duty; for they believe and preach as follows:—

The Romish Church is a house of lies.

Its decrees are worthless.

Neither ordination, nor dignity, make a man a priest, but merit. Ordination and office count for nothing; dignity being in proportion to moral goodness.

The soul, after death, ascends straight to heaven, or descends into hell.

The fire of purgatory exists nowhere.

Prayers for the dead are vain and superfluous, being only inventions created by the avarice of the clergy.

The images of the Deity and Saints ought to be abolished.

Holy Water is ridiculous.

Priests must lead a life of poverty, and be satisfied with alms.

The preaching of the Word of God must be free and accessible to all.

No sin ought to be tolerated ; not even for the purpose of avoiding a greater evil.

If anyone has committed a mortal sin, it is not necessary to obey him.

Confirmation and Extreme Unction ought not to be numbered among the Sacraments of the Church.

Baptism must be celebrated with clear water, without holy oil.

The use of cemeteries is needless ; it was invented for the purpose of traffic. It matters little how the dead are buried.

The temple of God is vast ; it embraces the whole creation, and to erect temples, monasteries and chapels, is an attempt to circumscribe His power, as if Divine goodness would be more propitious in them.[1129]

Ecclesiatical vestments, the decoration of the altars, cups, sacred vessels, all these have no significance as regards religion.

The Priest may consecrate and administer the body of Christ at all times and in all places. The Sacramental words are sufficient.

It is useless to invoke the mediation of the Saints, who reign with Christ in heaven ; for they know not what is going on ; they do not hear the prayers, and if they did, they could do nothing.

Singing and the repetitions of Canonical hours, is but lost time.

Work should be suspended only one day in seven, namely, on Sunday.

The solemn festivals dedicated to the Saints ought to be abolished.

The fasts established by the Church are of no avail.

Indulgences and censures should be looked upon as worthless.

Such are the dreams of the Poor of Lyons. Not content with propagating them in their little assemblies, they have the boldness to preach them and affirm them publicly.[1130]

It will be noticed that every one of these articles brings us
back to the general tradition of the Waldenses, particularly to
those of France.    There is nothing in this detailed enumeration
to indicate the slightest deviation.    They are, furthermore,
confirmed by the records of trials during the same period,
concerning the Waldenses of Freyssinières, a Barbe named
Martin, arrested at Oulx, and a woman belonging to the diocese
of Valence.[1131]    If we examine them with attention, this is what we
find :—

Catanée is right when he observes that the Waldenses
" throw no doubt upon the hidden mysteries," or dogmas, of the
Catholic religion.    Metaphysics and theology, properly so-called,
remain untouched.    It is the doctrine of worship and others akin
to it, that the principal divergences concern.    Purgatory is rejected
because it does not exist, except in this life,[1132] inasmuch as it
was invented by the avarice of the Priest.[1133]    Our fate is decided
here below : after death, devotions will in no way change it.[1134]
Worship belongs to God alone, as to the Creator ; [1135] the Virgin
Mary and the Saints being but creatures, have no share in it ;
besides, is it not doubtful whether they hear our prayers ?    At
any rate help can come from God alone.[1136]    What is to become
of the Ave Maria ?    Should it be repeated as a penance ?    No :
it is not a prayer like the Lord's Prayer, which being taught us
of God, should suffice.[1137]    Images are vain ;[1138] as to festivals we
must make a distinction.    There are the festivals, properly so-
called, which God has ordained, namely, Sunday and the festivals
of Christmas, Easter, Ascension, and Pentecost.    Of course we are
bound to observe those ;[1139] the others cannot be obligatory
nor do they exclude work.[1140]    Everyone is free to act according
to his own consience, but above all, let Sunday be observed ;
whilst the memory of the Apostles or of any who are among the
Saints may also be honoured.[1141]    However, God is not in the
Church more than elsewhere.    He may be equally well prayed to
at home, nay, even in a stable ; he is present everywhere.[1142]    The
Romish Church has become a Babel, a Synagogue of Satan ;[1143]
it is the Church of the wicked.[1144]    The Prelates are worldly
and lead scandalous lives,[1145] hence they are unsuited to their
office ; for legitimate power in the Church of Christ is always
in proportion to the holiness of those who exercise it.[1146]
The office of the Romish clergy is therefore an empty for-

mality; its practices are worthless, and its holy water very harmless.[1147] God blessed the waters from the beginning of creation, and He blesses them every year on Ascension Day, together with every one of His creatures.[1148] Rain water is just as good.[1149] Aspersions are, therefore, matters of indifference, as well as the singing that accompanies them.[1150] If this be so, has the Church a right to tithes and offerings? Certainly not. As for alms, we shall give them to the poor instead of handing them over to the curates. What matters it to us if these latter remonstrate? Clerical censures affect us but little; we are not bound to obey either the Church or her Prelates; not even her Pope, for he is very far from being holy.[1151] It is a long while since he usurped the power he is wielding; since Sylvester, of blessed memory, there has been no true Pope.[1152] Once we had the same ordinances: but the Priests having given themselves up to avarice and worldly vanities, we have been obliged to separate, in order to hold fast the rule of poverty.[1153] As we are not numerous, we live concealed, and for very good reasons;[1154] but, whatever may be said, we are the Church of God,[1155] and those who are not with us will go to perdition.[1156] We are but a handful of people; but it may be on our account that the world has not perished.[1157] Our rule forbids all swearing,[1158] even mitigated oaths;[1159] it also condemns the death penalty, except for the crime of killing a man.[1160] We recognize in our Barbes the power to bind and loose; it is to them that we are bound to confess our sins;[1161] that is to say, mortal sins.[1162] In pronouncing absolution, the confessor lays his hand on the penitent's head.[1163] Penance consists in repeating the Lord's Prayer a certain number of times,[1164] without the Ave Maria;[1165] in fasting—not on Saints' days, nor after the Lenten rule[1166]—but on the eve of the four great festivals and of Sunday, and at any rate on Friday.[1167] The Barbes do not receive the communion at Church any more than their flocks. They bless the bread, and that serves us as Eucharist. Their benediction is more effectual than ecclesiastic consecration. This latter is null and void;[1168] hence we desire no communion with Catholics. We avoid also uniting ourselves with them in the holy bonds of matrimony,[1169] were it only out of respect for this last Sacrament, which is not badly kept in the nest of the Alps.[1170]

If all this be true, how can we believe certain confessions of abominable practices, attributed to the Waldenses of Freyssinières,[1171] and even to Barbe Martin ?[1172] The very form of these confessions betrays, first of all, a contradiction,[1173] and then an absurdity.[1174] Let us not forget that a few years later the Waldenses did take notice of this cynical slander in order, in a letter to King Ladislas, to denounce it, complaining that an inquiry was not granted them.[1175] No, there can be no doubt; those infamous stories are the last resort of a clergy which avenges itself in its own fashion upon those who did not lay bare the corrupt practices of the priests to laugh at them, but to place in juxtaposition to them a pure life. It is true that thereby the scandal was rendered more publicly outrageous, and the clergy more and more hateful and unpopular.

So much having been determined, we must note a few historical details concerning Barbe Martin.

His father was named Girondin. From Spoleto, where he ordinarily resided, he had more than once visited the valleys of the Alps, in the capacity of a Barbe, preaching and hearing confession from village to village.[1176] To him Martin owed his early religious instruction.[1177] This was carried on by some other Barbes, belonging to the little town of Camerino, one of whom was named Barnovo, and another Josuè. Martin had accompanied them several times on their missionary tours, and eventually he was one day brought to the great teacher Jean Antoine, who lived in Cambro, on the territory belonging to the Pope.[1178] He was consecrated Barbe, and on the occasion, as was customary, exchanged his baptismal name for that of Martin. This is the way the ordination took place. When a Barbe is consecrated, Martin writes, the Master assembles a few other Barbes, and the candidate is required to swear as follows : " You, so-and-so, swear upon your faith to maintain, multiply, and increase our law, and to betray it to no one in the world ; you promise in no wise to swear, to observe the Sabbath, and to do to no one that which you would not have them do unto you ; finally, that you believe in God, who made heaven and earth."[1179] When the candidate had taken this oath, the great Master handed him a cup, and at that moment, he assigned a new name to him, saying : " Henceforth thou shalt be called thus."[1180] It is on this occasion, the accused adds, that I received the name of Martin, in lieu of my former one of François, for this ceremony takes the place of baptism.[1181] We learn furthermore, that Martin's co-religionists bore several names; beyond the mountains in France, they were called Poor of Lyons; on this side simply the Poor.[1182] He had set out that year, with a companion named Barbe André. They visited Genoa, Nice, Acqui, and Vivarais, as well as several districts of France; they held a Council in Lyons, with six other Barbes, and saw on their way home a goodly number of Waldenses in the mountains of Valence and the neighbourhood of Embrum and Gap. In the month of March last, Martin adds, we met near Acqui, three persons, refugees from Dauphiny, whence they had been exiled, who recognised us by our cloaks.[1183] We spoke of our business, they said they were waiting for pardon to re-enter their home, and continue as in the past. . . To return to my narrative, it happened that on my return from Lyons, with another Barbe, named Pierre, we arrived at Oulx. As we were crossing the mountain, towards Pragelas, we were arrested.

Did you know that there were people of your sect there?

We were told so, so we thought of utilizing our ministry in favour of the Waldenses.[1184]

The two Barbes, just mentioned, were not the only ones who has been seen arriving in the valleys of the Alps about the same time. A woman tells us that she received some into her house, while her late husband, Pierre Fournier, was living. One day she saw two of them,[1185] who from their speech would have been taken for foreigners, for they spoke Italian or Lombard; and they were dressed in grey.[1186] Her husband lodged them "for the love of God." After supper one of them pulled out a little book from his pocket, stating that this book contained the Gospel together with the precepts of the law, and that he was about to expound it to all present: that he had a mission from God for the reformation of the Catholic faith, and that to this end he went about the world after the manner of the Apostles, preaching quietly the mode of serving God and observing his commandments. Thereupon he began to read:[1187]

"What was their name?"

"I do not know."

"Have you seen them since?"

"It is twenty-five years since I saw them for the first time; I may have seen them altogether nine or ten times; not always at my house, however."

"Did you often confess to those men?"

" Every time that we received them at our house ; therefore four or five times. When they went away they sometimes gave us some needles, and my husband gave them some little money for their trouble."[1188]

" How much, do you know ?"

" I did not see it counted."

" Did you not hear these heretics preach at Barillonne ?"

" Yes, some ten years ago. My husband and I were visiting a relative, named Jean Favre. We lodged at his house. One evening we went to call upon his brother, Monnet Favre, and lo ! we found there our two preachers with the assembled family. Monnet, who was not expecting to see us, was quite put out. This was so evident that we soon withdrew."

" What did the preachers say ?"

" Nothing."

" Did they discontinue their preaching on your arrival ?"

" No."

According to these different testimonies we must conclude that the Chief of the Barbes at that time usually resided in Southern Italy.[1189] He presided at their ordination,[1190] assigning to each one a new name ;[1191] finally, after the example of our Lord, he sent them out, two by two, to preach repentance and feed the scattered sheep of persecuted Israel in the valleys of the Alps, in Liguria, Puglia, and other localities.[1192]

These somewhat lengthy details—but of importance here—bring us to this two-fold conclusion : first, dissent in the valleys of the Alps during the XV. century, is connected with that of the early Waldenses, whom we know ; secondly, it shows a certain fusion—already noticed[1193]—with the Cathari.[1194] The influence of these latter upon the Waldensian rule had been sufficiently marked to induce the Cathari in their turn to yield more than one point. One would think their dualism had gradually become melted down by the fire of the Crusades and the stakes. The fusion was complete ; the name, place, and future were all left to the Waldenses. The population thinned and partially dispersed, ebbed away in different directions, especially towards Calabria ; but at the time of the visit of the Brethren of Bohemia they had already got together again, and from the writings which emanated from them, we have seen that the faith of their fathers was far from being extinguished.[1195] A few more years, and we approach the Reformation. Luther had just boldly proclaimed his theses; and a broken-down Savoyard Prelate, at the end of his days—for he had served the French monarchy under three of its kings—had risen to the Archiepiscopal see of Turin. This was Claude of Seyssel. Though he did not visit the Waldenses, he made some inquiries concerning them, examined their doctrine, and undertook to discuss it in a treatise that was posthumously published in 1520.[1196] What did he find to reproach them with? This point has been studied by Jacques Cappel, "minister of the Holy Gospel and professor of theology in the Church and Academy of Sedan."[1197] He takes up the Archbishop's complaints in order; it must suffice us to sum them up.[1198]

The Waldenses accept only the contents of the Old and New Testament. They hold that the Pontiffs and Priests with their doctrines and commentaries have attacked the authority of the Scriptures. Tithes, first fruits, consecrations of churches, indulgences, benedictions, holy water—all are condemned as of human invention; even the mediations also, for, say they, "Christ is fully sufficient for all persons and things."[1199] Moreover, the saints do not know what is going on here below. Images and the sign of the Cross are destestable. It is idle to repeat the *Ave Maria*, as it is not a prayer, but a simple salutation. Marriage is permissible in all cases, except those of immediate consanguinity. Purgatory does not exist; everything done to deliver souls from it is labour lost and absurd. The Priests have not the power of forgiving sins; this belongs to every Christian who treads in the Apostles' footsteps, and the Waldenses, more than the Church of Rome, have a right to the name of Catholic. With respect to prayer, men ought to accept only that which was transmitted to them by the sacred authors. Lying is a mortal sin.

Here again the same characteristic traits remain; but we long to hear a witness who is not a Catholic. The last word on the subject under consideration naturally belongs to Barbe Morel. The reader has not forgotten that to more than one reformer he opened his mind on the religious condition of the Waldenses. He is so evidently candid, that to learn the plain truth we have but to listen to him.[1200]

After the usual salutations, Morel explains how the ministry is recruited. Ordination crowns the preparation; it is accomplished by means of the laying on of hands, and the administration of the

L

Sacrament of the Eucharist. Once consecrated, the young ministers set forth, two by two, to evangelize. That has already been mentioned.[1201]

Morel goes on : "As for rank we have regard to years of service; that is to say, the order of consecration determines seniority in everything, whether it be honour, dignity, or office. He who precedes is the master; he who follows, the disciples.[1202] It is our custom, and we think so much of it, that the latter does nothing without the former's permission, although it may be the most insignificant thing—to drink a glass of cold water, for instance.[1203] Not that we consider it sinful to act otherwise, we only desire that everything shall be done decently and in order. As a rule, our ministers do not marry; but I must confess —for I speak to you in all confidence—that chastity is not always the better kept for that.[1204] Bread and clothing in sufficient quantities, on an emergency, for our absolute needs, are furnished to us gratuitously by the people who receive our instruction. We work at different trades to please our people and to avoid idleness,[1205] but, to tell the truth, the time we give to that would not be of any profit in acquiring a knowledge of the Scriptures. We pray kneeling, at different hours : morning, evening, before and after dinner, before and after supper, at noon, and sometimes also during the night; and also after preaching. Our prayers last about a quarter of an hour. Before eating or drinking, we almost always repeat the Lord's Prayer; but our prayers are not the result of any superstition, or vain desire for formality, or of respect for the times. We have no other object than the glory of God and the good of our souls. Our temporal goods, which, as I have said, are—thanks to the alms of our people—abundantly assured to us, are managed in common. People, when on their death-bed, frequently offer us money and varied gifts ; I must confess that I never had the courage to accept anything at the hands of a dying person. Every year the ministers assemble in general council, to talk over their affairs, and we change our residence in pairs ; for we do not reside for more than two or three years in the same locality, unless perchance, in the case of some old man who may be permitted to have a fixed residence somewhere, for the remainder of his days. All we receive from our people in the way of money is handed over to this same general council, and placed in the common treasury, in the hands of our leaders.[1206] It is destined, in part, to cover the expenses of travelling, as they may deem necessary; sometimes a portion is reserved for the poor. Before separating, we unite in the mutual confession of our sins. If one of us falls into any carnal sin, he is excluded from our community;[1207] he is forbidden to preach, and he is directed to earn his bread by the sweat of his brow."

Thus far Morel has hardly spoken of anything but what has reference to the organization; however he mentions also the beliefs, religious practices, and manners.[1208]

" With regard to our articles of beliefs, we teach our people, as well as we can, the contents of the twelve articles of the Symbol, called the Apostle's Creed, and every doctrine deviating from it is looked upon by us as heresy. We believe in a God in three persons; we hold that the humanity of Christ is created and inferior to the Father, who wished by means of it to redeem mankind; but we admit at the same time that Christ is both very God and very man. We hold also that there is no other mediator and intercessor with God than Jesus Christ. The Virgin Mary is holy, humble, and full of grace; the same with the other saints; and they await with her in heaven the glorification of their bodies at the resurrection. We believe that, after this life, there is only the place of abode of the elect, called paradise, and that of the rejected, called hell. As for purgatory it was invented by anti-Christ, contrary to truth, therefore we reject it. All that are of human invention—such as Saints' days, vigils, holy water, fasts on fixed days, and the like, especially the mass—are, as we think, an abomination in the sight of God. We believe the sacraments to be the signs of a sacred thing, or a visible figure of an invisible grace, and that it is good and useful for the faithful sometimes to partake of them, if possible; but we believe that, if the opportunity to do so be lacking, a man may be saved nevertheless. As I understand it, we have erred in admitting more than two sacraments.[1209] We also hold that oral confession is useful, if it be observed without distinction of time and for the purpose of comforting the sick, the ignorant, and those who seek our advice, according to the Scriptures. According to our rule, charity ought to proceed as follows :—First, everyone must love God, above all creatures, even more than his own soul; then his soul more than all else; then his neighbour's soul more than his own life; then his own life more than that of his neighbour; finally, the life of his neighbour more than his own property."

Such are the articles of faith noted by Morel. The following details merely serve to amplify them.[1210]

We, continues the Barbe, once a year visit our people who are scattered over the mountains in different villages. Each one confesses to us in secret.[1211] On such occasions we exhort married people to live together honestly, and to give each other their due, to avoid evil and not from voluptuousness.[1212] Finally, we entreat everyone to abstain from all sin, and inculcate upon them, as best we may, the doctrine of original sin. If anyone be sick, if we are called, we visit him, to comfort him with our exhortations and prayers. At the time of being called we are sometimes asked to bring material assistance also, because of the sick person's indigence. When we preach two of us officiate. We sit near each other; the elder speaks first, then the younger. As we have no share in civil power and as—whether they like it or not—our people are subjected to the jurisdiction of infidels; we advise them to elect two or three men of recognized honesty, and to entrust them with the arrangement of their affairs.[1213] We excommunicate those who steadfastly refuse to accept our instructions and warnings; the consequence being that they cannot, after that, take part in business matters or listen to the preaching.[1214] If this be done it is to the end that they may be ashamed; for we remember, in connection with this, that it is not becoming to give sacred things to the dogs, or expedient to throw pearls before swine. Thus there are several, who, when readmitted to hear the preaching, have treated it with scorn. We ourselves do not administer the sacraments to the people—they are Papists who do this;[1215] but we explain to them as well as we can the spiritual meaning of the sacraments. We exhort them not to put their trust in anti-Christian ceremonies, and to pray that if they be compelled to see and hear the abominations of anti-Christ, it may not be imputed to them as a sin, but that such sort of abominations may soon be confounded to make room for truth, and that the Word of God may be spread abroad. Besides, we absolutely forbid our people to swear. All dancing is prohibited, and, generally speaking, all kinds of games, except the practice of the bow or other arms. Neither do we tolerate vain and lascivious songs, delicate clothing, whether striped or checked, or

cut after the latest fashion.[1216]    Our people are generally simple
folk, peasants, having no other resource but agriculture, dispersed by
persecution in numbers of places very distant from each other.
From one extremity of the district to the other is more than 800
miles.[1217]    Although we are everywhere subjected to Papist magistrates and priests, it seldom happens that one of us is called
in judgment or condemned, or that he frequents places of
debauch.[1218]

After these positive data, Morel states his doubts, which are
those of his co-religionists.   They bear upon forty-seven points.
Most of them have their importance, if it be a question of ascer-
taining the condition of beliefs, of practices in vogue, and even
current opinions.   Let us make a note of them, without, however,
wandering from the text before us.   These doubts suggest as
many questions.[1219]

1.—Ought we to admit degrees in the dignity of the ministers
of the Word—for example, those of Bishops, Presbyters, and
Deacons?[1220]   We clearly see that the Apostle commands it to
Timothy and Titus; Christ set Peter over the other Apostles,
giving him the keys of the kingdom of heaven; and among the
Apostles themselves some were pillars.   At any rate, those
degrees are not recognized amongst the Waldenses.[1221]

2.—What are we to understand by the keys which were given
to St. Peter?

3.—Can such ministers of the Word as lead a wicked life,
usefully preach the word of God to the people, if they teach it in
truth?

4.—Should we recognize Presbyters, who neither preach nor
teach, except by their exemplary life?

5.—Are the ministers of the Word permitted to possess anything of their own? seeing that it is written : " If thou wilt follow
Me, go sell that thou hast;" and elsewhere, " have neither gold
nor silver;" and, " the Son of God had not whereon to lay his
head."[1222]

6.—Are the ministers of the Word permitted to lead a life of
celibacy?

7.—May the said ministers take about with them women who
wish to devote themselves to celibacy?[1223]

8.—What difference is there between the ministers of the Word of the Old Testament, and those of the New ?

9.—Which are the books of Scripture we are to hold as truly canonical ?

10.—Is allegorical interpretation useful for the explanation of the Scriptures ?[1224]

11.—Were the judiciary and ceremonial precepts, given in the law of Moses, abolished by the coming of Christ, or should we still observe them?

12.—Must the ministers of the Word teach all that is contained in the Scriptures, without any distinction ?[1225]

13.—How are we to understand the true and faithful interpretation of the holy Scripture, so as not to be led astray by the numerous commentaries and different interpretations, now existing and daily accumulating ?[1226]

14.—Are there more than two Sacraments ?[1227]

15.—Can marriage be sacredly contracted by persons who have not reached years of discretion ?

16.—Is marriage legitimate in all degrees of relationship except those indicated in chapter xviii. of Leviticus ?

17.—Is a woman permitted to marry again when her husband has given no sign of life for a number of years ?

18.—If a man seduce a virgin, is he bound to marry her ? and if he do marry, must he give her a dowry ?

19.—We exhort the betrothed not to marry for the sake of luxury or avarice, and we tell them that such marriages are of the Devil. We admonish them to marry to the honour of God and for the begetting of children. Is this right ?

20.—Is it allowable for a woman to alienate a portion of her husband's property without his knowledge ?

21.—Do the Gospels contain certain teachings of Christ which should be called precepts, and other teachings which should be looked upon as counsels ?[1228]

22.—Would it be desirable that ministers should celebrate the rites and ceremonies of the Sacraments whenever they have an opportunity [1229]

23.—From the fact that Christ said " Swear not at all," must we conclude that every oath is forbidden as a mortal sin ?[1230]

24.—Is it allowable to mourn for the dead ? We read somewhere that the saints mourned for them, while again we read elsewhere that such is forbidden them.

25.—Is it allowable on Sundays to occupy oneself with manual labour ? Are there feast-days which we are bound to observe ?[1231]

26.—Is it allowable for a person, who may be assailed by evil men, to defend himself, even if he cannot do so without taking their lives ?[1232]

27.—If we recognize that Christ is our sole justification, and that we are saved only through His name and not by our own works, how are we to read so many passages of the Scripture, which rate works so highly ? The souls of the simple may easily be deceived thereby. Is it not written : " By thy words thou shalt be justified and by thy words thou shalt be condemned ?" Do we not read : "Not everyone that crieth unto me : Lord, Lord, shall enter into the kingdom of heaven, but he that doeth the will of my Father, which is in Heaven ?" And elsewhere : " Ye shall possess the kingdom for ye have given me to drink ?" And again : " As water extinguishes the fire, thus do alms extinguish sin ?"[1233] The alms and prayers of Cornelius seem to have had the effect of bringing about the appearance of the angel, and thus he may have been justified. We might think also that the publican who went up to the temple, went away justified through his prayers. If Jesus loved John particularly, is it not because the latter loved him more than the other disciples ? We read that Mary Magdalene experienced a better reception than Simon, because she loved more. We should conclude from this that works count for something. Moreover, do we not read that on more than one occasion God revoked his chastisements, upon seeing that the sinners repented ? Is it not written that we shall be judged according to our works ? And lastly it seems that there will be a difference, in paradise between the just. We pray thee to enlighten us, especially on this point.[1234]

28.—It is written : " Suffer little children to come unto me, for of such is the kingdom of heaven." Ought we not to conclude from this that children who have not reached the age when they can use their reason, will be saved by the grace of God and the merits of Christ, whatever people they may belong to? And on the other hand, as it is written that "it is impossible, without faith, to please God," and that "he that believeth not the Son, shall not see life; but the wrath of God abideth on him." Must we conclude that all those who have the use of reason, without faith in Christ, shall be rejected?[1235]

29.—Are civil or other laws invented by men, and by which the world is ruled, as to temporal things, legitimate in the sight of God? For it is written, "The laws of the nations are vain."[1236]

30.—Did God ordain that magistrates should inflict the death penalty on murderers, thieves, and other such evil doers, or does he wish that a punishment be inflicted upon them, which by subjecting them to a severe penance, shall make them better? For, according to the opinion of many, the magistrate carries the sword to inflict this punishment, but not the death-penalty, as God does not desire the death of the sinner, but rather that he should turn from his wickedness and live.[1237]

31.—Is it allowable for the faithful to plead before an infidel judge? That seems to be forbidden them by St. Paul.

32.—Is it allowable for anyone who has been unlawfully deprived of an article[1238] to regain possession of it, even without the knowledge of the one that has it in possession, in case he can not obtain it otherwise?

33.—If a labourer be treated with unjust harshness, is he permitted to retain anything which he may have promised to return?[1239]

34.—Does the inheritance of children revert by right to the mother, when there is no will? And if she marry again is it just that the inheritance should pass to the children of the second husband? We doubt it.

35.—Must all that is added to the principal be considered usury?[1240]

36.—Must all profit be considered illicit which, in commerce, exceeds that of labour?

37.—Is the distinction between mortal and venial sins legitimate?

38,—Is there any ground for distinguishing between inevitable ignorance and that which is simulated, or the effect of negligence ?

39.—Does ignorance make sin excusable ?

40.—Is the passion of our Lord only applicable to original sin ?[1241]

41.—Is the passion of our Lord of no advantage to those who abide in sin, and are the good works they do of any avail to them ?

42.—What council must be given to one who may have committed a deadly sin, like that of murder ; to one who may have children of another man's wife, which are fed by the husband who believes them to be his own ; or to one who has lived in sin to the last ?

43.—If one who has obstinately lived in sin, notwithstanding all the warnings he may have received, calls us on his deathbed, ought we to hear him and give him counsel ?

44.—Is a deathbed repentance, caused by fear alone, of any avail ?

45.—What advice must be given to one who has accidentally found an article of which the owner is unknown ?

46.—Can we, as ministers of the Word, accept food, money, or other earthly goods from the faithful ?

47.—Is it allowable for us to counsel our people to kill the false brethren in our midst, when they seek—as has happened—to deliver us into the hands of the papists that we may perish, and thereby to hinder the preaching of the Word of God ?[1242]

48.—Finally, the question which troubles us more than all the rest, is that of free will and predestination, upon which Luther and Erasmus are far from being agreed.[1243] What we have read upon the subject has troubled us ; we are, alas, so ignorant ! I confess that, thus far, we have believed that God has placed within every man a certain natural virtue, according to the individual capacity, as seems to be taught by the Parable of the Talents. Moreover, does not experience teach us that even inferior creatures are gifted with a certain capacity of their own ? Therefore, we believed that man must be able to do something ; he has only need to be excited and stimulated thereunto by God, as is done when He says : " I stand at the door and knock " ; so that he who will not open to Him, according to his innate capacity, will meet, by his voluntary refusal, the fate he has deserved. If not, how must we understand all those positive and negative commandments of which we are reminded by Erasmus ? So much for free will. As for predestination, we believed that before creating heaven and earth, the Almighty had foreknowledge of those who should be saved, as well as of those who should be lost, but that He nevertheless created all men unto eternal life, so that no one need be damned if he do not elect to be so, by refusing to obey His commands. But if, as Luther says, all comes to pass of necessity, then those who are destined to life cannot be damned, and *vice versa*, for Divine predestination cannot be without effect. In that case, what need of so many writings, preachers and physicians ? Nothing can change our destiny if everything be of necessity.[1244]

"We hope," Morel concludes, " that the Spirit of God will enlighten us through thee, O, Œcolampadus ! that you will come to our help, according to the grace that has been given thee. We entreat thee earnestly, knowing that the Good Shepherd will not leave helpless those sheep that seek Him. Is it not written that whosoever asks receives, that he who seeks finds, and that it shall be opened to him who knocks ? There is but one Shepherd and one flock. As the great Apostle felt himself to be debtor to everyone, so it is with thee, for thou walkest in his footsteps. Be it here or there, it is always a question of God's cause. Now, if there be with God no acceptation of persons, so will it be with thee ; for art thou not His vicar ?[1245] O that we might be firmly united together ![1246] After all, do we not agree with you in all things ? We always have had the same sentiment as regards the faith, from the time of the Apostles ; only, through our fault, alas ! we have neglected the study of the Scriptures, so that we have not understood them as you do.[1247] We therefore come to thee to be guided, instructed, and edified. Greeting. The same God is over us all."[1248]

Thus ends the confession of the Waldenses.[1249] It is touching, it is lacking in nothing, neither sincerity nor truth. Whilst reading it we feel the Waldensian soul to be in that critical hour that precedes the Reformation, when it opens like the virgin flower to the first rays of the sun, which gave it life. If this confession

indicate a certain decadence, let us not be in a hurry to read anything else in it. Isolation, joined to oppression, had condemned
the Waldenses of the Alps to comparative inaction. With light
still burning, they, like the sentinel, waited for the break of day,
and lo ! several went to sleep ; but the awakening was as rapid as
it was easy. In this awakening there is a movement of repentance and the earnest of a future about to commence. Thus everything is in harmony with the true history of Waldensian origin.
Those who prefer the legend are embarassed by it. They speak,
not of a relaxation, but of decadence, if not of original fall, in
order to be able to believe in a pre-historic, apostolic, and immaculate age of the Waldensian faith. As compared with their
ancestors, the Waldenses of this period show at least " a sensible
inferiority in the knowledge of things pertaining to salvation, and
especially in the profession of the evangelical faith."[1250] Why so ?
Because, we are told, they are invaded by Romish ideas to such an
extent that even oral confession becomes known among them.[1251]
But oral confession has been practised by the originators of this
work ; we have surely seen that. It seems to us, on the contrary,
that the Waldenses of the Alps profited by the Lombard and
Hussite reaction, and that with respect to Romish ideas, their
mode of thinking shows, here and there, signs of advance upon the
original tendency of France.[1252] After all, the rule always remains
the same. As we found the Waldenses at the dawn of the early
age, so we find them at the end, excepting as regards their zeal,
which has somewhat diminished, either because of the dispersion
or because of local circumstances. Still these variations, similar
to those which had distinguished other groups of the Waldensian
family, are so far from making a breach in the unity of the original
rule, that this latter is recognisable in the valleys of the Alps, as
it was in France, in Lombardy and to the confines of Germany.
This rule became moulded by a new general and powerful reaction,
that of Protestantism. Need this be regretted ?

We answer frankly, no. Infancy has its charms ; all origins,
seen from afar through the medium of the imagination, are clothed
in tender colours. They make us dream. Our recollection carries
us back to them, and we begin to mourn the good old days, as
in the song of St. Alexis. We have something better to do.
The days of the Apostles were not exempt from imperfections,
any more than those of Abraham and Waldo. Let us admire

them, but without preferring them to the future. The ideal is higher, for it is before us, and the road which leads to it is called progress. The idea of Waldo springs up like a fountain, it runs into the river of the Reformation, and the river flows on. Where is the river that flows back to its source? Is there any kind of civilisation which carries nations back to the primitive condition of wandering tribes? Can a man enter again his mother's womb? We have seen the Brethren of Lombardy separating themselves from the ultramontanes, because, weary of thinking like children, they wished to reason like men; and here we find Barbe Morel, who hails with inward joy the great day of the Reformation, which he at last sees breaking upon the horizon. Let us learn of our fathers to plough our furrow without looking back.

But, someone will say, beginning with Waldo, did they not go back? The legend of our apostolic origin, already deeply rooted in Morel's time, must mean something. It repeats to us in its own language the words of the prophet :—

> Ye that seek the Lord,
> Look unto the rock whence ye are hewn.

Certainly. But for the Israel of the Alps, that rock is Christ and His eternal Gospel. More than one child of His will proclaim the fact in a loud voice before the whole world, in some such words as these :—

" We believe all the commandments of God, as Jesus Christ taught them to His holy Apostles, and as the Holy Church holds and believes them, and God forbid that we should wish or undertake to increase or diminish, correct or reprove the law and doctrine of God, who is all-good, all-wise, and all-perfect; who never uttered an imperfect word or thing, in which there is anything to be repented of or to be amended; by which law, as sacred and perfect, we wish to live and die. And we take God to our witness that we hold no opinion of any particular sect, and that we believe and have believed neither in Waldo, nor Luther, nor anyone else, except inasmuch as he proclaimed the Word of God and not his own, provided we have been able to know. That is what we hold and believe, protesting before God and all the world, that if we have been made to say otherwise, by any means whatsoever, be it by cunning, threats, prisons, tortures, or torments, it was contrary to the truth and our faith and belief."[1253]

Now, who is there that does not know that on looking upon Christ we see, at one and the same time, Him who was, who is, and who is to come ? Yes, that look embraces the very life of the religion which will not be surpassed ; it contemplates the ideal. Waldensian legend expresses that continuous contemplation, and in that it is historical. We may even say that in that sense it is truer than history, " for it fits closer and translates the invisible ideal more correctly than real facts, which follow its evolutions only from afar, and with a slow step."[1254] It sums up beforehand, as it were, the programme of our destiny as a people ; it is like the anticipated vision of a golden age—believed in, hoped for, and continually being realized.

FINIS.

# THE WALDENSES OF ITALY.

## NOTES.

*When two numbers are found together, the one distinguished by an asterisk is the one which exists as the reference number in the text.*

1 Michelet, *Hist. de France* Edition 1855, vol. viii., ch. 16.
2 Readers of the writings of Reclus, the eminent geographer, from whom we have quoted, will discover in them many analogies of this kind.
3 Id. *La Terre*, vol. 1.
4 Titus-Livius had already said: "Datur haec venia antiquitati, ut, miscendo humana divinis, primordia urbium augustiora faciat."
5 Gretser, *Contra Valdenses*, iv. "Diuturnior," says the text. Michelet translates: "more durable."
6 Preger, *Beitrage*, etc., p. 6—8.
7 Almost all have been mistaken on this point, historians as well as polemical writers. It is surprising, however, that Michelet should not be an exception. See *Hist. de France*, ii., 401.
8 Ps. Isidore, *Edictum Constantani Imperatoris.*
9 "In donatione illa audita est vox angelorum dicentium in aere: *Hodie in Ecclesia venenum effusum est.*" Joh. de Parraisus. *De potestate regia et papali,* Paris, 1506 ; also Goldast, *Monarchia,* vol. ii., p. 108.
10 We know that Constantine deferred being baptised until the end of his life, and that the ceremony took place at Nicomedia, under the auspices of the Bishop of that city, who was the leader of an Arian faction. The legend originated at the end of the V. century from a baptistry in Rome, named after the Emperor. At the time of the commencement of our history, the legend was becoming less known ; but papal ambition was reaching its climax and had no longer any need of it.
11 Fleury, *Hist. Eccl.*, vol. xi., disc. 4.
12 "Mendacium vero illud et fabulo haeretica . . . ita delecta est, ut etiam mulierculae super hoc concludant." Wesel, disciple of Arnaldo, *ep.* 384 (ap. Mart. and Durand) from Rome, to the Emperor of Germany. The legend was only exposed by Laurent Valla, in the XV. century.
13 "In his successisti, non Petro, sed Constantino." *De Consid.*, vol. iv., ch. 6.
14 "B. Sylvestrum dicunt Antichristum fuisse, de quo in 2 Thess. ii., 4. A tempore illo dicunt Ecclesiam esse perditam." Bonacursus, *Vitae haereticorum seu manifestatio haeresis Catharorum*, ap. d'Achery, *Spicilegium*, vol. i., p. 208, and Baluz. Misc. vol. ii., p. 581. This witness is a competent one, for he came from the ranks of the Cathari.
15 "Quousque ipsi eam restaurarunt." *Summa*, ap. Mart and Durand.
16 "Quod semper fuerunt aliqui qui Deum timebant et salvabantur." *Ibid.*
17 "Instinctu diabeli fuit aedificator ecclesiae romanae primus." MS. of Clermont, ap. d'Argentre.
18 "In temporibus autem istis restitutum esse per ipsos, quorum primus fuit Valdesius." *Adv. Cath. et Wald.*
19 Preger, *Der Tractat D. von Augsb.*, Munich, 1878.
20 The expressions *quousque, temporibus istis*, of Sacconi and Moneta, are significant. They are quite irreconcilable with the idea of an historical transition, properly so-called.
21 "Non enim multum temporis est quod esse coeperunt. Quoniam, sicut patet, a Valdesio cive Lugdunense exordium acceperunt." Moneta wrote these words in Lombardy, in the year 1244.

22 "Illa pars a tempore Silvestri non fuit usque ad tempus Valdesu, quod tu possis ostendere."

23    *Adv. Cath. et Wald.*, passim.

24    *Valdesiani, Socu Valdesu, Societas Valdesiana.* Vide the *Rescriptum* relating to the conference of Berzamo, ap. Preger.    We shall return to this point.

25    Schmidt *Aktenstucke*, ap. *Hist. Zeitschrift*, 1852, p. 239., cf. MS. of Cambridge, vol. A., f. 236-238 and *Nobla Leiczon*, v. 403.

26    See the words of Barbe Morel, at the end of this volume. A transient allusion to the tradition may be noticed in the *Lib. sent. ing. Thol.*, p. 377 ; that is all.

27    "Non principium sed reparacio *nostri ordinis* fuisse dicitur." Letter of the year 1368. See below, p.    . Cf. R. Sacconi.

28    Cl. of Seyssel, *Disp. adv. errores et sectam Waldensium*, 1520.

29    Justinger, *Chron.*, year 1420, according to the original text, ap. Ochsenbein.

30    Michelet, *Hist. de France*, ii., 402.

31    This note refers to an Appendix to the French Edition, not included in the English Edition.

32    "Caudas ad invicem colligatas, quia de vanitate conveniunt in id ipsum." Inn. III., ap. Baluz. I. *ep.* 94 and 509.    The sentence is repeated by his successors.

33    C. Schmidt, letter of April 28th, 1850, ap. Muston, *Israel des Alpes*, preface.

34    One finds more than one indication of this in the ancient funeral inscriptions. One of them runs : "To the memory of a legionary veteran, paper merchant." See Michelet, *Hist. de France*, vol. ii., l. iii.

35    "Civitatis splendorem . . . longe superavit ecclesia lugdunensis." *Gallia Christiana*, iv., 3.

36    "Novam inducendo celebritatem, quam ritus Ecclesia nescit, non probat ratio, non commendat antiqua traditio." *Ep.* 174 *ad canonicos lugdunenses.*

37    " Patriæ est, non exilii, frequentia hæc gaudiorium." *Ibid.*

38    The Abbot of Clairvaux says of this same Church of Lyons, that "haud facile unquam repentinis visa est novitatibus adquiescere." *Ibid.*

39    "Cum per totam fere Galliam, non solum inter scholas, sed etiam triviatim . . . disputaretur." St. Bern. *opp.* i. 309. Cf. *ib. ep.* 88 *ad Cardinales.*

40    H. Martin, *Hist. de France*, vol. iv., b. xxiii.

41    See C. Schmidt, *Hist. et doctrine de la secte des Cathares ou Albigeois*, Paris, 1849. Tocco, who is reserved on the question of the origin of this sect, calls them "manichei imbastarditi." See his *Eresia nel Medio Evo*, p. 100, et seq.

42    " Eo quod aliae nationes hæreticos Provinciales Albigenses consueverint appellare." Math., Paris ap. Bouqet xxii., and P. Vaux-Cernay. *Hist. Albig.* ap. Duchesne.

43    See *Hist. Pontif.* ap. Pertz and Wesel's letter to the Emperor Frederick.

44    " Haeres nequitiae ejus . . . non quidem emendavit sed immutavit." *Ep. adv. Petrob. haereticos.*

45    "Evacuant sacerdotium Ecclesiae." Evervinus, *ep. to S. Bernard.* ap. d'Argentre I., 33.

46    "Nos pauperes Christi." Evervinus.

47    "Ipsum papam non esse quod profitetur, apostolicum virum." *Hist. Pontif.*

48    "Si fidem interroges, nihil christianius . . . Panem non comedit otiosus." *Sermo* 65 *in Cant.*, ap. Mabillon iv.

49    "Qui antea Apostolia et Continentes appellabantur, sine dubio postea Beghardi et Beguinea dicti sunt." Mosheim, *de Beghardis*, Leipsic, 1790, p. 122.

50    "Fratres Beghardi . . . qui udem et Alexiani, Coloniae ob. reliquias S. Alexu in eorum oratorio asservatas." Quotation ap. Mosheim, p. 552.

51    "Quis mihi det, antequam moriar, videre Ecclesiam. Dei sicut in diebus antiquis ? " *Ep.* 238 *to Eugene III.*

52    MS. poem of the Vatican on Arnaldo. *Coll. Ottoboni*, n. 1463.

53    Clerjon, *Hist. de Lyon*, iv., 176.

54    *Gallia Christiana*, vol. iv.

55    C. Schmidt notes several examples, ap. Muston, *ib.*, p. xxxiii., n. 2.

56    So says the *Rescriptum* ap. Preger. The less precise inquisitorial chronicles have Valdus, Valdensis, sometimes Valdius, etc.

57    It is known that family names were not as yet in use. The name of Peter is mentioned for the first time in a writing of the year 1368 wrongly

attributed to Pilichdorf ; and soon afterwards it is mentioned in the double Waldensisn MSS. of Cambridge and Strasburg, the Latin reading in which bears the date of 1404. The former says : " E regione Waldis Petrus nominatus ;" the latter still mere distinctly : "Lo propi nom del cal era Piero duna region dicta Vaudia," or " Cujus proprium nomen Petrus fuit, sed a quadam regione dice-batur Waldis." A more or less wooded locality was called Wald, Vauda, Vaudia or Vaud. As to deriving Valdez from Vallis, it is a mere waste of time and trouble. Sober men have taken in a serious light the puns of the monks, Bernardus Fontis Calidi and Eberardus de Retunia, the former of whom says that Valdenses comes from Vallis "eo quod profundis et densis errorum tenebris involvantur ;" and the latter that the name of Vallenses is accounted for " eo quod in Valle lacrymarum maneant." He also derives Montanists from "montani." We read again : " Valdenses dicuntur a valido mago, vel a valle, ut alu dicunt, quia in valli orti sunt quia alio nomine dicuntur pauperes de Lugduno." Schmidt *Acktenstucke*, etc., n. 1. " Petrus de Walle," says a letter of the Brethren of Lombardy, dated 1368. See below, note 740. After this we are not so much surprised that writers should have made *Valdesi* synonymous with *Vallesi*. But this latter word does not exist, although it is mentioned by Thou, Leger, Brezzi, Gilly, etc.

58 " He was born at Lyons," says the *MS. de l'Histoire Veritable des Vaudois*, n. 169, King's Library, Turin. But this MS., which is far from deserving its title, belongs to the XVII. century. According to the chronicles of the XIV. and XV. centuries, Waldo was born out of Lyons.

59 Guy Allard, for instance, claims that Waldo was a native of Vaux in the Velin or Viennese. Melia repeats this. *Origin*, etc., p. 15. Gauduel believes he came from the Briançonnais, according to A. Lombard, *Pierre Valdo et les Vaudois du Briançonnais*, p. 9.

60 According to documents of the XI. century. the territory of Vaud was called Comitatus and Pagus Waldensis, and its Lord was called Dominus Vaudi, or Lord of Vaut. See *Mem. et Doc. publies par la Soc., d'Histoire de la Suisse Romande*, vol. vi. and vii., passim.

61 Ochsenbein, *Der Inquisitions—process*, etc., p. 23.

62 Chastel says simply that Waldo is so called "from the Marquisate of Vaux, of which he was the first to bear the title." *Hist. du Christ*, iii., 479.

63 " Valdenses dicto a Valde cive lugdunense, in loco dicto vulgariter *Valgran* moram faciente." *Script. Inq. anon.*, ap. Allix. *Some Remarks*, etc., London, 1690. cf., Melia, *op. cit.*, p. 2. The author. who advances this opinion, wrote subsequently to 1494. It is as well to note that in 1492 some of the Barbes met behind the church of St. Nizier, for purposes of drill. See Allix, *op. cit.*, p. 314. Can this fact have given rise to the aforesaid idea? M. Berges is inclined to see in all this nothing more than a "mere play upon words." *Rev. Hist.* xxxvi., 2nd part.

64 " Per inquitatem foenoris multas sibi, pecunias coacervaverat." *Chron. Laud.*, ap. Bouquet, Recueil, xiii., p. 680—682, and ap. Pertz, *Mon. Germ. Script*, xxvi., 447—449. The reading of Pertz is more complete.

65 " Contigit cuidam ex eis mori subito coram eis." Anon. of Passau, ap. d'Argentre I., 92. Some add that this accident happened upon the threshold of his house (Rubuys, *Hist. de Lyon*, p. 268) ; others, under the porch. (Fl. Illyr. *Catal.*, 1666, p. 631).

66 Gaston Paris, *La Vil de S. Alexis*, etc., Paris, 1872. See *Rivista Cristiana*, No. for May, 1887.

67 " De multis modis eundi at Deum edoctus." *Chron. Laud.*

68 " Cui magister dominicano sententiam proposuit : *Si vis esse perfectus*, etc. Matthew xix. *Ibid.* It is known that these same words decided Anthony of Egypt to become a hermit.

69 " Immobilibus haesit." *Ibid.*

70 " De mobilibus iis a quibus injuste habuerat, reddidit." *Ibid.*

71 Fleury. b. lxv., c. 49.

72 *Ibid*, c. 50.

73 " Da pauperibus, non ribaldis." *Chron. de Salimb.*

74 "Non enim insanio sicut vos putatis." *Chron. laud.*

75 "Velut ameus affecta . . . arripiens virum suum per pannos. *Ibid.*

76 "Non licuit ei . . . in ipsa urbe cum alus cibum sumere quam cum uxore." *Ibid.*

77 " Currente an. MCLXIII.," so the narrative begins in the Chronicle of Lyons. The catalogue of the Gallia Christiana states that the successors of Humbert II. were Heraclius, Drogon, and this Guichard, who is elsewhere erroneously called Guilbert. The latter would be installed about the year 1165.

78 Stephen of Borbone, Richard of Cluny, and a nameless writer of Passau make him out a man of some literary knowledge; Gaguinus deems him quite illiterate, while M. Flacius Illyricus, Perrin. Basnage, etc., consider him learned.

79 "Audiens Evangela, curiosus intelligere quid. dicerent, fecit pactum cum dictis sacerdoribus." Étienne de Borbone, ap. A. Lecoy, *Anecdotes historiques*, Paris, 1877.

80 Our chronicler claims that he obtained these details from eye-witnesses, even from this Bernard, who was one of the richest men in Lyons and friendly to the monks. He adds that he often saw Stephen, and relates that he, in his turn, having become wealthy, thanks to his share of the benefices of the Chapter, died afterwards of an accident that happened while building his house. See if Ébrardus (*Handbuch d. christl. Kirch. u. Dogm. Gesch.*1865, ii., 317) is right in suspecting them of being Cathari or precursors of Waldo !

81 "Cum saepe legeret et corde tenus firmaret." *Ib.*

82 " Pauperes qui ad eum confluxerunt docuit N.T. textum vulgariter." An. of Passau. Cf. with St. de Borb.

83 " Cœperunt paulatim. . . . sua et aliena culpare peccata." *Chron.laud.*

84 Arnaldo da Brescia had already seen in these words : " beati pauperes spiritu " the "primum mandatum evangelicæ doctrinæ," the A B C of apostolic life. See Wesel's ep. to Frederick.

85 "Putabat . . . quod vita apostolica jam non esset in terra." Treatise *contra haer Wald.* hitherto attributed to Pilichdorf.

86 " Quod etiam Apostoli Christi non solum erant pauperes, imo etiam praedicatores. Coeperunt et ipsi praedicare verbum Dei." *Ib.*

87 " Multos homines et mulieres ad idem faciendum ad se convocando, firmans eis evangelia." Etienne de Borb.

88 " In giving alms he desired to preach sermons," jeeringly remarks Moreri. *Dict. hist.*, art. *Vaudois.*

89 According to the *Gallia Christiana*, iv., col. 126, he had condemned a certain Olivier at the Synod of 1176. The Synod in question is that of Lombers. The error has been rectified ; that Synod was held in 1165. See Gieseler *Lehrbuch*, vol. ii., part 2nd, paragraph 85.

90 " Vocati ab archiepiscopi Lugdunensi," says St. de Borbone. It is true that he adds "qui Johannes vocabatur ;" but he is mistaken, for John was not Archbishop of Lyons, under Alexander III.

91 " Prohibuit eis ne intromitterent se de Scripturis exponendis vel praedicandis." Et. de Borbone, Acts iv., 17 and 18.

92 " Magister sorum, usurpans Petri ufficium, sicut ipse respondit principibus sacerdotum, ait : Obedire oportet, etc." *Ibid.*, where reference is made to Acts v. and Mark xvi. 15.

93 " Post, expulsi ab illa terra." St. de Borbone, *Ibid.* The MS. of the *Hist. veritable des Vaudois* has it, that Waldo was sentenced by Guichard (whom it calls Guilbert) at this apocryphal Synod of 1176. Cf. Baronius, who falls into the same error. It is, perhaps, nothing but a confusion of names and dates.

94 According to the chronicle of Laon ap. Pertz, Waldo determined that very year publicly to proclaim his vow of poverty and to make proselytes.

95 Gregorovius, whose impartiality is recognised, thinks that the Pope may have been fortunate, but deserved no credit ; "sein Gluck. nicht sein Verdienst." *Gesth d Stadt. Bom.* 1862, vol iv., ch. 6.

96 At that time, the year began and ended at Easter. The Council was held from the 5th to the 19th of March, 1178, according to the chronicle, *i.e.*, 1179.

97 "Eos et defensores eorum et receptores anathemati decernimus subjacere." *Conc. Lat.* iii., *gen. can.* 27.

98 "Ad concilium quod fuit Rome ante Lateranense vocati." Et. de Bourbon, *Op. cit.*, p. 292.

99 " In concilio etiam Lateranensi in eos sententia excommunicationis lata est : unde eis etiam communicandum non est, cum sententia Apostolica ab Ecclesia praecisa sunt." Alanus. *Contra Haereticos, Waldenses*, etc. Schmidt persists in believing that this Alanus is " de Podio." He is mistaken. It certainly refers to " Alanus ab Insulis." or " de Lille," who died in 1202.—See *Chron. Alb. monachi. Trium. Fontium*, ap. Pertz. *Mon. Germ. SS.*, xxiii. Dieckhoff has held this passage to be interpolated, but he is far from having proved it. As to the inscription noticed by Buxhorn, Blair and Tron, to the effect that ." under the Pontiff Alexander III., and the Emperor Frederick I., the Waldenses were condemned as heretics," it has never been verified.

100 Besides the Chron. of Laon, see Moneta, Schmidt *Aktenstücke* quoted, and the MS. of Cambridge : finally the letter of the Brethren of Lombardy, of the year 1368, and Justinger ap. Ochsenbein, p. 86.

101   Aroux, *La clef de la comedie anti-catholique de Dante-Alighieri*, Paris, 1855.

102   "These Waldenses were simple enough to ask for authority from the Pope; which was equivalent to asking permission to secede from the Church." Michelet, *Hist. de France*, Paris, 1835-44, vol. ii., p. 401-402.

103   "He always lived in Rome, as if in an enemy's country."—Gregorovius, *ib.*

104   Besides Gregorovius see Comparetti, *Virgilio nel medio evo*, vol. i., ch. 7.

105   "Valdesium amplexatus est papa." *Chron. laud.*

106   The mention of this embrace is immediately followed by these words: "Approbans votum quod fecerat voluntariae paupertatis.'" *Chron. laud.* Given to a mere disciple of Waldo, as Tron, in spite of what the chronicle tells us, imagines it to have been, it undoubtedly becomes "benevolent," even "brotherly." The whole story savours of legend. It is inexplicable.

107   "E disputa devaut laresiarca." *MS. of Cambridge.*

108   "Era aqui un cardenal de Pulha lo cal era amic de lui e laudava la via de lui e la parolla, e amava lui." *Ibid.*

109   "Promisit servare iv. Doctores, scilicet Ambrosium, Augustinum, Gregorium et Hieronymum." Moneta v., 1.

110   The Beguins, for example, accused of usurping the office of preaching, resort to this distinction, which is less subtile than it seems. "In suam excusationem fictitie praetendentes quod non praedicant, sed loquuntur de Deo." Mosheim, *De Beghardis*, 1790, p. 206. This distinction is admitted by the adversaries, when they have an interest therein. See further on, at the dispute of Narbonne.

111   "Sic accepit a papa praedications officium." Moneta.

112   "Nen dement el meseyme predicant en la cipta fey plusors disciples."

113   "A primate ipsorum Valde dictos, qui fuerat civis Lugduni super Rodanum." This "fuerat" has puzzled the critics. According to Reuss (*Rev de Theol*, June, 1851) Map "says explicitly that Waldo did not attend the Council." Dieckhoff tries to evade the difficulty by referring the statement of Map to some other Council. We would observe that Waldo having been turned out of Lyons was no longer a citizen of that town. Although we cannot understand how Waldo being there, Map does not mention the fact. On the other hand, it being certain that Waldo did go to Rome—Reuss admits this—how can we account for his not remaining there to plead his own cause? Who could have presented it better than himself? After all we are obliged to leave this point undecided. Waldo may have been prevented by some hitherto unknown cause, from being present, at least on this particular day at the Council. On the other hand, Map's narrative does not explicitly deny his presence.

114   *Credere in* is seldom if ever employed in Church Latin, unless with reference to the persons of the Trinity. The answer to this last question ought to have been, according to the examiner, "We do not believe *in*, but *on* the mother of Christ." For that matter if men do anywhere believe *in matrem Christi*, it is in the Church of Rome. Moreover, the jargon of the schools did not always observe this rule. These grand theologians, in full session, strained at a gnat and swallowed a camel.

115   "Humillimo nunc incipiunt modo, quia pedem inferre nequeunt; quos si admiserimus expellemur." Mapes, *De nugis curialium*, rediscovered and printed by Wright, London, 1850.

116   "Inhibens eidem ne, vel ipse aut socii sui predicacionis officium presumerent nisi rogantibus sacerdotibus "*Chron. Laud.'* A la perfin receop repost en la cort que la gleysa romana non poya portar la parolla de lui." Cambridge MS.

117   "Facent camin per las regions de Ytalia fa aiostament." Cambridge MS.

118   *Chron. Laud* ap. Pertz. See above in Chapter iii.

119   "Quod preceptum modice tempore observaverunt." *Ibid.*

120   See note 745.

121   "Valdesium et Vivetum." *Rescriptum*, p. 19, 58. He has also been given, as colleague, a certain "socius Johannis" of Lyons. See note 740. Is there not some confusion here? Fuesslin (*Kirch. u. Ketzerhist*, 1170, part I., p. 137) observes that certain writers, having misread the name of Jean de Lugis, a Catharian, have converted it into Johannis de Lugduno. Moneta and others as far down as M. Tron seem to have repeated the error.

122   *Gallia Christiania* iv., col. 130-133. Stephen of Borbone calls him "aux Belles-mains."

123 "Anunente papa Lucio." *Ibid.*

124 "Vir magnæ litteraturæ et eloquentiæ." *Ibid.*

125 "Mandat dominus Apostolicus quod cessarent cum predicatio verbi Dei rubidus et illiteratis non conveniat." Anonymous writer of Passau.

126 Here again the passage from Stephen of Borbone, which we do not require to requote, would have its application.

127 "Eorum numerus octena millia excedebat." Ughelli, *Italia Sacra*, vol. iv., col. 1041, ed. 1719.

128 *Gallia Christiana.* There is no question of a crime of intolerance. We know that his two daughters had not passed the period of first youth. On the other hand, in the year 1218, at the conference at Bergamo, his death is spoken of as something quite recent.

130 "Qui se Humiliatos vel Pauperes de Lugduno falso nomine mentiuntur . . . anctoritatem sibi vindicant prædicandi . . . pari vinculo perpetui anathematis innodamus." *Lucu decü. c. hær.* ap. Mausi xxiv.

131 Thus far there are no certain indications of the origin of P. de Bruys, but he must have been born in the Alps of Gap. The letter of P. de Cluny, hereinafter mentioned, would lead us to think as much. We learn, furthermore, that there still exists in that territory a town by the name of Bruis (canton de Rosans (called Bruscum in 1147, Brosium in 1153, Brossium in 1294, Brueys in 1351, Bruys in 1516 ; which, according to the custom of the XII. century, may have given him its name. See *le Dict. topog. du Dep. des H. Alpes, by J. Roman* 1844, p. 22. He was not yet confounded with a canon of Lucca, as was done by Iselin and others before him. Fuesslin I., 191—194.

132. Peter the venerable, abbot of Cluny in his *Ep. adv. Petrob. haereticos.*

133 "Ex longinqua regione istuc accedere potuit et fortasse ex Italia, ut postea dicturi sumus," says Mabillon ; but he does not return to this subject. Pref. to his Ed. of *Opera S. Bernardi*, 1690, vi. Is his surname of Italicus truly historical, and if so, what justifies it? The description of his person is the only clue left us. It is of some value.

134 "Visa tantum eorum facie, cognosceret. . ᾽ . Asserebant quoque sibi a Domino Deo anticam et authenticam Prophetarum collatum fuisse benedictionem et Spiritum." See the *Chron.* ap. Mabillon III., 313.

156 The letter of P. the Venerable is addressed to the Bishops of Embrun, Die, and Gap.

136 "Facti estis velut columba seducta non habens cor et velut bos ductus ad victimam." *Ibid.*

137 "Duobus tantum homuncionibus . . . tam facile cessistis." *Ibid.*

138 "Tamen in eisdem vestris regionibus non parva semina reliquisse cognovi." *Ibid.*

139 "Ne putridae reliquiae reviviscere queant." *Ibid.*

140 "Ut de latibulis vestris ad publicum nostrum prodeatis invito." *Ibid.*

141 "Non habet veritas angulos, nec lumen sub modio vult latere." *Ibid.*

142 Hudry Menos. *Rev. des Deux Mondes* 1867—68, art *l'Israël des Alpes.*

143 Réveille, art. *Les Albigeois* in the *Rev. des Deux Mondes.* May 1, 1874.

144 Napoléon Peyrat, *Les Albigeois et l'Inquisition*, Paris, 1872. We note the more willingly the justness of this observation, as the book, from which we borrow it is full of more or less whimsical hypotheses.

145 "Quandoquidem cuivis sua religio debet esse libera." Perrin, b. ii., c. 8, and Sandius. *Nucleus hist. eccl.*, p. 410.

146 G. of Puy-Laurens, *Hist., neg. Franc, adv. Albigenses.* Vaissette reproduces it in his *Hist. du Languedoc*, iii., p. 129.

147 "Digito demonstrarent, nos apostatas, nos hypocritas, nos haereticos conclamantes," Baronius, an. 1178.

148 It was, according to him, the opinion also of the Toulousains. The Cathari, we know, passed for Arians. *Ibid.*

149 "Etiam evangelistas qui . . . nova illis evangelia cuderent. *Ibid.*

150 P. de Vause-Cernay, *op. cit.*,

151 Perrin, *op. cit.*, b. i., p. 1.

152 By representing them as united by the same faith, hence, one in all things, the Jesuit Gretser aimed at bringing the Waldenses into discredit ; Flacius Illyricus, Léger, Monastier, Basnage, Abbadie, etc., aimed at the opposite result. "Only ignorance or bad faith could have confounded them," says Hudry-Ménos.

153 Guill. de P. L. *Ibid.*

154 See *Contra Wald.*, ap. Bibl. P. M. vol. xxiv. Bernard, Prior of the Fontis Calidi on the confines of the dioceses of Narbonne and Béziers, has

woven the arguments cited in this dispute into his treatise, and has added a few notes at the end, which he expressly declares refer to other heresies. His aim thus far, he asserts, is to bring the principles of the Waldenses to the knowledge of illiterate ecclesiastics, and to show how they may be refuted. This leads one to suspect that if he reproduces in an abridged form the arguments of the dissidents, he also permits himself to amplify and complete those of his co-religionists. This possibility should be noted.

155 2 Thess. iii., 14 ; Heb. xiii.. 17; Matt. xviii., 17.

156 " Quia aliter quam S. Ecclesia docent." Gieseler observes that this must refer to their biblical method of teaching, inasmuch as they are accused of no heresy here, save that of *de inobedientia.*

157 " Non tamen debent nos prohibere."

158 " Multi laïci verbum Dei in populo fideli disseminaverunt."

169 " Isti omnes, licet laïci, verbum Dei praedicaverunt."

160 " Viri femineae debilitatis."

161 " Seducunt mulieres prius, per eas viros."

162 " Taurus vocent haereticos." Cf. Ps. xxii., 13, and lxviii., 31.

163 " Praeter errores jam dictos, graviter errant, quia feminas, etc. 1 Cor. iv., 34.

164 " Loquuta est de Christo . . . Non est idem praedicare et loqui." Luke ii., 36—38.

165 It took place about the year 1190. According to Vaissette (iii. 128) Gaucelin was Archbishop of that city from the year 1181 to 1191. A considerable interval must be admitted between the exile from Lyons and the disputation which took place, far away in Languedoc, and on the other hand, rather a short one between this disputation and the decrees which sanctioned its conclusions.

166 " Per scriptum definitivam dedit sententiam, et haereticos esse in capitulis, de quibus accusati fuerant, pronunciavit."

167 This name must be understood as alluding to the apostolic Sabates (or sandals), which they wore, as we shall see further on.

168 *Edictum Alph. reg. Arag. contra haereticos,* ap. Bibl. M. P., xxv.

169 *Stat. Syn. Odon.,* anno 1192, ap. d'Argentré, i.

170 See the *Bible de Guiot de Provins,* written in 1203, in the *Fabliaux et contes des poetes francais,* etc., ed. Meon, Paris, 1808.

171 " Pro toedio renunciare volentes." P. de Vaux-Cernay.

172 " Oporteret eos a praedicatione desistere." *Ibid.*

173 " Per omnia formam apostolicam imitantes." *Ibid.*

174 Guill de P.L., ch. 9.

175 " Ite, domina, filate colum vestram ; non interest vestra loqui in hujusmodi contentione." *Ibid.*

176 See epistles of Innocent III., b xi. to xv., passim, ap. Baluzius.

177 *Ep. ad Tarrag. Archiep,* January 15, 1209.

178 *Ep. ad Durandum,* same date.

179 *Ep. Helen episc,* June 7, 1213.

180 " Ne error novissimus fiat pejor priore." *Ep. ad Dur. de Osca et fratres ejus,* July 3, 1210.

181 " Cum essem astutus, dolo vos cepi," 2 Cor. xii., 16. This passage often occurs in Innocent's writings. *Ep ad Narb. episc, et suffrag. ejus,* same date.

182 *Ep. ad Narb. et Tarrag. et Mediol. archiep.,* May 4, 1211 ; *ep. ad Durandum,* May 3, 1211, and *ep ad Tarrac. et Narb. archiep.,* of the same day.

183 Hurter, *Hist. du Pope Inn. III.,* b. xiv. But this point does not come out clearly from the correspondence of the Pontiff.

184 Vidimus tunc temporis aliquos de numero eorum qui dicebantur Pauperes de Lugduno, apud sedem apostolicam cum magistro suo quodam, ut puto Bernhardo, et hi petebant sectam suam a sede apostolica confirmari et privilegiari." *Chron. Burchardi et Cuonradi Ursperg.,* ap. Pertz, xxiii., p. 396, and *Ep. d'Innoc. III.,* ap. Baluze, xiii., 94, xv., 137.

185 " Ipsi dicentes se gerere vitam Apostolorum, nihil volentes possidere aut certum locum habere, circuibant per vicos et castella. At Dominus Papa quædam superstitiosa in conversatione ipsorum eisdem objecit, videlicet quod calceos de superpedem præcidebant et quasi nudis pedibus ambulabant. Præterea cum portarent quasdam cappas, quasi religionis, capillos capitis non attondebant nisi sicut laici. Hoc quoque probrosum in eis videbatur, quod viri et mulieres simul manebant in una domo, et de eis diceretur, quod quandoque simul in lectulis accubabant." *Ibid.*

186 " Quæ omnia ipsi asserebant ad Apostolis descendisse." *Ibid.*

187 Letter of July 18, 1211, ap. Baluze.

188 Multo fortius . . . repellendi non sunt." *Ep. episc. cremon,* Aug. 15, 1213.

189   Cf., with the references given there *Chron. Burch. et C. Ursperg.*, ap. *Mon. Germ. Script.*, xxiii., p. 396.

190   " Exortæ sunt duæ religiones  . . . videlicet Minorum fratrem et Prædicatorum. Quœ forte hac occasione sunt approbatæ, quia olim duæ sectæ in Italia exortæ adhuc perdurant, quorum alii Humiliatos, alu Pauperes de Lugduno se nominabant." *Chron. Usperg. cf. Müller Aufange des Minoriten-ordeus*, ap. Brieger, *Zeitsch. f. Kircheng*, vol. vi.

191   Helyot *Hist des Ordres monastiques*, 1839, vol. ii., p. 238 et seq.

192   Hurter, *op. cit.*

193   See the two epistles of Innocent, dated January 15, 1209, and August 10, 1213. Hahn, while making this remark, goes so far as to take those, who favoured separation, for Manicheans, and this quite simply. See his *Gesch d Ketzer*, i., p. 186, n. 2. In order to account for certain points which, in their signed confession relate manifestly to Catharism, it suffices to suppose that the group of those favouring separation had admitted to their number a few converts from Catharism, and aimed at gaining adherents among them also. Hahn supposes that Innocent III. is mistaken, and that he gives the name of Waldenses to Cathari. But Durand and his associates declare that they separate " a Lugdunensibus," and Bernard and his acolytes are called " Pauperes de Lugduno " in the chronicle which mentions them. Besides, according to the Pontiff's correspondence, the above-mentioned confession was to serve as a banner for a general return. We shall see further on that it was again utilized in Milan.

194   Michelet, *Hist. de France*, ii., b. iii.

195   M. Berger remarks on this point : " If we had not, in this respect, the formal testimony of the chronicler Alberic, we should still know, by a number of other proofs, that under the episcopate of Bertram, the Waldensian heresy found its greatest development at Metz." *La Bible francaise du moyen age*, p. 39.

196   Cæs. Heisterb. Mirac.. dist. v., c. 20, ap. *Bibl. Cisterc.*, ii., 138.

197   " In urbe Metensi, pullulante secta quae dicitur Valdensium." Alberic, the author of the chronicle, is almost contemporary. See Pertz, *Mon Germ. Script.* xxiii., p. 878, an. 1199.

198   " Ipsi eis in faciem restiterunt." *Ep. Inn. III.*, b. ii., 141, ap Baluz, cf. Migne, *Sp.* 699, 793.

199   " Dicit Apostolus : Non plus sapere quam oporteat sapere, sed sapere ad sobrietatem." See Rom. xii., 3.

200   " Ut qui noluerunt obedire spontanei, discant ad quiescere vel. inviti." *Ibid.*

201   " Ut  . . .  quid statui debeat, melius intelligere valeamus." *Ep.* 142, *Ibid*, July 12, 1199.

202   " Obediendum esse soli Deo." *Ep.* 235 *aux abbés de Citeaux, de Morimond*, etc. *Ibid.*

203   " Injurias contumeliasque hac de re perpessus," *Gallia Christiana*, xiii., 754.

204   " Directi sunt ad praedicandum quidam abbates, qui quosdam libros de latino in romanum versos combusserunt et praedictam sectam extirpaverunt." Pertz.

205   " Omnes libri romane vel teuthonicé scripti de divinis scripturis in manus tradantur episcopi, et ipse, quos reddendos videri, reddat." This decree is from Bishop Guido, of Palestrina, Plenipotentiary of the Pope in Belgium. See Miraei, *Op. dipl. et hist.*, i., 564.

206   *Gallia Christiana*, xiii., 754.

207   Cæs Heisterb.

208   The *Fasti Corbeienses*, quoted by Harenberg (1762, i., p. 72), mention hostile laymen of " Suavia, Suicia et Bavaria," seduced " ab antiqua progenie simplicium hominum qui Alpes et viciniam habitant et semper amant antiqua." These are called Manicheans ; we read further that some came originally from Hungary. Half a century ago, Gieseler doubted whether we should recognise among them partisans of Arnaldo da Brescia. Others endeavour to twist the sense of this passage for the purpose of finding Waldenses. But it is proven that the whole passage, from page 45-89 of Harenberg's *Mon. Hist.*, is not authentic, as the above-mentioned *Fasti* does not contain it. C. L. Scheid was the first to notice this fact in 1758. Pertz, in 1839, laid the fraud bare, in his *Mon. Germ.* iii., p. 1, et seq.

209   *Chron.*, of Justinger, anno 1277 and 1399, ap. Ochsenbein, *op. cit.*, p. 95.

210   One hundred and thirty Waldenses were discovered in Berne, and fifty-three at Friburg, says Herzog, *Real Encycl.*, 1st ed., art *Waldenses.* Cf. Ochsenbein, *op. cit.*, p. 95-122.

211   " Um des Ungloubens der sekten Waldensium," dated December 9, 1400. See *Recueil Diplom. du canton de Fribourg*, b. v., p. 170.

212   One of the women accused of Waldensian heresy in Friburg, in 1430, confesses to having learned from her co-religionist, Conrad Wasen, that, in the Roman districts, there were a good number of people professing the same faith —" in partibus Romaniè." See Ochsenbein, *op. cit.*, p. 284.

213   The public called it "the beautiful street of the prelates—*die schone Pfaffengasse.*"

214   T. W. Röhrich, according to Specklin, *Mittheilungen aus der Geschichte der evangelischen Kirche des Elsasses*, 1855, 1st. vol.

215   *Chron.*, *Domin.*, *Colmar.*, ap., Urstisuis, *Germ. .Hist.*, ii., 5, 90 ; and *Chron. Hirsang.*, ap. Trithemius, i., 543.   Cf. Rohrich, *op. cit.*

216   Specklin thinks that these are Waldenses still.   "In the year 1230," he says, "the Waldensian heresy again raised its head here."   *Collectanea in usum chronici Argent.*, to the year 1230.

217   Mosheim, *De Beghardis*.  If we read, for instance, pages 115, 317, 482, 484, and 486, we cannot understand how M. L. Keller can pretend to rest upon the testimony of Mosheim, for confounding the Waldenses with the Beghins. Cf. his book *Die Reformation u. die ältesten Reformationsparteieu*, 1885, p. 23.

218   The recent researches of M. Müller have confirmed our conviction on this point, and on many others also.   We desire to offer him here our best thanks. See his book on the Orttieber, entitled : "*Die Waldenser v. ihre einzelnen Gruppen, bis zum Aufang des* 14 *Jahrhunderts,*" Gotha, 1886, p. 130 et 169.

219   That is to say, "Winkelprediger" litt. prædicatores augulorum," because "ipsi secreto *prædicant* et paucis hominibus *in angulis.*"   M. Haupt recognises in them Waldenses (see *Die relig. Sekten*, p. 26) and M. Müller shows that he is right, *op. cit.*, p. 165.

220   Et de Borbone *Anecdotes*, etc., n. 343.   Cf. Ing. of Passau, ap *M. Bibl. Patr.* xxv., p. 266—267.   There is no doubt Michelet borrowed his colours from here, in order with them to paint the Waldenses in such colours as he liked.

221   These are the "Sifridenses."   Anonymous writer of Passau, p. 266.

222   See Et. de Bourbon, *ibid.*, and the Inquisitor of Passau *ibid.*, p. 264.

223   Tocco *op. cit.*, p. 207, et seq.

224   "Recognovit quod bene noverat apud Mediolanum septemdecim sectas a se invicem divisas et adversas, quas ipsi eciam de secta sua omnes damnabant, et eas mihi nominavit et differencias earum."   Et. de Bourbon, *Anecdotes*, n. 330.

225   "Fuerunt schismatici judicati.   Postea in Provincie terra et Lombardiæ cum aliis hæreticis se admiscentes, etc.   *Ibid.*, n. 342.

226   See ante note 47.

227   Cf. the letter of his disciple Wesel, writing from Rome, ap. Mart and Durand, *Coll.* ii., 554, and Jaffe, i., 539, 543.

228   "Politicorum hæreticorum patriarcham atque principem se constituit." Baronius, *Ann. Eccl.*, ann 1141.

229   "Hominum sectam fecit, quæ adhuc dicitur hæresis Lombardorum." We read in the *Hist. Pontificatis* ap. Pertz, xx., p. 515.  On the other hand, Dav. of Augsburg, *op. cit.*, ch. 20, classes the "Arnostuste" among the sections of the Waldenses.  M. Tocco does not hesitate to affirm that "the Poor of Lombardy descended in a direct line from the Arnaldists," *op. cit.*, p. 187.  M. Preger, although more moderate in his language, is still positive on this matter. *Beiträge*, p. 31.  M. Müller hesitates to commit himself ; but he admits, in any case, the possibility of a connection between the movement of Arnaldo and that of the Waldenses.  *Die Wald.* p. 58.

230   "Sed ne conventicula ab eis fierent, signanter interdixit et ne in publico predicare presumerent districte inhibuit.  Ipsi vero mandatum apostolicum contempnentes, facti inobedientes, se ob id excommunicari permiserunt.  Hii se Humiliatos appellaverunt, eo quod tincta indumenta non vestientes, simplici sunt contenti."  *Chron. Laud.*, ap. Pertz, xxvi., p. 449, 450.

231   V. Tiraboschi, *Vet. Humil. Mon.*, *passim.* Cf. Preger, *Beiträge*, p. 32—34; Müller, *op.cit,,* p. 59 et 60.

232   "Humiliates *vel* Pauperes de Lugduno," says the decree of this Council, which we have before quoted.

233   "Quam bonæ memoriæ prædecessor tuus destrui fecerat." Ep. d'Inn. III. to the Archbishop and Chapter of Milan, 3rd April, 1210.

234   "Et nunc iterum est erecta."  *Ibid.*

235   "Pratum prædictum seu alium locum idoneum . . . concedatis eisdem sine gravi scandalo aliorum."  *Ibid.*

236   The letter of Innocent III. in which we find this is dated 14th June, 1210.  Buchardt was a witness of the reappearance of Bernard and his companions.  *Chron. Ursperg*, ap. Pertz, xxiii., p. 396.  Cf. Tiraboschi, *op. cit.*, i., 79.

237   "Cum olim una secta fuisse . . . conscissi in diversas hereses divisi

sunt." Dav. of Augsberg, ch. 20. We shall see in our last chapter that the celebration of the Eucharist was an invariable practice, before this division: " Eundem modum tenebant aute divisionem quæ fuit inter eos." Mart and Durand, v., 1775. Bernard Gui explains these words by adding : "Videlicet quando diviserunt se in Pauperes vocatos Lombardos et in Pauperos Citramontanos." See *la Practica Inquisitionis*, published by Canon C. Douais, Paris, 1886.

238 "Dividitur haeresis Leonistarum seu pauperum de Lugduno in duas partes. Prima pars vocatur Pauperes Ultramontani, secunda vero Pauperes Lombardi . . . Isti descenderunt ab illis." Sacconi, *Summa* ap. Mart. et Dur., v., 1775.

239 See note 924.

240 According to the *Rescriptum her. Lomb. ad Pauperes de Lugduno qui sunt in Alamanca*, ap. Preger. Cf. the examination of the three MSS. which contain it, ap. Müller, p. 22. The most ancient would probably be of XIII. century, or at latest the commencement of XIV. Cf. Preger, *Ueber das Verhältniss der Taboriteu zu deu Waldensiern des 14 Jahrhunderts*, Munich, 1888, p. 16—19.

241 The Ultramontanes were: "Petrus Relana et Berengarius de Aquaviva qui ambo tunc temporis accionem ultramontanorum annualem juxta suam consuetudinem procurbant, G. de Cremano et G. Turantus, Optandus de Bonate et Julianus." Those of Lombardy were: "Johannes de Sarnago et Thateus, Thoma set Maifredus, Johannes Franceschus et Jordanus de Dogno." *Ibid.*, n. 15.

243 "Pacem nobiscum habere non possent." *Ibid.*, n. 15.

243* "Si pro omnibus culpis satisfecerint . . . posse salvari." *Ibid.*

245 "Non homini sed verbis Dei virtutem attribuimus." *Ibid.*, n. 16.

245* "Cum nec sanctificari illic oblacio possit ubi spiritus sanctus non sit, nec cuiquam dominus per eius preces et oraciones prosit, qui dominum ipse violat." *Ibid.*, n. 24.

246 "Sacerdotes qui eucharistie serviunt et sanguinem eius indigne conficiunt, impie agunt in lege Christi putantes, eucharistiam imprecantis facere verba non vitam, et necessariam esse tantum solempnem oracionem et non sacerdotum merita, de quibus dicitur: sacerdos in quacunque fuerit macula non accedat oblaciones offerre deo." *Ibid.*

247 "Quomodo ergo si sancti non sunt, sanctificare alios possunt ? " *Ibid.*

248 "Audiant illi . . . dicentes : Ego non symoniacum attendo, sed verba benediccionis, quæ ex illius ore procedunt." *Ibid.*

249 "O miseri, omnibus hominibus miserabiliores, qui ore sacrilego talia audent fari nefaria . . . Dominus per Malachiam, quod malorum sacerdotum benediccio pro malediccione imputetur, ait : Maledicam benediccionibus vestris." *Ibid.*

250 "Breviter respondemus : Cum essem parvulus, etc." *Ibid.*

251 "Respondemus : quia contra veritatem scripturarum jam propalatam credere non possumus, nec eciam licet Valdesiani in hoc nos vellent cogere, volumus confiteri. Oportet emin obedire Deo magis quam hominibus." *Ibid.*

252 Cf. with another conference, apparently of Cathari, in Et de Bourbon, *op. cit.*, n. 329.

253 We have taken the facts respecting the conference from the Rescript itself. This is the address : "Oto de Ramezello del gracia confrater pauperum spiritu, I de Sarnago, Tadeus Marinus, G. de Papia, L. de Leganio, G. de Moltrasio, I. de Mutini, J. Franceschus, Jordanus de Dogno Bononius Atque Thomas dilectis in Christo fratribus au sororibus, amicis et amicabus tranus alpes pie degentibus in vero salutari salutem et dileccionis perpetue firmitatem." Preger supposes that this Rector was Thomas, but he is evidently mistaken. The letter must have been written a short time after the conference ; according to M. Müller, M. Preger still thinks it cannot have been written until about 1230, and gives reasons for his opinion. See *Ueber das Verhältuiss*, etc.

254 "Et ibi schole." We know already that these schools were places of meeting, where particularly the "magistri," who came from afar to visit the communities, were received. See Preger, *Batrage*, in appendix notice to n. ii., entitled *Orte in der Diocese Passau, wo die italischen Armen um 1250, Auhanger hatten*. The writing of said notice, as well as the one that follows, dates as far back as 1260.

255 "Et ibi schole et episcopus." *Ibid.*

256 "Et ibi schole plures (x) et plebanus occisus est ab eis." *Ibid.* The plurality of schools is an indication that, there as elsewhere, there was more than one sect at work.

257 Preger reproduces it in his *Beiträge*, no. iii., under the title of *Der Passauer anonymus uber die Kirchlichen Missbrauche.*

258 "Tempore interdicti exultant haeretici, quia tunc possent corrumpere christianos," said an Inquisitor quoted by Fl. Illyricus, *op. cit.*, p. 653.

259 Fr. Iostes, in his dispute with M. Haupt, had held that the Waldensian movement in Germany did not proceed from the ranks of the people. M. Haupt, in his reply, proves that it penetrated higher. *Der wald. Ursprung des Codex Teplensis*, p. 4—8.

260 "Nuncupaverunt se inter se *dy Kunden* et nos *dy Fromden.*" *Kunder*, in Latin, *noti*. These designations are ratified by usage, in Bavaria, Austria, and Switzerland. Haupt, *Die religiösen sekten*, etc., p. 24.

261 M. Haupt even thinks it was on the point of coming about, as it did, two centuries before, in the South of France. *Ibid.*

262 For details we refer to Haupt, *op. cit.*, and with regard to Pomerania and Brandeburg, to W. Wattenbach, *Ueber Ketzergerichte in Pommern u. der Mark Brandenburg*, ap. *Sitzungsber, d. kön preuss. Akad. d. Wiss.* 1886.

263 Ochsenbein, *op. cit.*

264 Duverger, *La Vauderie*, 1885, especially p. 17-27, and T. T. Altmeyer *Les Precurseurs de la Reforme aux Pays Bas*, 1886, vol. i., p. 54—62.

265 Haupt, *Die relig. Sekten*, etc., p. 26, and *Der wald Ursprung*, etc., appendix No. 4. Flacius Illyricus names still more in his *Catalogus*, p. 660.

266 Goll, *Quellen u Untersuchungen*, etc., i. p. 121, et seq.

267 From *calix*, cup. Also called *Ultraquists*, because they celebrated the Holy Communion in two kinds : *sub utraque*.

226* 268 M. Schmidt in his *Precis*, etc., remarks that *Tabor* in the Slavonic dialects signifies a *tent*. Being compelled to lead a rather nomadic life, on account of the persecution, they finally got that name applied to their sect, called *the Tabor*.

269 "I no longer doubt now but that Peter Chelcicky was acquainted with the doctrine of the Waldenses, from an early age, and found pleasure in it—u. daran Gefallen fand." Palacky, *Ueber die Beziehunger der Wald zu den Secten in Böhmen*, 1870. He adds, it is true, that he says not a word about it. M. Goll agrees in admitting that, when Chelcicky came to Prague from the South of France, he adhered to the views of the Waldenses, and that he continued therein —"u. habe in der Folge immer au ihr festgehalten." *Quellen*, ii., 42, n. 2.

270 M. Preger even thinks that they were numerous in Bohemia, on the eve of J. Huss's appearance. *Beiträge*, etc., p. 51.

271 Thus far the existence of any community had not been verified. Palacky, *ibid.*, Zezschwitz, *Die Katechismen*, p. 154 ; Goll, *op. cit.*, p. 37, n. 1.

272 Preger comes to the conclusion in his work, *Ueber das Verhältuiss*, etc., p. 110, that "that the Taborites are the spiritual offspring of the Waldenses." Lechler thinks this is an extreme conclusion. See *Theol. Literatur blatt*, 11th November, 1887. Cf. Haupt, *Husitische Propaganda in Deutschlaud (Hist. Taschenbuch*, sixth series, vol. vii., 1888, p. 235).

273 "Frederick, by the Grace of God, bishop of believers in the Romish Church, who reject the donation of Constantine." Haupt, *op. cit.*, p. 46.

274 "Il cuore, non la fibra." This expression is taken from Gino Capponi, who applies it to Savonarola, in his *St. di Firenze*.

275 Consult authorities ap. Iung and Böehm. This account is given here from Haupt, *op. cit.*, p. 44—46.

276 Wattenbach, p. 9—11.

277 *Réplique a Rokycana*, ap. Goll. *Quellen*, etc., ii., 42, n. 4.

278 "We have also heard from those who trace their origin back to the primitive Church, how even then, when Sylvester accepted those gifts his colleague Peter did not yield, but said: It is not in accordance with the doctrine and the example that Christ and our fathers, the Apostles gave us." Gregory, *Traite de l'Eglise*, ap. Goll., *op. cit.*, i., 10, 23. Cf. treatise *Wie die Menschen*, etc., ap., Goll. i., *Beilage*.

279 A bishop of the Brethren went so far as to believe that Waldo was the first founder of their opposition, and he was not the only one of that opinion. Goll., *op. cit.*, i., 49, n. 2.

280 F. S. Hark, *Die Entstehung d alten Brüder Unitat u ihres Bisthums*, in the *Brüder-Bote*, April and May, 1883.

281 "He performed the services secretly for the Waldenses among the Germans, and on that account he was burnt at the stake." "*Wil sie die Menschen*, etc., ap. Goll.

282 This is the thesis now maintained by M. Haupt, and to which we shall have to come back.

283 "Than has been recognised until now." Preger, *Beitrage*, p. 3.

284   "The history of the Waldenses has until now by no means received the attention which it deserves." Keller, *op. cit.*, p. 20, n. 1.

285   It is the watchword given to every departing missionary. Thus, Matthew Hagen confesses to his judges that his Bishop Reiser sent him " in order that he should proclaim the four Gospels, as the Apostles did, when Christ said to them : Go, etc." Wattenbach, *ibid.*

286   "Fere enim nulla est terra in qua haec secta non sit," Ing. of Passau, *op. cit.*, ap. Bibl. Max, Patr., c. 4.

281* 287   "Like a fire on the point of going out." These words are attributed to F. Reiser. Haupt, *op. cit.*, p. 46.

282* 288   Edgar Quintet, *Mélanges*, chapter on the *Avenu de la religion*, and *passim* in his book on the *Génie des religions*.

283* 289   According to Perrin, who had the advantage of consulting documents collected for him in the valley of Luserna and especially in Angrogna by Vignaux and other pastors of the Valleys (see Gilles, ch. li.), "it is believed by certain among them that they (the Waldenses) are sprung from the Waldenses of Dauphiny, Pragela, Fraissinières, etc." *Hist.* (*des Vaudois*, part i, p. 150? *ibid.* p. 5—64.

284* 290   It is the chronicle called the *Tranjetons de Molines.* These words are quoted after A. Muston. See *Le Temoie, écho des vallées vaudoises,* year ix., n. 47. The chronicle quoted by Muston, and which he dates back to the XV. century, is dated 14th February, 1816. The author was the person who founded the village of Font Gillarde. The copy of it which is preserved, presents, in the few lines that are known, some gross errors. Berger, *Rev. Hist.,* xxxvi.

285* 291   Muston, *ibid.,* n. 49.   Another village of the name of Villar is found further north, below Briancon.

286* 292   A MS. of Cambridge, entitled *Origo Valdensium,* by an Inquisitor of the XV. century, contains the following words, concerning our fugitives : " Lugduno fugientes ad ultimas Delphinatus partes, se transferentes in Ebredunensi et Taurinensi dioecesibus in Alpibus et intra concava montium accessu difficilia, plures ibi ex ipsis habitaverunt." Allix, *Some Remarks,* etc., at the end.

287* 293   "Minor Deo, major homine   . . .   Sicut luna lumen saum a sole sortitur, sic," etc.   Inn. III., *Ep.* 401, and *passim,* ap. Baluz. i.

294   " Pejores sunt illis."   *Ep.* 28, *ibid.,* xi.

289* 295   "Ad capiendas vulpeculas," writes Innocent, *Ep.* 149, *ibid.* x.

290* 296   Fauriel, *Croisade contre les Albigeois, par un troubadour,* p. 37. Peter Vallis Cernaü says the same thing.

291* 297   " Caedite eos, novit, enim Donimus qui sunt ejus." This expression is contested. See, for instance, *la Science Catholique, rev. des questions relig.,* 1st year, p. 224. But, " if the letter be incorrect, the fact is strictly true," we still say with Duverger, *op. cit.* p. 9. Moreover, it does not contradict the report written to the Pope by the same Arnaud, in which he relates this massacre of 20,000 persons, with the unction of a Mahdi, and closes by saying : " Facta hostium strage permaxima, spoliata est tota civitas et succensa, ultione divina in eam mirabiliter saeviente." *Ep.* of Inn., b. xii., 18.

292* 298   A. Muston, *ibid.,* n. 49.   Thus far we agree with our poet.   But from this to admitting " the Italian origin of the Waldenses of Piedmont," there is what is called *Saltus in probando,* a very long stride.

293* 299   *Hist. Veritable,* etc., MS., of Turin.   Cf. De Rubeis, after Perrin, *op. cit.,* b. i., ch. 3.

294* 300   Gilles, *op. cit.,* ch. i.

295* 301   *Les Vallées Vaudoises, étude de topographie et d'histoire militaires,* by A. de Rochas d'Aiglun, chef de bataillon du Génie, Paris, 1880.

296* 302   1 Kings, xx., 23.

297* 303   Hudry-Ménos, *l'Israël des Alpes,* Rev. des D.M., Nov. 15, 1867. However, some attention is occasionally paid to this. Monastier, for instance, admits that Pre du Tour is "unassailable," and that to attempt to attack Angrogna on a certain side, "is folly." *Hist. de l'Eglise Vaudoise,* i., p. 181.

298* 304   MS. of D. L. Garola in the archives of Count Emmanuel of Luserna, p. 19—23.

299* 305   Hist. Gén., b. i., ch. 1.   Cf. *Rev.* xii.

300* 306   Gilles, *ibid.*

301* 307   The documents of the house of Luserna are in manuscript, private, but accessible, thanks to the courtesy of Count Emmanuel. Moreover, their importance is infinitesimal, as regards this history. With respect to the act of donation of Adelaide, see *Mon. Hist. Patriae,* vol. i., p. 607.

302* 308   A. de Rochas d'Aiglun, *l.c.*

303* 309  Tron. *op. cit.*, ch. xii.
304* 310  Hudry-Ménos, *l.c.*
305* 311  The same, *ibid.*
306* 312  Gilles, *l.c.*
307* 313  Ill-timed, we say, for that testimony narrated in an inexact manner, is not a real testimony; such as it is, it weakens instead of justifying its own assertion.
308* 314  Recently it has again been advanced by Tron, *op. cit.*, ch. xii.
315  These tales are taken from Jacques Brezzi, Timoleon, and J. R. Peyran, Pierre, Bert, etc.
316  Brezzi, *Hist. des Vaudois*, preface. Cf. ch. ii., p. 46.
317  "Quando importava ai Valdesi di fare, per dir così, l'apologia della loro evangelica immobilita." A. Bert, *I Valdesi*, etc., p. 32.
312* 318  Leger, *Hist. Gen.*, etc., li., p. 131.
313* 319  *Hist. des Vaudois*, 1834, p. 160.
314* 320  *Ibid.*, p. 196.
321  *Op., cit.*, p. 137.
316* 322  "Non sectam doceo qui unitatem teneo. . . . Sectas et schismata atque haereses in quantum valui compressi, contrivi et pugnavi et expugnavi, et expugnare in quantum valeo prorsus Deo adiuvante non cesso." *Apol. adv. Theod.*
317* 323  "Quod homines colebant, ego destrui solus coepi." *Ibid.*
318* 324  Artiaco, *Fra Dolcino e la tradizione*, ap. *Riv Crist.*, v. 146.
319* 325  "It is possible," wrote Charles Hase, not long since, "that, since the time of Claude of Turin, a tendency, which anticipated the mission of the Waldenses, and assumed a definite form in consequence of its influence, was maintained among the labouring congregations of the valleys of the Alps." See his *Hist. de l'Eglise*, x. edit., year 1877, p. 276.   But when we asked the celebrated historian whether he had any evidence to give in support of his assertion, he confessed that those words expressed a timid hypothesis, to which he attached no special importance.
320* 326  Ex. Gilly in his *Wald. Researches*, Hudry-Ménos in his *Israel des Alpes*, ap. *Rev. des D. M.*, etc.
321* 327  *Etude sur l'origine des Vaudois du Piémont*, Geneva, 1871.
322* 328  "Non vi ha alcun cenno che in quei luoghi vi fossero eretici." *Un Episodio della Storia del Piemonte nel secolo* xiv., etc., 1874, p. 10—11.
323* 329  *Hist. de l'Eglise Vaudoise*, ch. iv.
324* 330  B. *Petri Dam. Epist.* 1606, b. vii., ep. 16, *ad Adelaidem ducissam et marchionissam Alpium Cotiarum.*
325* 331  "Permittis enim ut Ecclesiae tuae clerici . . . velut jure matrimonii confederentur uxoribus." *Ibid.*, b. iv., ep. 3, *ad Cunibertum episcopum taurinensem.*
326* 332  See his *Is. des Alpes* in the *Rev. des D. M.*
327* 333  *Gall. Christ.* iii., p. 178.  Cf. *Recherches hist. sur les Hautes Alpes* by the Abbot Guillaume, p. 108.
328* 334  *Is. des Alpes*, p. xxxii., n. 2.
329* 335  The verification is founded upon the very indications furnished by Muston.  The inaccuracy was established by F. Albert of Grenoble and F. Guillaume of Gap, to whom we hereby express our gratitude.  The Bull alluded to by Muston "says not a word about heresy or heretics."
330* 336  Monastier, *op. cit.*, ch. 4.  That is repeated by H. Martin, A. Bert, and others to the present day.
331* 337  These words are from the *Témoin, écho des Vallées Vaudoises*, anno 1881, in the course of a discussion upon the origin of the Waldenses.
332* 338  Pertz, *Mon. Germ.*, xii.
333* 339  *Op. cit.*, p. 324.
334* 340  Ag. de Gasparin, *Le Christianisme au Moyen-Age*, 1859, p. 141.
335* 341  *Lettre à A. Lombard*, July 12, 1865.  The latter published it in the appendix of his book upon *J. L. Pascale et les Martyrs de la Calabre.*
336* 342  Landulphi senioris, *Hist. Mediolani*, ii., 27, ap. Muratori, *Rer. Ital. Script.* iv.
337* 343  I allude to the house of Count of Foix.
338* 344  "Specialiter praedicat contra incarnationem Filü Dei," etc.  Brief dated Avignon, July 8, 1332.
339* 345  *Processus contra Valdenses in Lombardia superiori*, ap. Bibl Casan., Rome, D. iii., 18.  The notes of this trial appeared in the *Arch St. Ital.* 1865.
340* 346  "Quam plures conveni valles haereticorum tum Waldensium quam

Gazarorum perversorum." Vinc. Ferr. ap. *Raynald contin. ann. Baron.*, an. 1403, n. 24.

341* 347  "Quando veniebant ad dictas partes, pro majori parte temporis veniebant ad ipsum exponentum, et quando recedebant aliquantulum constituebant eum eorum Locumtenentem." State of Arch, Turin, Mat. Eccl., Inquisizione, mazzo i., categ. 9. This document was published in the *Rivista Cristiana*, October, 1881.

342* 348  Schmidt, *Hist. de Cathares*, etc., vol. i., p. 186—188.

343* 349  The Albigenses and the Poor of Lyons retired thither, says the MS. of D. L. Garola, which, moreover, is of a later date than Rorengo and Th. Belvedere.

344* 350  The existence of a Catharin current of emigration about 1250 has been ascertained. See Ch. Molinier, *L'Inquisition dans le midi de la France*, 1881, p. 253—257.

345* 351  Costa de Beauregard held that the Cathari in Italy "rejoined their co-religionaries of the Valleys of the Pignerol." *Mem. hist.*, quoted by Monastier, i., 42.

346* 352  "Me exinde foris expuli, absentem me feci," says the Duchess, in one of the acts of donation. Croset Mouchet, *Abbaye de Ste Marie de Pignerol*, 1845, Notes and Documents. Gilles (*op. cit.*, ch. xiv.) claims that the abbey "was founded in the year 606, by Adelaide, daughter of the last Marquis of Susa." This error, repeated by Muston (*Hist. d. Vaud.*, p. 7), is rectified by him (*Is. des Alpes*, i, 253).

347* 353  Among other privileges, the monastery had that of being classed among the abbeys, called *nullius diœcesis*, which are held directly from the Pope.

348* 354  "I vecchi conti di Luserna hanno avuto principio dai primi castellani che furono deputati assistenti ai marchesi di Susa alla custodia de passi dell Alpi." Della Chiesa, *Corona Reale*, part i.

349* 355  MS. of Garola, passim. We heard this last point from the mouth of Count Emmanuel of Luserna.

350* 356  It is represented by Alexander, Marquis of Angrogna, and Emmanuel, Count of Luserna.

351* 357  Garola claims to have kept the imprint of the seal of Count Manfredi, of the year 1256, and remarks as follows: "There was a small light surrounded by darkness," and the motto ran : *Sigillum Whelmi Manfredi de Lucerna*.

352* 358  From these coats-of-arms, Léger and Monastier go so far as to conclude that the Waldensian Church existed, *ab antiquo*. But the middle ages are full of such. We know that the coat-of-arms of the city of Geneva, before the Reformation, had for its motto : *Post tenebras spero lucem*. The sequins of Venice, as late as the XVI. century, had on one side the likeness of the Doge kneeling at the feet of Christ, with the inscription : *Ego sum lux mundi*. And does not the coat-of-arms of Leo XIII. bear a star with the words : *Lumen de Cœlo?* So true is it that the name and the thing do not necessarily go together.

353* 359  They were, moreover, rather whimsical. Here is an example : *Lucida lucenti lucescit, luxque, Lucerna, tua.*

354* 360  Besides the fact that the Waldenses have restored its true sense to this symbol, one might further question whether without them the coat-of-arms of Luserna would not be absolutely forgottten as that of Leo XIII. At any rate, we may be permitted to believe that the Waldensian name reflected credit upon it, when we hear the abbot Botero of St. Michael singing

> i Manfredi
> La cui virtù l'alta Lucerna ammanta
> Di Valdo e di Calvin contro gli eredi.

355* 361  "Angroniam . . . jam ad Delphinatus principe sollicitantibus Valdensibus praeoccupatum Ughelli, *Italia Sacra*, iv., 1051. If it were speaking of Pragelas, we might understand it more easily.

356* 362  Croset-Mouchet, *op. cit.*, p. 13.

357* 363  "Con gran disgusto dell Abate," says Cibrario, cited by Croset-Mouchet, *ibid.*

358* 364  "Territi monachi," says Ughelli, *l.c.*

359* 365  Such is the opinion of the author of the MS. of the *Histoire Véritable des Vaudois*, that of Garola, Monastier, and A. Bert; but there is absolutely nothing to justify it.

360* 366  "In quella valle non vi furono gentilhuomini ch'opponessers all'introduttione dell'heresie ma ben i monaci dell'Abbazia," Rorengo, *Mem.Hist.*, ch. vi.

361* 367   MS. of the *Hist. Véritable.*

362* 368   See Croset-Mouchet, *ibid.* p. 17—19, and the *Transazioni fatte tra li signori predecessori della serenissima Casa di Savoia e li Rev. mi Abbati ed nomini del Monastero di S. Maria in Pinerolo,* Turin, 1622.

363* 369   That does not make it necessary to represent the author of *Origo Valdensium* as saying that the Waldenses, who took refuge from Lyons, in the Alps, were "more than fifty thousand" (Lég. *op. cit.* ii., p. 32). This expression is not found in the text, as reproduced by Allix.

364* 370   According to Camerarius the date of the foundation of this colony must be brought back to the middle of the XIV. century; according to De Thou, to the middle of the XIII.

365* 371   The origin of the emigration into Calabria dates, according to Gilles, from about the year 1315; according to Perrin, about 1370; Muston, about 1340.   With Vegezzi-Ruscalla we incline towards the date indicated by Gilles. See *Riv. Contemp.,* Nov., 1862, p. 161, *et seq.,* art., entitled : *Colonia piemontese in Calabria.*

366* 372   Rorengo claims that he heard this detail from the lips of Gilles, who, by his family traditions, seems to us to be the best informed writer on this point.   However, Rorengo is far from doing him justice (*Mem. Hist.,* ch. xvi.) ; still his criticism is quite insignificant, and Vegezzi-Ruscalla alludes to it only to reject it.

367* 373   Gilles, *op. cit.,* ch. iii.

374   Comprising the natives.   See Jerome Zanchi, *Ep. ad Joh. de Lasco,* b. ii., p. 360.

375   See the two edicts of the year 1269, mentioned by Vegezzi-Ruscalla, *ibid.,* at the end, and by De Boni, the *Inquisizione ed i Calabro-Valdesi,* in the appendix.   The second of these decrees gives the names of about 70 heretics denounced by the Inquisition.

376   "Eodem anno (1210) Otho IV. Imp. Taurini aliquot diebus resedit, plurima privilegia ecclesiis concessit, maxime Ripaltae Abbatiae," Ughelli.

377   "Haereticos valdelses (sic) . . . a toto Taurinensi episcopatu imperiali auctoritate expellas." See *Mon. Hist. Patriæ Script.,* vol. ii., 1839, col. 488, by P. Gioffredo, according to the archives of the archbishopric of Turin, categ. i., mazzo i., n. 17.   The reading has been corrected by Manuel de S. Giovanni, *Un Episodio della St. del Piemonte,* p. 11—16, ap *Misc di Storia Ital.,* vol. xv. (1874).   Cf. as to the authenticity of the edict, Winkelmann, *Philip of Swabia and Otto IV.* Leipzig (Jahrb. d. deutsch. Gesch., vol. ii., 1878, p. 221) and T. Ficker, Die *Regenten des Kaisorreichs,* number 2, Othon iv., n. 363.   M. Manuel de S. Giovanni contests the authenticity of it ; Winkelmann hesitates to admit it ; Ficker accepts it, but without any proof ; Berger supports his view by the conclusions of these two last writers, whilst mixing them up together, *Rev. Hist.,* xxxvi., part 6.

378   "Statutum est quod si quis vel si que hospitaretur aliquem vel aliquam a'l esem vel Valdensam se sciente in posse Pinerolu dabit bannum solidorum accea quotiescumque hospitabitur." *Liber Statutorum civ. Pinerolu,* Aug. Taur., 1602, c. 84.

379   Vegezzi-Ruscalla, *Miscell. Patria,* vol. 122.

380   The collection of statutes bears the date of 1220, indicating the year in which the compilation was begun, by order of Thomas I.   This date does not refer to all the statutes indiscriminately.   A note at the end of the first book, p. 54, tells the reader that the different chapters were modified and sanctioned *per dominum in concione,* March 31, 1280.   On this point Cf. librario *St. della Mon. di. Savoia,* 1st ed., i., 263, with Manuel di S. Giovanni, *op. cit.,* p. 16.   From this decree, especially from the expression "Valdensem vel Valdensam," Herzog draws two conclusions : 1st, that the Waldenses were isolated ; 2nd, that the women still accompanied their preachers, *Rom. Wald.,* p. 272—3.

381   "Adjicimus insuper ut quilibet Archiepiscopus vel Episcopus, etc." *Conc. Lat.* iv., c. iii., § 7.

382   Tocco recognizes it very clearly.   *Op. cit.,* p. 170.

383   Thomas Aquinas, the angelic doctor, subsequently defined this point in unequivocal terms.   "Non solum ab ecclesia per excommunicationem separari, sed etiam per mortem a mundo excludi . . . Possunt non solum excommunicari, sed et juste occidi." *Summa* ii., 2, 9, xi., art. 3.

384   "Quod hostilis invaleat haeresis, proh pudor ! in partibus Lombardiae, quae plures inficiat." Message, dated March, 1224.

385   Raynaldi, ad an. 1226, n. 26.

386   "Hanc constitutionem nostram per totam Lombardiam facias publicari." Message quoted above.

387  "Vigor debet ecclesiasticus excitari," wrote Barbarossa, during the same year as the Waldenses were condemned at the Council of Verona. Frederick II. follows the same path, and says more resolutely : "A viris ecclesiasticis et praelatis examinari jubemus."

388  "Rogamus beatitudinem vestram . . . diligentem operam assumatis." Letter of Messine to Gregory IX.

389  See his Sicilian Constitutions, and Cantù, *Eretici*, discourse v.

390  That is to say : "Cut the head off a hundred thousand men placed in line." Verse of Guisti.

391  Vide Ante.

392  He was named Henry of Settala. His epitaph bears the words : *jugulavit haereses.*

393  Corio, *Storià di Milano*, part ii., f. 756 et seq.; according to Schmidt, *op. cit.* i., 156.

394  Cantù, *Storia Univ.*, Documenti ii., n. xviii. Cf. A. Lombard, *Pauliciens*, etc., appendix, letter L.

395  That is to say :  Thou who ascendest the royal steps of the great throne of the citizen of Lodi, protector and sword of faith, always call to mind on this spot the honours of Governor Oldrado, who raised this throne and burned the Cathari as it was right to do." Muratori, *Antiq. Ital.* v., 90. Guilini, *Mem. della città e campagna di Milano*, vol. iv.    Cf. Lombard, *op. cit.*, p. 210.  This equestrian statue is not in the best taste.  Galvano Flamma, although a monk, says, concerning it :  "In marmore super equum residens sculptus fuit, quod magnum vituperium fuit." Cantù, *Eretici*, V disc.

396  "Mediolanensium civitatem, quae pro maxima parte inhabitatur haereticis, contra, nos et Imperium manifesto favore tuetur." Pet. de Vineis, b. i., ep. 21.

397  "Mediolanenses autem, tunc temporis, formidine poenae potius quam virtutis amore, haereticos, qui civitatem suam pro magna parte inhabitabant, ut faman ¡suam redimerent, et accusationi imperiali liberius responderent, combusserunt." Matth. Paris, H. A., p. 366. Cf. Ripoll., *Bull. ord.fr. praed.*, i., 65. See Schmidt, *op. cit.*, i., 162.

398  Anon. de Passau, ap. F. Illyr, pp. 540 and 547.

399  The Counts of Luserna submitted to the Prince of Savoy that year, "A condizione d'esser mantenuti ne'loro privileggi, libero esercizio del culto a' Valdesi, oltre la confermazione senza dubbio delle loro proprieta ed immunita velle Valli." We give this quotation on the good faith of Sieur Gaston de Bez, who states that he read it in the MS. of Garola, entitled *Documenti Storici di Luserna e Valle* (January 5, 1831). We have had this MS. before us, but it seems that these lines escaped our notice, as was the case with Count Emmanuel and others. Monastier, who has not been in a position to see them, reads them in anticipation, as it were.  See his *Histoire*, vol. i., p. 92, 170, and 186.

400  "1297. Philippus libravit inquisitori Vaudensium pro medietate expensarum per eundem inquirendo Valdenses in valle Peruxie." Cibrario ap. Krömer, *Fra Dolcino u. die Patarener*, Leipzig, 1884, p. 22.

401  *Patenti di nomina*, etc.  State of Arch., Turin, Mat. Eccles., categ. ix., mazzo i.

402  "Recepit de xvii. sold. pro quodam parvo casali dirupto, sibi vendito pro parte domini, quod acquisitum propter valdesiam cujusdam valdesie combusti." Cibrario ap. Krömer, *l.c.*

403  "Quadam die quondam Gulielmum rectorem parochialis ecclesiae de Engravia Taurin diocesis celebrata missa per eum in platea dictae Villae nequiter occiderunt suspicantes quod dictus rector eos penes Inquisitorem praefatum de ipsorum haeresibus detulisset." Brief of John XXII., in the year 1332, ap. Raynaldus, ad. an. 1332, n. 31. *Engravia* is evidently an *erratum* which should read *Engronia*. With regard to *villa*, we do not see why Monastier wants to make a proper name of it, in order to read *Villar*.

404  "Praenominati haeretici ipsum Inquisitorem in quodam castello patenter et publice obsederunt, sic quod oportuit eum inde recedere inquisitionis hujusmodi officio relicto totaliter imperfecto." *Ibid.*  Muston arbitrarily attributes this fact to the Waldenses of the Valley of the Po. *Is. des Alpes*, i., 254.

405  Rorengo, *Mem. Hist.*, p. 17.  We there read that Jacques d'Achaïe, at the request of the Inquisitor, Pierre de Ruffia, gave orders in 1354 to different personages of the house of Luserna to cause the Waldenses in their valley to be incarcerated.

406  See upon this subject a letter of Gregory XI. to Amedeus VI., as given by Raynaldus, ad. an. 1375, n. 56. Cf. Rorengo, *ibid.*, p. 17.  The two reports do not entirely agree in the details.  This incident is mentioned in the *Processus*

*contra Valdenses*, ap. *Arch. St. It.*, an. 1865, p. 29—31, and so as to leave the impression that the murderer was not a Waldensian, but probably one of the Cathari.

407  See again the above-mentioned letter of Gregory XI. Cf. Rorengo, *ibid*.

408  Letter of Gregory XI., at the end.

409  Perrin, Léger, etc.

410  *Science Catholique revue*, etc., 15 March, 1888. Cf. Ch. Molinier, *L'Inquisition dans le midi de la France au XIII. et XIV. siècle*, part ii., ch. v.

411  Ex. Arnaud, Pons, Jourdan, Bonet, Maurel, Boer, Pascal, Maraude, Soulier, etc. *Ibid.*, passim.

412  Exempli gratia., the priest Jean Philibert, *ibid.*, p. 10.

413  " Vidit et adoravit pluries haereticos et in pluribus locis praedicationes eorum audivit, pluries recepit eos, dedit elemosinas Valdensibus . . . Includatur infra septa monasterii, etc." *Ibid.*, p. 71.

414  See Schmidt, *Hist. des Cathares,* 3rd period, ch. iii. Cf. Molinier, *op. cit.*, part ii., ch. vi.

415  The Dominicans were fond of having the double meaning, of which it is susceptible, attached to their name. *Domini cani* and *Domini canes*.

416  "Ad quos abolendos a Benedicto episcopus Valentinus excitatus, censores fidei zelum explicare jussi, denique Humbertus delphinus Viennensis." Raynaldi, ad. an. 1335, n. 63.

417  " Qui vocantur Waldenses, maxima multitudo, et quod quidam officiales tui dilectos filios inquisitores, non solum non juvant, ut deberent, in suo inquisitionis officio, immo multa impedimenta contra ipsos praestare presumunt." These obstacles are afterwards indicated. Raynaldi, ad. an. 1373, n. 20. The reproach is renewed two years later. See *ibid.*, ad. an. 1375, n. 25.

418  " Audivimus quod in eis (provinciis) haereticorum multitudo moratur etiam ab antiquo, contra quos vos et praedecessores vestri negligenter omisistis vestrum exercitium exercere ; unde fit quod multiplicantur execrabiles haereses, et haereticorum numerus, proh dolor ! adaugetur," Rayn., ad·an. 1375, n. 25.

419  Perrin, i., 113.

420  *Ibid.*, p. 114.

421  Perrin, *op. cit.*, p. 118—124.

402* 422  Perrin, i., 126.

423  " Vallem ipsam ecclesiastico supposueris interdicto." The papal brief, dated August 17th, is addressed to the Bishops of Turin and Nice ; to the Archdeacon of Vercelli ; and to James of Buronzo, a monk of the Order of St. Dominic, Inquisitor in Piedmont. Rorengo, *op. cit.*, p. 19. The absolution extends to all the heretics of the Valley of Luserna and especially to the Waldenses—"in Valle Lucernae Taurinensis dioecesis commorantes diversarum haeresum, et praesertim Valdensium seu Pauperum de Lugduno labe infecti." It is applicable to all the heretics scattered in the different dioceses hereabovementioned, even to those who had experienced more than one relapse—"pluries relapsi fuerint." What is most clearly shown by this brief, is not so much that the heretics are being converted, as he claims, but that they are numerous.

424  " Proclamari . . . alta et intelligibili voce faciatis." This decree, dated November 28th, 1475, was given at Luserna, "in ecclesia dicti loci, praesentibus testibus notaris . . . coram spectabilibus cum Dominis Lucernae videlicet Ugeta de Rorengis, Joanne de Giannoto, Gulielmo de Laia, Damiano de Nicia, Filipo de Bobio, Antonio de Campiliono potestate Lucernae, Jacobo de Beneitinis, ac Domina Catherina tutrix filiorum suorum condominorum ut supra." Rorengo, *ibid.*, p. 22—24.

425  Perrin, i., 151. It does not appear that all those names are there indicated in any order, the more so as Perrin makes mention of Catelan Girard. Gilles is silent ; Léger names only the first three ; Brezzi follows Perrin, and is followed by Monastier.

426  " Vobis sic omnino fieri volentes, ut potissime hi de Valle Lucernae ad gremium Sanctae Matris Ecclesiae venire possint." This word *venire* has excited the imagination of two writers ; they twist it to make it mean that it was not for the Waldenses a question of *re-entering* but of *entering* into the Church of Rome, and that, consequently, according to one, " the Duchess openly recognizes the antiquity of our origin, I had almost said our apostolic succession ;" according to the other, " at that time there was as yet no idea of calling in question the simultaneous and anterior existence of the Waldensian Church to that of the Romish Church." Cf. Brezzi, *Hist. des Vaudois*, part ii., p. 19, and Monastier, *op. cit.*, i., 174.

427  *Raccolta degli editti*, etc. Turin, 1678, p. i. Four pages further on, mention is made of four former edicts concerning the Waldenses ; two are by

Duke Louis, anno 1448 and 1452 ; the third by Duke Amedeus IX., anno 1446 ; the fourth by Duchess Iolante, anno 1473. Those edicts did nothing more than confirm existing privileges, relating to the valley of Luserna and the localties near Bubiane, Fenil, Campillon, etc. There is no question of religious liberty.

428   "Et quia tu Potestas Lucernae . . . illa ut supplicatur exequntioni demandare renuisti, imo illas retinuisti." *Ibid.* This podesta was Antonio di Campiglione.

429   "Perchè alcuni officiali e massime Antonio di Campiglione pedestà di Lucerna non procedeva con quel calore che richiedeva la causa," etc. Rorengo, *op. cit.*, p. 24.

430   Here is a request of the Lords of Luserna to the Duke of Savoy. The date is unknown. "Vobis illustrissimae, D.D., nostro Duci Sabaudiae, reverenter et devote exponitur parte spectabilium et generosorum Dominorum Lucernae et Vallis eius. Quod ipsi Domini exponentes, tanquam veri ac fidelis orthodoxi Christiani, conati saepe, et saepius fuerunt, omnem rabian, mamillam et labem heresial Gazariae et Apostasiae, de et a locis Engroniae, Sancti Joannis, Vilarü et Bobü praefatæe eorum Vallis, abstergere, expellere et exterminari facere, qua labe homines et personae ipsorum locorum erant et sunt infecti et infecta ; ipsis autem Dominis exponentibus, hanc materiam in honorem Dei sollicitantibus, homines et personae ipsorum quatuor locorum contra ipsos exponentes eorum immediatos Dominos et Superiores insurrexerunt, et arma acceperunt bellumque moverunt, etc." Rorengo, *l.c.*, p. 18. Is it not remarkable that heresy should there be designated as *Gazaria* or *Apostasia*, and the name of Waldenses not even hinted at? Rorengo concludes that his ancestors took " Gazari per Valdesi e Valdesi per Gazari." I do not believe them to have been as foolish as that. I am rather inclined to infer this : that the Cathari, as compared with the Waldenses, seemed to them more turbulent, and that it is the former who, in their opinion, deserve to be signalized as revolutionists.

431   " Ho avuta notizia d'altro ordine del Duca Carlo I. dell'anno 1484, col quale deputò alcuni delegati a conoscere sopra le violenze commesse ad Angrogna, Villaro e Bobbio, perchè i loro signori s'opponevano alle loro heresie, registrato nel protocollo del Bessone nell'archivio di Chiamberi." Rorengo, p. 25.

432   It is not necessary to be a Waldensian to feel this repugnance and to confess it. " I am happy," said a Catholic historian, " not to be obliged to recount the history of his reign." Cantù, *Eretici*, etc., xi. disc.

433   " Innocent was eight times father, without counting his eight daughters. By calling him father, Rome will only do him justice."

434   It is the Bull *Summis desiderantes*, of December 5, 1484.

435   Léger, who reproduces that Bull, gives by mistake the date of 1477. *Op. cit.*, part ii., p. 8—20.

436   "Nonnulli iniquitatis filii, incolae Provinciae Ebredunensis, sectatores illius perniciosissimae et abominabilis sectae hominum malignorum Pauperum de Lugduno seu Valdensium nuncupatorum, quae dudum in partibus Pedemontanis et alüs circumvicinis . . . damnabiliter insurrexit."

437   "Adversus Valdenses praedictos . . . insurgant, eosque veluti aspides venenosos conculcent ; et ad eorumdem haereticorum tam sanctam tamque pernecessariam exterminationem et dissipationem adhibeant omnes conatus."

438   This is what he says in his memoirs : "Simul ac Pontificis litterae ad eum perlatae sunt, presidibus Delphinatus mandavit, ne qua in re Alberto archidiacono ad negotium ex sententia conficiendum deessent." Godefroy *Histoire de Charles VIII.*, Paris, 1684, p. 277, et seq. The MS. there cited is in the Paris Bibliothique Nationale.

439   " Omnia enim juris ordine agebantur." *Ibid.*

440   "I miei, i miei faranno la passada." This saying is related by Perrin (*l.c.* 153). He quotes it undoubtedly from the memoirs of Vignaux which he had before him ; and he adds : " Voulant dire que ces soldats crioyent à eux pour les mettre à mort." This explanation seems to us the true one, because *passaa* is used in the Piedmontese dialect to signify death ; moreover, how could Perrin give it, who was ignorant of this dialect, if he did not take it from a competent author?

441   " Women and children, on their knees, crying out in their language : *O Dio, aiutaci.*" Perrin, *ibid.*

442   Gilles, *op. cit.*, ch. iv. Those are recollections derived from that traditon " which continually runs side by side with Waldensian history," as Hudy-Ménos says on this subject. Perrin and Gilles do not agree in the details. Thus, according to Perrin, the Black of Mondovi fell in the last attack, from an

arrow which hit him "in the throat," whilst, according to Gilles, he fell in the first assault, near Rocciamaneout, from an arrow that wounded him " between the eyes." If Perrin is correct, we might ask whether the pool called *Toumpi Ner* is not connected with the fate of the Black of Mondovi. Still, although Perrin had the memoirs of Vignaux before him, he may easily have made a mistake. He lacked in his interpretation the check of living tradition. Gilles wrote a little later, but upon the spot. The reminiscences attaching to the pool in which Saquet perished, have lived to this day. or very nearly. I observe further, concerning these Captains, that only one of them is named ; they came from the same province ; they fell, according to the first narrator, "at the same time," both, according to the second historian, imitated Goliath of Gath. But these data are far from sufficient to make us admit that it is simply a question of a single individual multiplied by the legend into two.

443  If the accusation made by the Nuncio be correct, wecannot conceive how 20 of those prisoners were spared.

444  Omnes incolæ Pratigelati et circumvicinorum locorum . . . . veniam petiere." *ibid.*

445  These words, so sublime in their simplicity, are handed down to us by the leader of the Crusade : they are undoubtedly authentic, and deserve to be quoted, even in the Nuncio's Latin : " Regi fideles obedientesque sumus et veri Christiani dici possumus. Præsti erunt legis nostræ Magistri—'Barbas ipsi vocant '—vitæ merito et doctrina insignes, qui sive in generalibus sive synodalibus conciliis, luce clarius novi et veteris Testamenti auctoritatibus probabunt nose recte de christiana fide sentire, nec insectatione sed laude dignos esse. Quia transgressores evangelicæ legis, longeque ab Apostolorum traditione recedente sequi volumus, et eorum pravis institutionibus obedire; sed paupertate ac innocentia delectamur quibus orthodoxa fides et fundata fuit et crevit. Divitias autem et luxum ac dominandi sitim, quibus nostri persecutores inhiant, aspernamur. Nam quod vobis statutum esse dicitis legem et sectam nostram extinguere, videte ne deo inimici sitis, neve eius iram in vos provocetis et, sub specie boni, ingens piaculum admittatis, ut Paulus quondam fecisse dicitur. Nos in Deo speramus, magisque ei quam hominibus placere studemus, nec timemus eos qui corpus occidunt, animam autem non possunt occidere. Et tamen scitote quod si Deus voluerit, nihil contra nos vires valebunt vestræ."

446  " *Se vera sentire, illos seductores esse* vociferautes." . *Ibid.* Catanée adds that they were even beaten. Is the Nuncio always well-informed, and does he always speak nothing but the truth ? We beg leave to doubt the fact.

447  " Omnia prius juris ordine expertus." *Ibid.*

448  " Hæretici natura loci tuti, per prona montium ingentia saxa devoluentes. Christianos repulerunt, ac nonnullis cæsis, multis vero vulneratis, ex rupe dejecerunt. Pugnatum tamen est summo nunc usquo ad vesperam magna contentione animorum." *Ibid.*

449  " Nova conpersio facti, unitati Catholicorum sunt restituti." *Ibid.* Muston attaches no importance to this fact, and, for this reason, Manuel of S. Giovanni handles him somewhat roughly, as may be seen in his *Memorie Storiche di Dronero et della valle di Maira*, 1868, part ii., p. 40, n. 2.

450  " De montibus descendentibus Archidiaconi misericordiæ se submiserint: cujus jussu ad veniam petendam misericordiamque consequendam Ebredunum petiere." *Ibid.* Chorier, *Hist. du Dauphiné*, vol. ii., p. 502, says the same thing.

451  " Archidiaconi nuntiis rupis altitudinem metiri jussis se inexpugnabiles esse, et pro secta sua mori decrevisse respondissent." *Ibid.*

452  " Super parvula quadam rupe, quæ tumulo Valdensium imminebat, vicissim se magno discrimine diræisere. Quod Valdenses qui . . . . aliquibus semper levibus præliis inferius tentabantur, et ad eos repellendos intenti erant, non animadverterunt." *Ibid.* If Muston had noticed this detail he would not have said that " nothing could have been more simple and natural than to have cut the ropes by which *they saw* their enemies descending." *Op. cit.*, i., 64.

453  " Cæteris venia concessa est." *Ibid.* " Ipsi vero," repeats another Inquisitor, " tunc quasi omnes . . . . ad gratiam benigne recepti fuerunt." *Scriptum Inquisitoris*, Cambridge MS.

454  Catanée is nearer right than he thinks, when he uses the word *tumulus* to signify the cave.

455  This is Perrin's version, followed by Chorier and Muston.

456  An anonymous writing, quoted in the *Bulletin de l'Academie Delphinale*, vol. i., Grenoble, 1846, p. 455.

451* 457  *Bulletin*, etc., *ibid.*

458  *Op. cit.*, i., 65.

459   Perrin, *op. cit.*, i., 131.  Cf. *Script. Inq. anon.*, ap. Morland and Allix, and Chabrand, *Vaudois et Protestants des Alpes*, Grenoble, 1886.
460   According to Monastier (i., 180), the soldiers came up from Bobi and were "detached from the papal army which occupied the Luserna." He does not follow Gilles' version, to which Muston brings us back.
461   Gilles.  The date of this inroad cannot be fixed.
462   See Perrin (i., 129, 152).; Gilles (i., 39); Monastier (i., 176, 186); Muston (i., 61).  Léger, who assigns no date, enables the reader to fix it more accurately.
463   Léger, ii., 20.  Innocent VIII. had succeeded to the pontifical See, 24th August, 1484.  It is true that Léger prints 1477, instead of 1487 ; but that is a *lapsus* which he himself corrects in the lines which precede the Bull.  See *ibid.*, p. 7—8.
464   See on this point Chabrand, *op. cit.*, p. 45—64.  He concludes that the Crusade must have raged against the Waldenses of Piedmont in 1487 ? against those of Dauphiny in 1488 ; and that it was brought to a close by the massacre of April, 1489, in the Val Louise.
465   According to Perrin and Gilles, this should be Philip of Savoy.  How shall we explain this *qui pro quo ?*  Philip, maternal uncle of King Charles VIII., was then "Governor of Dauphiny," according to the *Genealogie*, etc., before quoted.  Now Dauphiny included Val Pragelas.  Later, in 1496, he ascended the Ducal throne, after the death of Charles II.  He died in 1497.  Monastier tries to correct Perrin and Gilles ; but he also makes a mistake ; for he states that it is here a question of Charles II.  This prince was born 24th June, 1489 ; hence, rather late to receive the deputation, and he died in childhood, 6th April, 1496.  See Cibrario *Storia della Monarchia* in the *Specchio cronologico*.
466   Gilles, *l.c.*  Ricotti tells us of a compromise.  "On the intercession of the Bishop of Turin an agreement was come to between the Waldenses and the Duke of Savoy ; binding the former to lay down their arms, to defray the expenses of the war, not to erect Churches nor make any outward show of their form of worship, and moreover, to attend mass.  But this compact did not satisfy either party ; not the Catholics—because, under it heresy remained untouched—any more than the Waldenses, because, it involved the practice of degrading dissimulation.  *Storia della Mon. Piem.*, 1861, ii., p. 173.  The sources of information indicated by M. Ricotti do not bear out his opinion ; but the probabilities are sufficiently in its favour, and we should not be surprised to find it proved and established one of these days.
467   Gilles and Hudry-Ménos, *l.c.*
468   "Con sospetto di veleno," says Cibrario, *Specchio cronol, l.c.*
469   *Bulletin de l'Acad. Delphinale*, p. 454.  On the following page is inserted an extract of manuscript forwarded by the Mayor of Vallouise, according to which the Crusade took place in 1487, as the royal decree already infers.  It is true that the writing of this manuscript, whose author is unknown, is not contemporaneous with the event.
470   "Sine prejudicio causæ principalis et juri cuicunque acquisiti."
471   Perrin i., 137 à 144.
472   *Ibid.*, p. 145.
473   Perrin confines himself to stating that the Waldenses obtained a Bull, nay, a double apostolic Bull, through the mediation of Cardinal George of S. Sixt, then in France (i., 147).  Muston adds, but without proof, that the Bull was issued by Cesar Borgia, who had just received from the King of France, "with the title of Duke of Valentine, that part of Dauphiny which precisely comprised the valley of Freyssinière " (i., 76).  We hold to Perrin's version.
474   "Alexander sells crosses, altars, Christ.  Why should he not, since he first bought them ? "
475   Ricotti, who is not a fanciful writer, takes the liberty of asserting upon this point, what no authority indicated by him warrants him in saying, namely, that Crusaders were beaten in the valley of the Po as elsewhere.  See his *St. della Mon. piem.*, l. iii., ch. iii.  Cf. with Manuel of S. Giovanni, *Mem. St. di Dronero*, p. 40.  Gilles (ch. iv.) and Lèger (ii. 26) hardly say a word concerning the Crusade in that valley ; but it is an unfounded rumour, from which nothing can be inferred.
476   Baron Manuel of S. Giovanni imagines that this is not proved.  Mem. St. di Dromero, p. 39, et seq.  We refer him to Molinier, *op. cit.*, ch. vi., where mention is made of the Register of the Inquisition in Toulouse.  See especially the travels of Fournier, the Cathari.  Conclusive data are therein found, which justify the opinion of Ricotti on this point, and not the denials of his critic.

477 "In nonnullio partibus dicti marduonatus Salutiarum sunt multi heretici." Letter of the Inquisitor monks of Asti and of Turin, dated 8th May, 1417, to the Regent Valerian of Saluces. Muletti, *Memorie storico-diplomatiche appartenenti alla città ed ai marchesi di Saluzzo*, 1831, v. 6.

478 Muletti, *op. cit.*, vi., 28.

479 Anno 1440—1465. The Marquisate of Saluces, dated back almost to the time of Adelaide of Susa, and it was still a dependency of the house of Savoy.

480 Rorengo, *op. cit.*, p. 18. Cf. Fr. Arcangelo di Salto, *Idea di religioso serafico rappresentata nella vita del B. Angelo di Chivasso*, 1664, p. 103.

481 Such is the theory set up by Manuel of S. Giovanni. *Un Episodio*, etc., p. 17—21.

482 According to Gilles, the persecution of Margaret of Foix began in 1500, according to Muston in 1499. I do not find any reason for this discrepancy. Muletti, whose testimony Muston adduces, says expressly: "Le persecuzioni contro i Valdesi della valle del Po ebbero principio fin dal novembre dell' anno 1509, come imparo dal manoscritto che attentamente io svolgo." *Op. cit.*, vi., 381. Moreover, Muston wanders here more than once from the sources he alleges, and others before us have remarked it. See Manuel of S. Giovanni, *Mem. di Dronero*, p. 40—42, note 2.

483 "Iuvenis delicata, tota tristis ac languens." Muletti, v., 329. "Madama nostra era tuta del papa, et madama mandava ogni anno a dito papa (Jules II.) una trantena de botalli de vino de Pagno et del Chastellaro, perchè el bon vin gli piasia." *Ibid.*, vi., 388.

484 Muston, i., 255.

485 "Furono liberati d' ogni spesa di commissarii, di fanti e perfino *de lo borelo et de lo facinero*." Muletti, vi., 381.

486 "Uomo per assai vici che in lui regnaveno infamissimo," says the MS. of Giov. Andrea del Castellaro, quoted by Muletti, *ibid.*, p. 382. This MS. is the more interesting to us, in that we owe it to the pen of the "consignore" of Pœsane and Castellar.

487 "Incontinente senza martirio confessarono esser Valdesi." *Ibid.*

488 "Gienet Julian, Gienet Maria," says Muletti. Muston reads "Maria and Julia Gienet." Julian and Maria are family names, whilst Gienet is a baptismal name.

489 "Perche li altri fusiteno volseno pura fare qualche iusticia . . . et gli fu rotta pereo inquisitore la fede, et per Francesco Arnaudo che sedesia proquorore de la fede, et fu mal fato a mancargli alla promessa da poi che aviano chonfessato liberamente." MS. *ibid.*, p. 383.

490 "Chrossati et bandesati." *Ibid.*

491 "La chossa donda li Valdesi fasiano loro sinagoga era chossa bella a vedere, et era fata como esquasi un lanbarinto." *Ibid.*, p. 384. Muston sees in this house "the temple of the Waldenses;" whereupon Hudry-Ménos speaks of it as "the first Waldensian temple mentioned in the annals of the sect," and thinks that "this innovation" provoked the *razzia* we are narrating.

491* 492 Our MS. records that the nuns of Rifredo were also benefited by this windfall. Their monastery inherited the property of Jean Motos, condemned to perpetual imprisonment on account of heresy.

493 Gilles, *op. cit.*, ch. iv.

494 Muletti sums it up as follows : "Nel correre del 1512 non pochi di queqli alpigiani banditi dal marchesato, che si erano rifuggiti nella valle di Lucerna, vennero più volte alle loro case, e trovandone alcune in possesso dei nuovi acquisitori nè potendo riaverle, per dispetto le incendiavano. Nelle loro scorrerie uccisero cinque uomini e più di cento bestie ; terribili conseguenze di più terribili persecuzioni." *Ibid.*, p. 385.

495 "Madama avendo veduto la perdonansa et absolucione que avia fato el papa Lione a li homeni de Pravigliermo, etc." *Ibid.*

496 Muletti, *ibid.*. p. 386. These agreements were owing principally to the good work of François Violi of Saluces and Bernardin de Biandrata of Saint-Frout.

497 "If God be for us, who can be against us ?" Rom. viii., 31. The medal bears on one side this inscription : *Ludovicus marchio et Margareta D.*, Fois, 1503 ; on the other, an eagle with outspread wings, with the arms of Saluces and Foix, and the above-quoted biblical passage. Muletti, v., 381.

498 I allude especially to the prior Rorengo, who cannot find sarcasms sufficiently biting when speaking of the man with the long sword whom Gilles mentions. *Mem. Hist.*, p. 91. We can but say, every one to his taste. We leave to others the relish for large battalions—for the Nuncios and the captains, satiated with their easily acquired glory. When the Prior reproaches Gilles with

the fact that the Waldenses re-establish reform by the use of the " spadone," he forgets, in the first place, that such was not the purpose for which the Waldenses re-entered the valley of the Po ; moreover, he fails to observe that his argument strikes at the heart of the theology of the Church and her angelic Doctor, smiting at one blow the intolerance of the Popes, the feats of the Inquisition, and the Crusaders.

499   From the Latin *barbanus*, a word used in the middle ages with the idea of *patruus, avunculus*, uncle. Adelaide of Susa mentions two *barbani* in the act of donation before cited, in relation to the Abbey of St. Mary of Pignerol. Ducange adduces still further examples. See his *Glossarium*. Ménage remarks in his *Orig. Ital.*, that *barbanus* was derived from *barba*, " because they mostly wear beards, i. zü." It has also been observed, with greater humour than reason, that the Barbes preserved their beards when the priests began to shave. *Barbanus* was hardly employed anywhere except in Lombardy ; we know that the word *barba* is used in the Waldensian Valleys of Piedmont and in Venetia. Do not the modern Greeks designate the maternal uncle by the name, *Barba avunculus?* Again, it is Ménage who tells us this.

500   *Patruus*, according to the classics, meant uncle, censor, tutor, a grave and sober man. " Ne sis patruus mihi," says Horace. Most of those meanings are found also in the word *barba*.

501   *Presbyteros* indicated both the age and the gravity which render a man venerable, without the least particle of the real clerical notion of its derivative *presbtre*. Now *barba* preserves the same idea.

502   Father, abbot, pape, pope, etc., are so many synonymous titles, with which that of *Barbe* has no identity.

503   The Inquisition calls them *barba*, pl. *barbae*, or *magistri*. See *e.g.* the interrogatory of Regis, already cited, or further, Seyssel, *adv. errores et sectam Valdensium.*

504   Léger gives the list of the principal Barbes. It is not long, and, nevertheless, with the names of Pierre de Bruys, Henri de Lausanne, and Waldo, it includes those of several leaders of the Catharin communities, *op. cit.*, i., 202. Cf. Perrin, *op. cit.*, and Chabrand, *Vaudois et Protestants des Alpes*, 1886 p. 277.

505   *Ibid.*, p. 203.

506   This *di* we owe to the pen of Léger.

507   " We give the letter here textually, as follows : " La present és per advertir a la vostra fraternità, pagant lo meo debit, de mi a vos, de la part de Dio, maximament sobra la cura de la salù de las vostras armas, segond lo lume de verità departi a nos del Altissime, que la plaza a un chascun de lo mantenir, acreisser et favorir segond possibilità, et non venir a mens de tot bon principi, uzanças et costumas donàs de li nostres Antecessors, et a nos non degnes. Car poc profeitaria a nos esser muda de l'instantia paternal et dal lume dona de Dio a nos, per donar nos a la mundana et diabolica et carnal conversation, abandonan lo principal, que ès Dio, et la salù de las armas, per la breo vita temporal. Car lo Seignor di en l'Evangeli : *Qual cosa profeita a l'home si el gaigna tot lo mond, et suffre distruiment a la sua arma ; car meil seria a nos non aver conoissù la via de justitia, que avent la conoissua far lo contrari.* Car al judici de Dio-nos saren non escusivols e damna plus profondament, car plus fort torment serè donna a li plus fort e a li plus conoissent. Per la qual cosa yo prego vos per la carità de Dio, non voilla diminuir, ma accreisser la carità la temor et l'obedientia degna a Dio, et a vos entre vos, et totas bonas costumas apparterent et auvias et entenduas de la part de dio et nostra, et ostra et purgar d'entre vos tot deffect et mancament conturbant la paaz, l'amor, et la concordia et tota causa de vos ostar la libertà de servici de Dio, et la vostra salù ; et de l'administration de la verità, si vos desirà que Dio vos prospere li ben temporals e spirituals." (Here Léger inadvertently omits a few words, which he translates thus : " Car vous ne pouvez faire chose aucune sans luy." *Op. cit.*, i., 200). Et si cubità esser heritiers de la soa gloria, faça ço quel di : *Si tu voles entrar a vita, garda li meo commandament.* Item : *Fazé que entre vos non se musse juoc ni gourmandarias, ni ribauderias, ni bal, ni autras desordonnanças, ni questions, ni l'engan, ni barat, ni usura, ni malvolenças, ni discordias.* Ni voilla supportar entre vos, ni sostenir personas de mala vita ni que done scandol et mal example entre vos ; ma carità et fidelità regne entre vos et tot bon exemple, tractant l'un l'autre enaima un chascun volera esser faict per si meseime. Car autrament non ès possible alcon poer esser salva, ni haver la gratia de Dio ni de home en a quest mond, ni en l'autre la gloria. Et tot aiço s'apparten principalment mantenir et favorir a li regidors et gouvernadors. Car quand li cap son enferm, tuit li membres ensemp se dolon. Pertant si vos sperà et desirà possessir vita eterna,

et bona voouz, et bona fama et bon crédit, et prosperar en aquest mond en li ben spiritual et temporal, purga de tota vita desordonnà entre vos, loqual non abandonna unqua li sperant en si. Mas sapia aiçò per sort que Dio non exaucis, ni habita com li peccador, ni en l'arma malvolent, ni à l'home sotmès a li peccà. Bertant un chascun pause lo seo cor sobre la soa via, et fugia li perill si el non vol perir en lor. Non autre per lo present, sinon que vos mettas en effect acquestas cosas, et Dio di paaz sia com tuit vos et accompagne nos a las vrayas devotas et humils orations, salutant tuit li fidel et amà de Christ. Totus vester Bartholomeus Tertianus, ad omnia secundum Deum possibilia paratus."

508 See the *Processus contra Valdenses* of 1387, passim. Thus on page 40 it says :—" Magistris valdensibus missis a summo pontifice eorum de Pulia . . . Promisit servare ritum et omnia qui magistri valdenses predicant in manibus predicti Johannis Baridon de Pulia missi in partibus istis (a Barge) a papa eorum de Pulia." From this to deriving the Waldenses from the Pauliciens is but a step, according to A. Lombard. See his art. *Martyrs de Calabre* inserted in *Choses vieilles et choses nouvelles,* Lausanne, 1865, and his book entitled *Pauliciens, Bulgares et Bons-Hommes en Orient et en Occident,* Geneva, 1879.

509 Vincent Ferreri, after his visit to the Valleys, writes : "Nullus prædicaverat nisi Waldenses hæretici, qui ad eos consuetudine veniebant de Apulia bis in anno." Raynald., an. 1403, n. 24.

510 *Op. cit.,* ch. iii. Cf. Perrin, Léger, etc.

511 We should not be the first to make this supposition. V. Herzog, art. *Waldenser* in the *Real-Encycl.,* 1st edit., p. 518.

512 The *Processus contra Valdenses* invariably mentions the meetings as taking place in the house of one or another of the accused ; several are spoken of in the Valleys of St. Martin and Pragelas. Such an assembly would be exceptionally numerous. Thus we read on page 34 : "Martinus Carbonarius vidit modicum super Perruxiam unam congregationem valdensium numero ccxi., et unus magister sedebat super cathedram et prædicabat omnibus." There Jean Borelli is mentioned as the preacher, "filius condam Antonii Borrelli de Villari Pyonasche, cui pater fuit combustus." Pierre Pascal of Val St. Martin, François Zapella of Piossasque, Turin of Angrogne, etc. In the interrogatory of Regis, mention is made of " Co gros Amchel de Fraissinierè," of other Barbes of Méane, of Puglia, etc.

513 One of these contributions is noticed in the year 1431, with these words : "Nonne etiam in Delphinatu est quædam portio inter montes inclusa, quæ erroribus adhærens prædictis Bohemorum, jam tributum imposuit, levavit et misit eisdem Bohemis, in quibus fautoria manifesta hæresis prædictæ debet judicari ?" Mansi, *Conc. Coll.,* t. xxix., p. 402. Cf. Palacky, *Das Verhältniss der Waldenser zu den ehemaligen Sekten in Böhmen.*

514 *Op. cit.,* ch. ii.

515 See ch. iii., p. 92. To the examples indicated might be added the fact related by Heisterbach. This writer tells us that on the occasion of Emperor Otho's entrance into Rome, two ecclesiastics of his suite found a public meeting presided over by a heretic, and this is the way he expresses himself : "Simul in gressi sunt cuiusdam hæresiarchæ scholas. Locum quem tunc legebat is erat : *Jam judicium mundi venit ; jam princeps mundi huius ejicietur foras.* Quem locum ita glossavit : Ecce Christus diabolum principem huius mundi vocavit, quia hunc mundum creavit. Cum quo . . . satis diu disputavit." *Ill. Mir.,* l. v., ch. 26. It is evident, however, that this was a meeting of Cathari.

516 "De scholis Waldensium, quas inveni in valle quæ dicitur Engroiia (sic), et earum destructione . . . taceo de præsenti." *L.c.*

517 "Fuerunt enim in Longobardia veluti Scholæ seu Academiæ quædem hujus veræ Christi theologiæ . . . Habeo inquisitionem in Bohemia et Polonia contra Waldenses sub Rege Johanne circa 1330 Domini annum factam, ubi inter alia diserte fit mentio collectarum, quos fratribus et Præceptoribus suis in Lombardiam soliti sunt mittere, et in alia inquisitione invenio eos esse solito sex Bohemia causa discendi Theologiam, ad suos Præceptores Waldenses in Lombardiam proficisci, velut ad Scholam seu Academiam quandam." Matt. Fl. Illyr., *Catal. Test. Ver.,* Francof. 1666, p. 638 et 639.

518 Tron sees but one. *Op. cit.,* p. 63.

519 "This school was nothing else than the College of Barbes," wrote a Professor of Torre-Pellice, in June, 1866, in the *Echo des Vallées,* art., *Ecole des Barbes.* "Questo istituto era la scuola de'Barbi Valdesi," repeated another professor in Florence, in 1872, according to the *Resoconto Stenog. del Conf. Evangeliche,* p. 43. Both based their assertions upon an incomplete quotation of the words of M. Fl. Illyricus.

520    " Nauclerus narrat eodem tempore (1212) etiam Mediolani et circa fuisse ejusdem sententiæ ac doctrine homines, misisseque Alsatos Mediolanensibus, tanquam Praeceptoribus suas collectas, sive eleemosynas.    Unde licet conjicere utrosque fuisse Waldenses."    *Catal.* p. 639.

521    "Quod bene erant octodecim anni quod ab illa terra recesserat, causa heresis addiscende.    Qui. ut ipse recognovit nobis, per totum dictum spacium apud Mediolanum studuerat in secta hereticorum Valdensium."    *De Septem donis Sp. Sancti.* V. D'Argentrè, i., 86.    Cf. with the new edition of A. Lecoy de la Marche, Paris, 1877.

522    *Le Zémoin,* Dec. 22, 1876, art. entitled : *Une pierre précieuse in forme de Table,* signed E. Bonnet, pastor.

523    Perrin, *op. cit.,* p. 12.

524    See Tron, *op. cit.,* the chapter on the School.

525    It is called *lou collégé,* i.e., *the college.*    Those who visit Pra du Tour hear sometimes such language as this : *As-tu vî moun figl ?   Si l'ai vî passâ a mount vër lou Coulege.   Dount soun li tei maoutoun?   Isouu lai d'lai dar Coulege.*    The term therefore designates a well-known locality.

526    *Ibid.*    When M. Bonnet put his hand upon that table and had it transported by " twenty of the strongest men " to the place destined for it, namely, to a room adjoining the Waldensian chapel, it was covered with a damp dust, and evidently indicated the use made of it by its former owners.    *Horresco referens,* "they placed upon it their pans of milk."    Must we conclude from this that such was the original purpose for which it was designed ?    M. Bonnet answers : "They would not have taken so much trouble to prepare a place upon which merely to set milk pans, which are ordinarily placed simply upon a board that is not even planed."    As to the idea that this table was used at the meetings of our Church Board, "which, from this fact, perhaps, may have borne from ancient times the name of Waldensian table," it is simply ridiculous, notwithstanding M. Bonnet, in whose eyes historical probity is suspicious.    For an instance of his lucubrations, exhibiting such bad taste, see an article signed Barbet in the *Zemoin,* anno 1881, and certain bibliographic reviews on the occasion of M. Worsfold writing on Waldo and the Waldenses.    *Ibid.*

527    The letter of Morel exists in a two-fold reading, namely, in Waldensian dialect and in Latin, but with more than one variation.

528    " Cum genolh plega," or, " genibus curbis."

529    "S' ilh son de mauier as covenivolo e agradivols," or, "Si congrius praestent moribus."

530    "Hoc modo instructi ac edocti ad evangelizandum bini emittuntur."    For the Latin text see Scultetus, *Annalium Evangelii,* etc., p. 294—316, or Dieckhoff, *die Wald.,* app. n. 1 ; for the Waldensian text, the MS. of Dublin, entitled : *Epistola ad Oecolampadium.*

531    See art. quoted : *L'Ecole des Barbes.*

532    *Ov. cit.,* ch. ii.

533    This last is mentioned as "indoctus," and also under the name of Thomas of Landskron.    He had already visited the Waldenses of Brandeburg, who had finally taken refuge with the Brethren of the Unity.

534    " Vulgo ignotos," dit Lasitius, ap. Comenius, *Exc.* ix.    " Hi passim invenere in Italia, Roma quoque, aliquos vera pietate et religione Deum colentes, in profana atque superstitiosa gente, cum periculo et variis difficultatibus degentes, et clandestinis congressibus exercentes religionis studium."    Camerarius, *Historica Narratio,* etc., p. 120.

535    " Hoc ipsum cernens et clara voce : *Non sic Petrus* dicens, sacco protinus inclusus aquam Tiberis bibit."    Lasitius, *ibid.,* ou. ap. Goll. i., Beilage P.

536    " Malle se ita bestiam devorare, quam ab ea devorari."    *Ibid.*

537    "Tuebatur suam opinionem illo Josephi et Nicodemi, occultorum Christi discipulorum exemplo."    *Ibid.*

538    " Quod quidem sinceris Fratribus displicuit."    This word of comment and that which follows is from the pen of Comenius.

539    " Inciderunt et in Gallia in Waldenses," remarks Lasitius.    But Camerarius says : " in Gallia togata," otherwise called Cisalpine ; hence, in Piedmont.    Thereupon, discussion still continues, but without profit, for it is not necessary to pass our frontier to find one's self in communication with the Waldenses, both of Dauphiny and Piedmont.

540    " A quibus hospitaliter accepti sunt atque tractati."    Lasitius, *ibid.*

541    " Plurimi tunc sunt reperti.    Cum quibus gratulantibus tantam veritatis. scientiam Fratribus, et gaudentibus colloquio ipsorum."    Camerarius, *ibid.*

542    " Multum versati, et de religiouis negotio sententias contulerunt, et admonitione alicubi sua eos adiuverunt."    *Ibid.*

543 "Quædam aliquando audacius importuniusque disseruntur, quam rei temporique conveniebat." Lasitius thinks we shall have to return to this again. A MS. of Dublin, which we are using, contains a considerable fragment of the Waldensian text of this letter, beginning as follows : "Al Serenissimo princi Rey Lancelao."

544 "Car entre las autras cosas ilh predican enayma cans molestos, o renos, che nos haven per ley : dona te a tot demandant, che nos donen nostras deleictanczas per cavernas resconduas, o scuras, cum qual que qual nos occorra, o sia de mayre, o de filha, o de molher, o de seror, che e es de lor maniera, o costuma, e non de nos." *Epistola al Ser. Rey Lancelau.*

545 "Dio devant gardant e perseverant nos d'40 an e de plus non es auvia fornicacion non punivol enayma entre nos." *Ibid.*

546 "Ild dyon, o mot bon Rey, de gitta lor del vostre Regne aquilh pestilencials p. o. v. o. b., car petit de levan corromp tota la massa." Ces initiales se lisent ordinairement ainsi : "Picards ou Vaudois ou Béguards."

547 "Si alcun examine dreytament la nostra vita."

548 "O serenissime Rey . . . devant que nos habandonan la verita e segan la falsita, nos sostenren cum laiutori divin, ligam, carcers, exilhament, per grant temp pacientissimament."

549 "Non monte sobre lo teyt de la gleysa."

550 "Car de lome ilh han la natura, mas del demon las errors e lengan."

551 "Ilh benayczisson, e Dio maleiczis . . . Nos non intren en las gleisas de lor."

552 "Nos despreczen e fuye lor, car ilh son fait enayma stercora de la terra e enayma lo fum de la lucerna steincta, loqual manda neyror e pudor mortal."

553 "Nos haven conoissu per luoc de tota las cosas ia dictas per las sacras scripturas, per li script human e per predicacions de moti de la part de l' unità de li boemienc." *Ayczo es la causa del departiment de la gleysa Romana.* Dublin MS., p. 71.

554 "Proditores . . . inter plebeculam sæpicule pullulant." *Ep. à Ecolampade,* ap. Scultetus. It is true that these words were written later ; but they are referable as well to the generation preceding the Reformation as to the period when they were penned.

555 "Quantum vultis nobis dare, et in manus vestras Waldensium doctores trademus." *Ibid.*

556 "Sacramentorum signa plebeculæ nostræ non nos, sed Antichristi membra administrat." *Ibid.*

557 Gilles, *op. cit.*, ch. iv.

558 Born in Savoy, he became Bishop of Marseilles, then Archbishop of Turin, where he spent his last years, *i.e.*, from 1515 to 1520.

559 "Sed et dimittendorum peccatorum nullam sacerdotes nostros potestatem habere aperte protestantur, et proinde neque illis confitendum esse affirmant, neque sacramenta reliquia ab his suscipienda." *Adv. errores et sectam Valdensium,* éd. 1520.

560 "Quicumque ab his barbis et hæreticis decepti estis." *Ibid.*

561 "Hortamur et obsecramus ut ab istis falsis prophetis caveatis." *Ibid.*

562 "Salve mi Domine benedicte Œcolampadi . . . A longinqua regione animo vehementer exultanti ad te veminus, sperantes atque multum confidentes prædictum spiritum per te nos illuminare." Morel to Ecolampadius, ap. Scuttetus, *op. cit.*

563 "We are completely ignorant," says Ch. Schmidt, *op. cit.*, ii., p. 2, "whether any book of the Catharins escaped the flames." We should now perhaps add, except the Ritual discovered by Cunitz ; and according to others a version of the N. T.

564 Chabrand and Rochas d'Aiglun, *Patois des Alpes Cottiennes,* 1877, preface.

565 *Choix des poésiés des troubadours,* 1817, vol. ii., p. cxl. Let us notice in passing that Raynouard's opinion is in harmony with his theory of the early Romance Language, which need no longer be discussed, since we know it has been abandoned.

566 *Grammaire des langues romanes,* vol. i., p. 100. I have compared this passage again with the original.

567 "The Lyonnese," Fœrster writes, "is a dialect with a Provençal basis as regards the rules of sounds and the formation of verbs and substantives, as well as from its vocabulary. But to confine ourselves to a point that is quite elementary, the Latin *a* is transformed according to a phonetic proceeding peculiar to the French, and becomes *i* or *e* under the influence of the palatals. Its strong verbs also assume the French appearance. The Waldensian dialect.

on the contrary, does not know that kind of transformation ; it preserves its Provençal type even in the strong verbs.

568  It was Grüzmacher's opinion, according to his article upon the Waldensian Bible, v. *Yahrbuch f. rom. u. engl. Literatur*, 1862, p. 398. Diez accepted it, but with some attenuations.

569  *Ibid.*, p. 101. Diez notes here that Biondelli (*Saggi*, etc., p. 481) "refers it, without hesitation to the Piedmontese." But Biondelli has read our dialect in a bad version, *sui generis*, neither Waldensian nor Piedmontese, of the Gospels of SS. Luke and John, by Pierre Bert (London, 1832). Moreover, more than one master of the Neo-Latin languages has not yet gone beyond that point ; even Diez's grammar is not exempt from inaccuracies. For instance, he states that "the letter '*l*, after a consonant, becomes *i*, as in Italian." The words he quotes show that upon this point his researches stopped at La Tour. The Waldenses of the Valleys of Pérouse and St. Martin, do not say *ghiesia, kiar, piassa*, but *gleisa* or *gleiso, clar, plassa* or *plasso*. The affirmative particle is not *si* but *oui* in the Valley of St. Martin, and both *oui* and *si* in that of Pérouse.

570  *Waldensische Sprache*, in the *Archiv* of Herrig, 1854, vol. xvi., 4th book, p. 400.

571  *Rom. Wald.* p. 31, and *Die Wald. im Mittelalter*, 1851, p. 37, n. 1.

572  The examples taken by Montet from Diez, are precisely those we called attention to as being erroneous. *Hist. litt. des Vaudois du Piemont*, Paris, 1885, p. 11 and 12. *Page* 203.

573  *Ibid.*, p. 11. Montet has recently written some new remarks on the Waldensian dialect in his work, *La Noble Leçon, texte original d'apres le MSS. de Cambridge*, etc., Paris, 1888.

574  *Aperçu de l'antiquité des Vaudois des Alpes d'apres leurs poëmes en langue romane.* Pignerol, 1881, p. 11.

575  His aim is manifest. He is fond of concluding : "The origin of the indigenous Waldenses, is, therefore, anterior to that of the Waldensians who immigrated." *Ibid.*, p. 26.

576  See the article of W. Fœrster in the *Riv. Cristiana*, March, 1882.

577  "My demonstration might have been more conclusive," he confesses. See his *Examen de quelques observations sur l'idiome et les manuscrits vaudois.* Pignerol, 1883, p. 8. There is a very simple way of convincing him. He pretends that the most characteristic writings of our ancient literature are the ripe fruit of the dialect of our valleys, which he derives from the Italian stock, rather than from that of Provence, and that they take us back to the time of Waldo's appearance. Very good, we shall now proceed to place before our readers a specimen of a dialect of the pure Piedmontese, as it was spoken in the XII. century. It is an extract from a manuscript containing some notes of homilies delivered about that time. The subject is amusingly interesting ; the language is such that it was almost attributed to some Waldensian Barbe. The subject is the explanation of that passage of Scripture which speaks of our Saviour driving the money-changers out of the temple. "Aquesta sentenza e aquest flael dun Xrist catze cels qui vendean e acatavan el temple de so pare, oi en aquest iorn regnen, zo son li hereti qui acaten e venden les maisuns de Deu. Zo sun las ecclesias *qui est una* . . . Si cum dit Salomun in *canticis; Una est columba mea*, zo est gleisa. Aquesta columba sovent es vendua e achataa a *sqmoniacis hereticis*, qui son li mal volpil qui vasten e meten a vilta l'esposa de Xrist . . . *Capite nobis vulpes parvulas que demoliuntur vineas*, zo est prendi nos las petite volp qui catzun a mal nostre vigne . . . Lanzai lor las pere e catzai los de la vigna . . . Vos qui devez varder la vigna zo est sancta ecclesia, decatzai los heretis. E cum que los catzare ? Cum lo flael *de resticulis*. Zo sun le parole de Xrist qui dis : La mia maisun si est maisun d'oraciun, mas vos en avez fait balma de lairuns. Lo premer maistre d'aquisti larun simoniay si fo un encantaor qui avea num Symon Magus . . . Enquora regna en la xrestianta a questa heresia qui confunt e destrui la gleisa qui est maisun e vigna de Deu, mult la peora e aflevolis. E li pastor, zo son li evesque e li prever, non tenent plai, mas il meesme o fan o consenten. Or que deven far cil qui son bon homes e an lor corage vers Deu ? Dolent e corrozos en deven eser e preer Deu que el per la soa misericordia los fatza venir a emendement que il no seien dampnai . . . Or nos vardem que nos non abiam cum lor compaignis si nos volem aver la misericordia de Deu e aver part ab los saint apostoil, li quail foron car ami del nostre seignor Jhesu Xrist qui en la sancta cros sofri passiun per reemer l'umana generaciun." Between the above dialect and that of the Waldenses there is certainly not that affinity which connects the latter with the Provençal ; there are some analogies, which would betray contact, but not consanguinity. *Galloital-*

*ische Predigten aus Cod. misc. lat. Taurinensis D. vi.*, 10*ten Jahrhunderts her-ausgegeben von* W. Foerster, ap. *Rom Studien*, vol. iv., p. 1 ; and the following 14th Homily. It would be interesting to compare it with the *Sermons du XIIme siécle en vieux provençal*, published by Fr. Armitage, Heilbronn, 1884. Champollion Figeac had said : " This collection of sermons seems to me to belong to the dialect and to the church of the Waldenses of Piedmont." The professor of Bonn is of a different opinion. He demonstrates that the dialect of those sermons does not present the characteristic type of the Provençal, but the distinctive features of a Gallo-Italic dialect spoken in Piedmont, and that it is sufficient to compare these fragments with our ancient writings and our modern patois, to see that the Waldensian dialect is not found therein. *Ibid.*, p. 43. However, Preger, in his turn, from internal reasons—no longer linguistic, but historical—is brought to the same conclusion as the last witness : that those sermons are not Waldensian, but undoubtedly of a churchman speaking to churchmen. See *ibid.*, p. 80.

578   *Aperçu*, etc., p. 11. That is the end of Muston's first argument. The following page begins thus : " The Waldensian dialect is of an Italian and not a French formation."

579   Our venerable poet is now showing that French is " the chief of the languages which emanated from the Neo Latin;" which, however, does not hinder him from stating, on the same page, that it is " né du rapprochement de la langue d'oc et de la langue öil." He classifies the Roman de la Rose with Provençal literature, and brings forward Italian words to prove the Italian origin of the Waldensian dialect, without even asking himself whether these words do not belong to the Provençal as well. After that he quotes some Spanish, but at the same time Provençal, to prove that " the formation of the Waldensian dialect took place before the three languages (Italian, Provençal, and Spanish) became completely distinct." As if it were possible to judge of the character of a language from a few words of its vocabulary ! See *Aperçu*, etc., *passim*, particularly p. 2, 5—11 and 30.

580   That is what particularly explains the apparent, rather than real variations of Montet, who, however, after what we have read, admits that the ancient Waldensian is a " Provençal dialect," or " derived from the Provençal." *Op. cit.*, p. 13 and 17.

581   Letter of a Professor to the Collège de France to A. Muston. *Examen* etc.. p. 5.

582   Letter of P. Meyer to Muston, November 17, 1881. *Ibid.*, p. 7. We also wrote to Dr. P. Meyer. Here is what he had the kindness to answer: " To tell you the truth, I believe that the language of the Valleys, tends, in its development towards the Provençal and French, and that in its very forms it has a close connection with the idiom of Dauphiny ; but I do not know whether some linguistic affinities could not be shown to exist on the Eastern side. The documents which I possess for that part of Piedmont, where Pignerol and Saluces are situate, are not sufficient for me to decide." Moreover, he confessed to Muston that he had only looked at the MSS. of Cambridge and Dublin, "superficially and without taking any interest in them." So that, up to this point, at least, the opinion of M. Meyer is neither decided nor certain.

582*a*   Mention has been made to us of a discovery by Professor Ascoli of Milan. Some of his disciples in Italy support it warmly, and go so far as to imagine that it will soon bring about the classification of our dialect with a new group. The point is this. Ascoli affirms that he has observed near the Alps, but on the French and Swiss side, as far as the Jura and the Vosges, an interesting family of dialects, containing, besides certain characteristics of their own, some features common to French and Provençal. This family does not owe its formation to a tardy concourse of divers elements, but to its own historical and independent traditions, more or less like the Neo-Latin languages, whose type is recognized. It was waiting its turn to be established, and Ascoli has the merit of having described it, and even of assigning to it a name. It is called Franco-Provençal. Ascoli, *Schizzi franco-provençali*, in the *Arch-glottol. ital.*, vol. iii., pp. 61—120. Boehmer, nevertheless, continues to give it the name of " Burgundian." *Roman, Studien, passim*. But the description given by Ascoli, does not embrace the dialect of the Valleys; it passes quite close to it, on the frontier. This is not mere chance ; for that scholar could not be more explicit. Indeed, what is the distinguishing feature of the Franco-Provençal family ? This, namely, that the atonic or privative *a*, which is preserved intact in Provençal, is changed here, as in French, and is transformed after a palatal into *ie, i*, or *e*. That, says Ascoli, is one of the most characteristic phenomena of the Franco-Provençal patois. " L' antitesi più decisiva tra l' idioma provenzale e l' idioma francese, si manifesta ne' riflessi dell' A latino, così in accento come fuori di accento. L' A tonico rimane incolume, anche nel francese, quando egli sia in posizione ; ma fuor di posizione vi si suole alterare, e si riduce di solito ad e. Così, *arme* arma, âpre *asper*, *quart* quartus, *quattre* quáttor ; ma *aimer* amáre, *aimée* amata, etc. Nel provenzale, all, incontro, e nell' antico in ispecie, l' A tonico si rimane costantemente incolume : *aspre*, *amar*, *amada*, etc.  L' A essendo atono nella sillaba finale, riducesi nel francese ad un' *e* muta ; nel provenzale rimane *a* (che ne' moderni dialetti è prevalentemente *o*).  Così : fr. *couronne*, pr. *corona ;* fr. *aimée*, pr. *amada.*  Ora tra i fenomeni più caratteristici de' vernacoli franco-provenzali, egli è codesto dell' avervisi *ie, i, e* per l' antico A' preceduto da suono palatile." *Ibid.*, p. 70 et seq. Every Waldensian maydraw the conclusion. We say *couronna* and *courouno, amâ, cantá* or *ciantá, prijá, bucá, mingiá*, etc. Fœrster, noticing this, holds, therefore, that the group indicated by Ascoli includes the Lyonese and excludes the Waldensian ; which is the outcome, after all, of the foregoing observations. A. Rösiger, speaking of a Waldensian colony in Germany, places the written Waldensian of the Valleys, and of Dauphiny, *by the side* of the Franco-Provençal group, and explains its decadence by the intrusion of the French. *Neu-Hengstedt* (Bourset), *Geschiehte u. Syrache einer Wald. Colonie in Württemberg*, Greisswald, 1882. It is clear, then, that the Waldensian dialect—as, in this particular, it especially reproduces the Provençal type—could not be classed in the family described by Ascoli, so long at least as the distinctive trait which characterizes it remains such as he has described. *Romania*, anno 1875, p. 293—296. But is this definition justifiable and immutable ? Some doubts have been entertained ; nay, more, it has been seriously contested ever since its appearance.  Meyer held that the system of grouping set forth by Ascoli was erroneous in its foundation, and in this connection he adds an observation which it is well to recall. He says : " Does the new group proposed by Ascoli—one that offers no geographical unity —at least obviate the difficulty of grouping together very dissimilar dialects ? Not in the least.  He brings together dialects which offer a very small number of facts, selected among many, as being particularly specific. It is very evident that the Dauphinois resembles the Provençal more than the Franc-comtois and the Lorrain ; still, the Lorrain, Franc-comtois, and Dauphinois are embraced by the new group, from which the Provençal is excluded." *Ibid.* M. Ascoli has replied to M. Meyer in an article entitled : *P. Meyer e il Franco Provençal*, ap. Arch. Glott. Ital., ii., p. 385—395.  In it he maintains his thesis touching the definition of the group which he has described, without, however, succeeding in proving that the doubt enunciated by his critic is an arbitrary one. Whether this definition of Ascoli's be right or wrong—which is a point we need not discuss here—it is certain that the group characterized by it could not comprehend the dialect of the Valleys.  Meanwhile, the fact that this dialect bears one of the most characteristic traces of the Provençal language is well proven ; whereas the new combinations cannot prevail against it, as has been seen by the example adduced.  Professor Morosi, of the Florence Superior Institute, who is studying the Waldensian dialect, has agreed with this after the examination of a translation of the *Nobla Leiczon* into the principal patois of our Valleys and of Queyras which I have just submitted to him, and he permits me to record here his concurrence.

583  It is his old thesis, already brought out in his *Bibliographie*, p. 81—93, and p. 101.  He there said that " our dialect, in which the ancient Waldensian books are written (XII. to the XIV. century), was not the common language of France," by which he meant the dialects of Provence, Dauphiny, and Lyons together.  He added that it "approaches much more to the language used during the VIII. century, than to that of the XII."  According to his latest writings, Muston is still at that point.  Nevertheless, he admits that, compared with the actual dialect of the Valley of the Rhône, ours "presents the most similarities to the ancient Roman," from which it is not derived !

584  " We must certainly admit the possibility of the unknown documents having been written in a more ancient language, which is already rendered somewhat unrecognisable in the oldest of the copies which have come down to us." *Rom. Wald.*, p. 45. As an example of the application of this, see his study on the *Cantica.*

585  *Op. cit.* p. 13—17. It is true, Meyer observes, that this study "might, without harm, have been omitted." *Romania, XIV.*, 319. But thus far the Romanists have given us nothing better.

586  Strasburg is excepted ; the Waldensian MS. it contained having been destroyed by the burning of the library, August 23rd and 24th, 1870.

587  See Léger, vol. i., ch. 3. The catalogue we read there had been given by

Sir Samuel Morland in his history. See further, and especially Muston, *Bibliographie*, at the end of the last volume of his *Is des Alpes* ; Todd, *The Books of the Vaudois ;* Herzog. *Rom. Wald.*, p. 46—66 ; Montet, *Hist litt.*, p. 1—11.

588   Ch. Schmidt, *op. cit.*, ii., p. 117 and 274. Cf. Reuss *Rev. de Th. et de* Phil. *chrct.*, 18 2, p. 330.

589   With these [words commences the learned book of S. Berger : *La Bible française au moyen âge*, Paris, 1884. Cf. Reuss, *Fragm. litt. et critiques relatifs à l'histoire de la Bible française*, ap. *Rev. de théol. et de phil chrétienne*, 1851, page 322.

590   Even Perrin recognised this. " The point of departure of the Waldensian sect was the study of the bible," says this Jesuit at the 49th page of his pamphlet : *T Valdesi*, etc., Turin, 1871.

591   Tron, however, hesitates, *op. cit.*, p. 23.

592   *Ibid.*, p. 324.

593   See ante.

594   "Similiter multos libros Bibliae." This *similiter* seems to puzzle more than one reader. Berger, for instance, who translates it " également," *op. cit.*, p. 37.

595   Stephen of Borbone, a Dominican monk, was born in Belleville on the Rhône, toward the end of the XII. century ; he was Inquisitor for 25 years, and lived in Lyons, where he died about 1261. He can say : " Secundum quod ego (anclivi) a pluribus qui priores eorum (Waldensium) viderunt et a sacerdote illo . . . qui dictus fuit Bernardus Ydros." *Anecdotes historiques*, etc., p. 342. This incident is repeated by Echart and others.

596   "Like the translators of our own authorized version." *The Rom. version*, introd., p. c. He invents at pleasure on the subject of the composition of this committee. I noted a little way back that Ebrard believed these two priests to be Cathari. Gilly makes them out Lombards. "As their names indicate natives of Lombardy, Ydros and Ausa being towns in the North of Italy." *Ibid.*, p. xcix. Reuss confesses that his geographical knowledge "does not reach so far." Afterwards, Gilly gives them an associate, again "from Lombardy," namely, John "de Lugio ;" which is, in his opinion, an abbreviation of "de Lugduno." And then we have a disguised Manichean sitting with the Waldensian committee ! However, we have noticed above (note 121) the mistake which gave rise to the creation of this new personage.

597   Gilly, *ibid.* Tron remains of Gilly's opinion. See *Pierre Waldo*, p. 25.

598   "In quo textus et glossa Psalterii plurimorumque Legis utriusque librorum continebantur." *Op. cit.*, dist. i., c. 31.

599   *Revue*, etc., 1851, p. 332—334. The doubts there expressed by Reuss seem to us excessive. Cf. with his book, *Die Geschichte der heiligen Schriften N. T.*, 5th ed., § 465.

600   Berger is of the same opinion. *Op. cit.*, p. 37 and 38. Only, why does he think that those books and notes "differed in their origin and character ? " There seems to be no good reason for that exception.

601   As we observed before, it is the settled opinion of W. Foerster. Muston says that the Lyonnese in Waldo's time "was already the dialect of French, whence the Romance language was derived." *Bibliographie*, p. 101.

602   *Revue*, etc., 1851, p. 335. Muston is of the same opinion, from a different standpoint. See *l.c.*

603   Vide ante.

604   "Evangelia, Epistolas Pauli, Psalterium, Moralia Job et plures alios libros sibi fecit in gallico sermone transferri." Migne, Sp. 699. Another letter, addressed to the three abbots, has these words : "Multitudo gallicæ cuidam translationi divinorum librorum." *Ibid.*, *Sp.* 695.

605   Bertram undoubtedly replied ; but his second letter, like the first, is unknown. To get at the bottom of the matter it would be necessary to have the key to the private archives of the Vatican.

606   "Quis fuerit auctor translationis illius, quæ intentio transferentis . . . cum opinionem et vitam eorum penitus ignoremus qui sacras Scripturas taliter transtulerunt." *Ibid.*, Sp. 689.

607   "Magister Crispinus presbyter et R. socius ejus." *Ibid.*

608   " Multitudo non modica, tracta quodammodo desiderio Scripturarum . . *sibi fecit transferri.*" *Ibid.*

609   "In gallico sermone." *Ibid.*

610   "Quosdam libros de latino in romanum versos combusserunt." *Ibid.* This expression, which may refer to other books, must primarily refer to such as had been particularly forbidden, namely, the sacred books.

611  *Op. cit.,* p. 40—42.  The Evangéliare mentioned in these lines is found in the Bibl. de l'Arsenal, No. 2,083.

612  Reuss, who had not seen the MS. described by Berger, and knew it only from Abbé Lebeuf's mention of it, says at once: "If it did not contain more than the Lessons, it does not answer to the idea one has of a Waldensian version." *L.c.,* p. 341.

613  This point is settled now.  Berger disputed it.  "It is a mistake," he said.  In his opinion the author must have been Hamon de Landacob, a monk of Savigny, of the order of Citeaux, in Normandy.  *Ibid.,* p. 46—47.  But H. Suchier has proved that the person referred to is really Bishop Haimon.  See his art. *Zu den altfranzösischen Bibelübersetzungen,* ap. *Zeitschrift für romanische Philologie,* 1884, p. 413 and foll.  Berger now admits that, upon this point at least, his critic is right.  Montet followed Berger.  See *op. cit.,* p. 2.

614  With regard to the *Moralia Job,* besides Berger and Suchier, see some observations of Fœrster contained in his preliminary remarks to *Li sermon saint Bernart,* edited by him in 1885, p. 11.

615  Bibl. du Palais-des-Arts, A. i., 54.  For the description, see Gilly, p. 57—61 ; Muston, *Bibliog.,* p. 94 ; especially Reuss and Fœrster, who had it in their hands, one to analyse it, the other to transcribe the Gospel of John.  *Revue,* etc., 1852, p. 334 et seq., and the *Revue des langues romanes,* vol. v., n. 3 at the beginning.

616  That does not prevent the MS. from having a division by chapters, resembling that of the Codex Vaticanus.

617  They are : Rom. vii., 18 to viii., 28, and Luke xxi., 37 to xxiii., 14.

618  *Revue,* etc., 1853, p. 75.  Reuss adds the following marginal note : "The Limousin dialect (spoken by the Cathari) omits voluntarily the nasal *n,* forms the plural in *s ;* changes the *d* placed between two vowels into *z ;* terminates the first person plural of verbs in *m,* participles and generally all nouns absolute in *s,* and this *s* becomes *z* after *t* etc.  I have collected hundreds of examples from all parts of the New Testament, in order to compare the difference in words even amongst those in constant use.

619  *Ein Katarisches Ritual,* Jeua, 1852.

620  *Revue des langues romanes,* March 15, and April 15, 1878.

621  *L.c.,* p. 87.  It is true that in a subsequent article, Reuss claims that two passages must be excepted, namely : (1) The one which in the Lord's Prayer substitutes *panem supersubstantialem* (according to Matthew), for *panem quotidianum* (according to Luke), and adds the doxology, according to the Greek rite ; (2) Prov. viii. 22, translated from the Greek ho Kurios ektise, not from the Vulgate *Dominus possedit me.*  Reuss sees here an indication of the relations of Catharism with the tradition of the Greek Church.  *Rev. citée,* 1852, p. 327.  All that is very hypothetical ; is it not sufficient to admit that the version of the Lyons MS. is taken from a text different from our common Vulgate ?  Then we should not be led astray by the traces of Catharism, which Reuss sees in the Waldensian versions.  Haupt has demonstrated where these traces come from, namely, from his own pen.

622  Such is the opinion of Chelle, who has a note in the manuscript itself that reads : "This MS. contains a translation of the N. T., as used by the Waldenses, following the text and the order of the Vulgate.  It appears to belong to the commencement of the fourteenth century.  It has a Waldensian ritual at the end."  Now, remarks Reuss, we read the word Albigenses in two places instead of Waldenses.

623  See the *Rituale, passim.*  Cf. Reuss, *ibid.,* 1852, p. 338.  It is interesting to note here the interpretation given to the following passages : Jude 23 ; Matt. x., 8, and Mark xvi., 17, etc. ; Matt. iii., 11 ; John i., 26, etc., John xx., 21.

624  We are told that Reusch, whilst lately employed in putting Doellinger's papers in order, found a refutation of Cunitz's thesis.  But Doellinger could not in this piece of work have taken into account the *Practica* of Bernard Gui recently printed.  Let the ceremony of the *Consolamentum,* according to the *Rituale,* be compared with the report of that Inquisitor (*ibid.,* v., p. 1, 2, and 3), and it will be seen that Cunitz is right.  The Ritual is Catharin.

625  Bibl. Nationale, fonds français, n. 2425 (old n. 8086 of the Bibl. du Roi), For the description, see Gilly, *op. cit.,* introd. p. lxvi.—lxix., Reuss, *Revue,* etc.. 1852, p. 343.

626  Let us notice the following : All the Gospel of Matthew, the first twenty verses of Mark, 2 John v., 4 to the end, the 3rd Epistle of John, that of Jude, and the first three verses of the Epistle to the Romans, ch. ii. to iv. of 2nd Epistle to Timothy, and the first two verses of Epistle to Titus.  Finally, here are a few omissions : Mark xi., 1—11 ; Luke xvi., 1—12, xvii., 30—xviii., 10,

etc. Berger thinks these omissions were generally made for the purpose of abbreviation, or were caused by the negligence of the copyist.

627 We can hardly doubt but that this precious volume was about the XV. century, in the hands of a Waldensian hawker. *Revue historique*, January, 1886.

627* 628 Luke xii., 32 ; 2 Cor. vi., 16 ; James v., 8 ; Heb. x., 37.

628* 629 James v., 1. Here are some other passages indicated : Luke xv., 11, xix., 42 ; John ii., 17, iii., 18, vi., 51, xviii., 23 ; Acts xiv., 21, xv., 29, xvi., 18, xvii., 34 ; James ii., 8, v., 12 ; 2 Peter ii., 6 ; Rom. v., 12 ; 1 Cor. ii., 9 ; xv., 16, 54 ; 2 Cor. iv., 13, vi., 16 ; Eph. ii., 1 ; 1 Tim. i., 9, iii., 12 ; Heb. xi., 9, etc. We are indebted to the kindness of M. Berger for these notes.

630 *Revue de théol*, etc., 1852, p. 324.

631 University Library, Waldensian MS. Dd 15, 34, or vol. F. For description, see Bradshaw, ap. Todd, *Books*, etc., p. 214. This description, corrected by means of notes, which Bradshaw intended for us, has been revised and completed by his successor, Mr. Robertson Smith, to whom we here desire to express our gratitude.

632 Léger, Histoire, etc., i., p. 21—22. Cf. Morland *Hist*. of the Evang. Churches of Piedmont, p. 98.

633 The following are the omissions which have been detected ; viz., the beginning of Matthew as far as vii., 10 ; all of Mark ; Luke iii., 7 to the end ; John vii., 33—xiii., 28, and xv., 21—xx., 29 ; Epistle to the Romans ii. to Corinthians, Epistle to Colossians, and the 2 to Thessalonians, except the very first words of the i. ; written through carelessness and without a title ; 1 Timothy from commencement to ii., 7 ; Epistles to Philemon and that to the Hebrews ; Acts iv., 17—v., 4 ; xxii., 5—25 ; xxvi., from 5 till toward the end. Finally, the MS. ends at 2 Peter ii., 5. Nothing, therefore, of the Epistle of John, or the Apocalypse.

634 Bibl. de la ville, n. 488 (old 8595). For description see Champollion Figeac, *Nouv. recherches sur les patois ou idiomes vulgaires de la France*, 1809, p. 24 et seq. ; Gilly, *l. c.*, p. 45—51 ; Muston, who says in his *Examen*, etc., that it is " la seule Bible Vaudoise qu 'il ait étudicé up pen ; " *ibid*., p. 36, and Bibliog., p. 95 ; Herzog, *Rom. Wald.*, p. 62 ; Reuss, *Revue*, etc., 1852, p. 342.

635 Examen., etc., p. 36—37. Cf. Perrin, *op. cit.*, p. 57.

636 Ch. Figeac and Muston mention the Book of Songs instead of that of Jesus, son of Sirach. Gilly refers to these two writers. We follow Herzog, who saw the MS. after them.

637 This table is written on paper. It begins thus : " Aici commença lo registre de li evangeli de las Escripturas per lo cercondament del an premierament en lavenament del Segnor."

638 Generally speaking. According to Muston and Herzog ; but Reuss calls attention to the fact that if there are some divergences from the actual order, the same are also found in certain MSS. of the Vulgate.

639 Ch. Figeac believed this MS. to belong to the XIII. century, but he was led astray by Léger and Perrin, whom he accepted as guides in discussing and reckoning the age of Waldensian writings. Gilly notices it in passing : " C. F. follows the error caused by Perrin's mis-statements." Nevertheless, he adheres to his opinion upon this point, while Herzog clearly disposes of it.

640 Trinity College Library, Cl. A., Tab. iv., n. 13. For the description see especially an art. in *British Mag.*, by Todd, reprinted in his *Books of the Vaudois*, p. 1—7. Besides, Gilly, *l.c.*, p. xxviii.; Muston, *l.c.*, p. 95; Reuss, *l.c.*, p. 342; Herzog, *l.c.*, p. 55.

641 Perrin, *l.c.*

642 This copy consists properly of a revision of the Gospel of St. John, published by Gilly, and the immediately following transcription of the other books of the N. T.

642* 643 Herzog supposed this, from certain little omissions and slight mistakes which are not explained by any reading of the Vulgate. He indicates them in his *Rom. Wald.*, p. 55 and 56.

644 Todd, *Books of the Vaudois*, p. 190.

645 *Rom. version*, p. xxxvi.

646 City Library, c. 169, 706. For the description see Gilly, *l.c.*, p. lii.—lvi.; but especially Reuss, who examined it very thoroughly, *l.c.*, p. 344 and foll., and also Herzog, *ibid.*, p. 61.

647 " Guilemus Malanotus pastor pedemontanus valdensis hoc N. T. celeberrimae Tigurinae Academiae dono dedit die decimo Septembris, 1692."

648 " Per Barbetum quemdam, i. e. ministrum ejusdem ecclesiae."

649   Namely : the beginning of Matthew to iii., 17 ; Acts xxvii., 14—32 ; Rev. xx., 6—xxi., 23.

650   Reuss counted six of them.  *Ibid.*, p. 345.

651   There are no less that 32 books of the O. T. indicated in that manner ; with them Judith, Tobias, the 4th book of Esdras, Wisdom, Ecclesiastecus, the 13th chapter of Daniel, which is the story of Lusanna.  Herzog mentions also the book of Jesus, son of Sirach.

652   This kind of sub-division for the Old Testament, dates from 1490.  The division into verses was introduced from 1551 to 1560.  Reuss, *l. c.*, p. 347—349.

653   Reuss. *Revue*, etc., 18:3, p. 80—85.

654   This specimen is taken in part from the texts reproduced by Gilly, Reuss, Fœrster, Todd, and Chabrand.  We have made use of the manuscript corrections of Herzog upon Gilly's reproductions, and especially of his copy of the New Testament of Dublin.  But, still, our specimen would be incomplete and less exact also, without the co-operation of Professors Berger of Paris, Clédat of Lyons, and Ulrich of Zurich, of Dr. Ingram of Dublin, and the librarians Bradshaw and R. Smith of Cambridge.  We desire here to express to all of them our sincere thanks.

655   Lelong, *Bibl. Sacra*, i., 369.  Cf. Gilly ap. Todd *Books of the Vaudois*, p.164.

656   I allude to those recorded by Gilly (*Rom. vers.*, p. lxxviii.), and Muston (*Bibliog.*, MSS. bibliques ii., vi., and vii.).  People have been misled more especially by the title of *Bible des Pauvres*, of Paris.  This is definitely laid aside.

657   Gilles, *op. cit.*, preface and ch. ii.

658   Particularly in Val Pragelas.  Perrin. ch. iii., p. 57.  Cf. Léger, i., 23, 24.

652* 659   "May have been wholly or partially the productions of Waldo and his associates."  *Rom. vers.*, introd., p. xcvi.

660   This fact is well authenticated.  M. Berger writes us after his last researches : " I have been unable to discover either in the bible of the Cathari, or in the texts of the Waldenses, the slightest expression that would indicate a heretical origin, or that in any way gives a hint of the theology professed by the translators."

661   "Quia sensu proprio verba evangelii interpretari præsumpserunt, videntes nullos alios evangelium juxta literam omnino servare, quod se facere velle jactaverunt."  Dav. d'Augsb.

662   I take this statement again from his private correspondence, which I am authorised to use for my own benefit and that of my readers.

663   *E.g.*  "Ora Dio," to Acts x., 26 (Cf. Herzog, *Rom. Wald.*, p. 321), and "filh de la vergena," "pena," etc., *passim*.

664   "Arctis sime inhibemus," says the decree of the Council of Toulouse, anno, 1229.  Vaissette remarks "We find, in the informations laid and the judgments pronounced, that the heretics commonly called Waldenses, in the country read the Gospels in the vulgar tongue."  Hist. de Lanquedoc, iii., 411, anno 1237.

665   *Rev. Historique*, 1st art. quoted.

666   Muston makes Fœrster say that "this translation is, perhaps, by Waldo himself."  *Examen.* etc., p. 56.  But he is mistaken.  Not only does Fœrster not say that, but he could not do so consistently.  The dialect of Lyons and that of Provence are two different things.  What Fœrster admits. is, that the language of the MS. of Lyonsiis so far from being irreconcilable with our dialect, that it already contains it in a germ.  I would add, that according to Berger, it is to be hoped that the link connecting this version with that of the MSS. of XVI. century will still be found.  " I do not know," he says, "whether the MS. of Paris is not very near being this connecting link."  *Ibid.*

667   Reuss declared in 1851: "I find it impossible for the present to recognize the hand of Waldo in the Waldensian Biblical MSS. which now exist."  *Rev.* quoted p. 328.  Now, M. Berger recently wrote to us as follows : " There is no reason to think that there is any connection whatsoever between the Provençales versions, the Waldensian versions, and Waldo.  Everything tends to exclude this hypothesis . . . We must, then, until the contrary is proved, deny his paternity in the Provençal version, which was that of the Waldenses."  While quoting these words of the eminent Parisian professor, we feel constrained to acknowledge that he tries in every possible way "to prove the contrary."  We would offer him here our best wishes for his success, together with the expression of our heartfelt gratitude.

668   Library of the Convent of the Prémontrés of the Abbey of Teplis, near Marienbaden, Bohemia, vi., 139.  For the description see Preface to Codex Tepleusis, printed in 1881 to 1884.

669 Kraft, *Die deutsche Bibel vor Luther,* Bonn, 1883.

670 Biltz, *Die neuesten Schriften,* etc., article inserted in the *Archiv für das Studium der neuereu Sprachen u. Litteraturen,* vol. lxxvi., n. 1 and 2.

671 F. Klimesch, author of the publication of the Codex Tepleusis, had not mistrusted it at first. Biltz was the first to elucidate this point. See the *Sountags beilagen d. neuen Preuss, Ztg.* Nos. dated 3rd and 17th July, 1881. Let us remind the reader that there still exists another MS. preserving the old German version. It was described by Rachel, *Die Freiberger Bibelhaudschrift,* 1866. This learned man proves that the two MSS. have a visible bond of relationship as regards the text of the version.

672 See his work, *Die Reformation u. die älteren Reform parteien,* 1885, pp. 257—260.

673 In his pamphlet entitled : *Deutsche Bibelüber setzung d. mittelalterlichen Waldenser,* 1885.

674 His pamphlet is entitled : *Die Waldenser u. die vorlutherische deutsche Bibelüber setzung,* 1885.

675 It is first the turn of Haupt to reply with *Der waldensische Ursprung des Codex Teplensis u. der vorlutherischen deutschen Bibeldrucke gegen die Angriffe von Dr. Iostes.* 1886 ; then followed Keller : *Die Waldenser u. die deutschen Bibelüber setzungen,* 1886 ; and, finally, the new answer of Jostes : *Die Teplerbibelübersetzung, eine zweite Kritik,* 1886.

676 Berger, *Revue Historique,* two articles inserted in vol. xxx. and xxxii., 1886. He supports the theory of Keller and Haupt. Ph. Schaff, on the contrary, hastened to side with Jostes. See *The Independent,* October 8th, 1885. Karl Müller is inclined that way (see *Zeitschrift für Kirchen geschichte,* vol. viii., 3rd ed.), without giving any decisive reason. See, moreover, his article in the *Studien u. Kritiken,* 1887.

677 "Appears to me to be uncertain for more than one reason." Art. *Die neuesten Schriften,* etc.

678 *Die Waldenser,* etc., p. 84 et seq. Berger thinks that Keller there follows a dangerous road, which may lead him to very unexpected discoveries ; for, is he aware, upon what text the version he is analyzing is founded ? See the end of the second article of the *Rev. Historique.* Cf. Kolde, *Gött. gel. Anz.,* 1887, n. 1.

679 Biltz, for example, vaguely attributes it to the Friends of God, the more so, he says, that the preface to the German Bible, edition of Cologne, tells us that this Bible had been circulating for a long time in the valleys of the Upper Rhine. *Ibid.* We note, however, after Haupt and Berger, that the Waldenses of Strasburg (1400), and of Basle (1430) possessed the German Bible. The Synod of Tréves (1231) already finds that the heretics of that city had it in their hands. Now several among them seem to have been Waldenses. If, after this, we take into account the very small size of the Teplis volume, we shall not be far from recognizing in this one of those *little books* which the Waldensian evangelists carried with them. hidden under their rough cloaks.

680 Gilly had already remarked that the expression "lo filh de la vergena" is used in the same sense as indicated above in the version of Dublin, and that it is found also in that of Zurich, Grenoble, and Paris, and in several Waldensian writings, but not in the version of Lyons. *Rom. vers.,* p. xlii. and 95.

681 Allusion is here made to those which Ch. Schmidt published in 1852.

682 Indeed, we know that at the diet of Worms, the representative of the Roman court said to the Reformer : "Plurima eorum, quæ adducis . . . . Waldensium sunt, Pauperum de Lugduno sunt . . . hereses." P. Balan, *Mon. Ref. Luth.,* 1884, p. 182.

683 See a letter of the year 1368, hereinafter reproduced.

684 Dav. d'Augsb., ap. Preger, p. 29.

685 "Expositiones," says the inquisitorial record. Ochsenbein, *op. cit.,* p. 220. Cf. *ibid.,* p. 251 et 387.

686 "Finxerunt quosdam rithmos, quos vocant triginta gradus s. Augustini, in quibus docent quasi virtutes sectari et vicia detestari." Dav. of Augsb., ap. Preger, p. 35.

687 *Abriss der gesammten Kirchengeschichte,* 1879, vol. iii., p. 406.

688 "Articulos fidei septem de divinitate, et septem de humanitate, et decem precepta dechaloghi, et septem opera misericordiæ, sub quodam compendio et sub quodam modo ab eis ordinato et composito, dicunt et docent." Bern. Guid., *Practica inquisitionis hereticæ pravitatis* (Paris, 1886), p. 250.

689 It can hardly be a question of a compilation, from the Inquisitor's remark. See Montet. *Hist. Litt.,* etc., Pièces justificatives, *n.* 3. Compare

those seven articles of faith with the Credo, after Thomas Aquinas. See, more-over, the *Zweite Kritik* of Jostes, p. 9—10.

690  *Cod. S. Florian*, xi., 152.

691  At Strasburg it is a question of a book which the *magister* uses during the service ; at Friburg, divers writings in more than one language, especially a treatise, in which it is said that suffrages and other such works are of no avail to the souls of the dead.

692  " They were of a much later period." Rom. vers., introd. p. 35—37.

693  *Op. cit.*, ch. ii.

694  That letter is in Latin. See Cod. S. Florian, vol. xi., p. 152. The tran-scription was made by Professor Karl Müller, of Giessen, who had the kindness to send it to us. We are the more obliged to him as his task was a difficult one.

695  The quotation is taken from the Vulgate, which is not very correct. Segond translates : " Par votre persévérance vous sauverez vos âmes." Luke xxi., 19. Of course the letter ignores the division into verses.

696  Ps. lxvi., 10—11.

697  1 Cor. xii., 26.

698  Ps. cxxxvii., 9.

698*a*  Cf. Matth. xxi., 44 ; and Luke xx., 18.

699  " Parvulos motus animi nostri ad Christum debemus allidere."

700  Matth. xviii., 7.

701  Job ii., 1; and Ps. vii., 14—18.

702  See Prov. xviii., 19 ; but according to the Vulgate. In the English ver-sion the text is totally different.

703  Gal. vi., 2.

704  Ps. xx., 1—5, 7; cxix., 1; cxx., 1; cxli., 1, 2.

705  Ps. l., 15 ; lx., 11, 12.

706  Ps. li., 17.

707  " Fatemur enim nos, ut apostolus ait, imperitos sermone vel sermocinali scriptura, non tamen sine sciencia spirituali."

708  1 Cor., i., 19—20, 25—31.

709  These are the words of St. Paul, to which the editor had added a few complimentary words.

710  Matth. xi., 25.

711  1 Cor. viii., 1—3.

712  Ps. cxxxi., 1.

713  Exodus ix., 9.

714  Matth. xi., 29.

715  Rom. xii., 3.

716  2 Tim. iii., 7. The text of the letter contains an *ut*, instead of *ne*, but this is probably only a *lapsus*.

717  Ephes. iv., 20.

718  1 Cor. xiii., 2.

719  Widom vii., 13.

720  James iv., 17,

721  Matth. xxiii., 12. Compare also 2 Cor. iii., 5; Rom. xii., 3 ; 1 Cor. iv., 20: Eccles x., 1—6.

722  Matth xvi., 19.

723  Titus i., 5.

724  Matth. x., 1 ; xviii., 18.

725  Ps. xix., 4.

726  John xvii., 20, 22.

727  Matth. x., 9 ; xix., 21, 27.

728  " Nisi mecum manseritis, terram vobis prohibebo."

729  Matth. xix., 28, 29.

730  John xvi., 2. Cf. *ibid.*, v. 33, et xiii., 16.

731  " Terram vobis relinquimus, nos vero celum appetimus."

732  Ps. ii., 3.

733  Rom. xv., 4.

734  1 Cor. x., 6.

735  Rom. xv., 30 et suiv.

736  Matth. xxiv., 9.

737  Matth. x., 23 et suiv.

738  Ps. xxi., 11.

739  Job. xiv., 6—8.

740  " Petrus de Walle et ejus socius Johannis Ludinensis a Ludone civitate dictus (sic)."

741 " Tanquam ramus a vero trunco aqua sancti spiritus irrigato paulatim pullulans, non principium sed reparacio nostri ordinis fuisse dicitur."

742 John ix., 34.

743 1 Cor. iv., 3, 4.

744 " Dicti sunt Waldenses et postremum Ludinenses pauperes a Ludone civitate, in qua multo tempore conversati sunt . . . Viam scilicet paupertatis, quam predicti viri secuti sunt pauco ante eum tempore et adhuc sequentes eorum secuntur ut credimus juxta librum electorum."

745 " Tamquam leo a somno consurgens."

746 The MSS., which is very difficult to decipher, is here somewhat embarrassing. It seems to read : Sic in curiam ut habetis (or perhaps "hereticus ") est ingressus ab invidis reprobatus." " Curia " can only refer to Rome."

747 Matth. xviii., 19, 20.

748 Matth. vii., 1 ; 1 Cor. iv., 5.

749 Acts v., 38.

750 Rom. 1, 28.

751 1 Cor. xi., 19.

752 Jer. li., 6. Cf. Matth. x., 5 ; Ephes. iv., 17 ; Rev. xviii., 4.

753 " Ut audivi." This expression is found precisely in the historical frag-ment heretofore noticed. The sentence is : " Post autem anuos DCCC a Constan-tino, surrexit quidam, cujus proprium nomen Petrus, *ut audivi*, fuit, sed a quadam regione dicebatur Waldis." See my *Introd. alla Storia della Riforma in Italia*, appendix n. 1. There is evidently a connection between this fragment, or the writing from which it is taken, and the Book of the Just. The homo-genity of the matter in both, is, moreover, evident.

754 Col. iv., 6.

755 " Est duplex : prima est propter testium absenciam. Nemo enim hominum est qui audiverit seu viderit proprium rei principium, qui multum tempus jam est elapsum. Secunda racio magis principalis est propter persecu-ciones innumeras, quas passi sumus ; unde multociens producti sunt libri nostri quasi in nichilum, ita ut vix sacram paginam possemus reservare."

756 1 Cor. xi., 23. "Accepi . . . . quod tradidi vobis," dit la lettre.

757 " Et licet Petrus dictus Waldensis non accepisset, quod absit (fatemur enim fuisse presbyterum sacris ordinibus ordinatum cum Johanne suo socio sive confratre ejusdem ordinis et postmodum ab illo cardinali de quo audistis favente eidem confirmatum non dubitamus), tamen multi et innumerabiles sacerdotes qui hanc vitam sive fidem secuti sunt, nonne fratribus imponere poterunt ? " We know that this Cardinal is mentioned in the historical fragment.

758 Rom. viii., 28.

759 John x., 13.

760 1 Cor. i., 17.

761 *Ibid.*, ix., 13, 14.

762 John vi., 47, 54, 57.

763 " Crede et manducasti."

764 " Cum communio sit unitas Christi et sancte ecclesie."

765 " Auditis solum confessiones : pro reliquis mittitis ad ecclesiam popu-lum . . . Vos tamen unum semisacramentum." The letter is addressed : " Profunde speculacionis viris, fratribus in Italia, etc."

766 En voici l'adresse : " Dilectis, utinam in Christo fratribus universis et specialiter hiis quorum legacio ad nos usque pervenit, Johannes, Petrus et eorum consodales salutem in domino Jesu Christo."

767 " Vestra Regula narrat, ut ego memorie mee tradidi, quod sicut a tempore Abraham usque ad Christum nunquam deficit lucerna fidei, sic a Christo usque ad nunc. Dicitur eciam ibidem, quod in principio vestri ordinis vehementer mul-tiplicati fuerint fideles vestri qui aliquando M, aliquando verso (?) DCC in uno synodo congregatur . . . Et a Constantino et Silvestro usque ad inventorem vestre secte D(CC, additis CC annis ab invencione, quibus manifeste dicitur eam extitisse, remanent vix L anni usque nunc sc. anno domini MCCCLXVIII, inquibus predicare publice desit." Here we are brought back again to the historical fragment.

768 The Waldensian ministers and preachers were sufficiently acquainted in a general way with Latin, and bilingual readings, Latin and Waldensian, are not uncommon. We have an example of this at the present day, in the writings of Morel.

769 At least, according to the Genevan text published by Hahn, *Gesch.* d. Wald., p. 623—626.

770 *Aktenstücke*, etc., ap. *Zeitschrift f. die hist. Theol.*, 1852, p. 238, et seq.

Schmidt published them under the known title of *Regale secte Waldensium*, and considers that the whole forms a discourse.

771    " Vestra regula narrat, *ut ego memorie mee tradidi*," said the renegade Jean, whom we have just quoted.

772    "Trametament," says the MS.  See Montet, *op. cit.*, p. 136—139.

773    " Alcuns volon ligar la parolla de Dio segont la lor voluntà."

774    The allusion is in this passage : " Dont lo es script que Costantin dis a Silvestre e a tuit li successor de luy meseyme : Nos donen la nostra corona en la testa."

775    Montet, p. 57, et seq.

776    The discovery of this is due to Professor Alphonse Meyer.  The original treatise is in Greek.  Pitra published it in his *Spicilegium Tolesmense*, vol. iii., p. 338 et seq.  See the report of Mayer in the *Sitzugscerichte d. philos-philol u. hist. cl. d. k., Akad. d.   Wissenschaften zu München*, 1880, 5e liv.

777    *Op. cit.*, p. 76.   Cf. *ibid.*, p. 43—46.

778    *Op. cit.*, p. 72.   Cf. *Rivista Cristiana*, x., p. 235.

779    See *Rom. Wald.*, p. 72—76 ; but, above all, the detailed study he made of it, in the *Zeitschrift f. die Hist. Theol.*, 1861, 4th part.

780    *Op. cit.*, p. 64—68.

781    "Li 4 entendement czo es estorial, alegorial, tropologial, anegogial." *Cantica* iii., 10.

782    "Nos latin diczen," says the commentator.  See, moreover, the allusion to the meaning of the word martyr in Latin (iv., 1), and more especially the Latin verses at the end.

783    *Zeitschrift, l.c.*   Cf. *Rom. Wald.* p. 31—34 and 63—65.

783*  784    " Such a living picture of the condition of the Waldenses we shall be unable to find anywhere else." *Zeitschrift, l.c.*

785    Foerster, *Li sermon saint Bernard*, serm. xxi.

786    " Enquor n'est assez." *Rom. Studien, l.c.*

787    Traces of them are found in the *Gallo-Ital. Predigten ;* it may have been noticed that even that of *bons homes* is found there.  See our quotation in a note of the preceding chapter.

788    For example : the designation of people, flock, or Church of the Poor, already mentioned, and the passage concerning the *jus gladii* (v., 16), and such expressions as "filh de la vergina " (viii., 4), "devant pausa " (vi., 9), etc.

789    See following chapter, concerning the rule of faith.

790    " L'emburilh son li predicador " (vii., 2).

701*  791    Cf. vi., 9 ; iv., 4 ; vi., 2.

792    See above (p. 194—196).   MS. of Dublin.

793    See above, p. 186, or MS. of Dublin, p. 71.  We quote these two MSS. from a copy we have which belonged to the lamented Professor Zezschwitz.

794    On this point cf. the art. of Zezschwitz on the Bohemian Brethren. *Real Encyclo.*, 2nd edition, p. 655—658, and Goll, *Queller u. Untersuchungen*, part 1., p. 28.  Professor Goll informs us that instead of " Bohémiens " (see above, p. 196, n. 4), the original reads " Utraquistes."

795    According to three MSS., of Cambridge, Dublin, and Geneva.  Montet, p. 50—53, and *Noble Leçon* appendix.

796    *Purgatori soyma.*  Herzog, *Rom.Wald.*, app., n. i., reproduces the compared text of the MSS. of Geneva and Dublin.  The MS. of Geneva alone is complete.

797    Lydius, *Waldensia*, vol. i., p. 42 et seq., 90 et seq.  Montet is right in wondering how Léger could have given to this treatise the date of 1120.

798    Léger, in his history (i. 162), reminds the reader that the superstition of the worship of the Saints was an ancient one, and hastens to conclude : " It is therefore an obvious fact that the aforesaid feature of the Waldenses opposing the *newly-born* or *growing* doctrine of the invocation of Saints, must be of much older date than that of Antichrist," and he dates this back to 1120, namely, " fifty years previous to Waldo."

799    This in a writing, in the Trech language, upon Lucas of Prague.  See Montet, *Hist. Litt.*, p. 173—175.

800    Montet, p. 176.  We learn that Goll handed over to M. J. Müller, of Herrnhut, the duty of continuing the researches upon this point.

801    The Inquisitor who mentions these *Rythmes* indicates their object to us, and adds, that they are not the only attempts of this kind.  " Callide inserunt ibi ritus suos et hereses, ut melius alliciant ad ea discenda et forcius inculcent ea memoriter, sicut nos laycis proponimus symbolum, oracionem dominicam, et alia pulchra huius modi causa confinxerunt carmina."  Dav. of Augsb., ch. 17.

802    All but one have been published by Hahn, *op. cit.*, p. 560 et seq.

803 *Lo Despreeri del mont*, after two MSS.. one of Geneva, end of XV. century, the other of Dublin, beginning of the XVI. century. A Poem of 115 decasyllabic verses.

804 *La Barca*, after the two above-mentioned MSS., containing the preceding poem ; furthermore, a MS. of Cambridge, belonging to the beginning of the XV. century. A Poem of 56 stanzas of six Alexandrine verses, of which the 48th is irregular, being of 7 verses.

805 *Bibliographie*, p. 107.

806 See especially a few lines of the stanzas 17 and 19, which there is no necessity for citing.

807 Ex. " en général " and " pas " at the 74th and 314th verses. According to Tron, the Bark is of the XII. century.

808 *Oraçon*, according to the MS. of Dublin before-mentioned, fol. 47, a. They are 94 verses of uneven measure, sometimes even devoid of measure, with rhymes that are simply jingles.

809 See the *Echo des Vallées*, 1849, n. 10, p. 150 et seq., and the *Bibliog.* of the *Israël des Alpes*, p. 129.

810 *Bibliographie, l.c.* The editor of the *Echo des Vallées* does not hesitate to greet the *Oraison*, as a poem that comes to swell the list of the " numerous poems composed five or six centuries ago."

811 *Lo novel confort*, after the three mentioned MSS. Poem of 300 verses, or 75 " quatrains." The 40th lacks one verse.

812 *Lo Novel Sermon*, after the same three MSS. Poem of 408 verses, divided into 21 couplets. The length of the couplet as well as that of the verse is uneven.

813 Dante in his *Inferno*, v., 31—45, makes use of the same idea.

814 *L'Avangeli* or *li Evangeli de li quatre semenez*, after the two MSS. of Geneva and Dublin. Composition of 300 verses, divided into 75 mono-rhythmic quatrains.

815 *Lo Payre eternal*, after the three afore-mentioned MSS. Poem of 156 verses, divided into 15 sections, or 52 stanzas of three lines each. Every section is composed of 3 stanzas, the first of which refers to the Father, the second to the Son, the third to the Holy Spirit. The poet also addresses himself directly to the Trinity, twice in 2 stanzas during the course of the poem, and once at the end. A capital letter precedes every stanza, joining the three lines with a brace, and indicating the subject with a P. an F. or an S., and also a T. The title, therefore, does not correspond with the subject. It is taken from the first words.

816 *The Nobla Leiczon*, a poem in Alexandrin verse, after the three afore-mentioned MSS., and a fragment at Cambridge. Raynouard was the first to reproduce this poem with a translation. He took as his ground work the Genevan MSS., and made use of Léger's copy. Many an error has crept into this reproduction, as well as in that of Gilly, and later in that of Herzog ; which is, however, much less inexact. We have followed, in our first edition, the reading of Geneva, after the only diplomatic copy in existence, due to Appelstedt. We follow here the MSS. of Cambridge, recently published by M. Montet. It is more complete and more ancient than those of Geneva and of Dublin. It contains 481 verses.

817 Herzog suspects the interpolation of verses 439 to 456, and calls attention to the direct relation between the verses that precede, and those which follow. But this does not suffice to prove the fact. *Rom. Wald.*, p. 78—79.

818 These last two lines are wanting in the Genevan and Dublin MSS. They are reproduced from the MS. of Cambridge, according to Morland.

819 Cf. for the summary, Montet, *La Noble Leçon*, p. 11—18, which we have not made use of in our work. He concludes thus : " The poem is above all things an apology of the party, of which it sets forth, very plainly, the moral and religious principles. In the midst of the persecutions, it forms a confession of faith, a testimony which ought to demonstrate the innocence of the Waldenses, and at the same time a banner, a rallying point for reanimating their courage and confirming the hope they cherished, that justice would be done them. *Ibid.*

820 Sir Samuel Morland erroneously translates *car* by *for*, which corresponds to the French *car*. Léger does not fall into that mistake. We know that *car* had two meanings, one of which is rendered by *que*, the only one applicable in this case.

821 Ex. Léger, i., 161, and all the ancients ; Raynouard, ii., 137 et seq., Hahn, i., 65, Leroux de Lincy. p. 7 ; Muston, *passim ;* Flathe, i., 247 ; Monastier, i., 105 et seq.

822 *Rez. de Théol.*, etc., anno 1851, p. 325.

823 *Rom. Wald.*, p. 85. Cf. 1 John ii., 8, with verses 451 and 453. This last verse renders the expression of the Apostle to the letter. Montet adopts Herzog's opinion. That of Mandet, which establishes a relation between the verse of the Noble Lesson with passages of St. Paul, seems to be abandoned.

824 Todd, *op. cit.*, pp. 183 and 184, remarks that we do not read *ben han* but *ben ha*, and that we should say in Latin : *Undecies centum anni completum est.* He adds that the Provençal, did not any more than the Latin, admit of the agreement of a verb in the singular, with a noun in the plural. After that, is it necessary to demonstrate the force of the two adverbs joined together : *ben* and *entierament ?*

825 See the new Preface which Muston adds to the edition of his *Israël des Alpes* lately put into the market, and which has been neither revised nor reprinted. He stops there, for he says on p. 16 of his *Examen*, etc.: " I only wish to maintain here that the *Noble Leçon* had already appeared, or did appear, at the time of Waldo's arrival " in the valleys.

826 H. Bosio, *La Nobla Leyczon considérée au triple point de vue de la doctrine, de la morale et de l' histoire*, ap. *Bull. de la Soc. d' Hist. Vaudoise*, n. 2, p. 20—36.

827 See the chapter on the *Fraticelli*, in my *Introduzione alla Storia della Riforma in Italia*, 1881, p. 285 et seq.

828 He claimed : (1) That the Noble Lesson does not bear the seal of the Waldensian reaction. (2) That the Waldenses did not call themselves by that name before the XV. century. Herzog had no difficulty in showing that the Goettingen critic was in error as to the first point, and that as regards the second, the Noble Lesson does not authorize us to imagine that the Waldenses called themselves by that name, but rather to conclude that it was inflicted upon them by their adversaries at an early period. Cf. *Die Waldenser*, etc., p. 339, and *Rom. Wald.*, p. 80—81.

829 The foolish statements given currency to by the *British Magazine*, concerning Morland and Léger ; who are there suspected of having sent the Cambridge MSS. to Geneva, would, on the Continent, be sufficient to discredit any Review whatever. Todd, *Books, etc.*, p. 135—150. It is, therefore, not right to quote them as specimens " worthy of the school of critics," as has been done by M. Bosio, *Bullettin de la Sociètè d'Hist. Vaud.*, n. 2.

830 " It is highly satisfactory." *Discovery*, etc., after Todd, *op. cit.*, p. 210—223.

831 *Op. cit.*, p. 1°2.

832 *Ibid.*, p. 132—133. Montet, however, adopts the same method for the interpretation of the other reading. Can this be sustained ? He tells us afterwards, in his *Noble Leçon*, p. 5, that he has changed his opinion. The *terminus a quo* is now interchangeable for him with the Christian era. Berger was already inclined to swallow this hypothesis, as more likely to be true. *Rev. Hist.* xxxvi., 2nd part. Léger is avenged.

833 *Examen*, etc., p. 45.

834 " This name was probably introduced in a later revision." *Rom. Wald.*, p. 84.

835 P. Meyer wrote to Muston, 17 Dec., 1881 : " Since writing my article of 1866, I have seen the MSS. of Dublin and of Cambridge ; but only superficially and without taking any interest in them. All of them appeared to me to be of the XV. century at the earliest." How is this ; even those whose date is fixed at the beginning of the XV. century and at the end of the XIV ? That is going a little far. But Meyer will not long be of this opinion. He wrote to us recently : " Some day I intend to set to work on the Waldensian literature, as I am but very little satisfied with all that exists on this subject." Moreover, Fœrster also pledged himself to this. Some 5 years ago he wrote, that, in his opinion, the text of the Noble Lesson did not date back further than the XIV. century, and he proposed to prove it one day ; desiring first to publish a grammar of the Waldensian dialect. See *Riv. Cristiana*, 1882, p. 102. We hear that promise is about to be fulfilled. Mr. Boehmer, after reading what we have above said, writes : " The impression made upon me—which I informed you of—that the *Nobla Leiczon* might be very much older than is generally supposed, has been increased by your exposition of the matter.

836 See Montet, *passim*, and after him Bridel, Anderson Scott, etc.

837 We had just written these lines when we read the opinion given by Professor K. Müller upon the origin of our literature. " All that has been given out as Waldensian literature, before the Hussite period, is, without exception, of Catholic origin, and has never been Waldensian." *Zeitsch f. Kircheng*, by Brieger, 1886, p. 506. Here we have a thesis going thoroughly to the root of the

matter. It is a pity, that, thus far, the author has not seen fit to justify it, and that he has not had the time to do so as he had announced in his preface to his book. *Die Waldenser*, etc.

838 "Avea l' istinto del riformatore religioso, e ben sapeva trasfondere altrui l'intimo suo convinclmento." Tocco, *op. cit.*, p. 169.

839 Tocco appears to find nothing but that. "Come ad imitazoine dei Poveri di Lione sorsero i Poveri d' Assisi o frati minori, cosi ad imatazione dei predicatori valdesi nacquero i frati predicatori." *Ibid.*, p. 170.

840 According to two MSS. of Cambridge and Dublin. See Montet, p. 85.

841 *Nobla Leiczon*, v., 19, 217.

842 *Ibid.*, v., 287—288.

843 Some were not far from leaving the Old Testament on one side altogether. "Vetus Testamentum non recipiunt ad credendum," observes Dav. of Augsburg, "sed tantum aliqua inde discunt, ut nos per ea impugnent et se defendant, dicentes quod superveniente evangelio vetera ommia transierunt. One reading gives simply : "Vetus Testamentum non habent vel recipiunt, sed evangelia." Ch. 5.

844 For ex., in the treatises concerning *Antichrist* and the *Cause of the Rupture*, an inferior rank is assigned to the 2nd and 3rd epistles of St. John than to the 1st. Cf., upon this point, the letter of Œcolampadius to the Waldenses.

845 Thus Herzog and Montet, v. *Rom. Wald.*, p. 130—135, and *Histoire Littér.*, p. 81—84.

846 In our days, L. Desanctis held that the interpretation of the Holy Scriptures was not necessary ; this he did from a practical standpoint, and to put an end to the sophistry of the Romish theology. Whatever is true in this opinion was practised by the early Waldenses.

847 "Nec aliquam expositionem super eis recipiunt." *Practica*, p. 252. It is here a question relating to the oath, etc.

848 "Sensu proprio verba evangelii interpretari presumpserunt, videntes nullos alios evangelium juxta literam omnino servare, quod se facere velle jactaverunt . . . Mysticum sensum in divinis SS. refutant." They give their believers the impression that they are following the true reading : "boni et sancti homines, qui haberent rectam scripturam." Wattenbach, *Ueber die Inquisition gegen die Wald. in Pommern u. der Mark Brandenburg*, Berlin, 1886, p. 44.

849 "An sensus allegorici sint admittendi, et si ad plebem docendam sint utiles." Scultetus, *Ann. Evang.*, etc., 1620, p. 295—315, vers la fin.

850 *Nob. Leiczon*, v. 426—428.

851 *Ibid.*, v. 454—455.

852 The teaching of the "duae viae " is constantly found in the Waldensian writings. It is proven, moreover, by the inquisitorial documents. It is, therefore, characteristic. Is it necessary, in order to account for it, to find in it a link with the Didaché so-called of the twelve Apostles, as L. Keller does, for instance? See Harnack, *Texte u. Untersuchungen*, vol. ii. It is in our opinion more natural to recognise in it one of the maxims of the Sermon on the Mount.

853 "Dicunt et docent quod anime, quando exeunt de corporibus, immediate vadunt, vel in paradisum . . . vel in infernum, et non est alius locus animarum post hanc vitam nisi paradisus vel infernus." *Practica*, p. 252.

854 Montet confesses that "there is no question here of our most ancient documents. The word *purgatori* is not to be found in any rescript of that period." *Op. cit.*, p. 89.

855 Thus in the treatise of the *Purgatori soyma*.

856 According to Bern. Fontiscaldis, one would imagine that the ideas of the Waldenses of his acquaintance on this subject were not definite. *Op. cit.*

857 "Primo . . . purgatorium esse non credunt." *Aktenstücke*, dans la *Hist. Zeitschr.* 1852, p. 253.

858 "It is in this sense that St. de Borbone mentions " poenam purgatoriam," and Renier Sacconi the " presentem tribulationem."

859 "Dicunt et docent quod vera pœnitentia et purgatorium de peccatis est tantummodo in hac vita et non in alia." *Practica*, p. 252. Cf. Limborch, *Lib. sent. inquis. Tholos.*, Amsterdam 1692, *passim*.

860 "Negant post hanc vitam esse purgatorium." *Practica*, p. 247. "Dicunt non esse purgatorium." Dav. d' Augsb., ch. 5.

861 "Consequenter orationes et elemosinas ac missarum celebrationes et alia suffragia pietatis que fiunt a fidelibus pro defunctis, ipsi asserunt non prodesse." *Practica*, p. 247. Cf. *ibid.*, p. 246, 248, 252, et *Lib. Sent.*, p. 208 ; *Cons. Tarrac*,

p. 1,800; *Alanus.* ch. 12, p. 387—388 ; Wattenbach, *Ueber die Inquisition,* p. 57—59, 60—61.

862 " Non concedunt sanctos intercedere pro nobis, sive pro vivis vel defunctis." *Aktenstücke,* etc.

863 Montet, p. 91.

864 Homily on Herod and Herodias, quoted by Montet, *ibid.* Cf. the treatise on the *Tribulations.*

865 " Venerationem sanctorum dicunt esse ydolatriam." *Aktenstücke,* etc. Cf. Ochsenbein, *op. cit.,* p. 110; Preger, *Beiträge,* p. 246.

866 " Si pro nobis deberet orare, et alii sancti, quid tunc gaudii haberent ? " Wattenbach, *ibid.,* p. 55.

867 " Quia beata Maria nullam haberet potestatem, nec sancti." *Ibid.*

868 " Quia non averterent faciem suam a Deo et a facie sancte Trinitatis." *Ibid.,* p. 56.

869 Haupt, *Der wald. Ursprung,* p. 36.

870 "Ideo solum Deum invocaverit . . . In solo Deo figere fidem." *Ibid.* The passage from the Glosa Pater was corrected in this sense by the Waldenses. *L.c.*

871 *Nov. Sermon,* v., 10 et seq.

872 *Hist.* des Variations xi., 37.

873 *Nobla Leiczon,* v., 434—436.

874 Tocco, *op. cit.,* p. 139—150 ; K. Müller, *op. cit.,* p. 136—138.

875 Keller has strongly emphasized this point. *Die Reformation,* etc., p. 48 et seq. Cf. Dieckhoff, *op. cit.,* p. 189, and Zezschwitz, *Die Katechismen,* etc., p. 102, where we read : "For the Poor of Lyons the Sermon on the Mount possessed the importance of a Gospel."

876 *Nob. Leiczon,* v. 369—373.

877 " Dicunt quod homo non debet mentiri ; quod omnis qui mentitur occidit animam." *Practica,* p. 251 et *passim.* Cf. Alanus, ii., 15—17; Limborch, *Lib. Sent., passim* ; *Consult. Tarrac,* p. 1,797 ; Rén. Sacconi, *l.c.,* etc.

878 See, for instance, the Practica, vp. ii., 78. A distinction is drawn between sophisms "per verborem equivocationem, per conditionis adjectionem, per responsionis extorsionem, per admirationem, per translationem, etc." Cf. Dav. D'Augsb., ch. 42.

879 " Quia Deus prohibuit omne juramentum in Evangelio . . . . Et ista verba multum imprimunt credentibus suis." *Practica, ibid.,* ch. 6. Cf. *ibid.,* ch. 3, et iii. part, ch. 34, where we see that the Waldenses' rest upon the words of James v., 12.

880 " Si aliquis de credentibus ipsorum compellatur." *Ibid.*

881 Cf. Alanus, ch. 18—19; Limborch and Pierre de Valdis Cernaü, *passim,* and the *Consult. Tarrac.* de l'an 1242, etc.

882 " Pauperes Lombardi concordant . . . in juramento." R. Sacconi, *l.c.* " Dicunt illicitum esse omne juramentum, etiam de vero, et peccatum mortale. Sed tamen dispensant ut juret quis pro evadenda morte corporis vel ne alios prodat vel secretum revelet perfidie sue." Dav. of Augsb., ch. 5. Cf. Anon. of Passau, p. 547.

883 " Per hoc facile tunc poterant deprehendi et multi de medio auferri." Dav. of Augsb., ch. 18 et 31.

884 " Pro se vel alio a morte defendendo." *Ibid.,* ch. 18. Some accused persons think that they are allowed to swear, if it be a question of witnessing to the truth ; but this is deviation from the Waldensian usage. Wattenbach, *Ueber die Inquis.,* p. 63—65.

885 " Dicunt enim esse crimen inexpiabile et peccatum in Spiritum Sanctum prodere aliquem de secta sua perfectum." *Practica,* Vme partie, 3. Cf. Dav. d'Augsb., ch. 5.

886 " Hereticos deprehendere vel convincere modo est valde difficile, ut quasi desperent." Dav. d'Augsb., ch. 28.

887 " Exceptis valde raris, qui pertinacius errores suos aperte confitentur, qui eciam perfecti apud eos reputantur et pro magistris reputantur vel habentur." *Ibid.,* ch. 31.

888 " Sine expositione debita." *Practica, l.c.,* Cf. Alanus, ch. 20—23, and the other sources indicated by us.

889 " Concordant cum primis . . . in justitia sœculari." R. Sacconi.

890 " Dicunt non licere occidere maleficos per judicium seculare." Dav. d'Augsb., ch. 5. Cf. Anon. de Passau, ap. Flacius, *Catal. test. verit.,* 1597, p. 547.

891 " Quidam quadam supersticione asserunt, quod eciam animalia et bruta non liceat occidere, ut pisces, oves et huiusmodi. Cum autem volunt talia man-

ducare, suspendunt ea super ignem in fumum, donec per se moriantur. Pulices eciam et huiusmodi animalia excuciunt contra ignem vel vestem ipsam intingunt in aqua calida, et tunc nolunt ea occidisse, sed dicunt ea per se mortua esse." Dav. d'Augsb., *ibid.*

892 "Dampnant et reprobant imperatores, reges et principes, marchiones, lantgravois, duces, barones, justiciarios juratos, judices et scabinos propter quodcunque homicidium qnamcunque judicialiter et juste factum." P. Célestin, ap. Preger, *Beiträge*, etc., n. 72. Cf. Anon. de Passau, *l.c.*, et Wattenbach, *op. cit.*, p. 65.

893 *Index errorum*, n. 8, ap. *Max. Bibl. Patr.*, xxv., p. 308.

894 It may be said that the resistance of the Waldenses in times of persecution does not go to prove this horror. We answer that the deeds of those who were only termed the faithful, must not be attributed to the early and properly called Waldenses, in addition to which, while theory may be easy, practice is difficult. As for criticism, not only is it easy, but odious in this case, especially on the part of Catholics.

895 "Ipsi inter se vocant se Fratres seu Pauperes Christi." *Practica, l.c.*, n. 9.

896 Matt. v., 6. "Vocant autem se pauperes spiritu, propter quod Dominus dicit: Beati pauperes spiritu." *Anecdotes*, etc., n. 342. Cf. *ibid.*, n. 330.

897 More correctly *Valdésiens*.

898 See above, note 57. It is to legend we owe the idea of deriving "Waldenses, a valido mago, vel a valle," and the name of "Petrus a Valle."

899 St. de Borb., who procured information in Lyons itself, writes: "Dicuntur Valdenses a suo heresiarcha." *Op. cit.*, n. 330. Map, who examined the Waldensian deputation at Rome, says: "Waldesü a primate ipsorum Valde dicti." *De nugis curialium, l.c.* Alanus, Gui, Valdis-Cernaü, etc., testify to the same thing.

900 See especially the *Rescript* of the Poor of Lombardy.

901 In the letter of the Waldenses of Provence to the Protestants of Germany, of the year 1535, we read: "Valdenses olim invidiose nominati." Schmidt *Aktenstücke, l.c.*

902 *Histoire*, etc., ch. ii. Perrin had enunciated the same opinion. He says: "Waldo commenced teaching the people, who were afterwards called by his name." And on the subject of those of the Alps, who had fled from Lyons, he adds: "Who from Waldo, were called Waldenses."

903 Dieckhoff had noticed that; he had even partly proved it. But to Professor Müller belongs the honour of setting it forth clearly in the aforesaid book, p. 11 et seq.

904 Müller asserts that the name of Waldenses does not, any more than that of the Poor of Lyons or of Lombardy, designate in the primitive literature of the Inquisition, dissenting communities, or their faithful members, but merely the preachers. He quotes in support of this the testimony of Bernard de Fontiscaldis, Alain de l'Isle Ebrard of Bethune, Peter of Valdis-Cernaü, Peter of Tarragona, the *Doctrina de modo procedendi*, Bernard Gui, and the *Liber Sentent-Inquis. Tholos.*, ap. Limborch v. *op. cit.*, p. 12—15. The German Inquisitors would still make the same distinction, according to Müller; they were, however, the first to extend those appellations to the adherents of the "sect." M. Préger is not of this opinion. He has shown that the above distinction has been at the least exaggerated. See *Ueber das Verhältuiss*, etc., p. 57 et seq.

905 See *passim*, the authorities quoted. It was also called the "Family."

906 "Perfecti enim inter eos . . . ; imperfecti vero . . ." Inq. anon of Passau, *l.c.*, p. 266. Concerning the désignation "credentes," see St. de Borbone, *l.c.*, p. 294; the *Practica*, iii. part. n. 34; v. part, ii., 5 et 9, and elsewhere.

907 "Ex tunc debent servare castitatem et non habere proprium, et vivere de elemosinis." *Practica*, Vme partie, ii., 5.

908 "Dedit pecuniam . . . Pluries vendidit bladum in foro quod datum erat Valdensibus et reddidit eis pecuniam." *Lib. sent. inquis. Tholos.*, p. 224, 233. Cf. *ibid.*, p. 232; Dav. d'Augsb., ch. 7, et Wattenbach, *Ueber die Inquis.*, *passim.*

909 "Legavit in infirmitate, de qua decessit, clamidem suam Mandine Valdensi et viginti solidos societati pauperum de Lugduno." *Form. inquis. Carcass.*, n. 14.

910 "Ambulant inquiete nil operantes," dit Bern. de Fontcaude. "Non laborant manibus suis postquam sunt facti perfecti, nec faciunt aliquod opus ad lucrandum." *Practica, l.c.* Cf. Alanus, ch. 24; Ebrard de Béthume, ch. 25.

911 "Nisi forsitan in casu ad dissimulandum." *Practica, l.c.*

912 *Rescriptum her. Lombard.*, n. 6 et 7, quoted above in ch. iii.

913 "Comedunt panem otiosum, nil operantes; nos vero manibus opera-mus," say they, according to the Inquisitor of Passau, who observes that such is their principle : "Omnem clerum damnant propter otium dicentes eos manibus debere operari sicut apostoli fecerunt." *Bibl. Max. Patr.*

914 1 Cor. ix., 4 ; 2 Thess. iii., 7.

915 Müller observes that at the end of the XIV. and the beginning of the XV. century, the abstaining from work is considered by the Waldenses of Germany as an advance. *Op. cit.*, p. 125. Cf. Röhrich *op. cit.*, p. 42 and 51, and Krone, *Fra Dolcino*, p. 201, on the subject of the "Regulœ Valdensium."

916 Dicunt quod uxor a viro recedere eo invito et e contrario, et sequi eorum societatem vel vicim continencie." St. of Borbone, *ibid.*, n. 342. Cf. *Mart, and Durand*, v., 1754 et seq,, and *Aktenstücke.*

917 "Non salvatur nisi per voluntatem utriusque, nisi occasio justa inter-venerit secundum quod communi videbitur." *Rescriptum*, n. 12.

918 "Credimus legitime coniugatos nisi ob fornicacionis causam aut utri-usque consensum neminem debere separare et hoc obsecramus fratres ultramon-tanos credere et fateri." *Ibid.*, n. 9.

919 "Nec coniuges (habere), quas, si antea habuerunt, relinquunt." Dav. of Augsb., ch. 7.

920 It is to these regular sisters, we believe, the following words of Alanus refer : "Mulierculas secum ducunt et eas in conventu fidelium prædicare faciunt." Cf. *Aktenstücke.*

921 Thus might, perhaps, be explained the following declaration related by the Inq. of Passau "Sed unusquisque nostrem uxorem suam habet."

922 See the superabundant indication of confirmatory testimony, ap. Müller, *op. cit.*, p. 73, n. 3.

923 "Magister eorum," says St. of Borbone.

924 "Sciendum quod dixerunt quod Valdesius ordinem habuit ab universi-tate fratrum suorum." Moneta, *Adv.* Cath. et Vald., p. 403. Thomas, the Lombard, admits the fact, since he strives to justify it, in opposition to the Romish Church. In fact, he says : "quilibet de illa congregatione potuit dare Valdesio jus suum sc. regere seipsum et sic tota congregatio illa potiut conferre et contulit Valdesio regimen omnium, et sie creaverunt illum omnium pontifi-cem et prœlatum." Moneta replies to this, that if this reasoning justifies the office of Rector, it does not legitimatize that of Priest, which office Waldo could not have received in that manner, from a Catholic point of view. Dieckhoff did not recognize in Waldo the priestly office, and Preger was the first to point out this error. *Beiträge*, p. 19—21.

925 "Se nolle aliquem in societate ultramontanorum aut ytalicorum fratrum fore prepositum in vita sua nec post mortem." *Rescriptum*, n. 4. The reader will remember that the Lombards had their "prepositus" for life, called Oto de Ramezello, who signed himself : "Dei gratia confrater pauperum spiritu."

926 *Rescriptum*, n. 15. Cf. Müller, *op. cit.*, p. 33.

927 "Qui ambo," we read concerning them, "tunc temporis accionem ultra-montanorum annualem *juxta suam consuetudinem* procurabant." *Ibid.*

928 An accused Waldensian declares : "quod in Ecclesia non sunt nisi tres Ordines ; episcopalis, sacerdotalis et diaconalis." *Lib. sent.*, p. 290. Cf. *ibid.*, p. 289, 291, etc. Moneta writes : "Ordinem ecclesiasticum ipsi ad minus tripli-cem *confitentur*, scil. Episcopatum, Presbyteratum et Diaconatum, sine quo triplici Ordine Ecclesia Dei non potest esse, nec debet, *ut ipsi testantur.*" *Op. cit.*, 1, v., ch. i. "Peregrinantur," says the Inq. of Passau, "et ita Lombardium intrantes visitant Episcopos suos." We shall see further on that Bishops were not recognized by the Waldenses of the Alps.

929 "Ad cujus potestatem pertinere dicunt sacramenta penitentie et ordinis et eucharistie ministrare, nen con Evangelium ubicumque voluerit predicare, et potestatem predicandi Evangelium et confessiones audiendi presbiteris dare." Bern. Gui, *Practica*, iii. p., ii., ch. 35, entitled : *Ordines quos dicunt Valdenses esse in sua ecclesia, scilicet episcopi, presbyteri et dyachoni.*

930 "Licet communiter hoc non fiat." *Ibid.*

931 "Ad potestatem presbiteri pertinet confessiones peccatorum audire, non tamen potest penas peccatorum remittere, nec potest celebrare." *Ibid.*

932 "Taliter ordinatus dyachonus efficitur de eorum statu cum voto quod facit paupertatis, castitatis et odedientie ; nec ante receptionem dicti ordinis aliquis est perfectus in eorum statu." *Ibid.*

933 "Alii qui non sunt ordinati vocantur credentes et amici eorum, a quibus etiam recipiunt sustentationem." *Ibid.*

934  " Ad dyachonum pertinet ministrare tam majori quam presbiteris necessaria corporis." *Ibid.*

935  Non tamen habet potestatem audiendi confessiones." *Ibid.*

936  Thus says Müller, *op cit.*, p. 86—88.

937  " Major omnium," says Gui.  He mentions him also as " majorem seu majoralem."  Do these two titles indicate the same office, or is that *seu*, which means *or*, used there in the sense of *and*, according to a frequent custom in the Middle Ages?  Cf. *Lib. sent. ing. Tholos* p. 346 and 377, where mention is made of a certain Crispinus " qui erat major inter eos."

938  This point will be brought out by what we shall have to say further on about ordination.  Gui supposes that the participation in this ordination by other " majores " was possible, and he says that the Presbyter was allowed to lay hands on him only in case of the absence or decease of colleagues " majores." Hence " major " and  Bishop are interchangeable titles.  But is the " major " necessarily " majoralis ?"  We are inclined to think not, and that " majoralis " is equivalent to " major omnium."

939  Such is the opinion of  Müller, which we think he justifies very clearly. *Ibid., l.c.*

940  " Valdenses habent et constituunt sibi unum superiorem super se, quem vocant Majoralem suum, cui omnes tenentur obedire sicut omnes catholici sunt sub obedientia domini Pape." *Practica*, v. partie, ii., 5.  Cf. *Lib. sentent,* etc., p. 291.

941  " Singulis annis tenent aut celebrant unum vel duo capitula generalia in aliqua sollempni villa occulte quantum possunt, convenientes in aliqua domo conductam per aliquem vel aliquos de credentibus diu ante." *Practica, l.c.* The same instinct is to be found also in all dissenting bodies.  These words correspond, for instance, in a striking manner with what the Venice Inquisition teaches us concerning an Anabaptist reunion, held in that city, in 1550.  See *Riv. Cristiana,* 1885, January and March.

942  For instance, in the case mentioned above, Müller is not of that opinion.  He believes the idea of admitting the presence of laymen to the Chapter held in the Valleys in the XIV. century, to be absolutely erroneous, *op. cit.*, p. 89.  But is it proved that the rule does not admit the faithful?  We doubt this somewhat.  See ante, n. 767.  According to our interpretation, the number mentioned, either by John XXII. or the separated brothers John and Peter, is more easily explained.

943  " In illis capitulis major omnium ordinat et disponit de presbiteris et dyachonibus et de mittendis ad diversas partes et regiones ad credentes et amicos suos pro confessionibus audiendis et elemosinis colligendis, et audit et recepit rationem de collectis et de expensis factis." *Practica, l.c.*

944  See Dav. of Augsburg, ch. 9.

945  " Bini et bini circumeunt."  Map. *l.c.*  Cf. Wattenbach, *Ueber die Inq.,* p. 44.  They were the " major " and the " minor," the " senior " and the " junior " the " payre religios major " and the " menor," called also the " devant pausa," and the " menor pausa."  This " minor " or " junior " seems to have been a deacon.

946  *Practica,* v. part, ii. 5.  The *Benedicite* has already been mentioned in the *Consult. Avinion.,* 1235, and the *Tarracon,* 1242.  The custom was not adopted everywhere.  " They do not pronounce the blessing," confesses Anguilla Brechiller of Friburg in his interrogatory, March 23, 1429.  See Ochsenbein, *op. cit.*, p. 186.

947  " Facta predicatione, flexis genibus." *Practica, l.c.*

948  An accused person being asked " an cauticum ecclesiasticum crediderit magis valere quam simpliciter sub silenti celebrari," answers that he had learned " quod melius esset sub silencio fieri."  It is a question of the mass, but this avowal is none the less significant.  Another one declares to the judges that " melius secrete orare," and that " esse cantum sicut grimnitum porcorum ante portain."  A third confesses that he sang, in the Church, of course, but not to be observed.  A fourth says that he does not think singing glorifies God, and that it is preferable to serve him in the secret of one's heart.  Wattenbach, *op. cit.*, p. 31, 34, 62, 63.

949  " Unum Paternoster plus valeat quam decem campanarum sonitus, et plusquam Missa."  Inq. of Passau.

950  " Nullam aliam orationem dicunt tunc nec decent nec habent nisi orationem *Paternoster.*" *Practica, l.c.*

951  " Non orant aliud nisi Paternoster, non addendo Ave Maria vel symbolum." *Aktenstücke* de Schmidt.

952  Montet, p. 92.

953 " Nec aliquid reputant salutationem beate Marie Ave Maria." *Ibid.*

954 One of the accused avows that his Waldensian confessor directed him to recite the Lord's Prayer a hundred times, and not the Ave Maria ; adding, however, that the Ave is from the Gospel : "esse evangelium et non esse peccatum si diceret." Wattenbach, *Ueber die Inquis.*, p. 33.

955 The confessions of the two accused persons, are as follows : (1) " Quod dixerint sibi heresiarce, quod Avemaria scire deberet propter homines ; " (2) Jusserunt tamen ei scire Avemaria propter sacerdotes de hoc fortasse quesituros." *Ibid.*, p. 56.

956 " Plurimi eorum ignorant Ave Maria." *Index*, etc., ap. Bibl. M.P., p. 307. Witness this woman, who recites it thus : " Ave *Marge* gracia plene Domine *deken ey* benedictus Jhesus Cristus amen." Wattenbach, *ibid.*

957 " Nec symbolum apostolorum *Credo in Deum.*" *Practica, ibid.*, Cf. Inq. of Passau, ap. Fl. Illyr. who notes : " Id est negant Symbolum esse orationem." So true is it that they do not recite it, that Gui observes that in order to surprise them, one has only to ask them : Can you repeat *I believe in God ?* They will answer : "Nescio, quia nullus me docuit ita." According to Et de Borbone, or to the interpretation of him given by M. Müller, it is not the same in Alsace, any more than in the valleys of the Alps.

958 " Dicunt illa per Romanam Ecclesiam et non per Christum fuisse ordinata seu composita." *Ibid.* How shall we reconcile those words with the legend of the Creed, composed of 12 articles, each having an Apostle for its author ? Hahn gives it as Waldensian, because he found it in a so-called Waldensian writing, but of Catholic origin. *Op. cit.*, p. 605 - 611. Cf. with the *Articles de la Fe*, reproduced by Montet, *op. cit., Pieces* justificatives, n. 3.

959 " In illo plurimum gloriantur." *Ibid.*

960 "Non orant Psalmos ac orationes alias quantumcunque devotas." *Index*, etc.

961 "In orando non habent numerum determinatum, sed senior inter eos incipit orationem et facit eam vel prolixam vel brevem, secundum quod sibi videtur expedire." *Aktenstücke, l.c.* The author had just remarked that the Waldenses made use of no other than the Lord's Prayer. As a private penance, this prayer was repeated a great number of times, as we shall see.

962 " Prædicatio vel lectio." *Conc. Tarrac* of 1242. Cf., on this point, Montet, *Noble Leçon*, p. 18.

963 " Omnes scilicet viri et feminæ, parvi et magni, nocte et die, non cessant docere et discere. Operarius enim in die laborans, in nocte discit vel docet." Inq. of Passau.

964 "Apud nos vero," says a Waldensian hawker, "tam feminæ quam viri docent et discipulus septem dierum docet alium." *Ibid.*

965 Ochsenbein, *op. cit.*, p. 284,387, etc., and Röhrich, *op. cit.*, p. 40, 49, etc.

966 It is difficult to admit that this book they were anxious to be able, if need be, to conceal, contained the whole Bible ; although it may all have been translated in Germany at least. Indeed, the Inq. of Passau says : " Novum Testamentum et Vetus vulgariter trans tulerunt."

967 " Pro maiori parte sunt illiterati et scripturum lingua materna in corde retinentes et experimentes." *Aktenstücke*, etc.

968 "Habente Evangelia et Epistolas in vulgari communiter et etiam in latino, quia aliqui inter eos intelligunt, et aliqui sciunt legere, sed ea corde tenus didiscerunt." *Practica, ibid.*, ch. 6.

969 "Expositiones sanctorum respuunt, et tantum inhærent textui." Inq. of Passau.

970 " Quicquid prædicatur quod per textum Bibliæ non probatur, pro fabulis habent." *Ibid.*

971 *Consult. Avinion.*, 1235.

972 " Puellas parvulas docent verba evangelii et epistolas, ut a puericia consuescant." Dav. d'Augsb., ch. 15. Cf. ch. 5.

973 " Alter alteri ruminat . . . Ruminant aliis." St. de Bourbon, *op. cit.*, n. 349.

974 " Disce quotidie unum verbum." Inq. of Passau.

975 *Anecdotes*, etc., n. 349.

976 " Et plures alios, qui N. T. totum sciverunt perfecte." Inq. of Passau.

977 "Statim offerunt se promptos ad respondendum de fide sua." *Practica*, v., part ii, 5.

978 "Qui tria capitula continuata N. T. literaliter sciat corde." Inq. of Passau.

979 "Omnis gloriacio eorum est de singularitate, quod videntur sibi pre ceteris sċioli, quod aliqua evangeli verba vel epistolarum sciunt ċorde vulgariter

recitare. In hoc preferunt se nostris non solum laycis sed eciam literatis, stulti, non intelligentes quod sepe puer XII. annorum scolaris cencies plus scit quam magister hereticorum LX. annorum, dum iste sola illa scit, que usu corde affirmavit, illo vero per artem grammatice mille libros scit legere latine et ad literam intelligere quoquo modo." Dav. of Augsb., ch. 13.

980 See John, i., 11. "Pius jocus," says Flacius.

981 "Dicendo et allegando : Istud dicitur in Evangelio, vel in epistola, sancti Petri." *Practica, l.c.*

982 "Dicta Sanctorum nihil curant, nisi quantum pro secta eorum confortanda retinent : sed tantum Novum Testamentum ad literam observant." *Index,* etc.

983 We see, therefore, that the notion which attributes this maxim in its negative form to the Gospel, is not likely. It is not likely it was the work of people who committed the Scriptures to memory. So that it would seem that it is the Judge who displays his ignorance in this case. *Practica, l.c.*

984 "Dicunt et docent credentibus suis quod confiteantur sibi peccata sua et audiunt confessiones eorum." *Ibid.*

985 "Predicationem suam faciunt in domibus credentium suorum, aliquando in itinere, seu in via." *Ibid.*

986 *Op cit.,* p. 36.

987 "Matrimonium dicunt esse fornicacionem iuratam, nisi continenter vivant." Dav. of Augsb. ch. 5. "Mortaliter peccare conjuges, si absque spe prolis conveniant." Inq. of Passau. We must here note an isolated opinion : "Quod erraverit Ecclesia clericis matrimonium prohibendo, cum etiam orientalis concedat ut contrahant." *Ibid.*

988 "Confirmacionis sacramentam respuunt. Unctionem extremam respuunt et oleum consecratum et crisma nil valere plus quam aliud." Dav. of Ausgb., *ibid.* Cf. Inq. of Passau, *Ibid.* It was not the same at Friburg. See Ochsenbein *op. cit.* p. 187. According to Dav. of Augsb., *l.c.,* "magistri eorum imponunt manus discipulis vice illius sacramenti." The imposition of hands, therefore, occasionally took the place of confirmation. Another Inquisitor says the same thing, according to Preger, *Beiträge,* p. 69, n. 14.

989 This perfect momentary agreement between the Waldenses of France and those of Lombardy is noticed in the *Rescriptum.* It is there really a question concerning baptism "aque materialis." It is valid, not only if it be administered "per homines layeos et maliciosos," but also "per mulieres etiam meretrices." *Ibid.,* n. 8, 11, 17.

990 We see by the tone of the Lombard brethren, that they are preoccupied by it in their Rescript. "Dicimus quod nemo aque materialis baptismum respuens potest salvari, parvulos vero non baptizatos minime credimus salvari et hoc oramus eos credere et fateri." *Ibid.,* n. 8. There were, therefore, some Brethren who rejected this doctrine.

991 R. Sacconi, writing some years later, says : "Pauperes Lombardi . . . . dicunt quod infantes salvantur sine baptismo." Dav. of Augsburg, *l.c.,* adds : "Quidam dicunt baptismum non valere parvulis eo quod nondum—one reading gives *nunquam*—actualiter possint credere." We read again : "Quod ablutio, quæ datur infantibus, nihil prosit." Inq. of Passau. Cf. St. of Borbone, *op. cit.,* n. 343. This latter writer says, on the subject of the Cathari : "Dicunt baptismum parvulis non proficere ad salutem, qui nec motum nec actum habent fidei." *Ibid.,* n. 346.

992 See ante, p. 254.

993 "Certe non habetis. Auditis solum confessiones ; pro reliquis mittitis ad ecclesiam populum. Cum igitur ecclesia populis ministret et sacramenta et multa alia beneficia et vos tamen unum semisacramentum. . . ." *Cod. S. Flor., l.c.*

994 Ad. Franck, *Réformateurs et Publicistes,* 1864, p. 162.

995 "Sicut Apostoli laici erant." Inq. of Passau. Cf. Bern. of Fontis Caldis and Alanus.

996 Unordained laymen are distinct from the community. "Quidam dicuntur perfecti eorum, et hii proprie vocantur Pover de Leun." Dav. of Augsb., ch. 7. "Alii qui non sunt ordinati, vocantur credentes et amici eorum ;" but not "brethren." *Practica,* iii. p., 35.

997 "Sic, sine aliquia talia forma verborum . . . per solam orationem et manuum impositionem apud eos episcopus ordinatur." *Practica,* iii. part, ch. 1, intitulé : *Ordines quos dicunt Valdenses esse in sua ecclesia, scilicet episcop., presbyteri et dyachon.*

998 "Potest tamen ordinare majorem seu majoralem ipsorum." *Ibid.*

999 "Tam layci et ydiote, quam etiam litterati, dummodo probati prius

fuerint in dicta secta et electi postmodum, sicut superius est expressum." *Ibid.*
1000 "Prius per aliquod tempus examinant eum." *Aktenstücke.*
1001 "Nec omnes ad hanc formam assumuntur sed prius diù informantur, ut et alios sciant docere." Dav. of Augsb., ch. 7.
1002 "Quia alias nullus suscipitur nisi sit castus et ab omni consortio mulierum immunis, quoad opera carnalia." *Aktenstucke*, etc.
1003 "De aliis articulis nullam faciunt omnino mentionem." *Ibid.*
1004 "Vota vero que ab eo requiruntur sunt hec ; primo, ut promittat obedientiam Deo ; secundo castitatem . . . ; quarto, quod nullam habeat spem seu sustentationem manuum suarum, sed paupertatem voluntariam imitetur." *Ibid.* The third point relates to the oath, and the fifth to the relation with parents.
1005 "Non redimat vitam eorum, in captivitate constitutus, vel quocunque mortis periculo preventus, falso juramento vel aliquo peccata mortali . . . Quod non habeat maiorem confidentiam de consanguineis suis, quam de aliis hominibus ejusdem secte." *Ibid.*
1006 "Credunt quod a beato Clemente citra exclusive, nullus successit B. Petro apostolo aut Lino vel Clementi, qui haberet potestatem ligandi vel solvendi usque ad Don Valdense." See Martène and Durand, v., col. 1754.
1007 "Ponunt solum Deum a peccatis absolvere." Et. of Borbone. "Sacerdos non est nisi pronunciator. . . . Non valent indulgentiæ prælatorum. cum nullus peccatum possit dimittere, nisi solus Deus." *Index errorum.* Cf. *Lib. Sent., passim.*
1008 Ille cui fit confessio peccatorum, solummodo dat consilium, quod debeat homo facere, et injungit poenitentiam, et hoc potest facere homo sapiens et discretus, sive sit sacerdos, sive non." *Lib. sent., inq. Tholos.*, p. 290. Cf. *NoblaLeiczon*, v. 408—413, the *Barca*, etc., *passim.*
100 "Ipsi esiam ad ecclesiam ficte vadunt, offerunt et confitentur et communicant ficte." Anon. de Passau. ap. Flacius, p. 547. Cf. Dav. of Augsb., ch. 14 and 21.
1010 See Röhrich, *op. cit.*, p. 39, 53 et 68. However, all do not make this distinction between venial and mortal sins. "Dicunt quod omne peccatum sit mortale, et nullum veniale," notes the Inquisitor of Passau.
1011 "Non tenetur quis confiteri sacerdoti, si præsto sit laicus." Alanus, l. iii., ch. 9 et 10.
1012 "Bonus laicus potestatem habet absolvendi." Inq. of Passau.
1013 Wattenbach, *Ueber die Inq.*, p. 35, 36, 42, etc.
1014 From the age of 10 years. *Ibid.*, p. 36.
1015 Some of the accused expressed themselves thus : "Tenuerit eos pro confessoribus melius presbiteris potentibus dimittere sibi peccata . . . Sanctos homines, melius peccatoribus dimittere peccata presbiteris," etc. *Ibid.*, p. 30, 42.
1016 "Tanquam a pueritia . . . Sicut quando quis nascitur de ventre matris." *Ibid.*, p. 42, 44.
1017 "Si moriretur ipso anno, statim evolaret ad celum . . . Cui loqueretur semel in anno, non posset dampnari. *Ibid.*, 45, 43.
1018 "Non ordinatos presbiteros, nec missos ab ordinario . . . Habent potestatem a Deo . . . ab ore Dei." *Ibid.*, p. 42, 44.
1019 "De septennio ad septennium venirent ante paradisum ad audiendam sapientiam . . . Semel in anno venirent ad paradisum duo ex ipsis et reciperent ibi a Deo autoritatem melius presbiteris dimittendi peccata." *Ibid.*, p. 44.
1020 "Dicit ita : Deus te absolvat ab omnibus peccatis tuis, et ego injungo tibi contritionem de peccatis tuis usque ad mortem, et talem pœnitentiam faciendam." *Practica*, iii., p. 35.
1021 *Aktenstücke*, etc. This form is borrowed from an ancient German dialect.
1022 "Dicunt confessionem in morte facile abolendam, vel per manus imposicionem alicuius doctoris ipsorum." Dav. of Augsb., ch. 22. Cf. Anon of Passau, p. 545.
1023 Some cases of falling away are accounted for by the excessive rigour of the penances imposed. Ex. Wattenbach, *Ibid.*, p. 47.
1024 "Puta orationes, vel jejunia, vel utrum que," adds Gui, after quoting the formula of the Bishop's absolution. This expression corresponds exactly to the penances which we find in the trials.
1025 Wattenbach observes, that, as a rule, penitents were to repeat this prayer as often as 50 times on working days, and on Sundays about 100 times. *Ibid.*, p. 45. Cf. *Lib. sent., passim.*

1026 "Ne ceteris veniant in horrorem, quia dicunt quod carnes concedere quacumque die non est peccatum, quia Christus non prohibuit vesci carnibus nec precepit ab eis abstinere." *Practica*, v., p., ii., 5.

1027 "Quidam autem . . . affligunt se multum ieiuniis et vigiliis et huiusmodi." Dav. of Augsb., ch. 5. Cf. the words of Siegfried, ante, p. 255.

1028 "Quatuor dies in ebdomada, jejunant, videlicet 2, 4, 6 ferias et sabbatum, unum illorum dierum in pane et aqua, scilicet feriam sextam, nisi in itinere vel in alio gravi labore sive alia causa rationabili impediantur." *Aktenstücke.* Cf. Fl. Illyricus, p. 559.

1029 "Jejunandum in pane et aqua." Wattenbach, *Ibid.*, p. 46.

1030 "In pane et cervisia . . . In pane et tenui cervisia." *Ibid.*

1031 "Supra celarium in camera." *Ibid.*, p. 49, 42. Penitents frequently did not know the names of the confessors. *Ibid.*, p. 41.

1032 "Quod concessum est cuilibet homini sine peccato mortali consecrare illud." R. Sacconi. "Quidam dicunt tantum per bonos fieri, alii autem per omnes qui verba consecracionis sciunt." Dav. of Augs., ch. 5. "Quod bonus laicus, etiam mulier, si sciat verba conficiat." Anon. of Passau, ap. Fl. Illyr., p. 545.

1033 "Quod sacerdos in mortali peccato non possit conficere." Anon. of Passau, *l.c.* In France there is this expression, taken from *Consult. Tarracon.*, *l.c.*, p. 1800 : "Quod in sacramento altaris panis et vinum postquam consecratum est, non efficitur corpus et sanguis Christi, si sacerdos sit peccator, et quemlibet reputant peccatorem, nisi sit de secta eorum." These words are repeated in *Practica*, v. ii., 3.

1034 See what we said on the subject of the Ortlieber in ch. 3, p. 83, and cf. St. of Borbone, *op. cit.*, n. 343.

1035 "Corpus Christi et sanguinem non credunt vere esse, sed panem tantum benedictum, qui in figura quadam dicitur corpus Christi, sicut dicitur ; Petra autem erat Christus, et simile." Dav. of Augsb., ch. 5. Cf. Haupt, *Der Wald. Ursprung*, p. 36, n. 8.

1036 "Sicut in cena Christi." Dav. of Augs.. *ibid.* "Conficiunt in vulgari et dant sacramenta." Anon. of Passau, p. 546.

1037 "Conficiunt in picario, *i.e.*, poculo domestico, pro calice." Anon. of Passau, p. 547.

1038 "Ille qui præest inter eos, si est sacerdos, convocat omnes de sua familia," that is to say of the community, thinks Müller. See appendix to the *Disp. inter cathol. et pater*, hæreticum, ap. Mart. and Durand. *Thes. nov. anecdot.*, vol. 5, 1754; Gui reproduces this excerpt but with some variations. *Practica*, v. p., ii., 4.

1039 "Unum bonum scyphum de bono vino puro et unam fugaciam azimam." *Ibid.*

1040 "Credunt firmiter et confitentur quod istud est corpus et sanguis Domini nostri Jesu Christi." *Ibid.*

1041 "Nisi panem benedictum et vinum." *Ibid.*

1042 "Omnes Pauperes utrius que sectæ eumdem modum consecraudi tenebant, scilicet prœdictam ante divisionem quœ fuit inter eos." *Ibid.*

1043 Müller, *op. cit.*, p. 82. These details are gathered partly from the *Summa* of R. Sacconi ; partly from the *Disputatio inter Catholicum et Patarinum hœreticum ;* finally, from the *Doctrina de modo procedendi contra hœreticos.*

1044 "Dicunt quod malus sacerdos non potest conficere." Along with this, the predominating principle, diversities of opinion are to be found ; thus : "Quilibet potest absolvere, conficere et ligare, dummodo sciat verba." *Aktenstücke, l.c.* Again : "De corpore vero Domini sentiunt (Pauperes Lombardi) etenim pejus quam primi (Pauperes Ultramontani) dicentes quod concessum est cuilibet homini sine peccato mortali consecrare illud." *Reg. Vald.*, ap. Krone, p. 202. Cf. Ren. Sacconi. This right appears to have been recognised, even in women. "Bonus laicus, etiam mulier, conficiat." Inq. of Passau, ap. Flacius. Et. de Bourbon says : "Quidam . . . dicentes quod ordo requirit sexum virilem : alii non faciunt differenciam . . . Vidi hereticam que super arcam ad modum altaris paratam consecrare. . . ." *Op. cit.*, n. 343.

1045 "Sibi mutuo partecipantes." Dav. of Augsb., ch. 5.

1046 "Quo facto, tam asserem quam cochlear in ingem projicit comburenda." *Index*, etc.

1047 "Plurimi tamen magistrorum suorum abhorrent hoc . . Abscondentes se . . . paschali tempore, ne a Christianis agnoscantur." *Index*, etc.

1049 Müller has collected the following : "Credentes qui comederunt anpem et *picem* in die cene juxta maledictum morem suum a Valdensibus benedictum, cum firmiter existiment ipsi consiliarii quod Valdenses tunc credunt conficere corpus Christi." What is this *picem ?* Perhaps a derivative of *picari-um* or of *piceum*, the cup. V. *Consult. Avinion.* 1235. Cf. Ducange on this expression. " Si cum eis (that is to say, with the Cathari and the Waldenses) comedit aut bibit vel de pane benedicto ab eis accepit." *Consult. Tarrac*, 1242. " Si pacem ab hæreticis vel Valdensibus vel panem ab eis benedictum a quocun-que sibi missum vel datum scienter et dampnabiliter receperunt." *Consult Nar-bon*, 1243. " Accepisse pacem a mulieribus valdensibus, comedisse eciam de pane in cena domini ab ipsis Valdensibus benedicto . . . Et multociens pacem ab eis accepit et comedit de pane et *pisce* benedicto a Valdensibus in die cene." *Form Inq. Carcass, n.* 8.

1050  Schmidt, *Hist. des Cathares*, ii., 130, 131.

1051  If Müller had examined attentively, would he not have found that the origin of this rite is, after all, less mysterious than he thinks.

1052  " Quando audiunt confessiones, dicunt confitentibus quod quando con-fitebantur sacerdotis non dicant nec revelent eis quod confessi fuerunt ipsis Valdensibus." Again : " Si confitebantur peccata sua semel in quadragesima vel ante pascha proprio sacerdoti." *Practica*, v. part, ii., 6 et 9. This does not pre-vent us from comprehending that believers neglected to confess to the Priests of the Church. *Lib. sent.*, etc., p. 241 and *passim.*

1053  " Eatis ad ecclesiam, solvite decimas et jura sua clericis." *Consult. Tarracon*, an. 1242.

1054  See the quotations mentioned by Müller, *op. cit.*, p. 95, n. 1.

1055  " Non esse subjectos domino pape . . . nec aliis prelatis Romane Ecclesie." *Practica, ibid.*, chap. 3.

1056  " Asseverant se non posse excommunicari ab eisdem romano pontifice et prelatis." *Ibid.*

1057  " Sanctiones canonicas decretalesque constitutiones summorum pontifi-cum et statuta de jejuniis et de festis colendis ac decreta Patrum predicta secta devians a via et recta semita non recepit nec valere reputat, sed spernit et respuit et condempnat." *Ibid.*

1058  " Melius esset vobis quod essetis custos porcorum quam quod celebratis missam, quia estis in peccato mortali." So says Crispin to a Priest. *Lib. sent.*, p. 253.

1059  " Ecclesia malignantium et bestia et meretrix quæ leguntur in Apoca-lypsi." Ren. Sacconi. Cf. Anon. of Passau, ap. Fl. Illyr., p. 544, and Dav. of Augs., ch. 5.

1060  " Omnes obedientes dampnari." Dav. d'Augsb., *ibid.*

1061  " Quod ipsi sint Ecclesia Jesu Christi . . . Ipsi soli juste vivant." Anon of Passau, *l.c.* " Se solos esse Christi Ecclesiam et Christi discipulos affirmabant." Dav. of Augsb., *l.c.*, Cf. *Index*, etc. " Dividunt unitatem Ecclesie credentes et dicentes hominem virtuose viventem solum in sua fide salvandum." *Aktenstücke, l.c.* Keller interprets this passage arbitrarily, for the purpose of attri-buting to the Waldenses the doctrine of salvation by faith alone. *Die. Ref.*, p. 249.

1062  " Haec omnia dicunt agi propter quæstum." Inq. of Passau.

1063  " Velle etiam potius sepeliri in campo quam in cœmeterio, si Ecclesiam non timerent." *Ibid.* Cf. *Index*, etc.

1064  " Ornatum Ecclesiæ dicunt esse peccatum, et quod melius esset vestire pauperes, quam ornare parietes." Inq. of Passau.

1065  "Universitates scholarum . . . reputant inutiles et temporis per-ditionem." *Index*, etc.

1066  " Omnen clerum damnant propter otium, dicentes eos debere manibus operari." *Ibid.*

1067  " Quod omnes observantiæ religiosorum sint traditiones Pharisæorum. Quod traditio Ecclesiæ sit traditio Pharisæorum." Inq. of Passau.

1068  " Hoc vocant decem precepta." *Ibid.*

1069  " Quod nemo cogendus sit ad fidem." *Ibid.*

1070  " Sicut nos non posse vivificare, sic non debere occidere." *Index*, etc.

1071  " Quod omne peccatum sit mortale." Inq. de Passau.

1072  "Quod missa nihil sit, quia Apostoli eam non habebant." *Ibid.*

1073  "Nisi tantum verba Christi vulgariter," *i.e.*, the sacramental words. *Ibid.* Cf. *Index*, etc.

1074  " Ecclesiam vocant *Steinhauss* vel *Strohhauss* . . . Ecclesiam muratam reputant ut horreum . . . nec Deum ibi habitare autumant " (See Acts xvii., 24).

1075  " Quod terra et populus non sit per Parochias dividendus . . . Quod omnia jura parochialia sint tantum ad inventiones." *Ibid.*

1076   Quod doctrina Christi, sive Apostolorum, sine statutis Ecclesiæ sufficiat ad salutem." *Ibid.*

1077   " Omnes consuetudines Ecclesiæ approbatas, quas in Evangelio non legunt, contemnunt." *Ibid.*

1078   " Omnia Statuta Ecclesie post ascensionem Christi dicunt non esse servanda nec alicuius esse valoris." Dav. of Augsb., ch. 5.   This principle is a radical one, but still Waldensian.   Cf. among other sources upon the polemics, the 92 articles enumerated by the Inquisitor Peter ap. Preger. *Beiträge,* p. 68.

1079   This detail, which is true of the Waldenses of Germany, would not, generally speaking, have been so of the Waldenses of France.   The rest is susceptible of a general application.

1080   " Casti etiam sunt, maxime Leonistæ."   *Max. Bibl. Patr.,* xxv., col. 272.   This reading is doubtless more correct than that of Fl. Illyricus, who says : " Casti etiam sunt Leonistæ."   *Catal.,* p. 658, 659.

1081   " Semper operantur, discunt et docent, et ideo parum orant." *Ibid.* We read also, in the same volume, col. 263 : " Operarius enim in die laborans, in nocte discit vel dicet : et ideo parum orant propter studium."   Instead of " semper operantur."   Fl. Illyricus says : " Si autem operantur vel discunt vel docent," etc.

1082   " Ut capiant in sermone." *Ibid.*

1083   " Cognoscuntur etiam in verbis præcisis et modesta." *Ibid.*   In lieu of these words, Fl. Illyricus reads as follows : " Consimiliter et mulieres eorum sunt modestæ."

1084   " Nec dicunt *verè* vel *certè,* et similia : quia hæc reputant juramenta:" *Ibid.*

1085   " Stinserunt lumina dicendo : Quilibet faciat pro quo est ibi quis habebit tenrat."   See the trials of the year 1387, inserted in the *Arch. St.* Italia, anno 1865, and examined in the *Revista Cristiana,* 1876, p. 169 and 217 ; the trial of Philip Regis in the same Review, 1881, p. 363 ; that of Barbe Martin, reproduced by Morland and Allix, and which we shall analyse further on ; moreover, vide ante and Rorengo, *Mem. Hist.,* ch. 2, and Léger, b. i., p. 182. etc.

1086   Gaston Boissier, from whom these words are borrowed, adds : " Five centuries before, the fanatics assembled for celebrating the Bacchanalian feasts, had been reproached with the same crime." *Rev. d. D.M.,* 15th April, 1876.   The origin of the calumny is, therefore, Pagan.

1087   See Mùnitius Felix, *Octave,* ch. 8 ; Athenagoras *Leg.,* ch. 3 ; Tertullian, *Apol.,* ch. 2 and 7, etc.

1088   " Aliquando faciunt extingui lumen, si sit ibi, propter hoc, ut dicitur, ut non videantur vel deprehendantur ab extraneis seu exterioribus non consentientibus in facto eorum." *Practica,* v., p. ii., 5.

1089   " In nocte maxime perterrebatur," confesses a woman, " propter ablacionem luminis in commodo ubi sedebat."   Wattenbach, *Ueber die Inq.,* p. 40.

1090   " Dicitur," says Gui, in recording the circumstance we have just mentioned.   Elsewhere, he shows clearly that he has not rejected the calumny.

1091   Thus do we account for the depositions of Galosna and Bech in the *Processus contra Valdenses,* ap. *Arch., St. It.*   The first recants.   The second contradicts himself in two ways : first in his testimony itself, and then where he states that the heretics, of whom he speaks " nunquam tangent mulierem, et mulier unquam virum nec aliam personam quamcunque."   Moreover, the heretics there called Waldenses are principally Cathari.

1092   " Quod autem ut dicitur . . . extinctis lucernis pariter fornicentur, non puto istius esse sectæ, nec aliquod horum veraciter, intellexi ab illis, quibus fidem adhiberem."   Dav. of Augsb., ch. 10.   This was said of the Cathari : " Cathari dicuntur hoc facere."   Cf. *Ibid.,* ch. 5.   The same is repeated in the Practica, v., part ii., 5.

1093   See the observations of G. Amati upon the above noted trials, in the *Arch. St. Ital.,* and what the procurator Pagano of Cosenza stated not long ago, in speaking of the sect of the Saints of Calabria. *Tribuna,* 12 January, 1887.

1094   " Magnam habent speciem pietatis, eo quod coram hominibus juste vivant."   Inq. of Passau, *ibid.,* p. 264.   " Speciem sanctitatis et fidei pretendentes."   Et of Borbone, n. 342.

1095   " Could greater praise be given to the Waldenses, from the mouth of one of the Inquisitors who was persecuting them ?" exclaims Haupt, *Die relig. Sekten,* p. 25.

1096   " Laneis inductis," says Map.

1097   See above on the subject of the Poor Catholics, p. 71 and 73.

1098 " Sandaliis desuper perforatis." Innocent III., Epist. xii., *l.c.*
1099 "Insabbatati dicti sunt, quia . . . speciale signum in modum quasi scuti in parte superiori cotularium deferebant, in quo signo ab aliis suis complicibus et credentibus differebant." *Practica*, v. part, ii., 2.
1100 " Eb. de Bethune, *Contra Valdenses*, ch. 25, ap. *Bib. M. Patr.*, xxiv., p. 1572. C. P. Valdis Cernaii, ap. Duchesne, Hist. Franc. SS. v., 557, or Bouquet, Recueil, vol. xix., 6.
1101 " In domo tua te presente in loco multo suspecto plures latentes heretici cum libris et sandaliis et varia supellectilia sunt invecti." *Form. inq. Carcass.*, n. 8. This is how a presbyter, who came from Dauphiny to Avigliano is described a century later : " Niger, cum quadam oppellanda de panno bruno et uno mantello de blaveto scuro." *Processus*, ap. *Arch. St. It.*, n. 39, p. 8.
1102 " Vadunt autem in diversis habitibus vestium . . . ne agnoscantur, et cum transeunt quandoque de domo forte in domum, aliquod onus deferunt palee vel vasis, et in obscuro vadunt, ne quis perpendat quid agant." Dav. of Augsb., ch. 8. Cf. ch. 17.
1103 " Aliquando quidam maximus inter eos fuit captus, qui secum ferebat multorum artificiorum indicia, in que quasi Proteus se transfigurabat." St. of Borbone, *op. cit.*, p. 293.
1104 "Si quereretur in una similitudine, et ei innotesceret, in alia se transmutabat. Aliquando ferebat habitum et signacula pegrini, aliquando bacculum penitenciarii et ferramenta : aliquando se fingebat sutorem, aliquando barbitonsorem, aliquando messorem." *Ibid.* Cf. *ibid.*, p. 280.
1105 We take this description from its source, namely, the writings of the Inquisitor of Passau, *Max. Bibl. Patr.*, xxv., col. 273.
1106 " Habeo pretiosiores gemmas."
1107 " Tantum rutilat, quod amorem Dei ascendit in corde habentis eam."
1108 Luke i., 26 ; John xiii., 1.
1109 Matth. xxiii., 2, 13 ; Mark xii., 38—40.
1110 " De clericis et religiosis."
1111 " Rabbinos vero tales non quærimus."
1112 Already quoted, note 921. We should be inclined to conclude from this statement that there is here no question of ministers. But it is well to bear in mind that this took place in the centre, where universal priesthood was most marked, and where they condemned the enforced celibacy even of the Priests. See ante, note 987.
1113 Cf. the following passages. Luke vi., 24 ; Matth. xxiii., 14 ; Rev. xiii., 10 ; and Luke xi., 52.
1114 " Quia veram fidem Christi habemus, et sanctam vitam et doctrinam docemus omnes nos, ideo . . ." etc.
1115 " Nos vero omnia facimus quæ docemus."
1116 "Nos vero tantum doctrinam Christi servare suademus et Apostolorum."
1117 " Per manus impositionem omnia peccata relaxamus."
1118 " Eligite eam."
1119 See *Echo des Vallées*, 1st year, n. 7.
1120 That was the idea on which is founded the graceful poem of the late Professor G. A. de Félice, entitled, *Le Colporteur Vaudois.*
1128 "Audivi ab ore credentis cujusdam, quod quidam hæreticus, quem novi, ad hoc tantüm, ut cum a fide nostra averteret, et ad suam perduceret perverteretque, nocte hyemali tempore per aquam, quæ dicitur Ibsa (Fl. Ill. dit : *Ibis*) natavit ad ipsum." The astounded Inquisitor here exclaims : " Erubescat negligentia fidelium Doctorum . . . Observa fervorem in docendo et discendo." Inq. of Passau.
1122 " Hoc tu Valdensis hæretice non facis ; non vadis ad mundum, non prædicas peccatoribus magnis . . . sed solos illos attrahis, quos audisse esse pacificos, quietos, silentiosos, compositos." *Contra Vald.*, ap. *Bibl. M. Patr.*, p. 277-299, ch. 10, et 11.
1123 " Non possum esse talis lucerna publica propter instantes persecutiones, quia vocant me hœreticum." *Ibid.*, ch. 13.
1124 Seven, twelve, or twenty persons, according to Wattenbach, *ibid.*, p. 49.
1125 " In locis occultis docent et discunt, nec aliquem admittunt, qui non sunt fidei eorum. Cum in unam conveniunt, primo dicunt : *Caveto ne inter vos sit curvum lignum*, id est, ne aliquis extraneus adsit, et suam doctrinam prœcipiunt occultare clericis." Inq. of Passau. This figurative expression was doubtless agreed upon, and, moreover, it may have implied that they had but little hope of "depriving the lion of his talons."
1126 In Piedmont the conventional sign consisted in the men touching the

little finger, saying : " Welcome." The woman touched two fingers : " De more ipsorum est quod mulieres tangunt duos digitos et homines digitum auricularem ad cognoscendos se ipsos hereticos intra se." *Processus,* ap. *Arch. St. It.,* n. 39, p. 6, 7, 32.

1127 " Quod haberent potestatem a Deo predicandi hominibus, sed non omnibus." Wattenbach, *ibid.,* p. 44.

1128 The Inquisitor of Passau says, concerning the preaching of the Waldenses in Lombardy, Provence, and other places, that crowds gathered to hear them, " et in publico disputabant, et populum vocabant ad stationes solennes in foro, et in campo, et prædicabant in tectis." Ap. Fl. Illyr., p. 642.

1129 " Templum Dei late patere, orbem terrarum illud esse ; coarctare ejus potentiam qui templa, monasteria, sacella construunt, tanquam divina bonitas magis favens et magis propitia in illis sit."

1130 " Hæc sunt Pauperum de Lugduno opiniones et deliramenta. Nec jam satis habebant in conciliabulis communicare, sed propalam prædicare atque adstruere audebant." *Op. cit.*

1131 Here are three pieces which refer to it : 1. *Scriptum Inq. cujusp. anon.* 2. *Proc. Inq. contra Barbam Martinum.* 3. *Proc. Inq. contra Peyronettam.* They are reproduced by Morland and Allix, after the Cambridge MSS.

1132 " Tantum Purgantur viventes in præsenti." *Scriptum,* ap. Allix, p. 300. Cf. the trials, *ibid.,* p. 311, 323, 324.

1133 " Ad extorquendas pecunias pro missis et orationibus dicendis quæ de nihilo prosunt." *Ibid.,* p. 311.

1134 " Bona opera quæ fiunt ante mortem hominis plus prosunt quam omnia quæ fiunt post mortem." *Ibid.,* p. 323.

1135 *Ibid.,* p. 301, 309, 310, 322.

1136 *Ibid.,* 301, 310, 322, 323, 324. We read there that the Apostle Peter was worthy of credit, but not Paul : " S. Paulum vero non credunt quia fuit assassinus ! " Have we not here an indication of the influence of the Cathari ?

1137 " Ave Maria non est oratio sed annunciacio et salutatio, et ideo non injungunt in pœnitentiam eis qui sunt de eorum secta quod dicant Ave Maria, et quod Solus Pater Noster est vera oratio, quia a Deo facta fuit oratio illa." *Ibid.,* 310—311. Cf. p. 317.

1138 *Ibid.,* p. 324.

1139 " Festa quæ sunt praecepta a Deo, prout est Dies Dominicus, festum Nativitatis Domini, festum Paschæ, Ascensionis et Pentecostes, sunt celebranda." *Ibid.,* p. 311. Cf. p. 301.

1140 " De festivitatibus Sanctorum et Sanctarum per Romanam Ecclesiam introductis non est curandum, quod licitum est omni die opus servile exercere." *Ibid.,* p. 310. " Alia autem festa Virginis Marie et Sanctorum sunt festicula. et qui non vult, non tenetur illa celebrare, quia non sunt præcepta." *Ibid.,* 311.

1141 " Dies Dominicales Super omnia alia festa . . . solemniter coli, Alia vero festa dicebant fuisse per Ecclesiam inventa, quæ non erant de necessitate colenda, imo poterat aliquis operari in ipsis, exceptis festivitatis Apostolorum et aliis majoribus." *Ibid.,* p. 323. Cf. p. 309, where we read : " Credunt in S. Petrum, et post ipsum in S. Gregorium," etc.

1142 " Quia Deus est ubique." *Ibid.,* p. 300, 311, 324.

1143 " Domus confusionis, Babylon, meretrix et Synagoga Diaboli." *Ibid.,* p. 300.

1144 " Ecclesia malignantium." *Ibid.,* p. 299.

1145 *Ibid.,* p. 323.

1146 " Quantum quis habet sanctitatem, tantum habet facultatem et potestatem in Ecclesia." *Ibid.,* p. 299. Cf. p. 311.

1147 *Ibid.,* p. 300, 311, 323.

1148 " In die Ascensionis Domini." *Ibid.,* p. 311. Cf. p. 324.

1149 " Aquæ pluviales sunt ejusdem virtutis." *Ibid.,* p. 301.

1150 *Ibid.,* p. 300, 323, 324.

1151 " Summus pontifex, ex quo non observabat sanctitatem quam debebat observare, non habebat aliquam potestatem, dicendo de eodem in hæc verba : *Autant malvais est le Pape comme nengun autre.*" *Ibid.,* p. 323. Cf. p. 300.

1152 " A beato Silvestro non fuit verus Papa." *Ibid.,* p. 299.

1153 " Ipsi prædicatores sive magistri hujusmodi sectæ et sacerdotes seu viri ecclesiastici olim solebant esse unius et ejusdem legis et ordinis ; sed cum ipsi viri ecclesiastici voluerunt insequi avaritiam et vanitates hujus mundi, et ipsi prædicatores in ipsa paupertate manere voluerunt, ideo fuit facta inter eos divisio, et effecti fuerunt inimici." *Ibid.,* p. 324.

1154 " Cum numerus ipsorum prædicatorum et aliorum hominum justorum

**N**

qui hujusmodi sectam tenuerint adhuc esset parvus atque rarus, ideo eis erat necesse incedere occulte, sicut faciebant Christus et ejus Apostoli." *Ibid.*

1155 "In ipsis tantum sit Ecclesia Dei qui vivunt in paupertate." *Ibid.*, p. 299.

1156 "Credunt quod extra eorum sectam nemo salvatur, et qui sunt eorum sectæ sancti esse dicuntur." *Ibid.*, p. 301.

1157 "Ces ung plen pung de gent que sosten tot le monde, et si aquello gent non era tot le monde saria a fin." *Ibid.*, p. 325.

1158 "Pre quacunque re, vera vel falsa, non licet jurare." *Ibid.*, p. 300. "Est peccatum mortale." *Ibid.*, p. 313.

1159 "Jurare pro quavis occasione vel causa Deum, pro vero vel mendacio, aut aliud quodcunque facere juramentum ubi poneretur ista locutio *per*, erat magnum peccatum." *Ibid.*, p. 322.

1160 "Pro quovis delicto quantumcunque gravi, quis noti tradendus est morti, nisi sit homicida." *Ibid.*, p. 313. This is the only exception that we know of to a rule which was hitherto far more absolute. From this to admitting that the Waldenses did not hold themselves bound to obey temporal rulers, " unless they were of their own sect " (*ibid.*, p. 301) is a long stride. At least it would be necessary to use some discrimination.

1161 "Credunt quod eorum Magistri et Barbae potestatem habeant ligandi et solvendi, et quod illis et non Presbyteris Romanæ Ecclesiæ confitenda sunt peccata." *Ibid.*, p. 299. Cf. p. 323.

1162 *Ibid.*, p. 317.

1163 "Ipsa confessa est peccata sua alteri ex eis, genibus flexis ac si fuisset coram suo proprio sacerdote, et inde, facta confessione, ipsam absolvebat manum ad caput imponendo more sacerdotum." *Ibid.*, p. 327.

1164 "Aliquibus vicibus Pater noster pro pœnitentia . . . Frequenter Pater Noster, et hoc tantum quantum possem. *Ibid.*, p. 317, 327.

1165 "Non autem Ave Maria." *Ibid.*, p. 317.

1166 *Ibid.*, p. 301, 311.

1167 *Ibid.*, p. 324.

1168 "Viri ecclesiastici sunt mali et pessimæ vitæ et peccatores . . . Non possunt consecrare corpus Christi, et non valet consecratio per ipsos facta . . . Ipsi Barbæ, et qui sunt de eorum secta, non recipiunt eucharistiam, sed loco eucharistiæ benedicunt panem et dicunt quod illa benedictio est majoris virtutis quam dicta consecratio, ex eo quia tantum quantum quis habet bonitatis et puritatis, tantum habet et potestatis." *Ibid.*, p. 311.

1169 "Credunt quod non licet hæreticis eorum sectæ cum catholicis matrimonia contrahere." *Ibid.*, p. 301.

1170 "Dicebant quod sacramentum matrimonii debebat fideliter et firmiter custodiri." *Ibid.*, p. 323.

1171 "Credunt quod licitum est libidinose convenire, et participare etiam cum omni personi sibi in quovis consanguinitatis vel affinitatis gradu conjuncta, saltum quando conveniunt cum aliis ejusdem sectæ in eorum prædicationibus, et extinctis luminibus." *Ibid.*, p. 300.

1172 To this Barbe are attributed distinctions regarding the different degrees of consanguinity, and the avowal that his penitents lived in incestuous relations, "tamen extra Synagogum." *Ibid.*, p. 311—313 and 317.

1173 The dissidents accused the Priests of the crime of impurity. "Nimis lubricitur et in honeste vivebant," they said, "tenendo meretrices . . . Sic malum exemplum ostendendo in populo." *Ibid.*, p. 323. In fact, that was one of their motives for dissidence. Would it have been logical for them to abandon the priests in order that they might imitate, nay, surpass them in crime?

1174 Thus Barbe Martin is made to say that according to the commonly received opinion of his co-religionists, "si in dicta Synagoga generetur filius, ille filius erit in futurum aptior ad exercendum officium Barbarum, prædicationum et confessionum quam aliquis alius quia genitus est in dicta Synagoga." *Ibid.*, p. 312.

1175 See Ante, note 544.

1176 "Ipse ejus pater, qui erat Barbe, ibat ad confitendum et prædicandum gentes in illis montibus." *Ibid.*, p. 307.

1177 "Sunt sexdecim anni elapsi quod Girondinus ejus pater ipsum loquentum ipsam fidem Valdensium et hæresim docuit." *L.c.* Here we have a proof of the marriage of the Barbes, some may say, but let us see. If Martin's education as a Waldensian had only commenced sixteen years previously, the above may signify that Girondin, the father, had not embraced the Waldensian rule before his marriage. Morel will tell us something farther on, which does not incline us to believe in the marriage of the Barbes.

1178 " Duxit ipsum ad eorum magnum magistrum qui vocatur Joannes Antonii et qui suam residentiam facit in loco de Cambro de dominio Popæ." *Ibid.*, p. 308.

1179 " Tu talis jura supra la fide tua de mantenere . . . nostra lege et de non la discoperire a persona del monde et qui tu prometes de non jurare Dieu a nul modo, et que garda la domenega." *Ibid.*, p. 313. It is, therefore, a question of a formal oath. Cf. p. 308. Peyronette says, in her turn, that, as they mistrusted her, they made her swear to keep silent." *Ibid.*, p. 325. Here we have, therefore, another exception to the rule.

1180 " Magnus magister dat eidem Barbæ, sic facto, ad bibendum modicum vini. Ex tunc mutat sibi nomen, dicendo · *Des en la te chameras tal.*" *Ibid.*, p. 313.

1181 " Quod illa solemnitas habetur loco baptismi." *L.c.*

1182 " Dixit quod de ultra montes in Regno Franciæ appellantur Pauperes de Lugduno, de citra vero montes in patria Italæ appellantur Pauperes Mundi." *Ibid.*, p. 314.

1183 " Qui tres agnoverunt ipsos Barbas in habitas eorum, videlicet in mantellis." *Ibid.*, p. 315.

1184 " Animo exercendi eorum officium et ad consolandum dictos Valdenses ibidem commorantes. *Ibid.*, p. 316.

1185 *Ibid.*, p. 312. Two as a rule. *Ibid.*, p. 297, 298. Sometimes it was one or the other, or three together. *Ibid.*, p. 322.

1186 " Duo homines extranei, induti vestibus grisei coloris, qui, ut sibi visum fuit, loquebantur lingua italica, sive lumbardica." *Ibid.*, p. 322.

1187 " Hora nocturna post cœcam unus ipsorum legere cœpit unum parvum librum quem secum deferebat, dicendo in eodem descripta fuisse Evangelia et præcepta legis, quæ ibidem dicebat se explicare et declarare velle in præsentia omnium ibidem circumstantium, quia dicebat se fore missum ex parte Dei ad reformandam fidem Catholicam, eundo per mundum ad instar Apostolorum pro prædicando bonis et simplicibus gentibus de modo et forma serviendi Deo et vivendi secundum ejus mandata." *L.c.*

1188 " Dum recedebant a domo sua aliquoties dabat sibi certam quantitatem acuum sive *d'aiguilles*, et ejus quondam maritus dabat ei pecunias pro pœna ipsorum." *Ibid.*, p. 329.

1189 It is as we have seen sometimes at Cambro (?) in the territory of the Pope ; sometimes at Aquila, etc. *Ibid.*, p. 298.

1190 " Barbæ creari solent per eorum supremum in civitate Aquilæ in Regno Neapolitano." *L.c.*

1191 The evil disposed said it was to mock the Pope : " In desirum Romani Pontificis eis nomina mutantur cum ad magisterium hujusmodi afficiantur." *L.c.*

1192 " Quemadmodum Christus redemptor noster discipulos suos binos mittebat ad prædicandum, sic et idiota et bestialis illius sectæ Magniscius alios magistros inferiores per ipsum creatos et probatos, quos vulgo Barbas dicimus, ad docendum . . . hinc inde binos mittere solitus fuit." *Ibid.*, p. 297—298.

1193 See Ante.

1194 The name of *mundi*, which is the literal translation of *Cathari*, is particularly significant. " Mundos se coram populo . . . esse simulant," is what we read in a writing attributed to Joachim. See Schmidt, *Hist. de Cathares*, ii., 155.

1195 See Ante.

1196 *Adversus errores et sectum Valdensium tractatus.* The author died in June, 1520. Cl. Coussord, theologian of the University of Paris, again dealt with the same subject, but according to the pamphlet of Seyssel.

1197 *La doctrine des Vaudois représentèe par Cl. Seissel archevesque de Turin, et Cl. Coussord theologian de l'université de Paris avec notes dressées par Jacques Cappel*, etc. Sedan MDCXVIII.

1198 See *ibid.*, ch. 4 : *Ce que Seissel reprend aux Vaudois.*

1199 " Christo omnibus ad omna abunde sufficiente."

1200 See the Latin letter of Morel to Œcolampadius, according to *Scuttetus*, *l.c.*, and the *Memoires de Morel*, in the Waldensian dialect, according to a MS. in Dublin, to which Perrin alludes in these words : " The book of George Morel, containing all the doubtful points, paid by George Morel and Pierre Masson before Œcolampadius and Bucer, concerning religion and the replies of the aforesaid personages." Herzog examined the MS., and he quotes it in his *Rom. Wald.*, p. 340 et seq.

1201 See Ante.

1202 " Eique magister constituatur."

1203 " Ut verbigratia bibere aquam." According to the Memoirs " semil hantament li devant pausa non devon far alcun cosa sencza la licenzia de son compagnon."

1204   "Inter nos nemo ducit uxorem : tamen, ut verum fatear (tecum enim cum multa omnia loquor), non semper caste nobiscum agitur." Let us remind the reader that Morel also alludes to: "nonnullæ nostræ mulierculæ, quas dicimus sorores," which "agunt vitam in virginitate." The *Memoires* have a different reading : "Item alcuns de nos ministres de l'evangeli ni alcunas de las nostras fennas non se maridan."

1205   "Ad plebis obsequium." Doubtless, in order to spare the pockets of the contributors, the popular reading has omitted this passage.

1206   "Colliguntur a majoribus nostris."

1207   "A nostro consortio."

1208   We have thus far followed the order of the Latin version according to Scultetus. For this particular point, we follow, with Herzog, the order of the popular version, which is more satisfactory ; although the difference is not great.

1209   "In hoc, ut andio, erravimus, credentes plura quam duo sacramenta."

1210   We revert to the Latin version for the order of the subjects.

1211   "Nos annen per tuit li an una vecz per vesitar nostre poble en lor meysons, car ilh habitan en las montagnes per diversas borcas e villages ; e li auven d'un en un la confession auricular." The Latin version says : "clandestine audimus."

1212   "Debito proprio honeste, et tantum ad medicinam, non ad voluptatis societatem." No doubt we ought to read here "satietatem" for the popular version has : "a medicina de lor debit e nou a la saciota (sic) de la volunta." Morel mentions a very practical warning, as old as the law of Moses ; but we must be excused for not quoting it here.

1213   The choice fell upon as many Barbes, so that Morel adds, according the popular version : "Emperczo sen forcza de l'auvir quasi en totas sas difierencias."

1214   "Excommunicamus a prasi populi et ab verbi auditione." Herzog gives up the attempt to translate *prasis*, which is, undoubtedly, derived from "Prazis."

1215   "Li papista." The Latin version has a stronger expression : "Sacramentorum signa plebeculæ nostræ non nos, sed Antichristi membra administrant."

1216   "Neque ullo vestitu, colore diverso, superfluo, scutulato, aut delicato, sive consciso utetur." How shall we translate this *consciso* or *ensemptalha*. We know that the sumptuary laws of this period regulated even the cut of trousers.

1217   "Nam ab unius extremitate ad aliam intersunt plusquam octingenta milliaria." Herzog supposes an error here. Perrin (i., 106) thinks that Morel intended to say that the number of the inhabitants amounted to 800,000 !

1218   "Per tot sotmes, volha o non volha, a las segnoriias e a li preyre papistica."

1219   "Peticions." We follow both readings.

1220   "Enayma d'episcopa, de preverage, de diacona."

1221   "His tamen gradibus inter nos non utimur." In dialect : "Emperczo nos non usen d'aquisti gra entre de nos."

1222   "Cum lo sia script : si tu voles venir enapres my, vay e vent totas cosas."

1223   "Si li dit ministre pon licitament amenar fennas, las quals volhon viore en vergeneta." We read, furthermore, the question : "An mulieres juvenes, requirentes et volentes vitam in virginitate agere, sint in religionem introducendæ." There is there an asylum a class of sisters. Morel expresses himself on this point, thus : "Ducuntur prædicti recipiendi ad quendam locum, ubi nonnullæ nostræ mulierculæ, quas dicimus sorares, agunt vitam in virginitate." The same passage is to be found in the popular reading with this variation : "La cals son las nostras serors en Jesu." A stroke of the pen has eliminated the passage from the popular version.

1224   "Si li sen alegoric se son recebu per treyt de l'escriptura sancta profeytivolment." See for the Latin reading, ante n. 849.

1225   The question is exemplified : for instance, says Morel, "what we read concerning the daughters of Lot, concerning Judah and 'soa nora Tamar,' and concerning the wives and concubines of Solomon."

1226   "A czo que non sian deceopu per tanti e divers commentaris e interpretacions que son ese fan de jorn en jorn."

1227   "Si son plus de duy sacrament, con czo sia que li papista diczan esser sept." This question is addressed to Bucer. Morel omits here the avowal made to Œcolampadius : " In hoc, ut audio, erravimus, credentes plura quam duo Sacramenta."

1228 That is at least the sense which we think ought to be given to the words : " Si son alcunas scripturas de Crist, lasquals poissan esser ditas comandament e alcuns conselh."

1229 " Si sara cosa profeytivol que ministres administressan li rit e las ceremonias de li sacrament aqui hont o poyrian fur."

1230 " Si tot jurament es defendu sot pena de pecca mortal, diczent Crist, non volha jurar al postot." The Latin version has an identical expression.

1231 Si es licit de far alcuna cosa manual al jorn de li diamenja e si al postot se deo gardar alcuna festa." In his second letter to Œcolampadius Morel asks whether it is permitted to work on a feast day.

1232 Elsewhere Morel supposes the case of a person attacked in a wood. See the above-mentioned second letter.

1233 " Enayma l'aiga steng lo fuoc, enaymi l'almona steng lo pecca." Il est clair, par ces citations, que la différence entre les livres canoniques et les livres apocryphes est encore à faire.

1234 This same point is touched upon in the second letter to Œcolampadius, with the expression : de meritis.

1235 " Non havent fe de Crist, son reprova."

1236 " Si las leis civils e las semilhant atrobas de li home . . . sian valeronas enapres Dio. Car es script : las leys de li poble son vanas." Here we surely have one of the consequences of the oppression under which the Waldenses had so long groaned.

1237 " Car alcuns dison . . . Dicunt enim nonnulli."

1238 " La soa roba." Herzog translates " Kleid," i.e., clothing, robe. He is wrong.

1239 To his masters, of course. Here again Herzog's translation is incorrect.

1240 " Si tot quant es ajosta al principal, es husura." Cf. Nov. Serm , v. 95—96.

1241 " Si la passion de Christ es tant solament ista per lo pecca original." This idea is enunciated in the Cantica.

1242 " Si lo es licit a nos menistres de conselhar al nostre poble qu'ilh tuon li fals frayres, lical son entre de nos e cerchon e an cercha de liorar nos menistres en li mans de li papista, a czo qu'lh fessan nos morir e que la parolla de Dio non sia anuncia entre lo poble, e moti de li fidel sian destruyt par dit papista d'arma e de cors e de la roba." The Latin reading gives more details. See Ante.

1243 " Outra las predictas demandas non hy a alcuna cosa que contorbe mais nos frevols que del libre arbitre e de la predestinacion de lio o, de laqual cosa Luter e Erasme en son tant different."

1244 " Quia necessario contingunt omnia." These last words are wanting in the popular version.

1245 " Qui vere es illius vicarius."

1246 " O utinam inter nos firma essemus unitate conjuncti."

1247 " In omnibus tamen vobiscum convenimus, et a tempore Apostolorum semper de fide, sicut vos, sentientes concordavimus, in hoc solo differentes, quod culpa nostra ingeniique nostri pigritiæ, scripturas tam recte quam vos neutiquam intelligimus."

1248 " Omnibus Deus idem." This conclusion is taken, like the rest, both from the popular and Latin version.

1249 This is Herzog's expression : " Thus did they confess it to them." Rom. Wald. p. 365.

1250 Monastier, op. cit., I., 195—197.

1251 Ibid.

1252 Herzog, Rom. Wald., p. 297 et passim.

1253 Letter of the Waldenses of Cabrieres to John of Roma, Inquisitor, 3rd February, 1533. Herminjard. Corr. des Reform, vol. vii., p. 466.

1254 Cf. Emile Montegut, Milanges Critiques, Paris, 1887, p. 195.


END OF NOTES.